THEORIES OF SICKNESS AND MISFORTUNE AMONG THE HADANDOWA BEJA OF THE SUDAN

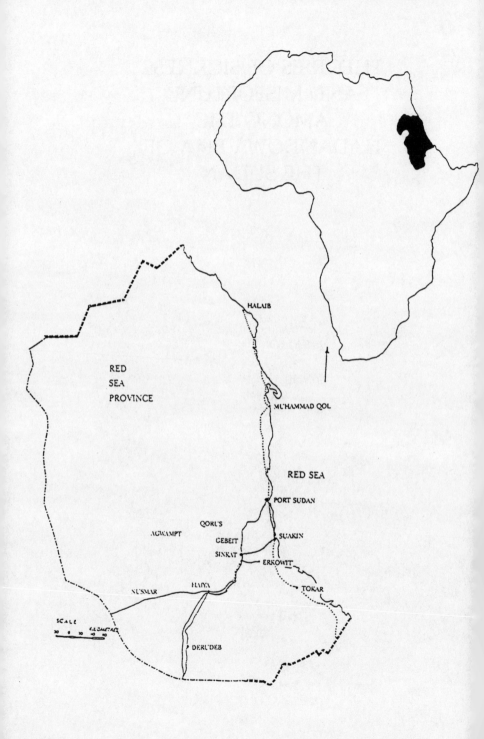

RED
SEA
PROVINCE

RED SEA

HALAIB

MU'HAMMAD QOL

PORT SUDAN

QORU'S

AGWAMPT

GEBEIT

SINKAT

SUAKIN

ERKOWIT

TOKAR

NU'SMAR

HAIYA

DERU'DEB

SCALE
KILOMETRES
30   0   10   20   30

THEORIES OF SICKNESS AND MISFORTUNE AMONG THE HADANDOWA BEJA OF THE SUDAN

Narratives as Points of Entry into Beja
Cultural Knowledge

FRODE F. JACOBSEN

KEGAN PAUL INTERNATIONAL
LONDON AND NEW YORK

First published in 1998 by
Kegan Paul International
UK: P.O. Box 256, London WC1B 3SW, England
Tel: (0171) 580 5511 Fax: (0171) 436 0899
E-mail: books@keganpau.demon.co.uk
Internet: http://www.demon.co.uk/keganpaul/
USA: 562 West 113th Street, New York, NY 10025, USA
Tel: (212) 666 1000 Fax: (212) 316 3100

Distributed by

John Wiley & Sons Ltd
Southern Cross Trading Estate
1 Oldlands Way, Bognor Regis
West Sussex, PO22 9SA, England
Tel: (01243) 779 777 Fax: (01243) 820 250

Columbia University Press
562 West 113th Street
New York, NY 10025, USA
Tel: (212) 666 1000 Fax: (212) 316 3100

© Frode F. Jacobsen 1998

Phototypeset in Palatino 10 on 12 pt
by Intype London Ltd

Printed in Great Britain
by TJ International, Padstow, Cornwall

British Library Cataloguing in Publication Data
Jacobsen, Frode Fadnes
Theories of sickness and misfortune among the Hadandowa Beja of the Sudan:
narratives as points of entry into Beja cultural knowledge
1. Beja (African people) – Health and hygiene.   2. Social medicine – Sudan
3. Beja (African people) – Social life and customs
I. Title.
306.4'61'089935

ISBN 0710305915

Library of Congress Cataloging–in–Publication Data
Jacobsen, Frode F. (Frode Fadnes) 1961–
Theories of sickness and misfortune among the Hadandowa Beja of the Sudan:
narratives as points of entry into Beja cultural knowledge/Frode F. Jacobsen.
p. cm.
Includes bibliographical references (p. 380) and index.
ISBN 0–7103–0591–5
1. Philosophy, Hadandowa–Red Sea Hills (Egypt and Sudan)   2. Hadandowa
(African people) Health and hygiene.   3. Hadandowa (African
people)–Diseases.   4. Oral tradition–Red Sea Hills (Egypt and Sudan)   5. Red
Sea Hills (Egypt and Sudan)–Socal life and customs.   I. Title.
DT155.2.H32J33   1998
306.4'61'089935–dc21   97–37375
CIP

CONTENTS

Acknowledgments   xi
Preface   xiii

1. Introduction

1.0. Some considerations for departure   1
1.1. The fieldwork   4

2. Approaches

2.0. In defense of 'jumping the fence'   7
2.1. Learning culture   9
2.2. Focusing folk theories in the context of social practice   12
2.3. Cultural categories and classifications revisited   13
2.4. A simple story is never a simple story   16
2.5. A general outline of the analysis   18

3. Some Aspects of the Hadandowa Beja World

3.0. The Beja   20
3.1. The crane who married the crow   24
3.2. Of animals and men   26
3.3. Placing men's honor in the hands of women   27
3.4. Beja culture in a precarious pastoral adaptation   29
3.5. Bad things will come to you on their own   35
3.6. Evil from within and evil from outside   36
3.7. Recent changes: Beja people in a ruralized urban
     setting   43

CONTENTS

4. Health, Sickness and Healing Among the Beja

4.0. The occurrence of sickness among the Hadandowa
Beja   51
4.1. Traditions of Treatment and Practitioners   62

5. Beja Sickness Narratives and Culture   75

6. Beja Theories of Sickness in the Context of Anthropological Discourse

6.0. Introduction   80
6.1. General theories of herbs and herbal treatment   83
6.2. General theories of sicknesses   92
6.3. Theories of human physiology and sicknesses   116
6.4. A preliminary conclusion: bodies, societies and
     processes of trans-substansiation   132
6.5. Stings and bites from animals and insects   133
6.6. Food, places and sicknesses   134
6.7. Theories of spirits and the spirit world   144
6.8. Sicknesses of indirect influences from humans and
     animals   157
6.9. Fright and sicknesses   172
6.10. Mother's work and the health of children   175
6.11. Sins, failures and sicknesses   178
6.12. Traditional knowledge and treatment   180
6.13. Some conclusions   181
6.14. A further discussion: metaphors, metonyms and
      theories of essence   189

7. Two Case Studies

7.0. Introduction   204
7.1. The case of Musa Osman   206
7.2. The case of Ahmad   210

8. Return to the Stories

8.0. Introduction   214
8.1. Personal narratives: the story of Halima Umar   215

vi

CONTENTS

8.2. The politics of language and the strategy of
     open-endedness   246
8.3. A different story: *Busarā* stories and other
     mythical stories   267

9. Arrivals

9.1. Basic assumptions   305
9.2. Narratives, folk theories and the pragmatics of
     sickness negotiation   307
9.3. Notions of 'essence' and 'contagion' in the context of
     Beja culture and society   310

Appendix 1: List of Sudanese Arabic terms used   313
Appendix 2: List of Beja terms used   316
Appendix 3: Al-Khatmiyya: Its origin and its
            development   320
            in the Sudan
Appendix 4: Questions from the first round of
            semi-structured interviews 1993   329
Appendix 5: Second round of semi-structured interviews
            1994   332
Appendix 6: Marriage patterns among Hadandowa Beja   335
Appendix 7: Child mortality in the aftermath of drought   337

Bibliography   334
Subject Index   360
Author Index   364

FIGURES

Figure 1. The family of Musa Osman   206
Figure 2. The structure of 'The story about the wandering
          dervish'   281
Figure 3. The structure of 'The three sons and the
          inheritance problem'   284
Figure 4. The structure of 'The basīr and the surgeon'   290
Figure 5. The structure of 'The basīr and the Egyptian
          officer'   292
Figure 6. The structure of 'The basīr and the child who
          lacked a mouth'   293
Figure 7. The structure of 'The lizard who clung to
          the brain'   295

TABLES

Table 1. Physical qualities of human blood · 98
Table 2. Substance qualities of sicknesses · 99
Table 3. Symptoms of *kosúlt* · 101
Table 4. Causes of *kosúlt* · 101
Table 5. Treatment of *kosúlt* · 102
Table 6. Symptoms of *hāf* · 103
Table 7. Causes of *hāf* · 103
Table 8. Treatment of *hāf* · 103
Table 9. States of the stomach *heminéit* · 120
Table 10. Fertility and mortality · 338

ACKNOWLEDGMENTS

The bulk of this research was made financially possible by a grant from the Norwegian Research Council. I am also grateful for financial support for an initial visit to the field provided by Center for Development Studies and The Faculty of Social Science, University of Bergen, Norway.

I want to thank the University of Khartoum and the staff of Norwegian Red Cross and the Sudanese Red Crescent in Sinkat for invaluable help making practical arrangements for staying in the field. A special thanks to Dr. Mohammad Abu Amna and his family in Port Sudan for their hospitality, kind assistance and good advice. Most of all, however, I am indebted to the many local people in the Sinkat province who shared their lives with us and to my local research assistants Eisa, Fatna and Aisha.

The finalization of this study would not have been achieved without the advice, support and cooperation of a number of fellow researchers. First of all, I want to thank Professor Roy D'Andrade, who made a nine months stay in the Department of Anthropology possible at the University of California, San Diego. The present work owes much to his sensitive criticism. I am also very thankful to Professor Frederick J. Bailey who gave numerous helpful suggestions and helped preparing the manuscript for publication. I also want to express my gratitude to Professor Melford Spiro, Professor Theodore Schwarz, Professor Marc Swartz, Professor Michael Meeker, Professor Thomas Levy, Professor Guillimo Algaze and Dr. Daniel Fessler for sharing their knowledge with me in numerous discussions. A special thanks to Kristi Porter who did the final proof-reading of my manuscript.

At my home institution, the University of Bergen, too many people have been of help to mention them all by name. Firstly,

ACKNOWLEDGMENTS

I want to express my gratitude to Professor Sigurd Berentzen who has been my supervisor for two theses. His sudden death in November 1996 has been a great loss for his colleagues, friends, and to anthropology in general. I also want to give a special thanks to Professor Jan Petter Blom, Department of Social Anthropology, for his continuous support throughout my research as well as encouragement and fruitful suggestions, and Dr. Sharif Harir, Center for Development Studies, for his invaluable ethnographic commentaries.

Finally, I want to express my gratitude to my wife, Janike, who endured the ups and downs of my research together with me and who, by making observations in the female settings from which I was excluded, made valuable contributions in the field.

PREFACE

This study focuses on Beja cultural knowledge of health and sickness. The central question which is raised is, 'What does one as an anthropologist have to know in order to understand a Beja sickness narrative?' A vast amount of knowledge is taken for granted when a Beja sickness story is told. Some of this knowledge consists of variably externalized cultural theories and propositions, which may be viewed as inter-linked cultural schemata. A knowledge which is wholly non-conscious and not externalized, however, seems to underlie the cultural models Beja people make explicit. An implicit 'theory of essence' seems to be a crucial aspect of this latter kind of knowledge. Basically the 'theory of essence' contains two related general assumptions. Firstly, things which resemble one another are thought to have the same 'essence'. Secondly, many of the properties of a thing are seen as being produced by its 'essence'. Recent research in psychology and psychological anthropology points toward assumptions of 'essence' as cross-culturally central to cultural thought and reasoning.

These quests lead me to ask, 'how are their cultural repertoires expressed in narratives and what are the consequences?' Mythical narratives, in combining a strict and internal logical structure with little room for alternative interpretation, continue to legitimize Beja healing traditions by being repeatedly retold in an authoritative fashion. Beja personal sickness narratives, in contrast, as a rule leave out the greater bulk of knowledge needed in order to understand them. Often several theories and propositions may equally well render a given sequence in a narrative meaningful, a fact which allows for flexibility with regard to interpretation of real life occurrences of sickness. In other words, the structural flexibility of Beja personal narratives allows for flexibility in the narrative structuring of reality for Beja people.

Finally, the narrative analysis will serve as evidence for the validity of my presentation of Beja forms of knowledge and grammar of knowledge in two ways. Firstly, the adequacy of the folk theories will be supported by their explanatory potential for the stories. Secondly, the relevance of the folk theories will be demonstrated by showing how they, by narrative means, are pragmatically linked to real-life situations.

1

INTRODUCTION

1.0. SOME CONSIDERATIONS FOR DEPARTURE

'Every intellectual has a very special responsibility. He has the privilege and the opportunity of studying. In return, he owes it to his fellow men (or "to society") to represent the results of his study as simply, clearly and modestly as he can. The worst thing that intellectuals can do – the cardinal sin – is to try to set themselves up as great prophets vis-à-vis their fellow men and to impress them with puzzling philosophies. Anyone who cannot speak simply and clearly should say nothing and continue to work until he can do so' (Popper 1992:83).

Scientific work resembles art. Painting or drawing are ways of seeing. To paint is to see what is there to be painted, to see its details and its larger features, to see it from different angles. Importantly, to paint is to look for hidden features, that seemingly are not there, which with the artist's glance turn out to be astonishing patterns, that may be more influential for the process of painting than features that were very clearly perceived at the outset.

This I will argue is the case for scientific work as well. To study people's behavior, whether it be storytelling or engagement in political disputes, is to see. In order to see, one has to make symbolic representations. Like the endless sketches of the painter before the final motif appears, one has to make representations and representations of representations. Every representation involves simplification. So, of course, representations of representations entail simplifications of simplifications.

In my work I try to make such simplifications and simplifications of simplifications as conscious as possible. At the same time I try to involve the reader in some of this process, in my own seeing process. One might argue that this process involves simplifying too much and leaving out many interesting details, to which I will respond 'yes, that is precisely my intention.' There are too many things to be explained in the world, and even in a small village in the Red Sea Hills there are endless features to be studied. My intention is to focus on a narrow range of things, but, hopefully, to be able to offer some good explanations of the phenomena I focus upon. In other words, my strategy is intensive rather than extensive. If my explanations are of this kind and so clear that they are subject, in whole or in part, to refutation, I will feel that I reached my aim.

The construction of symbolic representations of Beja[1] knowledge necessarily involves using different kinds of notational systems. Those notational systems should, of course, not be mistaken for structures within the heads of Beja people. I am making no such claims. For this reason, I think it is probable that my notational system may be improved to make better representations of how Beja reason about health matters. To the extent that the semantic structures I outline make the Beja stories I present understandable to the reader, however, I will hold it plausible that these structures probably have something in common with the way Beja represent their knowledge to themselves.

My present views on Beja culture and society have slowly evolved over a period of more than three years. Although grounded in extensive fieldwork, in many meetings with Beja people and in numerous chattings and interviews, those views cannot be separated from my experiences in the anthropological community and with scientists in other related fields. My account is hence more than just a description of the Hadandowa Beja socio-cultural features. It also represents an attempt both at regional comparison and at relating my observations to anthropological discourses on sickness and health, narration and on human thinking and reasoning.

The subject of my discussion is in many ways complicated. I have tried to make both my observations, and the different methods through which I have used them as data, as transparent as possible. I do not know whether I approach Popper's ideals of simplicity, modesty and clarity. However, this has been my aim, and it is up to the reader to evaluate to what extent I managed this.

As already mentioned, I want to focus and explain a narrow

range of things. However, I would like the things I explain to be of true importance for the lives of the Beja. I would like to point to some ways in which Beja make order in their life world and how they go about problematizing uncanny and troubling experiences. I would like to go about this by looking at stories they tell about healers and sickness,[2] both through histories 'from former times' and narratives of personal experiences. In analyzing the stories, I first and foremost want to ask the following question: what does one as an anthropologist have to know in order to understand these stories? As I will argue knowledge probably has much in common with the knowledge the Beja have to have in order to grasp the same stories. Needless to say, Beja knowledge of healers and sickness has relevance for other realms of experience than sickness and health. The knowledge base, which in many ways is a 'taken for granted' knowledge by the narrator, is too broad to be confined to an artificial realm of health and sickness. In order to reach my aim I necessarily had to employ some rather brave speculations and interpretations. I will, however, as far as possible, try to make it clear to the reader at what points I am on empirically uncertain ground.

Why am I then focusing on experiences of sickness and health? Part of the answer to this question is that I find health and sickness to be, not unexpectedly, a topic of much discussion, attention and involvement among the Beja. Also, a heavy investment in terms of effort, time and material resources is employed to restore good health in people. This is again, of course, linked to the fact that for the Beja, like other people, health and sickness are of acute concern. For this reason I found this field a convenient point of entrance in looking at some ways in which Beja people employ different cultural resources in making their world meaningful. Since so much knowledge concerning health matters is implicitly employed by the Beja when they tell stories or when they choose among treatment options, looking at those activities seemed to me to be a more tangible point of entrance into Beja reasoning than for example looking at religious beliefs per se or 'culture' at large.

I could of course have looked at other relatively demarcated fields like the traditional political management of usage and ownership of different kinds of natural resources, which involves a clear tradition and a vast body of knowledge. However, this is a field which involves a great deal of secrecy. As an example,

Beja people will never be willing to truly state the number of their animals, both because they fear the 'evil eye' and because they are afraid that this knowledge may be misused by other households. They will also never reveal the number of children they have or the amounts of different sources of income for their households.

Having a background in health work as well predisposes me to an interest in questions related to health and sickness. Further, I am inclined to think that since the occurrence of sickness is such an acute and disturbing experience, people will draw upon as many cultural resources as possible in order to restore health, or failing that, to make sense of sickness and death.

I have another important aim with this study, which is to 'de-exoticize' the Beja and make them appear familiar to the reader. When I first went into the Red Sea Hills, I felt like 'landing on the moon.' The reason for this was not so much that the environment in this arid to semi-arid area was so unfamiliar to me, but rather my unfamiliarity with their social life. People behaved toward me and each other in such very different and unexpected ways that it seemed unlikely that they could be driven by similar motives and have the same inclinations as, let us say, my fellow Norwegians. After living with them for a while, however, their reactions became familiar to me. We could understand each other's jokes, even if not always, and I could understand some of the circumstances and situations which made them happy or angry and I could recognize them as familiar to me. This does not mean that I shared all their opinions and aspirations or that they shared mine. I could, however, clearly make the inference that if I had the same opinions and aspirations, I would have reacted in the same ways as I saw them reacting.

To this end, I might stress the unexotic rather than the exotic, the familiar rather than the unfamiliar. If I am to be accused of simplifying too much, I would rather be found simplifying in order to show the common human-ness of Beja reasoning and meaning-making than adding to an existing body of exotic portraits of places and people.

1.1. THE FIELDWORK

My fieldwork was conducted over three periods: the summer of 1993, the summer of 1994 and for six months beginning in

4

January 1995. While in the field I worked closely together with male and female research assistants. Without their help, this work could not have materialized. We sat together for many hours nearly every day in order to write down conversations and observations while they were still fresh in our memories. In some instances we had the opportunity to make tape recordings of conversations. Anyone familiar with the task of analyzing audio recordings, however, will know that this is a time consuming task which put a heavy strain on the research assistants.

In my fieldwork I have combined different kinds of methods. In some instances, I conducted semi-structured interviews (see Appendix 4 and 5). In other cases, I did longitudinal follow up studies on a few selected households where chats and conversations rather than interviews were the sources of information. My wife Janike and my female research assistant Aisha were of invaluable help in this task. Finally, the 'method of hanging around' was an indispensable method without which this type of research would be impossible to conduct. Many kinds of questions are impossible to ask directly to a Beja, for reasons of politeness and other things. Also, like humans everywhere, the Beja do not experience a neat correspondence between the ideas they hold and the manifestations of these beliefs in verbal and other kinds of behavior. It was therefore necessary to combine these various methods of observations.

NOTES

1 When I speak about Beja (sometimes called Bega in various types of literature), it is usually in the sense Hadandowa Beja, Hadandowa being one of the five main subsections of the Beja tribe. Since I have not carried out fieldwork in provinces other than Sinkat province, which is predominantly Hadandowa, some of my conclusions may not be as valid for other areas. The term 'Beja' is a non-native term not used by Beja themselves, who will usually refer to themselves as Bedawiét.
2 'Sickness' here will mean a native conception of ill-health, involving the native conception of diagnosis, symptoms, causation and treatment. I deliberately avoid using the illness/disease distinction which, e.g. Kleinman (1978, 1980) advocates, where 'disease' relates to an objective state of affairs while 'illness' is the patient's experience of the disease. Although I agree that one might fruitfully distinguish between the patient's experience and some basic biological underlying bodily processes like a bacterial infection and related immunologic

responses, I do not think that the terms 'illness' and 'disease' clear the picture. My stance will be made clear later on in the introduction to Chapter 6.

2

APPROACHES

2.0. IN DEFENSE OF 'JUMPING THE FENCE'

Many anthropologists seem to be of the opinion that the outcome of what is done within cognitive science, of which cognitive anthropology in some respects constitutes a branch,[1] reflects the strict methodologies of its practitioners more than what is 'out there' among the people they study. Even anthropologists admitting that cognitive anthropologists produce new knowledge find this knowledge rather trivial and uninteresting. 'What cognitive anthropologists investigate has nothing to do with the real lives and concerns of people' is a common complaint.

Cognitive anthropology is often described by people outside the field as if it is a theoretically unified field. In fact it is quite pluralistic with regard to theories employed. However, it may be seen as having a unified agenda, defining agenda as 'a direction of work' (D'Andrade 1995:4). By this I mean to imply that cognitive anthropologists generally seek to explore the way in which culture is learned and transmitted, as well as memorized and retrieved by individuals of a culture. I will argue that since cognitive anthropologists are the only ones systematically undertaking those quests, other anthropologists would benefit from relating their research to what is achieved through the agenda of cognitive anthropology. In reviewing the field of cognitive anthropology, Maurice Bloch (1994) expresses an even stronger version of this view:

'If culture is the whole or part of what people must know in a particular social environment in order to operate efficiently, it follows first, that people must have acquired this knowledge, either through the development of innate potentials, or from external sources, or from a combination of both, and secondly that this acquired knowledge is being continually stored in a manner that makes it relatively easily accessible when necessary. These obvious inferences have in turn a further implication which is that anthropologists' concerns place them right in the middle of the cognitive sciences, whether they like it or not, since it is cognitive scientists who have something to say about learning, memory, and retrieval. Anthropologists cannot, therefore, avoid the attempt to make their theories about social life compatible with what other cognitive scientists have to say about the processes of learning and storage' (Bloch 1994:276–277).

Supporting his position I am inclined to say that anthropologists criticizing contributions in the field of cognitive anthropology for being too detailed without reflecting the genuine concerns of real people, should rather engage in a cross-fertilization by relating their research to what is achieved in this field. Pascal Boyer's attempts of relating findings in cognitive psychology to anthropological studies of religion represent in my opinion a clear advance in making even laboratory findings relevant for human systems of beliefs cross-culturally (Boyer 1993, 1996a, 1996b).

As an anthropologist I was raised within a tradition where cognitive anthropology was not represented as a separate field of investigation. I have, however, for a couple of years tried hard to 'look over the fence.' I discovered that many of the questions I had in relation to my own fieldwork have been asked before and in better ways by cognitive anthropologists. The endless curiosity of people in this field both with regard to small details as well as in creating 'big pictures' has attracted me. I am heavily indebted to cognitive researchers working on language and culture in their own societies. They have supplied me with very useful ideas concerning the making of hypotheses about how stories are told, how they might be analyzed in different ways and how they seem to relate to the overall culture. Since I have been working in an alien culture with only partial proficiency in the local languages, their contributions have been invaluable to me.

8

2.1. LEARNING CULTURE

A nagging question which repeatedly haunts the mind of an anthropologist concerned with philosophy of science is: how do I know that I know what I think I know? This question pertains both to the validity of ones findings as well as to the proceedings which lead to one's conclusions. It leads one to ask: by what means did I explore the culture and society in question, and how have I at various times represented this knowledge to myself?

In order to protect oneself from the uneasiness of such self reflexivity, one might employ what I will label the 'immersion' model of fieldwork. This model is brilliantly accounted for by Moerman (1969:450, in: Hutchins 1978: 29):

'It is perhaps charmingly naive for the discipline which prides itself on having realized that it would not be a fish who discovered water to assume that cultural immersion (the longer the better; one just soaks it up) produces scientific knowledge.'

Through immersion one ideally learns to understand the way natives understand and to experience the world the way natives experience it. To the extent one is successful in this enterprise, it is not without great costs. By internalizing the cultural means of natives, their cultural schemas, propositions and theories, one may acquire parts of the same 'taken for grantedness' by which natives encounter their world. Having the knowledge, however, does not make one any more able to specify the way the knowledge is represented, or how one came to have these understandings, than a native is able to do through introspection.

My argument is that one should rather turn the inward-looking questions of the bothered philosopher of science towards the natives, in my case the Hadandowa Beja: how do *they* know what they know? How did *they* come to acquire this knowledge? How is this knowledge represented to *them*? How do they employ *their* knowledge in real-life situations? One of the tools that the ethnographer may employ toward answering these questions, is to be self-conscious about how he acquires Beja culture at various stages in his research. As it will turn out, looking at culture as 'a unified whole' becomes less tenable. 'Tearing culture into parts' allows for addressing new questions of individual minds as well as questions related to cultural sharing.

In order to achieve this goal, the anthropologist has to strive to detect as well as represent the knowledge structures by which the natives understand their world. This is largely what cognitive anthropology is all about. However, this is not an easy task, and various suggestions of how people acquire, represent and employ knowledge in real-life situations have been proposed.

D'Andrade (1995) nicely sums up various efforts both by earlier ethnoscientists and later cognitivists. Advances within symbolic anthropology as well as linguistics in the early 1950s led to a 'culture as knowledge' position where researchers tried cross-culturally to explore the content and organization of cultural knowledge. In this period theoretical and methodological foundations were laid for achievements in the second period extending from the late 1950s to the early 1970s. In this second period the main efforts were directed towards method and formalization. A large body of work concerned with taxonomies and feature analyses of kinship terms was created. Although it might be said that during that period culture and meaning were too much attributed to individual minds, the individual mind became a matter of investigation for anthropology for the first time. This led to a cross-fertilization between disciplines like psychology, linguistics, anthropology, philosophy and neurology, a collaboration which still goes on in several academic environments.

The third period was initiated by Eleanor Rosch in the mid-1970s when she introduced her prototype theory, involving a psychological theory of categories. In her view categories are 'fuzzy' and organized around 'a set of properties or clusters of correlated attributes that are only characteristic or typical of category membership' (Rosch 1975, in: Medin 1989). Psychological theories became increasingly more important than linguistic features. Schema theory and the notion of 'connectionist networks' were developed. A schema[2] may be defined as 'an organized framework of objects and relations which has yet to be filled in with concrete detail,' in contrast to a prototype, which 'consists of a specified set of expectations' (D'Andrade 1995:124). The concept of 'cultural models' is often used for such 'learned schemata' (Strauss & Quinn 1992). Within anthropology a focus on cultural models during this period has produced new knowledge on how such models function as basis both for making inferences and producing metaphors (c.f., Mathews 1992;

Holland & Quinn 1987; Quinn 1992a, 1992b; and Strauss 1992 on 'cultural models'; Johnson 1987, Lakoff 1987, Lakoff & Johnson 1980; and Lakoff & Kovecses 1987 on metaphors). Schema theories have in various ways been applied to the analyses of narratives as well. A schema theory which proposes universal schemas and inter-linkages of schemas cross-culturally underlying narratives, is proposed by the cognitive psychologist Jean Mandler (1984). Her approach will be fully accounted for later on. Holly Mathews (1992) has tried to show how morality tales in the Oaxaca state of Mexico are structured by schemata in two senses. She finds that Jean Mandler's universalistic schema seemingly underlies all the stories she analyzed. In addition, Mathews finds that the narratives can fruitfully be analyzed as being based on inter-linked cultural models as well. A more extensive discussion of her research and possible applications of it will follow later on.

The fourth period is still too recent to be described in a definite way. However, D'Andrade (1995:248) proposes two characteristics of this new development:

'There appears to be a trend towards the study of how cultural schemas are related to action. This brings to the front issues about emotion and motivation, along with a general concern about internalization and socialization. At the same time, there is growing involvement in issues concerned with the way cognitive structure is related to the physical structure of artifacts and the behavioral structure of groups.'

Edwin Hutchins' (1995) research related to distributed cognition most prominently represents the latter type of development. The trend toward incorporating issues of emotion and motivation is a general concern shared by many contemporary cognitive anthropologists, such as Naomi Quinn in her investigations of the motivational force of models of marriage in United States (Holland & Quinn 1987; Quinn 1992a, 1992b; Strauss & Quinn 1992).

I am tempted to add another development represented by the cognitive psychologist Douglas Medin (1989). He argues that both the classical view, that concepts have defining properties, and the probabilistic view, that conceptual representations may be based on properties that are only typical of category examples, account for real-life classifications only to a limited extent. Instead he proposes that a greater stress be placed on folk theories, theories by which people culturally organize their world, a view he shares with the cognitive anthropologist Roy D'Andrade (personal communication).

2.2. FOCUSING FOLK THEORIES IN THE CONTEXT OF SOCIAL PRACTICE

In an earlier study by D'Andrade, Quinn, Nerlove and Romney (1972), a feature matrix analysis of standard American and Ladino Mexican categories of sickness was developed. Taking different American and Mexican sickness terms as a point of departure, systematic questions were asked related to how one could catch a specific sickness, what the symptoms of it are and how the sickness might develop. They presented their findings in two-dimensional matrices, one of them scaling sicknesses according to perceived seriousness, the other to perceived contagiousness. One of the significant findings was that Ladino Mexicans rated many more sicknesses as 'not contagious' or 'not very contagious' than Americans.

There was one clear problem with this approach. Although many facets of sicknesses were accounted for, in the words of D'Andrade (personal communication), 'there was no theory of germs in there.' I had a similar experience when trying to elucidate native Beja sickness terms in the initial stages of my research. I started out asking people questions about what they called the condition, what they thought were the causes behind it and what possible treatment solutions there could be (see Appendix 4). Later I tried, on the basis of a list of native sickness terms acquired from this first round of questions, to ask people to suggest both symptoms, etiologies and treatment solutions for those sicknesses. After this I tried to match etiologies and forms of treatment with different native sickness terms. In addition to not being able to elucidate important Beja sickness theories, I found the classification system itself very difficult to obtain. An important reason for these difficulties will become evident in Chapter 6, in its concluding part 6.13. In this conclusion I argue that 'open slots' in Beja theories and propositions may be filled in by several possible labels of sicknesses as well as several options for treatment. Furthermore, a given Beja sickness label may fit into schemas belonging to different cultural theories.

Instead of trying to find a system for classifying sickness terms or types of treatment, I rather focus Beja folk theories in the context of their social practice. By trying to account for native theories and levels of theories, I was able to discover some salient pattern of relationship between how Beja people perceive causes of sicknesses and how they seek treatment for them. And, not unimportantly, focusing on theories brought into view ways in which sickness diagnosis is embedded in a social and cultural setting. In this regard my work to some extent may be seen as moving backwards from the end toward the beginning.[3] I started out pondering stories and how to understand them. This led me to analyze theories underlying them. Analyzing the theories highlighted cultural and social features which I had not been aware of before. Hence, the third chapter represents my view of Hadandowa culture and society as I came to see it after working out their cultural theories of sickness and health.

By focusing on theories, I was also able to better account for people's strategies and changes of strategy in real sickness cases, as will be discussed in Chapter 7. This approach offered explanations for why people sometimes radically changed forms of treatment while still using the same diagnostic label in the case of actual sickness or why a physical sickness sometimes may be treated in the same manner as a psychological disturbance. By focusing Beja theories, *post hoc* changes of etiologic explanations after a specific form of treatment has proved to be effective or ineffective were also rendered meaningful.

2.3. CULTURAL CATEGORIES AND CLASSIFICATIONS REVISITED

By focusing on theories, however, one does not totally avoid addressing problems of classification. Theories make linkages between perceived categories in the world. Folk theories also to some degree account for linkages between entities which make up a category, e.g. by posing how different spirits relate to each other socially. However, analyzing folk theories does not give a real clue to why those very categories exist *per se*. Although my primary task is not to account for the ontology of Beja cultural categories, I found it difficult to totally avoid the question. Since

I am not able to mount any real evidence for the ontological accounts I present in Chapter 6, however, those accounts should be seen as more or less plausible speculations rather than real findings.

Eleanor Rosch's psychological approach to prototype categorization clearly represents an advance over earlier linguistic feature based theories. However, theories of prototypes, such as Rosch's, are problematic for several reasons (Medin 1989). Firstly, they treat concepts independently of social contexts. Secondly, if people state that two particular attributes are the most typical of a given object, this does not necessarily mean that they perceive the *combination* of those two attributes as typical for this object. As an illustration of this problem, Medin & Shoben (1988) noted that even if people in the United States tend to rate small spoons as more typical than big spoons and metal spoons as more typical than wooden spoons, people still find large wooden spoons to be more typical than small wooden or big metal spoons. Thirdly, goal-oriented categories like 'things to eat while on a diet' may be seen as having typicality effects as do other prototype oriented categories. By this I mean that diet foods can be ranked with regard to how typically they represent the category of diet food. With closer investigation, however, ideals rather than prototypes seem to be found for such categories, e.g. a zero calorie food item is an ideal rather than prototypical diet food. Instead of totally disregarding theories of prototype, however, these problems ought to inspire a search for linking similarity driven cognitive processes to real social and cultural processes.

Prototype theories may be seen as a specific kind of theory of essence. Some kind of 'chairness' makes various chairs an instance of a chair and an essence of 'giraffeness' makes a giraffe a giraffe, even if it has a short neck. It is impossible to pose a list of attributes that have to be removed from the giraffe in order for it to become something other than a giraffe. Such theories of inner essences are typical of Western cultures and may underlay, for example, perceptions of different human races as 'natural kinds' (Boyer 1993, 1996; D'Andrade 1995).

While Rosch takes the position that some inherent structures and attributes of objects make people distinguish between different natural kinds, Scott Atran takes an evolutionary approach. Throughout evolutionary time humans acquire intuitive beliefs

about animals, plants and non-animate objects through prolonged interactions with them and learn to distinguish between
them as different natural kinds with different inner essences
(Atran 1990, in: D'Andrade 1995). Some evidence for such
intuitive categorization taking place has been mounted by the
cognitive psychologist F. C. Keil (1979, 1983, 1986 in: Boyer 1993).
Building upon Sommers' (1959, in Boyer 1993) philosophical
argument that ontological distinctions are made manifest by
predicate restrictions, he designed research projects aimed at
detecting how small children make ontological distinctions. It
appeared that the children were able to make fine distinctions
between, for example, living things and artifacts, even when
presented with objects unfamiliar to them:

> 'Keil used stories which make a passing mention of objects
> called "hyraxes" and "throstles," which were never defined
> or described. The only thing said about them is that the
> hyraxes "are sometimes sleepy" and that the throstles "need
> to be fixed." Kindergarten children, who have never heard
> of those things, nevertheless infer, on the basis of such sen-
> tences, that it is possible that a hyrax might be "hungry,"
> and that a throstle might be "made of metal"; on the other
> hand, they constantly deny that a hyrax could be "made of
> metal" (Boyer 1993:144).

Later other cognitive psychologists have shown that even preschoolers assume that category membership of an object is more
important than observable features (Gelman & Gelman 1986,
Massey & Gelman 1988, Becker & Ward 1991). Building upon
these works, the cognitive anthropologist Pascal Boyer (1993,
1996) has expanded the notion of natural kinds by suggesting
that humans cross-culturally project ideas of one category of
natural kinds like humans to another category like, for instance,
plants, attributing faculties like memory and intention to plants.
Supernatural notions may be created by violations of specific
expectations for natural kinds, like creating the notion of invisible
humans. Boyer's theory will be discussed at length in Chapter
6, where I will try to explore its potential fruitfulness in illuminating Beja theories of sicknesses. Other theorists, like Rozin &
Nemeroff (1990, 1994) have demonstrated how an 'inner essence'
of natural as well as 'pseudo-natural kinds' may be perceived by
humans as spreading to or transgressing the borders of different

natural kinds, a theory which proves fruitful for discussions about Beja sickness etiologies as well as forms of treatment. Before pursuing discussions about folk theories, however, I would like to present some questions related to narrative which I find intriguing. Indeed, these questions triggered much of my investigation of Beja folk theories.

2.4. A SIMPLE STORY IS NEVER A SIMPLE STORY

For a given sickness term, I found that the Beja often conceived of different possible etiologies which were mutually exclusive. When looking at real sickness cases, I detected that, depending on the etiology they hypothesized at a given moment, they pursued the treatment option which was in accord with the assumed etiology. Conversely, I found that a given treatment form may apply to different labels of negative physical or psychological states depending on the perceived etiology. Eventually, I sought to elicit by various means the theories and propositions that Beja people seem to employ when dealing with sicknesses or when trying to prevent them. The results of these investigations are presented in Chapter 6. Many findings presented in Chapter 6 stem from the knowledge I gained by asking the question: what do I as an anthropologist have to know in order to understand a Beja story? As I argue, this knowledge is not too different from the knowledge Beja people themselves employ in understanding and constructing stories. This has been a guiding question in a line-by-line analysis of several Beja sickness narratives.

This question is similar to those initially raised by the cognitive psychologists Roger Schank and Robert Abelson in their seminal book *Scripts, Plans, Goals and Understanding* (1977). Their original question was: what is the nature of knowledge and how is this knowledge used? By way of computer simulation, they tried to arrive at what information a computer needed to be fed in order to process and 'understand' simple stories and how this knowledge was represented. Their findings suggest that even a simple sequence in a story like 'John ate lobster at Lundy's' required complicated interlinked schemas in order to be comprehended, such as a restaurant schema, which again is connected to an overarching customer schema and so on. Proceeding from computer simulations, they asked a three and a half year old child Hana some questions related to the following story (p.231):

'John went to a restaurant. The hostess seated John. The hostess gave John a menu. John ordered a lobster. He was served quickly. He left a large tip. He left the restaurant.'

Based on this story they asked her some questions:

Q: Why did the hostess give John a menu?
A: Because you need a menu. (Why?) Because you want to eat food. You can't order food unless you have a menu.
Q: What did John eat?
A: Lobster.
Q: Why did John go to a restaurant?
A: Because he was hungry.
Q: Did the waiter give John a menu?
A: Yes.
Q: Why did John leave the waiter a large tip?
A: I guess he didn't give the waiter a bill.
Q: Did John pay the bill?
A: Yes.
Q: Why did John go to a table?
A: Because he has to eat at a table.

Evidently Hana's answers seem to be quite independent of the actual story. Indeed, even when presented with a more complicated story, her answers seem to build on pre-required scripts. When they tried to present the same story to her twice, she again showed disregard for the story itself and presented answers in the same independent way the second time.

At least four lessons can be drawn from their experiments:

1. Even simple sequences of a simple story requires vast cultural knowledge which is taken for granted in the story itself.
2. Since this knowledge is not itself present in the stories, an extensive contextual analysis has to be performed.
3. Such knowledge seems to be structured in the form of interlinked cultural schemas.
4. A careful sequence by sequence analysis has great rewards for narrative research.

17

2.5. A GENERAL OUTLINE OF THE ANALYSIS

These four kinds of insight presented above will have some clear implications for my further analysis. My study of narratives will serve a double purpose. Personal and mythical narratives will be analyzed through a line-by-line approach in Chapter 8. That chapter will serve two aims. Firstly, the narrative analysis will serve as evidence for the adequacy of my representations of Beja theories outlined in Chapter 6. Secondly, I want to demonstrate how Beja narratives serve as a pragmatic means for the linking of folk theories to real-life situations. Naturally, the practical use of Beja folk theories cannot be predicted from the inherent grammar of those theories.

The outline of native theories in Chapter 6 is the result of my efforts to elucidate the implicit knowledge in Beja sickness stories. Such an approach generated many questions which served as guidelines for me both for interviews and for raising topics in informal chattings. A substantial part of my analysis concerns investigations into the characteristics of the folk knowledge thus gained.

Chapter 7 illustrates how various theories may be cultural resources in a given case of sickness. Two case studies of sick children are presented in order to show how relatively fixed cultural schemata may be flexibly and pragmatically employed in order to create meaning in a complex world of daily life experiences. Together with the narratives presented in Chapter 8, the case studies serve as evidence for the validity of the theoretical outline in Chapter 6.

Before proceeding in my attempts at analyzing different kinds of Beja narratives and what one needs to know in order to understand them, some relevant facets of the lives of Beja people have to be accounted for. In Chapter 3 several general aspects of the cultural, socio-economic and natural world of the Hadandowa Beja will be presented. In Chapter 4 various healing traditions as well as native sickness categories will be accounted for and explained. As will be seen throughout my discussion, Beja cultural theories cannot be properly understood without relating them to larger cultural, social, socio-economic and ecological constraints which impinge on the lives of all Beja.

NOTES

1 Partly cognitive anthropology has its own history as a separate field of anthropology with antecedents like linguistics, anthropology (the language and culture school) and ethnoscience.
2 Pl. schemata.
3 This is of course only partly the truth, since I naturally had aquired some cultural background knowledge which helped me in paying attention to the stories and raise some fruitful initial questions.

3

SOME ASPECTS OF THE HADANDOWA BEJA WORLD: BEING A PASTORALIST THE BEJA WAY

3.0. THE BEJA

My aim in this chapter is twofold. Firstly, I want to present a broad and short ethnographic description of facets of Beja culture and society. Secondly, I discuss why Beja people use only a narrow range of their cultural models in explaining real instances of sickness and misfortune. By considering them as 'total social facts' (Mauss (1925) 1954) I aim at providing some holistic forms of explanations. Before taking a brief look at Beja theories of sickness and misfortune I want to provide a short and general introduction.

The Red Sea Hills are located in a mountainous semi-arid to arid area in the north-eastern Sudan. It is mainly inhabited by the nomad and semi-nomad Beja pastoralists herding goats, sheep and camels.[1] In addition to keeping animals most Beja seasonally cultivate sorghum in the areas of the seasonal brooks called *khoors*.[2] Outside the urban centers the population is thinly dispersed. Normally one encounters five to twenty huts within view of each other, occasionally more, and in rare cases one finds single huts out in the bush a long walking distance away from the nearest neighbor. The vegetation is sparse and the annual rainfall is low and normally occurs in the Fall.[3] In some years the rain is nearly absent. If two or more such years occur in a row, a serious condition of drought may result, which the Beja have experienced several times during their history.[4] In the second most recent drought, in 1984, the loss of animals for the Beja was enormous; estimates by researchers suggest that between 75 and 90 % of all domestic animals perished.[5]

For an outsider, it is impressive to recognize that Beja people

20

have been able to make a living in an area so seemingly unfit for human habitation.[6] Beja people, however, have vigorously defended this area as their ancestral land for thousands of years[7] (Paul 1954; Trimingham 1949). Throughout history they have provided fierce resistance against invading Roman, Egyptian and British troops (Newbold 1935, Paul 1954).

Beja people have been described by various writers as 'traditional' and 'clinging to their ancestral ways' both generally and when dealing with sicknesses. Their conservatism in matters of health and opposition to 'modern' health care was noted by British colonial medical officers like Balfour,[8] Bloss (1948) and Bousefield (1908) as well as the famous Wolff sisters,[9] serving as midwives in the Red Sea Hills and other parts of the Sudan for more than twenty years. This situation is nicely summarized in the words of the British historian and colonial officer Paul (1954:132): 'We have introduced him [the Beja][10] to the benefits of modern medical research: he prefers still his own more drastic remedies of knife and branding iron.'

The present-day Beja consider themselves Muslims. The islamization of the Beja people is, however, comparatively recent. Although Beja individuals and smaller subsections probably were influenced by Islam as early as the 10th century, the first real move toward Islam was made in the early part of the 17th century (Paul 1954; Trimingham 1949; Voll 1969). The extent of the islamization up to present day has been a matter of discussion among historians. Trimingham (1949:15-16) makes his position in this debate very clear:

> 'The Islam of the majority of the Beja cannot be regarded as more than skin deep. None are particularly religious, though like most of the Sudanese they are extremely superstitious and show credulity of any fekis[11] who gain amongst them a reputation for possessing baraka.[12] ... [The] majority of the nomads care nothing for the religious orders which play so vital a part in the religious life of the settled population of the Sudan.'

One might argue against the position of Trimingham that Islam, like any of the 'religions of the book,' occur everywhere as local phenomena with many local traits and characteristics. Further, since the majority of the Beja people still are non-literate, there is no reason to expect that most Beja should follow the written prescripts of Islam very strictly. Indeed it would be strange to use this as a measure of the seriousness of the Beja in the pursuit of their religion stating that 'none of them are particularly religious.'

I once witnessed a couple of Muslim teachers of Islam coming from Suakin to a remote rural area in Sinkat to preach the observance of basic duties of Islam to what they recognized as ignorant rural Beja people. Among other things they wanted them to pray at the prescribed times. Learning that they had been following the wrong time schedule for their prayers, the rural Beja tried very eagerly to correct their mistakes. This is in line with most of my observations, which point out that most Beja took their religion seriously. However, this does not mean that they are receptive to all ideas propagated by Islamic learned men. The veneration of saints and holy men seem to be an area where people are not willing to change their practices whatever efforts various ʿulama[13] might go to in persuading them that this is not in accordance with proper Islam.

The description by Trimingham (ibid.) of Beja as showing 'credulity of any fekis who gain amongst them a reputation for possessing baraka' could also be said about most Sudanese Muslims, although I regard the statement as an exaggeration both as a characteristic of the Beja as well as other Muslim peoples in the Sudan, Ethiopia, Eritrea and Somalia (Holt and Daly 1979; Lewis 1955, 1966, 1969; Trimingham 1949, 1976; Voll 1969). When Islam was first introduced successfully in the Sudan, it was by way of Sufi orders from the Hejaz and Northern Africa (Holt 1977; Karrar 1992; Voll 1969). The veneration of saints and deference to living religious leaders found more than fertile ground in the Sudan. Such traits, although present in all islamized societies, are especially strong and prominent in the Sudan (Karrar 1992; Trimingham 1949; Voll 1969). (For a more thorough discussion of this see Appendix 3.)

The concept of baraka is indeed very central to religious beliefs of the Beja, and Trimingham (ibid.) rightly observed that Beja people pay special attention to people said to have baraka. The Beja concept of baraka, or héequal in Tu Bedawie, is said not only to be something a person has, but also something a person is. The concept has many of the same connotations like the Arabic baraka, meaning 'giving prosperity, increasing fertility, mediating blessing from God, bringing good luck to people.' As will be

22

discussed at length later, however, the luck-bringing dimension seems to be especially prominent among the Beja.

My point here is that asking whether Islam has a light or heavy impact upon the Beja is asking the wrong question.[14] In some respects, facets of the Islamic tradition are lacking among the Beja. However, other aspects are paid a good deal of attention and are greatly elaborated by the Beja.

Before going into any depth in analyzing salient features of Beja culture, however, some facets of their social organization ought to be outlined. The Beja consist of several major and minor tribal units. The three most prominent ones are the Bisharin, the Amarar and the Hadandowa. The Bisharin live in the north and north-western parts of the province. The Amarar inhabit the coastal plains north of Port Sudan as well as the slopes of the hills. The Hadandowa, who represent the largest tribal section,[15] live in the area between the Red Sea Hills and Atbara river.

A fourth group living on both sides of the border toward Eritrea, the Beni Amer, is sometimes considered to be a Beja tribe (Paul 1954). Indeed they tend to share many Beja socioeconomic and cultural traits (Ausenda 1987). However, those who speak of them as Beja usually do not consider themselves as either Beja nor Beni Amer (Dahl et al. 1991). While most Beja speak the northern Cushitic language of Tu Bedawie,[16] most Beni Amer speak the Semitic language of Tigré. A further difference lies in the fact that the Beja, throughout known history, have mainly maintained an egalitarian type of social organization, while the Beni Amer have traditionally had a more stratified society (Paul 1954). In the words of Trimingham (1949:14), 'whilst the other Beja give full equality to all members, the Beni Amer social organization is based upon a form of caste system. . . .'

Since the beginning of the islamization of the Beja, more and more references to them have been made by historians, geographers, travelers and others. They are usually characterized as 'wandering nomads with no paramount chief, but divided into groups headed by sheikhs' (Ausenda 1987:45). Indeed the lack of politically effective higher levels of organization is a striking feature of the Beja tribes. In a sense, the Beja do not at present exist as a political entity and are perhaps better labeled as a linguistic unit, as speakers of the Tu Bedawie language.[17] Furthermore, the bigger tribal groups like Hadandowa are not mobilized as wholes in conflicts over land and natural resources. In such

23

conflicts, neighboring subtribes will organize against each other, regardless of whether they consider themselves as subtribes of the same tribe or as subtribes of different tribes. In such a conflict between people of the Garib subtribe of the Handandowa and a subtribe of the Arteiga, one of my Garib informants was asked why he did not mobilize for war together with his tribal brethren: 'Why are you not coming with us? Are you not a Garib? Are you not a man?'[18] The Arabic term *gabīla* is increasingly used by Beja people denominating a tribal affiliation at this sub-tribe level.

Beja conceive of their tribes and subtribes as people related through patrilineal descent, although in practice their recruitment involves 'many aberrations of bilateral consanguinity' (Dahl *et al.* 1991). Ideally each tribal and subtribal group is affiliated with a piece of land in such a way that one's closest neighbors tend to be one's closest relatives from the perspective of patrilineal descent. However, the most important herding and land-using group, the lower level *diwáb*,[19] is ambilineal in its recruitment. This is the only effective corporate group claiming customary rights to a grazing territory. A similar complexity was noted by Barth for the pastoral Basseri nomads of southern Iran (1961). However, while the social organizational complexity among the Basseri primarily seems to stem from lower level herding groups using affinal ties as a resource for creating effective herding management units, both affinal ties as well as matrilineal ties are relevant in creation of the *diwáb* (Ausenda 1987; Dahl *et al.* 1991; Salih 1971, 1980).

Beja ideas about the nature of their own *diwáb* as opposed to its social surroundings is, as we shall see, of key importance for contextualizing their theories of sickness and misfortune. Inseparable from Beja ideas of the *diwáb* is also a cluster of attitudes which I label a Beja 'culture of honor.'

3.1. THE CRANE WHO MARRIED THE CROW

'Do not marry strangers, your own people are better.' This is a prominent theme among Beja, 'strangers' not referring to non-Beja, but to people outside a Beja's own minimal lineage group, the *diwáb*. The Beja folktale about the female crane who married the male crow illustrates this point (Roper 1928). Straight after their marriage the crane proposed that they should go for a long journey over several oceans. Since the crow is a poor long-distance flyer, he had to ask the crane for assistance. Her family persuaded her to support him several times, but after a while they withdrew their support and left him far away from home.

The word *diwáb* has different layers of meaning. It may be translated as 'home,' 'house,' 'family,' 'relatives,' or 'wife' as well as 'group' at the lowest level of tribal division (Roper 1928). The exact meaning always depends upon the context in which it is used. However, even when used as here, to denote a tribal subsection, it conveys the connotations of nurturance, trust and intimacy.

The *diwáb* is the corporate group proper by which one, through shared descent, is entitled to share rights to a piece of land and all its productive resources. The main efforts of a Beja in socio-economic terms, are directed towards his own *diwáb*. Although matrilineal principles with regard to inheritance and recruitment to the *diwáb* are of importance, the Beja practice of close endogamy contributes to keeping the resources within this lower level group (Salih 1971, 1980). A *diwáb* may vary in size from 50 to 200 households, according to Ausenda (1987).

The *diwáb* is the most important group of belonging for any Beja and their main social point of reference. It is this fact Dahl *et al.* (1991:3) allude to when they characterize Beja social structure as 'extremely familistic.' Like the Basseri (Barth 1961) and in contrast to African cattle nomads (Murdock 1959; Dahl *et al.* 1991) they are, as a rule, endogamic within their lowest level subtribe unit.[20] While various kinds of alliances exist between tribal and sub-tribal groups in many other East African pastoral societies, as in the Basseri case (Barth 1961), strong mutual distrust exists between different Beja *diwábs*.

A visitor among Beja will, as I myself experienced, note their lavish hospitality more than their distrust. 'As a guest you are allowed to be a king for three days,' a Beja friend told me. Being a guest, however, one is being a guest in contrast to being a 'trusted friend.' And not being a 'trusted friend' means that the hosts will be alert and zealously control the amount of information to which the guest has access. In this regard it makes little difference whether one is a foreigner, a non-Beja Sudanese or a Beja from another *diwáb*.[21]

3.2. OF ANIMALS AND MEN

There are two pervasive themes in Beja traditional songs. One has to do with love, praising the beauty of particular women, commenting upon features of a man's beloved like her big and beautiful dark eyes, the gracious way she holds her head lifted when walking, the lightness of the color of her skin, or her youthfulness. The other main theme has to do with animals, in particular camels. The relationship between a Beja man and his camels is a matter frequently talked about. Camels are praised extensively in songs, where the shape, movement and individual characteristics of each camel is described in great detail. Camels and camel herding can be said to be a key symbol of Beja pastoralism. Herding camels represents the prototypical tough and independent life of a Beja.

Within the *diwáb* the social and spatial segregation between the sexes is profound. Like the ownership of animals, herding and milking are purely male prerogatives. Young, unmarried men are said to become 'strong, virile and attractive to women from their diet' (Dahl *et al.* 1991:131). Camel milk is said to be both a most healthy food and a means of protecting oneself against various kinds of sicknesses.

Life among animals is solely men's world. A woman, in contrast, is expected to spend most of her time in the tent. Much of her work consists of preparing food, performing activities like grinding sorghum for *o'tam*,[22] the most important staple food of the Beja. It is made with water and most often eaten with milk. She makes clarified butter oil from milk, which in the present day precarious situation is often sold or exchanged for other food items. She bears the responsibility for maintaining the tent by making mats from *burūsh*[23] or weaving woolen carpets. And, last but not least, she has the primary responsibility for nurturing and taking care of young children.

On several occasions, while in periods living in Sinkat town, I heard the singing of a woman passing by, carrying a basket toward the outer limits of town. When I asked people about the meaning of this, I was told that the basket contained the afterbirth[24] of a newborn boy. The basket is hung on a suitable branch of a tree. Asking what people do when a girl is born, they explained to me that people will bury her afterbirth in silence in the ground inside the tent or hut. As Vågenes (1990, 1995) observes, this tradition is a neat and apt illustration of the dif-

26

ferent role expectations for males and females. The work of females is confined to the tent and its near surroundings, while men's work is connected to the bush and the 'outside world.' The only exception is cultivation work, where women sometimes take part in sowing and harvesting.

For a man it is considered shameful to cook or to build or maintain huts. In general he should avoid hanging around the campground unnecessarily and instead enjoy the company of fellow men working outside the camp or drinking *jábana*[25] under a tree or in a 'men's hut.' In the towns men will gather in the market place and in coffee shops nearby. The market place is a strictly male domain where women should not venture. Buying and selling goods is supposed to be taken care of by the husband or by close male relatives.

The Hadandowa women are guarded by fathers, brothers, sons and husbands throughout their lives. Their protection and control is a constant concern of their male relatives. The honor of male relatives as well of their whole *diwáb* is strongly tied up with the conduct of their women (Ausenda 1987; Dahl *et al.* 1991; Vågenes 1990). In particular the sexual conduct of women is zealously guarded by men. Most Beja women are circumcised the Pharaonic way (see El-Dareer 1982), sometimes as early as one month of age. The vaginal opening is then sewed together in order to ensure virginity. They will always be accompanied by men, or, more often, female guardians reporting on their behavior when moving outside their compound. Although their faces are not usually hidden, the hair is always expected to be covered. Despite of all precautions, conflicts related to questions about the chastity of women are frequently occurring in the area.[26] Beja people perceive the conduct of women in sexual matters as profoundly affecting the collective honor of their *diwáb*. An illegitimate sexual relationship between a woman and a man from outside her own *diwáb* is expected to cause a violent response and a claim for substantial compensation from her relatives toward the male offender and his relatives.

3.3. PLACING MEN'S HONOR IN THE HANDS OF WOMEN

Noting the strict sexual division of labor and the confinement of women's movements, one may safely conclude that 'men and women live their lives in separate realms of activity, in a male external sphere and a female domestic sphere (Vågenes 1990). While this clearly is an important feature of Beja society, there are informal ways in which females extend their sphere of influence both inside and beyond their households. As several informants made clear to me, however, the politics of maintaining social relationships is, to a great extent, in the hands of women. An important facet of maintaining social ties is visiting during important life cycle events – such as childbirths, wedding ceremonies and mourning periods of *furāsh*.[27]

Failing to pay a visit at these times is not a very severe breach for men; a man can always send a greeting or an apology with another person. A man may leave after 'showing his face.' Female relatives, however, are expected to show their presence. A woman's absence signals deteriorating social ties within the *diwáb* or between *diwábs*. By attending, but not staying for the appropriate length of time, she shows that the relationship is not as important as it once was and is of diminished priority. Taking this, together with the fact that the honor of individual men as well as *diwábs* and tribal groups is so dependent on the conduct of women, one may indeed conclude that 'men place much power in the hands of women.'

In some realms of experience, the power of women is quite noticeable. Following Weber's definition of power as 'the probability that one actor within a social relationship will be in a position to carry out his will despite resistance' (Weber 1947, in Swartz 1991:243), numerous examples can be found to support the claim that Beja wives have substantial power in relation to their husbands in questions related to health and sickness, circumcision, and in the use of the household budget. In regard to circumcision, there is a general change in men's opinion, as they are coming to see Pharaonic circumcision as un-Islamic. However, as told by local health workers, men have to trick female relatives in order to achieve a Sunna circumcision.[28] Sometimes men will go with their daughter to a midwife, telling her to do the Sunna circumcision and tying the feet of the child together by wrapping pieces of clothes around the traditional way. The female relatives will then, too late, discover that a 'complete' circumcision is not performed.

Beja male informants frequently expressed the belief that women are less logical than men, so it is no use in trying to deny

28

them what they want. This belief is also noted brilliantly by Swartz (1991:266) for the Mombasa Swahili: 'Since women are expected to be emotional by their God-given natures, there is no advantage in denying them what they want in hope that they will learn from the denial.' Shana[29] told me the following story which illustrated this point very well:

> 'I am not sure whether he is the grandfather of us or a relative of him. He was very good and religious. In former times men did a lot more for their wives than now! This man had some problems with his wife, the problems got solved, and on such occasions it was customary to do some good things for the wife, so he slaughtered a goat for her, only throwing the spleen away. The wife said: 'Oh, this is good, but something is missing.' 'No', the man said, 'nothing is missing.' 'There is something missing,' she said, 'there is no spleen here. I cannot consider this a goat, I want another one.' By saying this, she created a great problem, because animals are expensive. From this time the man never ate spleen and he said to his relatives that if they ate spleen from that time on, they will lose their teeth!'

As is evident in this story, men may go to great lengths in fulfilling the wishes of their wives. Further, if they are not capable of doing this, they will remember the painful experience of displeasing their wives. It is not improbable that the woman in Shana's grandfather's story exercised subtle political power by exploiting her husband's beliefs about women. Whether or not this was her conscious strategy, it seems clear to me that Beja women exercise power in more subtle ways than Beja men. As a final point, I think that the position of women in various kinds of negotiations is important to acknowledge in order to understand their contribution in the field of maintaining the health of children and other family members.

3.4. BEJA CULTURE IN A PRECARIOUS PASTORAL ADAPTATION

Hadandowa Beja people, as I came to know them, stress politeness in social relationships. They are also very sensitive to personal insults from people and are easily aroused to anger. This is not to say that Beja people will readily attack a person physically for insulting them, even though I will suggest that it is more likely to occur among Beja pastoralists than in an agricultural society.[30] More characteristically, however, it is extremely difficult to restore a social relationship with a Beja one has insulted.

In one incident Ibrahim[31] made comments on the behavior of Mousa, a Hadandowa Beja visitor from a neighboring town. Mousa tried in a friendly way to establish relationships with some local Beja. However, Ibrahim did not think it likely that he would succeed. Mousa, in Ibrahim's opinion, tried too often to argue with people. He insulted people by saying things like 'you promised to come a long time ago, why are you late?' or by starting to complain about the local conditions. 'If he continues to insult people like this, he might find it very difficult to restore a relationship with them again, if he succeeds at all. If one creates a problem with people, it may be impossible to get into a friendly relationship with them later on,' Ibrahim concluded.

The problem, in Sinkat as elsewhere, is that other people possibly might have witnessed the insult. For this reason making an apology in privacy is naturally not enough. In order to re-establish the relationship, one has to make a clear apology which is witnessed by other people. Two things have to be achieved: the relationship must be restored and the personal honor of the insulted person has to be maintained.

People may go to great lengths in bearing the costs of breaking a social relationship. In one instance I witnessed a researcher trying to get help from a local inhabitant, Mohammad, in assisting his research. By the local standard, the researcher was willing to pay a more than reasonable salary. However, because he often had insulted Mohammad during previous employments and, more importantly, because Mohammad's friends knew about those insults, he refused to be employed again. He refused in spite of having a severe lack of money, a condition which is not untypical in the present harsh living conditions in the Sinkat area.

Some researchers maintain that pastoral people or people with a pastoral heritage are cross-culturally more concerned with questions of personal honor and hence more sensitive to insults. Edgerton (1971) together with five anthropologists and one geographer conducted a study of four East African peoples each of which consisted of a group with a predominantly pastoral

adaptation and another group with a predominantly agricultural adaptation. Although they concluded that the cultural
differences between the different societies were greater than the
differences within an ethnic group between the pastoralists on
one side and the agriculturalists on the other, they were able to
delineate some significant differences related to the mode of
production. One of the most outstanding differences had to do
with the concept of honor. The pastoralists were more sensitive
to insults and more concerned with politeness in social behavior.
They were more likely to act with direct aggression towards
people insulting them than were the agriculturalists.[32] How could
such differences be explained?

In order to suggest an answer to this question I want to present
some findings from a study which compares the rate of homicide
between the Northern and the Southern states of the USA
(Nisbett *et al.* 1995). Although highly speculative in their use of
ethnographic and historical material the researchers in this study
present an innovative idea which begs further research from
social scientists. Nisbett *et al.* (1995) made the following significant discovery: while the rate of African-American offenders was
nearly the same in the Northern and the Southern states, the rate
of white non-Hispanic offenders (almost always male) was on
average much higher in the South than in the North. The less
urbanized the population, the more significant the difference
was. In cities with less than 200,000 inhabitants, the rate of argu-
ment-related murders in the South was more than double the
rate in the North. The felony related murders were also higher
in the South than in the North, but not nearly as significant.
Historically, in the words of Nisbett *et al.* (1995:135), 'the sober
Puritan, Quaker, and Dutch farmer-artisans settled in New
England and the mid-Atlantic states,' while 'the dominant economic and cultural influence on the South came from the herding
peoples on the fringe of Britain . . . [the] so-called Scotch-Irish.'

The explanation, they suggest, has to do with the pastoral
mode of production. Since in pastoralism the risk of sudden loss
of all animal capital and the risk of loss of one's herd by theft is
great, a culture of honor may be adaptive. By establishing a
reputation for aggressiveness, toughness and capability of
responding to threats and insults with immediate violence, a
herder may secure his way of living. The researchers do not
reach their conclusion in a dogmatic fashion. They render it

31

possible that a variable co-varying with pastoralism may explain their data. Given lack of established data on the topic cross-culturally, however, they hold their theory to be the best explanation posed by researchers so far.[33]

The concept of honor is very pronounced among the Beja (Morton & Fre 1986; Dahl *et al*. 1991). It is expressed both at the individual level and as the collective honor of the *diwáb*. At the individual level, the expectation of honorable conduct is primarily placed on men. An honorable man is expected to show self control and working for the common good of his *diwáb* instead of serving his personal interests. He is expected to be hospitable and generous towards visitors. This expectation seems in many ways, however, to be an extension of his general capability to protect people who are perceived as being in a weaker position, like children, women and dependents. In order to gain people's confidence in his ability to do so, he has to gain a reputation for toughness and aggressiveness in situations where the interests or honor of his dependents are at stake. Failing to do so in a situation where he is expected to show open aggressiveness will clearly undermine his long-term position by making it less attractive for others to seek his help and by making him an easier target of others' aggression. His honor is also tied up with his ability and willingness to maintain the honor of others when being their guest.

A Beja man should also be very careful about giving away information about his *diwáb*, information which other people could use to harm his *diwáb* or otherwise use to their own advantage. The level of secrecy in matters of economic significance is notably high among the Beja pastoralists. They will never give away the actual number of their animals to anybody outside their *diwáb*. It is also considered impolite and a sign of lack of cultural competence to ask such a question or to ask any questions related to the property or income of a Beja. In addition a Beja will avoid mentioning the actual number of his children and their names.

If people from outside the *diwáb* attempt at investigating into such matters this is perceived as an insult threatening its honor. A swift and aggressive response is required for the males belonging to the *diwáb* in order to maintain a reputation for toughness and willingness to defend its honor as well as its people and material resources. As already mentioned, such

32

threats and shows of aggression mostly do not proceed to actual violence.

Storå's (1996), in his study of pastoral nomads in Turkana, Kenya, also stressed keeping secrets of economic significance as a prominent feature of their pastoral adaptation. Since the very means of existence are so easily taken away from pastoralists, it may be reasonable to assume that secrecy and control of information is cross-culturally more at stake for them than for agriculturalists.

The names of females are never mentioned in public. As an example, when I once asked a person about a woman whom I hoped could assist me in future research the person got very surprised and exclaimed 'you are not supposed to know the names of any women!' Not to make women's names public has as well to do with the Beja concept of honor. To mention the name of one's mother people would say is 'like making her a prostitute.' Most Beja I met are quite self-reflective in this and other cultural matters which set them apart from other surrounding ethnic groups. As an example, I witnessed one time when Mousa, one of my informants, met a friend and close relative, Ahmad, he greeted Mousa by saying 'hey Amna' in a low voice when passing by. Amna was the name of Mousa's mother. Mousa first flushed and then laughed and smiled, telling me that 'Ahmad is a very good friend!'

By way of preliminary conclusion one might say that having a culture of honor is highly adaptive for pastoralists like the Beja. This of course does not mean that the pastoral mode of production in any way determines a culture of honor. Hadandowa Beja are described by other Beja as more easily raised to anger by insults than other Beja (Paul 1954). And, their habit of keeping names of females secret is not shared by neighboring Rashaida pastoralists and nomads. The Beja habit of keeping their number of children and animals secret also clearly has to do with their belief in the power of the 'evil eye,' a point to be discussed later. However, in line with the thought of Nisbett et al. (1995), I will pose the hypothesis that once a 'culture of honor' is established among pastoralists like the Beja, this becomes a cultural resource which make them better adapted to their precarious mode of subsistence and, in the case of the Beja, the harsh environment of semi-desert and unpredictable rainfall.

When speaking with individual Beja persons about their plans for the future, the most striking feature is the picture they give of their life world as capricious and unpredictable. After the drought in 1984, when most of their animals were lost, this conception of a world with so many unpredictable forces at work which may suddenly change their whole destiny has probably not been weakened. Not only are they in constant danger from the aggression of other people, they are, as well, in danger of harsh and 'aggressive' natural forces which in a short while may destroy the whole basis of adaptation and survival of many Beja households.

The Beja world is also inhabited by other capricious and sometimes malicious forces. The cultural world of the Beja is a world inhabited by a host of spirits. Although there are Muslim and good intentioned spirits, most Hadandowa Beja are mainly concerned with the malevolent ones as well as the capricious ones which occasionally create problems. There is, as will be discussed later, a concern with a spirit world not very different from the world of the Beja pastoralists.

Beliefs concerning spirit aggression and spirit possession are widespread all over the world. In all pastoral societies and most non-pastoral societies surveyed by Murdock (1980), spirit aggression is seen as significant.[34] I will suggest the hypothesis that spirit aggressiveness towards humans fits the precarious lifestyle of pastoralists generally and pastoral nomads in particular. One might argue that in all kinds of situations characterized by high stress and little control, humans may employ supernatural beliefs of all kinds. However, as I will come to argue later on, not all kinds of supernatural beliefs seem to fit the pastoral adaptation of Beja people.

Sorcery and witchcraft, however, seem to be negatively correlated with spirit aggression cross-culturally (ibid.). This holds for the Hadandowa Beja as well. In the Beja case, like for the Azande (Evans-Pritchard (1937), 1985), it makes empirically sense to distinguish sorcery from witchcraft as modes of folk explanations.[35] Sorcery as a technique involving conscious manipulation of certain objects is available among the Hadandowa as well as among other Sudanese Muslims (Holy 1991). It is seldom encountered, however, in explanations of misfortune in real-life situations. Witchcraft as an unconscious, illegitimate and evil force emanating from specific individuals is absent as an available theory (see also Ausenda 1987). A frequent occurring theme in the region, however, is the 'evil eye' as an unpredictable force which may be activated occasionally by any individual.[36]

To summarize, so-called 'non-natural' causes of sickness and misfortune are frequently employed in Beja etiology. These forces normally stem from the unpredictable spirit world or from any person who unpredictably activates an evil force. There are other 'mystical' forces at play as well which may account for sickness and bad luck. These forces have to do, in various and complicated ways, with fertility of humans and animals, and they will be discussed at length later on.

3.5. BAD THINGS WILL COME TO YOU ON THEIR OWN

'You have to seek out good things, but bad things come out of their own accord.' Beja proverb.

A lot of changes have affected the Beja since the devastating drought of 1984. There is nothing new about serious droughts in the Red Sea Hills. Droughts have frequently visited the Beja, and many such droughts are remembered by means of oral narratives. The last droughts, however, have had a heavier impact upon the Beja than earlier catastrophes. The high child mortality after the drought of 1984 is a clear indicator of this, as will be discussed in Chapter 4.

In the aftermath of the 1984 drought, the urbanization of the Beja has taken place quickly. The North-Eastern region of the Sudan traditionally had by far the largest percentage of nomads. According to Eltay & Hashmi (in Ertur & House 1994:42), 53.5% of the population were considered nomads in 1956. By 1983, however, the percentage declined to 25.3%, a reduction of more than 50%. Urbanization means leaving the ideal nomadic way of life and adapting to the negatively evaluated towns, described by Beja as filthy, unhealthy, unstable and full of immorality (Ausenda 1987; Dahl *et al.* 1991).

Generally, whether living in urban centers or rurally, the changing socio-economic situation means that most Beja can no longer rely solely on pastoralism. Burning wood for charcoal has traditionally been looked upon as an inferior and despised activity. Many Beja are, however, now forced into this activity in order to survive. While seasonal migration for work to Port Sudan and Gaash has long offered additional income for many Beja (Paul 1954), the changing living situation has forced many Beja males to stay away for seasonal work for great parts of the year, leaving behind what are essentially female headed households (Vågenes 1990). This leads to women seeking sources of income outside their home, a situation evaluated negatively by women as well as men.

Women leaving home and taking young children out of the compound is perceived by many Beja as detrimental to the health of their children. Also, new food items brought into the area by relief organizations are often perceived as not being nutritious, and in some cases directly dangerous to people's health. For example, even many urbanized Beja believe that the relief cooking oil brought into the area after 1984 caused dangerous skin sicknesses as well as hepatitis.

Throughout the history of the Beja, outside intervention in their areas usually meant trouble. By distrusting non-Beja people in general and people not from their own *diwáb* in particular, in addition to spending economical and social resources in relationships to people from ones own *diwáb*, Beja may be said to have engaged themselves in a self-fulfilling prophecy. By seeking out friendship and cooperation with near kinsfolk, one will get good things in return. From outside ones *diwáb*, however, one can only expect problems and quarrels over land and resources. For this reason it is perhaps no wonder that many Beja people asked themselves, when foreign relief organizations arrived in the area: 'Why are they here? What do they want from us?' Both human and spirit encroachment from outside the Beja *diwáb* put the health of humans in danger (see Chapter 6).

3.6. EVIL FROM WITHIN AND EVIL FROM OUTSIDE

Sorcery by means of conscious manipulation of objects representing the victim like a piece of his hair and related sorcery concepts are, as already mentioned, available as a cultural resource among the Beja. It is also mentioned in Islamic scriptures available to literate Beja by the term *'amal*, a concept which is widespread in the whole Islamic world. The Beja only very seldom, however, employ the notion of sorcery in situations of misfortune in daily life.

Witchcraft, as a malevolent substance causing harm to others without the witch being conscious of it, is virtually non-existent among the Beja. There are old stories about the 'werehyena' which is similar to witchcraft stories in other societies (Ausenda 1987). Certain humans are said to become werehyenas at sunset. According to an informant they are believed to steal babies or suck the blood out of them. At dawn they become ordinary humans again. This belief is not a specific Beja one and is widespread throughout a wider region including southern Ethiopia (ibid.). Although the notion is present among Beja people, however, I never heard about a concrete episode where people applied a specific incidence to a witch. When I asked people about stories of werehyenas, some answered that 'people used to believe in such things in former times,' while others said that 'those are just stories.'

How could this be explained? Whiting (1950), in her cross-cultural study of witchcraft or sorcery, proposed that absence of institutionalized ways of solving conflicts in a society may explain why witchcraft and sorcery explanations[37] are frequently invoked in such societies.[38] This co-variation may be valid for many societies, but does not seem to apply to the Beja. The Beja have no institutionalized ways of *enforcing* solutions in conflicts. The tribal leaders can persuade conflicting parties to meet and discuss their differences. They may also persuade people to accept a given solution, although what often happens is that people agree on meeting again later and 'cool down' their moods in the meantime (Ausenda 1987; Bonsaksen 1991; Paul 1954). As an example, some conflicts over the right to cultivated land is said to follow unsolved from generation to generation. Steadily new tribal meetings are held where all members of the disputing groups are welcomed and where everyone may voice his opinion in an egalitarian fashion regardless of his social standing.

The traditional tribal leaders have no means of enforcing solutions or coercing any of the parties. If no preliminary agreement is reached, an open violent conflict may, in the worst case, break out. Cases of actual violence are infrequent, however, which also may be due to the presence of police and other state authorities present today. Even before such modern institutions were represented, though, cases of violence were not that frequent among Beja people (Paul 1954). In other words, Beja people are used to living in a world with a lot of unresolved conflicts. However, they do not resort to witchcraft or sorcery models in explaining those problems.

Nadel (1952) in his seminal article 'Witchcraft in Four African

Societies' posed another explanation. If there are structural conflicts with no possible solution among close relatives or among
people in close co-operation in any society, people may invoke
witchcraft explanations for various types of misfortune. Ausenda
(1987) proposes that the absence in Beja households of structurally derived tensions similar to those posed by Nadel explains
why witchcraft accusations are absent among them. Since Beja
are patrilineal and endogamous, 'women are consanguineal both
with their children and with their husbands' (p.428). According
to Ausenda structural lines of conflicts are thus avoided.

The degree to which Beja spouses are relatives, however, is a
matter of discussion. In quite a number of cases (see Appendix
6) a Beja marries his classificatory cousin,[39] meaning that their
stated relationship may go back several generations. This
relationship may be figured through women as well as men. In
other words, although most Beja may be said to marry endo-
gamically with regard to the same *diwáb*, the households the
spouses represent may be spatially and genealogically quite
distant from each other and hence allow for potential conflicts.

Another source of conflicts is the relatively strong emotional
tie between siblings. If a conflict arises between, let us say, a wife
and a sister of the husband, the brother-sister tie might prove to
be most persistent (Dahl *et al.* 1991). The following incident
shows how a conflict between a wife and her sister-in-law might
occur in one of the few sorcery cases I encountered:

'In one instance I heard about where sorcery accusations
were actually voiced, a married woman, Lesha, died of sickness. Her relatives went to a *fagīr* in order to confirm their
belief that one of the sisters of Ibrahim, the husband, had
practiced sorcery against Lesha because Lesha cared too
much about her husband and contributed too little support
for her own siblings. Lesha's relatives got their suspicion
confirmed by the *fagīr* and they went to the family of the
accused sorcerer to receive compensation. Both Lesha and
Ibrahim belonged to the same *diwáb*.'

Yet another source of conflict is strife among co-wives. In practice
there are very few Beja men who can afford to have more than
one wife, although they hold the belief that as Muslims they are
ideally allowed to marry up to four. One other incident of sorcery

accusations I heard about was sorcery accusations against a senior wife when the younger wife got sick and died.

I think that it is part of the truth to state that there is a source of potential conflict inherent in the social structure of many Beja households. The other half of the truth is, however, that Beja people maintain a state of affairs of potential and real conflicts outside their *diwáb*, while they downplay inner conflicts.

I agree to some extent with Ausenda if his statement is given a weaker form, stating instead that some kinds of structural conflicts between close relatives are avoided since the Beja are both patrilineal and endogamous. This might partly explain the absence of witchcraft accusations among Beja, at least within the *diwáb*. However, instead of stating that there are no potential structural conflicts within the household, I would rather like to expand the scope of Ausenda's argument and state that the Hadandowa Beja in general expect no evil from inside their own *diwáb*. The people inside their own *diwáb* are the ones they support and may expect help from in times of need. They are the ones who in practice cooperate in cultivating fields and herding animals. If some members of the *diwáb* should be struck by catastrophe of any kind, the other members are expected to share their expenses. When marriages, mourning rites and burials are performed, the people in the same *diwáb* will support each other. In a rather hostile natural and social environment where the play of natural forces is often unpredictable and where other groups compete for scarce natural resources, the *diwáb* is the only stable element which one can count on. Its people represent 'one's own kind' as illustrated in the story 'the crow who married the crane.' As a further example, although camels are individually owned, camels and land are seen as the property of the whole *diwáb*, a property which should never be given to women, since it then potentially may pass out of the group (Salih 1971, 1980).[40]

The animal and grain products from ones own *diwáb* are perceived to promote good health. Even sticks from the huts or tents from members of ones *diwáb* are used to cure sickness caused by spirits.[41] The Beja conception of sharing in an egalitarian manner mainly pertains to their own *diwáb*. Beja people never feel completely relaxed and secure when traveling away from their own sub-group (Dahl *et al.* 1991).

One might say that the main conflicts among Beja arise between people belonging to different *diwábs*, in contrast to, for example, the Muslim Swat Pathan people in North-Eastern Pakistan as described by Barth (1965). Although they have a segmentary lineage model similar to Beja ideology, among the Swat Pathan the main conflicts arise between close relatives in the fashion of more distant cousins unite against closer cousins. Beja channel conflicts outside their own sub-group, which in turn contributes in making their wider social surroundings conflict ridden and insecure. In many ways the peaceful and harmonic inner life of the *diwâb* then becomes a self-fulfilling prophecy. To the extent that non-natural evil forces operate inside it, it is mostly in the form of a random person coincidentally casting an 'evil eye,' but not usually being ascribed the 'power of the evil eye' as a personal attribute, and hence different from typical witchcraft accusations. Moreover, as already shown, the bulk of the 'personalistic'[42] and supernatural forces concern spirits and mystical influences from outside. This is in concert with the view Beja hold of the social and natural environmental surroundings and in concert with their adaptation to them.

By way of preliminary conclusion, Whiting's (1950) argument does not account for the absence of witchcraft and the low incidence of sorcery among the Beja. Her argument might be strengthened by taking other factors like conflicts between close relatives into consideration. Nadel's argument, however, seems better to account for the relative absence of such explanations of misfortune among the Beja, if it is applied at the level of the *diwâb* instead of individual households.

Like Nadel (1952) and Whiting (1950) I have been concerned with intra-community accusations of witchcraft and sorcery. My arguments so far do not exclude the possibility of inter-*diwâb* or inter-tribal witchcraft and sorcery accusations. The absence of such accusations in social practice in Beja society may, however, be due to the availability of other etiological explanations which better fit their culture and pastoral adaptation. As already argued, Beja theories of spirit possession and spirit aggression seemingly better fit their *diwâb* ideology, conceptions of honor and, in general, their pastoral adaptation.

Up to now, I have dealt with the question of theories of sickness and misfortune at four levels:

1. The level of Beja sentiments and *diwâb* ideology: theories of spirit aggression fit their view of an insecure, unpredictable

and mainly hostile outside world. Theories of witchcraft involving close relatives does not fit their view of the *diwáb* and its people as stable, peaceful, benign, sharing and nourishing.

2. The level of social structure: by the custom of intra-*diwáb* marriages the possibility of strife between a spouse and people in an affinale relationship to the spouse is less likely than in a society with exogamy. There is, however, an important socio-economic premise for this feature: the *diwáb* unit is a corporate unit in sharing important material resources as well as having an ideology of 'sharing blood.'

3. This leads us to the third level: since the *de facto* corporate units among the Beja, the *diwábs*, function as the basic socio-economic units in competition with each other for scarce material resources, internal strifes within a *diwáb* would be a disaster. Since inter-group sorcery and witchcraft accusations are prone to trigger potential conflicts within this unit, people avoid them. For this reason Beja traditionally may have favored 'evil eye' explanations of a type which stress its incidental nature more than 'evil eye' explanations which stress 'evil eye' as an inherent attribute of specific individuals.

4. The fourth level concerns the pastoral mode of production: pastoralists, as a result of their mode of production, are more inclined than agriculturists to be on guard against encroachment from the outside and hence seek to gain a reputation for aggressiveness and ferocity (Nisbett *et al.* 1995). Therefore mystical theories of spirit aggression from outside seem to better fit their general style of life than theories of witchcraft and sorcery, whether concerning inter-*diwáb* or intra-*diwáb* accusations. The findings of Murdock (1980) pointing towards a 100% correlation between pastoralism and prominence of theories of spirit aggression may support this claim.[43]

There is still a broader kind of explanation which I have not yet explored, an explanation which relates both to the Beja socio-economic adaptation and to Beja ideas of their *diwáb*. In the article 'Ghosts, Ifaluk and Teleological Functionalism,' Spiro (1952) addresses the question of the absence of witchcraft and sorcery among the Ifaluk people in the Micronesian region. He states that such theories would be incompatible with their practice of helpfulness, sharing and co-operation. However, this is not the explanation he poses. His argument builds upon some important premises: all humans have aggressive impulses which either have to be openly expressed, projected to others, and hence transformed, or repressed, the latter at great personal costs. Sorcery accusations, witchcraft theories and theories of spirit aggression can all be seen as different opportunities for projection. Since the Ifaluk people live on a very small island, however, there may be many opportunities for 'fight' but absolutely no avenue for 'flight.' Pursuing a cultural evolutionary approach, Spiro poses the explanation that given these circumstances, projection of evil motives towards fellow Ifaluk is not sustainable as a mode of projection and would lead to undermining their socio-economic adaptation on that small island, an adaptation which depends upon sharing, co-operation and kindliness towards others.

Although Beja people are not circumscribed by natural hindrances like the Ifaluk, they may in a sense be seen as 'socially circumscribed' in the way Carneiro (1988) suggests for the Yanomamo. Unlike the Nuer of the Southern Sudan (Evans-Pritchard (1937), 1985), the Beja people traditionally have had no effective higher level segmentary political mobilization of patrilineal groups making them able to effectively invade bordering territories. The Beja have adapted to a territory with scarce and vulnerable resources and are surrounded by other tribes towards which they generally have had a hostile relationship. In other words, the Beja people as a whole may be seen as socially and politically circumscribed.

Given the traditional inter-*diwáb* strifes and hostilities, however, as well as the extreme dependency of an individual Beja upon his or her smallest segment group for support and, indeed, survival, one might look upon each Beja *diwáb* as, in a sense, socially circumscribed. In other words, a Hadandowa Beja *diwáb* may be seen as surrounded by a 'sea' of a socially hostile and insecure world over which one has absolutely no influence. Given such a situation, inner-group witchcraft or sorcery accusations would be as untenable for the Beja as for the Ifaluk from a cultural evolutionary perspective. Stating that this is a cultural evolutionary argument, I trust I have made clear that this mechanism is not pointing to sentiments of individual Beja people at all. If it is a real mechanism, it is per definition not present in the mind of any individual Beja.

By way of concluding, several explanations may in combination account for the absence of inter-personal mystical explanations and the strong presence of theories of spirit aggression among the Beja. None of the possible explanations I have explored so far exclude each other logically. I readily admit, however, that one question remains unexplained: why are accusations of witchcraft cross-culturally generally not invoked between groups of non-relatives or distant relatives?[44] At the present time, I can only acknowledge that the position of Nadel seems tenable, but with one important modification: witchraft accusations are probably not employed related to social 'stress-points' in societies with small populations which are ecologically or socially circumscribed.

3.7. RECENT CHANGES: BEJA IN A RURALIZED URBAN SETTING

It has been argued more generally that prevailing Beja modes of explanations for sickness and misfortune stress the haphazard nature of evil forces rather than sources of evil connected to specific individuals and specific social relationships. Moreover, Beja cultural explanations of evil stressing evil forces as intruding the *diwáb* from outside has been portrayed as more prominent than folk theories of evil sources from within the *diwáb*. Both arguments fit the picture given of the social and cultural life world of the socially circumscribed Beja pastoralists and may even have gained increased relevance in the aftermath of the last severe droughts, which have made the Beja pastoral adaptation more precarious than perhaps ever before.

The discussion so far has been related to pastoral and rural Beja. Beja people are increasingly becoming city dwellers. Fewer and fewer Beja are depending upon pastoralism as their primary source of livelihood (Bonsaksen 1991, 1993; Vågenes 1990). The impact of written Islamic sources is greater in the cities (Ausenda 1987; Dahl *et al.* 1991; Paul 1954; Trimingham 1949). These factors may, for example, possibly account for the instances in Sinkat town where specific individuals were attributed 'the power of the evil eye,' a practice which to some degree approaches the tradition of pointing out personal witches. That notions of witches and witchcraft may gain new relevance in African urban settings is supported by several recent anthropological studies (Austen 1993; Bastien 1993; Ciekawy 1990; Geschiere 1988). Other differences between cultural theories encountered in towns vs. rural areas will be discussed later on.

Although living in a town clearly has some impact on rural people moving in, the towns themselves may also be changed in the process. Instead of echoing the usual point of view that people in the Red Sea Hills are getting increasingly urbanized, one might state that the towns in some senses may be becoming increasingly ruralized. This is at least the case with Sinkat, where the population has drastically increased during the last few years. As an example, the Sinkat suburb of Dinayet according to official statistics increased from 1023 persons in 1983 to 2579 in 1993.[45] In contrast, while the number of households were counted as 240 for Dinayet in 1957, the number of households in 1983 were 505.[46] Briefly, a greater increase in the population may have taken place during the last ten years than during the 26 years from 1957 to 1983.

According to an informant who for a time served as a Sinkat council member, the city council of Sinkat has changed drastically during the last three or four years. While the tribal background of the council members used to be somewhat haphazard, a close matching between the size of the subtribe and its representatives in the council is now steadily negotiated.

Different parts of Sinkat may be clearly marked as inhabited by specific subtribes. The general trend is that new migrants tend to settle near their relatives (Vågenes 1990). This generates the trend that people from the same *diwáb* tend to live closely together. As an example, all the nearest neighbors of my informant Mariam from Dinayet belong to the same *diwáb* as her. This process may be even more marked in more recent quarters than in the older, central part of Sinkat.

Some processes may weaken the intra-*diwáb* ties in the towns. While funeral and marriage ceremonies lasted for up to seven days, a steadily declining economy has contributed to people making ceremonies of shorter duration, from one to three days. While the host used to provide up to three meals a day as well as accommodation for relatives from the same *diwáb*, traveling guests only rarely stay overnight nowadays. According to an informant, whilst people sitting at a truck stop or restaurant in

44

former times used to invite relatives passing by for a meal, nowadays they only briefly say 'hello' because they cannot afford to pay for a meal for them. 'When having a guest, the guest will pay nowadays, and he will not blame his host,' he states.

The declining economy, however, also has effects which may strengthen intra-*diwáb* relations. In order to keep the expenses of marriage ceremonies as well as the bridewealth low, people nowadays tend to encourage marriage of as close relatives (not only agnates) as possible. In addition, several couples from the same *diwáb* may be married at the same time in order to econo- mize the ceremonial expenses, which again give additional occasions for intra-*diwáb* co-operation.

With the growth of institutional state agencies for conflict man- agement, tribal and subtribal level traditional means of solving problems may be weakened. In a situation of both rapid socio- economic changes and a general decline in people's standard of living, the small-scale *diwáb* may, as shown for marriages, increase in importance for urbanized Hadandowa people though. This reinforces the traditional place of the *diwáb* as a much more important aspect of tribal life for Beja than higher levels of sub- tribes and tribes.

Hall (1981) comments in her book *Sisters under the Sun* that

'The notable absence of women in the streets and country- side around such population centers as the township of Sinkat in the Red Sea Hills is proof enough that the practice of women walking in public and being seen by male strangers is not sanctioned by tribal tradition' (p.125).

I am inclined to argue, however, that the tribal traditions are not weak in the towns. They may even grow in importance as the towns get increasingly 'tribalized.' The significance of differences in sex roles do not seem to become less important in the town than in the countryside. Quite the contrary, as people move into towns and live in densely populated quarters, the need for keeping the sexes in separate spaces makes people who can afford it build houses with separate quarters for men and women. The need for protecting the women with regard to out- siders is partly taken care of by building high walls around the individual properties. This makes movements in and out of the houses clearly visible as well as shielding the space of the women from onlookers. While men in rural areas gather under trees, separate shelters or huts, the urban Beja utilize coffee shops as 'men's houses' or gather at the market place, which is prohibited for women. The spatial separation of the sexes is possibly greater in the towns than in rural areas.

All this means that changes in development in cultural concepts and theories are not easily predictable from socio-economic changes among urbanized Beja. If the town of Sinkat is increasingly becoming 'tribalized,' one should expect that this would facilitate a prolonged life of cultural features typical of the pastoral and rural kind of adaptation. For this reason a pastoral 'culture of honor' and of *diwáb* ideology may live on for a long time in towns like Sinkat as well as in rural areas. If this is the case, the arguments made for Beja theories of sickness and misfortune may largely be as valid in an urban as a rural setting. My own findings so far also indicate that Beja theories of 'evil eye' as an unpredictable force not connected to specific individuals, spirit attacks and spirit possession have real-life relevance in both urban and rural areas. Conversely, accusations of witchcraft and sorcery are as absent in urban as in rural areas.

NOTES

1 In lowland areas like the Gaash, cows are more common. In Sinkat province only a few Beja in urban areas owned dairy cows.

2 Sudanese Arabic word.

3 Most of the precipitation falls in July and August. The mean annual amount varies from 5 mm in the Northern parts to around 200 mm in the South (Walker 1987).

4 The first drought still remembered by Beja was in the 1880s and 90s, which furthermore was coincidental with the Mahdist war. Later periods of drought were recorded in 1925–27, 1941–42, 1948–49 and 1955–58 (Dahl 1989). The latest drought occurred in 1984 and in 1990–91. The last two droughts brought international attention, and several relief organizations have been operating in the area since 1984 (see, e.g. Dahl 1991).

5 See Bonsaksen 1991.

6 Several Beja told me that the area in earlier times probably has been much more fertile with more vegetation and annual rainfall than now. However, until now I have not come across scientific research mounting any evidence for this.

7 The name Beja (Bega) related to nomads in the Red Sea Hills appears for the first time in an Axumite inscription of the second century A.D. (Christides 1980:130, in Ausenda 1987). Roman references to 'the Blemmyes' in the third century A.D. are regarded by several

historians to be identical with the Beja (Paul 1954). Also earlier hunter-gatherers in that region are possibly related to present day Beja (ibid.). There is, however, no present evidence to support this claim.

8 Personal letters 1897–1931. See list of literature for references.

9 Personal letters 1914–37. See list of literature for references.

10 My addition.

11 From the Arabic word *faqīr*, meaning 'holy man' or 'poor man'. In Sudanese Arabic the word is pronounced *fagīr*, pl. *fugarā*. According to Trimingham (1949:141) the word may have four different meanings:

(1) A pious man in the sense that he strictly observes religious practices.

(2) A holder of a religious offices like being the leader of a Sufi order.

(3) A schoolmaster of a Quran school.

(4) A religious healer.

In the present citation the meanings (2) and (4) seem to apply. See further discussion in Chapter 4.

12 The Sudanese Arabic word *baraka* may be translated as 'blessing', 'holiness', 'abundance' and 'prosperity' (See Catafago 1975). The concept will be discussed repeatedly later on in this discussion.

13 Used here in the meaning of 'a person who has acquired Islamic education'.

14 This is to say, if one does not specifically have the spread of written Islamic texts in mind.

15 According to 1970 figures they numbered approximately 260.000 (Salih 1980).

16 For simplicity, I will mostly refer to their language by the term Beja language.

17 The label 'Bedawiét', strictly meaning speaker of Tu Bedawie, is of importance for Beja people as a label of common identity as against other ethnic groups in the Sudan. As well, there is historical evidence for political mobilization cross-cutting the various Beja tribes against enemies from outside. Seen over a long time span, however, such mobilizations have been extremely rare.

18 Fortunately this conflict was solved by mediators in a peaceful way, which to my impression is the usual case when conflicts threaten at this level.

19 Another form of the word, *díwa* (as spelled by Roper (1928)), is also heard in daily usage among Hadandowa Beja.

20 In more urbanized settings like Sinkat town Beja people do not seem as strict as in rural areas in adhering to intra-*diwáb* marriages. However, marriages between people of different Hadandowa sub-tribes (above the *diwáb* level) are very rare in towns as well.

21 Some Beja told me that being a foreigner I am at an advantage rather than disadvantage for two reasons: Firstly, I am not a competitor for their natural and social resources, and, secondly, I am excused

for asking questions which would be regarded as impolite if asked by another Beja.

22 Similar to *asīda* (Sudanese Arabic), but much thicker in quality.

23 Plural form of *birish*, Sudanese Arabic name for dried leaves of the local *doom (A)* palm, *Hyphaene theabaica*.

24 Called *whálas* in Tu Bedawie.

25 The Beja name for traditional coffee served in small cups following a strict ritualistic procedure. One is supposed to drink one, three, five or seven cups. The cups are served in a special order, giving priority to guests and men of seniority.

26 If the woman in question is married, this will in many cases result in divorce. In severe cases a husband may kill his wife for being unfaithful. In one case I came across, a man killed his wife on mere suspicion. He was imprisoned by the local police. His relatives were, however, negotiating paying a ransom to the local authorities. Some informants told me that it seemed likely they would succeed in getting him out of prison.

27 Period of mourning after death of a person before burial.

28 Where 'only' the clitoris is removed. Whether this is a practice which has some support in the Quran, is a matter of discussion in present day Sudan.

29 A local female research assistant.

30 Some researchers have tried to test the hypothesis of whether people in pastoralist societies are more inclined to react with violence to personal insults. Although it is not yet proven in any way cross-culturally, some findings to be discussed later on clearly supports this hypothesis.

31 All the names used here are pseudonyms.

32 This may often mean a show of aggression more than actual violence. Jacobs (1979) in his study about aggression among Maasai pastoralists reaches the opposite conclusion. He maintains that earlier descriptions of Maasai people as more aggressive and violent than their agro-pastoralists and agriculturalist neighbors have no roots in reality. He even concludes that incidents of violent acts are more frequent from mixed-farmers against the Maasai than *vice versa*. Jacobs (ibid.) like Nisbett *et al.* (1995, see below), however, makes his argument of the background of accounts of real episodes of violence. In the case of Beja people, for example, most shows of aggression do not end in violence. I argue that aggressive responses to insult may be culturally valued without necessarily being directly reflected in statistics of violent episodes.

33 Most of the white Southerners Nisbett *et al.* describe are no longer herders and pastoralists. Central to their theory is the assumption that once a society establishes a 'culture of honor,' it will maintain itself by making it extremely costly for singular individuals to not act accordingly. As shown from studies in predominantly black inner-cities in the USA, only a small proportion may actually hold such values, but the vast majority will have to adapt in order not to be victimized (see i.e. Hannerz 1969).

34 In societies discussed by Murdock (1980) where pastoralism was not predominant, in 121 of 127 (95.3%) societies spirit aggression theories are described as being important. In all (100%) of the 12 pastoral societies which he presents, theories of spirit aggression are important. As one might expect, pastoralism is not in any way a prerequisite for spirit possession. In the majority of agricultural societies discussed by Murdock, belief in spirit aggression is prominent. I am aware that the quality of the different works he cites differs a great deal. I also admit that the number of pastoral societies is not large enough for making good statistics. However, the pastoralist connection he makes regarding the prominence of belief in spirit aggression and the pastoral societies is statistically significant enough to render it plausible for making hypotheses.

35 In many African societies an analytical distinction between sorcery and witchcraft is probably not useful or, alternatively, has to be defined differently than Evans-Pritchard did for the Azande (see, e.g. Turner 1967).

36 Sometimes specific persons are ascribed 'the power of the evil eye,' as has been described for the Islamic, Christian and Jewish traditions and characteristically encountered around the Circum-Mediterranean area (See, e.g. Brøgger 1989, Dundes 1981, Sachs 1983). However, in the Red Sea Hills this seems to be a predominantly urban phenomenon in my experience. I never encountered such an idea in rural areas of the Sinkat province. The rare occurrence in urbanized centers like Sinkat could be explained by a stronger influence of Islamic written sources in towns as well as more influence from the greater Middle East.

37 Like Baxter (1972) she does not distinguish analytically between these terms.

38 A similar point is made by Mary Douglas (1970:xxxv) where she states that 'where social interaction is intense and ill-defined, there we may expect to find witchcraft beliefs.'

39 *Door érr* in Tu Bedawie.

40 It may seem strange that Beja people should be concerned with the danger of losing property to women for several reasons: Firstly, most of the marriages are intra-*diwáb* marriages. Secondly, the recruitment to the *diwáb* is ambilineal. Thirdly, ideally Beja are matrilocal in their pattern of settlement, which should mean that in a inter-*diwáb* marriage the man will tend to move to her relatives. According to several of my informants, however, this period does not last long. Often the couple would live for 1–3 years with her relatives, and then establish themselves near his relatives. If this is usually the case, then there is a real danger of losing *diwáb* property in inter-*diwáb* marriages, if the property is delegated to women.

41 See later discussion in Chapter 4.

42 See later discussion in Chapter 4.

43 Recent studies among the pastoral Barabaig and the agro-pastoralist Iraqw in Tanzania lend support to this claim (Rekdal & Blystad, forthcoming; personal communication). While witchcraft or sorcery

accusations are frequently occurring among the Iraqw they are nearly absent among the Barabaig. Conversely, while spirit aggression is a common explanation for sicknesses and misfortune among the Barabaig this theme plays a less prominent role among the Iraqw.

44 There may be some exceptions to this rule. As an example, in present day Botswana witchcraft accusations are increasingly occurring between non-relatives or distant relatives according to Professor Benedicte Ingstad, University of Oslo (personal communication).

45 Those were the registered numbers given in 1995 from the Sinkat Council. There are a lot of uncertainties connected to these statistics. E.g. the number for 1993 is based on 'housing cards' for obtaining sugar at low official rates, which of course encourage people to give a higher than factual number of household members. However, the counting took place at a time when many people were cultivating their land in rural areas (September), which could contribute to giving a lower than the actual number. However, since similar sources of faults may have operated in 1984 and since the increase in the number of individuals is more than double that in 1984, the statistic may be significant enough to show the general trend.

46 In both registrations the counting of the households is questionable, however. Whether a house is counted as inhabited or empty unfortunately often seems haphazard. Since the same source of fault was present in both countings and the differences between the numbers is significant, however, I believe that the countings clearly show a general tendency.

4

HEALTH, SICKNESS AND HEALING AMONG THE BEJA

4.0. THE OCCURRENCE OF SICKNESS AMONG THE HADANDOWA BEJA

4.0.1. An introductory commentary on the health situation in the Red Sea Hills

The question of which sicknesses are most frequent among the Beja can be approached in two different ways: firstly, one can look at what diagnoses are most often given by medical doctors in the area or, secondly, one can look at what native labels of diagnosis are most often employed by Hadandowa in the area. In this work I will mainly be concerned with the latter approach. There is very little reliable statistical material based on biomedical research available for the Red Sea region. Dr. Mohammad Abu Amne,[1] a Beja pediatrician working in Port Sudan, gave me this list of diagnoses of the ten most frequent sicknesses occurring among children. The list is ordered according to the frequency of the condition, 'nutrition deficiency' being the most frequent, 'anemia' the second most frequent and so on.

1. Nutrition deficiency: lack of protein usually leads to the sickness of kwashiorkor, characterized by body thinness combined with a big, swollen stomach. General poor nutrition may lead to marasmus, an even more serious loss of strength and body mass.
2. Anemia: many Beja do not have vegetables in their diet. Cows' milk, which contains iron, is often not available. If milk is available at all, it will most frequently be goat's milk, which, unfortunately, does not contain any significant amount of iron. For this reason, severe enlargement

51

of the liver in children as a result of anemia is sometimes encountered in hospitals.[2]

3. Vitamin deficiencies.
4. Gastroenteritis. At the time of the fieldwork, UNICEF was carrying out a program to prevent child mortality as a result of diarrhea. Despite their efforts, diarrhea continues to be a serious problem in the Red Sea province.
5. Bacterial respiratory tract infection.
6. Whopping cough.
7. Measles.
8. Tuberculosis, including chest, bone and skin tuberculosis: although tuberculosis is not the most frequent complaint, many health workers regard it as the most or one of the most serious health problems for several reasons. The diagnosis is considered socially shameful by Beja, so people often do not report it. Since it has a long period of treatment (at least 6 months), it is often difficult to persuade patients to continue heavy medication for such a long time. If not treated, it will usually lead on to death. Because it is so contagious, often several family members will contract the sickness. The spread of the sickness is also facilitated by general weakness related to lack in proper nutrition. For this reason, decrease in food supply during a period of drought will lead on to an increase in the prevalence of the sickness.
9. Tetanus: tetanus may be caused by animal feces coming in contact with a skin wound. Since animals and people are living densely together in most households, the high frequency of tetanus is not astonishing.
10. Lung infections.

It is illuminating to consider that the four most frequent sickness states are all connected to nutrition and nutritional states. After the recent severe droughts in the area, undernourishment is the primary problem in children as well as adults.

4.0.2. Hadandowa Beja sickness diagnostization

Beja people are themselves well aware of the connection between nutrition and sickness. Abu Aisha, an old rural *omda*,[3] expresses his thoughts like this:

'Sicknesses have now become more frequent, in former times they were few. If a person was wounded in former times, we did not take him to the hospital, but gave him butter oil and local treatment. But now, if a person receives a very small wound, he will pass away! And if you give a sick person meat and butter oil, it will harm him! Now all sicknesses are increasing. I know the reason for this increase: It is because people use coffee beans and snuff, which were less usual before. Also people now use less butter oil and meat. People do not use nutritious things like relief oil, which sometimes even makes *herár*.'[4]

General lack of food as well as the change in food habits are often related to the increase of sicknesses of Hadandowa Beja people. If new food items are introduced in an area, people are inclined to relate seemingly new sicknesses to them. However, the relationships Beja make between nutrition and sickness are complex and, from a Westerner's point of view, often unexpected. In order to get an understanding of how Beja people make etiological connections between sicknesses and different causal agents, one first has to explore the knowledge base from which Beja make their inferences of causal[5] connections. In order to make it easier for the reader to follow my lines of thought, however, I will introduce a limited list of the most frequently occurring native sickness labels I encountered in the Sinkat province.

A common theme in treatment traditions in the Middle East and the Circum-Mediterranean areas has been the division of sicknesses into 'hot' and 'cold' sicknesses. This division is pervasive among the Beja as well, although many traits of their traditions deviate from a 'classical' humoral tradition.[6] This will be discussed in detail later on. At this stage it is sufficient to state that Beja people tend to think of 'cold' sicknesses as resulting from cold weather, cold water, cold body states or kinds of food considered to be 'cold,' and 'hot' sicknesses as resulting from hot weather, hot body states and various 'hot,' spicy or strong-tasting food. Generally 'hot' sicknesses are treated by 'cold' means, while 'cold' sicknesses are treated by 'hot' means. The terms 'hot' and 'cold' refer to more than temperature attributes, as will be discussed presently.

For the sake of simplicity, I will try to divide the physical sicknesses in the list below as far as possible into the categories of 'hot,' 'cold,' and 'sicknesses caused by spirits and mystical influences.' As will become clear later on, however, the divisions given here represent an oversimplification. For example the sickness of *táflam* (see below) may result from 'cold food' as well as from spirits or tainted food. In addition, it may be caused by the 'evil eye.' The terms given in the list represent only the most frequently occurring sickness labels.

Old Islamic scriptures concerning health matters are present among the Beja. However, only a very few literate people in the Red Sea Hills are able to read classical Arabic. Despite being few in number, because they are seen as 'men of religion' they are in a position to influence people more than could be predicted from the size of their group. The classical book *The Medicine of the Prophet*,[7] written by Ibn Qayan al-Juwziyya written in the 14th century A.D., is the most basic point of reference for local Islamic healers *(fugará)* in Sinkat.[8] For this reason I will try at various points in the coming discussions to refer to this source of influence from the classical humoral tradition. The English translation of it is done in the field by my research assistant Eisa Ali Jelani.[9]

i. Hot sickness states

Kosúlt

Kosúlt is conceived of as a 'hot sickness' eating body tissue and making people lose weight and feel feverish. It is often spoken about as a 'fire within the body' which may stem from heat like the hotness of the sun and may as well transfer into other 'hot' sicknesses.

Kosúlt may be treated by using things with cold temperature in order to counteract the heat. This is in accord with thoughts represented in *The Medicine of the Prophet*, where cold water is recommended for conditions of fever: 'When this cold water touches the hotness of fever, it [the fever] is destroyed' (p.24). However, the concepts of hotness and coldness are, as will be discussed in Chapter 6, linked to other physiological dimensions in Beja theory other than classical humoral thinking. *Kosúlt* may also be treated by various kinds of heat extraction, as for example letting the patient be wrapped in goatskin from a newly slaughtered goat in order to let the skin absorb the heat.

Heminéit

Heminéit is the Beja word for a substance with a sour taste which Hadandowa people conceive to be in the stomach of all humans. They often talk about it as a kind of 'fuel' for the body without which humans cannot survive. However, this heminéit may be of a bad quality or there might be too much of it. These conditions cause sickness, and the sickness is also called heminéit. It is characterized by a state of laziness, stomach pain, headache and a 'burning throat.' The sickness of heminéit may lead on to many other sicknesses, most of which are 'hot sicknesses.'

Gúrda

Gúrda is the Beja name for a sickness characterized by fever, generalized body pain and tiredness. The pain is often described as 'pain in the bones.' Periods of chills and body shaking from fever are common, and sometimes people report headache and vomiting. The symptoms people describe and their onset are often very similar to the symptoms of malaria.

The smell of green grass after periods of good rain is thought to be the main cause behind the sickness. However, the milk and meat of animals feeding on this grass and vegetation may also cause gúrda in humans.

Milaria[10]

Although most Beja recognize the utility of anti-malaria drugs, traditional treatment similar to the treatment of gúrda is often sought out, especially in rural areas. Often people conceive of both mosquitoes and the smell of green grass etc. as causes for malaria.

Koléit

Koléit is the most common Beja word for gonhorrea. According to local informants, the word bájal is used for a later and more complicated stage of the sickness. The common symptoms of the sickness are well recognized by Beja. Sexual relations are thought to be the main mode of transfer. However, a 'hot substance' and not germs is transferred. Women with the hot sickness of kosúlt are most frequently mentioned as the source of it. The 'hot' substance creating gonorrhea may also be transferred through handshaking, clothes and through smoking the same water pipe.

ii. Cold sickness states

Táflam

Táflam is a Beja word for a stomach sickness usually described with symptoms like stomach pain with a 'knocking' sensation and severe diarrhoea which often contains blood. It is a very frequent condition in the area, a condition which is often diagnosed as dystentaria by local health workers. It may stem from spirits as well as tainted food or from drinking cold water on an empty stomach.

Watáb

Watáb is a Beja word for a 'cold' non-serious condition characterized by headache, tiredness and laziness. It may result from prolonged lack of nourishment, from tiredness, postponement of breakfast or from walking for a long distance without eating a meal. It may easily be treated by making small cuttings on the legs in order to 'let out cold blood' as well as by burning all the finger- and toe-nails lightly with a small burning stick. The condition is very frequent, and people seldom seek the advice or help of a specialist for it.

Herár

Herár is a Beja concept similar to the Sudanese Arabic concept of *yeraghān*. Both concepts are denoting the symptoms of yellowish coloring of the skin and sclera. From a biomedical point of view, this symptom, of course, applies to a broad range of negative physical states like obstruction of the bile tract, various malfunctions of the liver, pancreatic or liver cancer, destruction of red blood cells from malaria and so on.

If the cold sickness of *watáb* lasts for a long time, it may develop into the sickness of *herár*. *Herár* is treated by specialists only. Thirteen brandings are made at specific places on the body with a piece of hot iron. In addition, the patient is advised to avoid fat food and eat a lot of sugar.

Hāf and háf masóob

Beja think of *hāf* as a very dangerous 'cold' sickness which may often kill the patient. The sickness is characterized by abdominal swelling. This swelling is sometimes asymmetrical, showing more on one side of the stomach than the other. Most people describe 'solid parts' which contain 'black, solid blood' and can be palpated on the surface of the stomach.

Hāf masóob is a children's sickness which is less severe than *hāf*. Like *hāf* it is a cold sickness, but one cannot always feel any 'solid parts' on the stomach. The child will typically have a swollen stomach and diarrhea. People think that this condition may develop into *hāf* if not treated properly.

Hāf is not among the most frequent conditions. However, since people think that it is difficult to cure and often leads to a painful death, it is utterly feared by all Beja. When its name is mentioned, people employ protective formulas or spit on the ground in order to repulse the sickness. *Hāf masóob*, by contrast, is a frequently employed diagnosis by Beja parents and not so much feared.

Áfram

Áfram is a Beja term for a severe disease where 'knots,' sometimes described like 'fists', can be palpated on the surface of different parts of the body. The patient will most often die from this 'cold' sickness.

iii. Sicknesses of spirits and mystical influences

Sirr

A usual explanation for this state is that a person X saw another person Y having a meal which X would like to share, but for reasons of politeness or other reasons X did not accept an invitation from Y. The food will then harm Y's stomach and cause *sirr*. The Beja do not think that the influence is caused by the illegitimate emotion of envy *per se*. X does not envy Y the food but only experiences a wish to taste it, and the wish itself transforms the quality of the food. Like *táflam* it is a very usual complaint which all Hadandowa people experience now and then.

Tesérimt[11]

Tesérimt is a mystical sickness, but it is not caused by spirits. Usually only small children are afflicted. A wide range of symptoms is described, although most people state that skin wounds are usual. The wounds are most often characterized as 'dirty' and stemming from rashes filled with water. A circular discoloring of the skin around the wounds is often described. In other cases the child will die before any wounds appear. The child often has a bloated stomach and cries ceaselessly. Sometimes the child, if affected before birth, might die in the womb. In dramatic cases it is described as 'being born without skin.'

The sickness of *tesérimt* has two possible sources. Firstly, it may result from influences mediated by mystical food. If the mother eats meat, butter oil or milk from foreign animals or eats food items which the Beja are not used to, the child may get the sickness in the womb or through mother's milk. Secondly, some native camels are treated in a special way in order to make them more fertile. Unfortunately this increase in fertility is dangerous for people other than the owners of the camels, and the products of them or their mere presence may cause sickness and death in children of other households. In the rural area of Odrus, on average roughly one child in every household[12] is said by parents or close relatives to have died from *tesérimt*. In Sinkat, people living in the center of the town tended to speak more about *t'háasimt* (see below) than *tesérimt*, while people on its outskirts still frequently experienced sicknesses and deaths of children as resulting from *tesérimt*.

T'háasimt

The spirit world is thought to be a reflection of the ordinary world in many ways. There are spirit herbs, spirit animals as well as spirit humans. For example, there are ordinary spiders and there are spirit spiders. Both of them may bite people and cause skin rashes. Both of them are called *t'háasimt*, which is also the name in the Beja language which is used for the sickness resulting from bites of spiders. However, the most serious sickness and the sickness of most concern to Hadandowa people results from bites of the spirit spider. The main symptom of *t'háasimt* is skin rashes, which may be localized to one area, like the forehead, or be spread all over the body. If the sickness is not treated properly, the rashes may 'go inside the body and eat the liver' and the person will then die. In case of spirit spider attack, like other spirit sicknesses, treatment by *fugarā'* is the only possible treatment. The sickness is a frequent complaint both in rural and urban areas, and *fugarā'* are often consulted for this sickness.

Mírquay

Literally meaning 'fright' in Beja language, or *khoof* in Arabic, is also the name of a childhood sickness resulting from a frightening experience, like seeing a spirit in sleep or while awake or being surprised by a dog suddenly barking behind it. The sudden appearance of a person whom the child has not seen before may also cause the sickness. Most informants told me that the symptoms of fright from spirits are more severe and persistent and require the intervention of a *fagīr*.

Another Beja word used for the condition is the word *míngay*. This word strictly means 'left alone,' but it is used as well in characterizing a sickness by saying that a child suffers from 'left alone-ness.' In this use of the concept there is a hidden cultural proscription that a small child should never be left out of sight of the parents or a close adult relative. As soon as it is left alone, bad things might happen to it.

Shagīga[13]

Shagīga is a condition of intense headache affecting only one side of the head. It is described in *The Medicine of the Prophet* (p.66–69) as a sickness which results from 'air' or 'a kind of fluid' proceeding from the stomach to 'the vessels of the head.' It may be treated in some instances by provoking vomiting. To my knowledge none of those notions of etiology are shared by Beja people, although, as we shall see, they share the conception of a direct relationship between the stomach and the blood. According to Beja theories, *shagīga* may result from spirit affliction, from a 'bad smell' like the smell of animal excrement or from cold things, the 'common cold' or cold weather. In all cases people usually seek the help of a *fagīr* for this sickness. Although the condition is not uncommon, specific individuals tend to experience it from time to time. The symptoms described, like intolerance of daylight and intense localized headache with nausea, are rather similar to those of migraine headache.

Toordíp

Toordíp is a Beja word for epilepsy, *saraʿa* in Arabic; literally it means 'falling down.' Nearly all Beja people I met believed spirits to be behind this sickness. Some Beja believe spirits to be dwelling in the head of the sufferer. When the sick person has a fit, people usually do not dare to interfere or even touch him, but immediately call for a *fagīr*.

Although the belief that spirits cause epilepsy is widespread in many Muslim societies, other societies, like in rural parts of Turkey (Good 1994), allow for other causal explanations like frightening experiences, lack of sleep or worry. A combination of explanations is also put forward in *The Medicine of the Prophet* (p.51), where epilepsy may stem from spirits, or alternatively, from lack of balance between the four kinds of bodily fluids. Although some urban Hadandowa people allow for physiological explanations, in my experience most of them consider spirits to be the sole cause of epilepsy.

Kelay t'áat

Keláy is the Beja word for 'a bird.' The word *t'áat* means 'struck.' The expression *kelay t'áat* thus means 'a bird struck.' *Kelay t'áat* denotes a condition of half-side facial paralysis. The sickness is thought to be caused by a spirit bird slapping the face of its victim with one of its wings. Although in principle everybody may get the sickness, the actual cases I came to hear about all concerned adolescent girls of ten to fifteen years of age who were approaching the marriageable age.[14] According to two Islamic healers (*fugarā'*) who treat such cases from time to time, all of them recover from the condition after a period of treatment. Although people often spoke about this sickness, the prevalence of the condition did not appear to be high in Sinkat and surrounding areas.

Háale

The Beja word *háale* may be translated 'madness.' People labeled by this word are usually described as showing one or more of the following traits: speaking strangely, displaying strange behavior like walking out naked or dressing in a strange way, seeing things not experienced by others, not being able to take care of their daily needs like eating, dressing, or finding their way back to their home, or being abnormally aggressive. People behaving in this manner are perceived to be possessed by spirits, not merely afflicted by them.

The usual treatment consists in a *fagīr* trying to expel the spirit by various means like reading the Quran, whipping the patient, or making the patient observe specific dietary rules (see later discussions). In some cases the sick person will live together with the healer in his or her house for a period of time. This concept of madness, its etiology and treatment is shared by other Muslim societies in the Sudan as well as beyond.

Although the condition is linked to spirits and spirit possession, people are not as afraid of 'mad' persons as they are of a person having an epileptic fit. Since there is no kind of psychiatric care in the area, 'mad' persons receive no type of medication or hospitalization in a medical institution. They intermingle with other people in the market place or on the streets. Mostly people will talk with them in a friendly manner, and sometimes people entertain themselves with their 'craziness.' In one instance a 'madman' was told that I was a great healer. The man instantly treated me with due respect and asked me to lay my healing hands on his head, to the laughter and applause from the audience!

In some cases, a 'mad' person is believed to be especially benevolent and not capable of any kind of evil. The person is thought to bestow blessings[15] on people meeting him or her on the street. This is a common Northern Sudanese theme well known from the famous novel *The Wedding of Zein* by Al-Tayyib Salih (1968). Some women will even supply them with gifts of money in the same manner as wandering Muslim preachers and holy men are treated.

Waswás

A person with *waswás (A)* is seen as more lightly psychologically afflicted. The term applies to a broad range of uncommon behavior, like having paranoia, performing excessive rituals of cleanliness, experiencing a long-lasting depression of mood or, not the least, isolating oneself from other people. Indeed, social isolation in the socially very 'dense' Beja society is the key feature people mention when describing symptoms of psychological malfunction. Although people sometimes believe spirits to be behind the condition, personal worries and difficult life circumstances are also invoked as modes of explanation. In addition, the sicknesses from *zār* spirits (see below) may often involve symptoms of *waswás*.

Zār

Zār is an example of what Lewis (1971, 1989) calls a 'cult of affliction.' It is a possession cult typically involving politically marginalized social groups like women or slaves in Muslim societies across Northern Africa and the Middle East. In zār, once possessed, one will continue to be possessed. Healing consists of trying to please the zār spirits so as not to harm their hosts.

Clearly, among the Beja, more women than men are afflicted by zār. The symptoms often involve minor complaints like a minor swelling, paralysis in one hand, excessive or irregular menstrual bleeding, 'low mood' or infertility. In addition, marriage problems may be ascribed to zār spirits. However, both men and small children may get the sickness of zār. This happens much more frequently among the Beja than is reported in other Muslim societies, where the proportion of women afflicted is more prominent (Boddy 1988, 1989; Cloudsley 1984; Constantinides 1977, 1982; Hall et al. 1981; Lewis 1969, 1971, 1986, 1989; Lewis et al. 1991; Kenyon 1991; Makris 1991; Natvig 1992; Safa 1988; Schneider 1988).

4.1. TRADITIONS OF TREATMENT AND PRACTITIONERS

4.1.1. The basīr

The term basīr is said by Arabists to mean 'one who can see the unseen.'[16] The busarā'[17] are traditionally linked to the practice of bone-setting in various literature. Bone-setting as a traditional specialized skill is found in Latin America (Huber & Anderson 1996) and the Far East (Kleinman 1980) as well as in Africa (Bishaw 1991) and the Middle East (Gallagher 1983). Bloss, a former British colonial medical inspector in the Sudan, describes his impressions of busarā' and other traditional healers in the following way:

'Of the native methods of treatment at that time the following points are interesting. Surgical procedures were carried out [Mahdi's time, not own experience] by a man called the basir (lit. a skilled person). Hakims were the wise men who compounded the mysterious mixtures that were prescribed for non-surgical cases. In addition there was a sort of barber surgeon, who armed with circumcision clamp and a bleeding horn did a good trade visiting and soliciting custom from door to door. It used to be the custom to be "bled" every six weeks or so which is rather reminiscent of England 100 years ago. Wounds were treated by the *basir* who having washed them, put ground coffee, gunpowder or butter in them and bound them up. Fractures were splinted with palm leaves, but these were put on so tightly that in many cases gangrene supervened. When a limb had to be amputated for surgical reasons, it was stretched through a hole in the wall of a house and severed with a blow of a sword. The stump was then plunged into hot oil to stop the bleeding. For headaches, melted tallow was poured down the nostrils and for infantile diarrhoea the teeth of the child were extracted and the tooth sockets fired with cautery' (Bloss 1948:42).

The role of the *basīr* as a person mainly treating wounds and mending bones is predominant in other parts the present-day Sudan as well.[18] However, in order to get a proper view of a typical *basīr* in the Red Sea Hills, one has to combine Bloss' description of the *basīr,* the 'hakim,' and the 'barber surgeon' and add to it the role of the traditional 'herbalist.' Although *busarā'* in towns like Sinkat sometimes specialize in mending bones or treating stomach sicknesses, typically a Beja *basīr* uses a range of techniques for treatment and also treats a range of sicknesses. Indeed they are more similar to the Cushitic general practitioners *(ogeessa/wogeessha)* described by Slikkerveer (1990) from the border area between Somalia and Ethiopia than *busarā'* as generally described in the Middle East:

> '... his medical practices involve a number of techniques and instruments geared to treating mainly naturalistic illnesses ... [He has] a wide knowledge of medicinal plants and traditional remedies which he grows himself or gathers from special places in the mountains. In addition to fractures and wounds, [he also] treats hemorrhoids, abscesses, ulcers, headaches, swellings on the head, ear infections, muscular cramps, lumbar complaints and various forms of cancer. His methods of treatment range from counterirritation by means of singing, cauterization and having patients inhale the smoke of burning leaves ...' (Slikkerveer 1990:177).

Hadandowa Beja *busarā'* whom I encountered used a broad spectrum of herbal remedies as well as animal products like butter oil from animal milk or the contents of animal intestines. They made skin brandings with a heated piece of iron for dysentery and various other sicknesses. For sicknesses of 'bad blood' (see later discussions) they made cuttings or used a 'bleeding horn' for letting blood. This remedy is widespread cross-culturally in the Islamic world (Gallagher 1983; Paul 1975), and is strongly recommended in the book *The Medicine of the Prophet* (p.44–49).

If one looks at their individual careers, some of them inherited their practice from their fathers, or, in some cases, from their mothers. A particular sub-tribe of the Hadandowa, the Hamdab, has a special reputation for providing good *busarā*. While this tribal background is supporting ones position as a *basīr*, it is not a necessary condition. Although numerous *busarā* are not Hamdab, however, their practice usually has a limited local scope mainly serving people of their own sub-tribe, neighborhood or *diwáb*.

A *basīr* practice does not need to be inherited. In many cases I encountered, a person gradually became known as having special skills in traditional treatment. Some of those persons were women. In such cases it is difficult to say at what point of time the person became a 'specialist' from a former position of being a clever 'non-specialist.' In this regard the *busarā* tradition differs sharply from the *fugarā*[19] tradition, which is soon to be discussed. Indeed, the knowledge of *busarā* is often indistinguishable from ordinary folk knowledge.

When talking with Beja people or interviewing them about the symptoms, causes and possible treatments of sicknesses, the answers of *busarā* 'specialists' did not usually deviate in content from 'non-specialists.' However, the *busarā* were generally more knowledgeable than most Beja and could provide more detailed accounts and present a wider range of solutions than the average Beja. Especially concerning forms of treatment, the *busarā* tended to be the most knowledgeable. In questions regarding etiology, however, their knowledge was not much greater than that of most adult Beja. In addition, many *busarā* depended upon sources of livelihood other than being a *basīr*. The *busarā* tradition is clearly a 'tradition of the people' representing one kind of traditional Beja wisdom and knowledge.

In most sickness cases I came across, people would have tried out their own means of treatment within their own household before consulting a *basīr*. Mostly, the means they employed were of the same kind as the ones employed by *busarā*. If their treatments fail, they may seek the help of a *basīr*. However, some techniques, like making brandings or deep cuttings, are usually not performed by non-specialists.

Usually, people have the choice of consulting a range of different *busarā*. What *basīr* they choose is naturally dependent upon his or her perceived skills and reputation. However, there is one special type of reputation which is difficult to connect with skillfulness. Some *busarā* are said to be *héequal*, a Beja word having the connotations of blessed, holy and luck-bringing. The word is also connected to increased fertility in people and animals. The theory of *héequal*-ness is important when people make choices about which healer to consult, whether a *basīr*, a *fagīr* or a cowry-shell woman. This theory, however, will be discussed thoroughly in Chapter 6.

4.1.2. The cowry-shell woman

The profession of predicting people's destiny or condition from throwing cowry-shells[20] is an entirely female profession. Although most women in Sinkat from time to time entertain themselves by throwing cowry-shells, relatively few are considered professionals. Seven shells, whose convex sides have been cut off, are thrown on the ground and analyzed from their positions as well as on which side they land. Ha'isha, an elderly Hamdab woman, is one of the few cowry-shell specialists in Sinkat. She explained that in some cases she provides sickness diagnoses, as well as predictions about what type of treatment and practitioner to seek for. The type of divining system she represents is common throughout the Sudan (Ausenda 1987).

Ha'isha told me that people come from all over Sinkat to visit her, although most of her clients live in Dinayeet, her own suburb. Although people do not visit her daily, she states that more people are seeking her advice nowadays than before. In her case she inherited her trade from her mother. However, as the case of Amna shows us, this is not a necessary condition:

> Amna is presently practicing as a female *fagīr* in a relatively well-regulated area of Sinkat town. She is a talkative and friendly woman who makes friends easily. Before starting a

career as a *fagīr*, however, she made a living as a successful
cowry-shell woman. She explains, 'Before I became a professional in cowry shells I was very poor. After I was
divorced from my first husband, I took a loan of 50 [Sud-
anese] pounds to sell eggs. From the profit of the eggs I
wanted to pay back the loan. Then, unfortunately, in the
middle of this work I became sick with malaria. In this
malaria period I had a dream. In that dream I saw a bird
and a 50 pound note in his mouth. This bird said to me,
"Give these fifty pounds back to the person from whom you
took the loan." I did. This bird then advised me to be a
cowry-shell woman. At first when I began as a cowry-shell
woman, my brothers and my [second] husband told me to
stop this business, but I did not listen.'

4.1.3. The *fagīr*

Amna's story is quite typical of stories I heard from some *fugarāʾ*
explaining why they became practitioners. By contrast, similarly
validating stories were never to my experience told by *busarāʾ*.
In Amna's case, she gained a good reputation as a cowry-shell
woman because, according to an informant Saleimin, 'she used
to tell people the truth and told no lies.' Saleimin is a personal
friend of Amna. Her success made her expand her practice, and
she then became a *fagīr*. Amna continues her story:

> 'After this I married and had a child. I then changed my job
> and became a *fagīr*. People used to come to me in my
> home, and I gave them *mihaya*.[21] As *fagīr* I also used one
> part of the Holy Quran to begin with, but now I use the
> whole of it.'

'People believe she is *héequal*,'[22] Saleimin states, and 'people come
to visit her from far away.' 'There are always many people
waiting for her in her home.' If stories like hers are generally
accepted by people, such stories clearly strengthen and probably
help establish a reputation for *héequal*-ness. While being *héequal*
is good for the practice of a *basīr*, it is a necessary precondition
for being a *fagīr*.

The Sudanese Arabic term *fagīr* stems from the word *faqīr* in
classical Arabic, meaning 'a materially poor person'. This term
has traditionally been applied to Muslim holy men in general,

not primarily to people doing healing. In the Sudanese setting, however, a *faqīr* is almost always considered first and foremost a healer, which might be a particular feature of the 'Sudanized' version of Islam (see, e.g. Trimingham 1949). Although a *faqīr* in the Red Sea Hills sometimes uses herbal remedies, they mainly employ 'treatment by the Quran' in their practice. This treatment may be administered by different means, the most usual being:

1. *Waṣl (A):* A Quranic inscription is made on a piece of paper, which is then burned. The ash is mixed with water, which is given to the patient to drink.
2. *Mihaya (A):* Quranic verses (often seven) are written in ink on a piece of paper or wood. The inscription is washed away with water afterward. This water is carefully collected and the patient is given the water to drink.
3. *Hejāb (A):* A piece of paper with a Quranic inscription is wrapped inside an amulet as protection against attacks from evil spirits. The use of *mihaya* as well as *hejbāt*[23] are common all over the Muslim Sudan (Holy 1991) as well as the rest of the Muslim world (Gallagher 1983; Slikkerveer 1990; Trimingham 1949, 1976; Wikan 1982).
4. Readings from the Quran by the *faqīr*. The *faqīr* sometimes makes the readings more effective by holding his right hand on the head of the patient, by spitting on the ground after each word or by spitting directly in the face of the patient.

While the *basīr* knowledge to a great extent may be considered 'folk knowledge,' this is not the case with *faqīr* knowledge. While most *busarā* I encountered tended to be illiterate, most *fugarā* had at least some proficiency in reading Arabic. The three *fugarā* with whom I had the opportunity to establish personal contact, all spent considerable time reading books on Islamic medicine, and, in general, Islamic literature. While two of them inherited their practices from their famous fathers and grand-fathers, the third one, Mohammad, started his own practice. Although his father's reputation for piety clearly helped him, Mohammad has a distinct personal story explaining his career:

'My career started in 1962 when I was a manager of an irrigation scheme. One of the officers got bitten by a scorpion. To drive by car to the nearest hospital would have taken two hours, and, besides, the car was not there. I felt bewildered about what to do, and suddenly the thought came to me that I could try to read some Quran for him and lay my hand on him. I did, and the man improved immediately.

At first the man was laying on the ground breathing quickly and superficially. Later he sat among his companions playing cards and walking around with no symptoms at all. In the lowlands of irrigation-schemes scorpions represent a big problem, and people often get bitten. This particular officer got bitten beside the door of his office at two o'clock in the afternoon when he was about to close the office!'

His story is not untypical, although his high social standing may be exceptional. Similar stories are both told by and about *fugarā*, as another story told about a female *fagīr* by an informant is an example of:

'One *fagīr* in Sinkat, not so many years ago, died, and he had many books, but none of his sons took over his work and the books he used for his work. One of his daughters became very sick, and she told people that she wanted very much to become a *fagīr*. She took over the work and the books, and then she became well. After this incident a man was brought to her because he was unable to move. She treated him and he became well, and finally he married her. Now she is a famous *fagīr* in Sinkat.'

This female *fagīr* is presently living near the center of Sinkat town. She is from the Ashraf tribe, a Beja tribe claiming direct descent from the prophet Mohammad (Paul 1954). People from this tribe generally have a reputation for piety, and Ashraf *fugarā* have a similar standing among *fugarā* as Hamdab *busarā* among *busarā*.

Beside from the distinguishing facts that *fugarā* generally are literate, supposed to build on written Islamic sources, usually inherit their practice, and have a clear and legitimized point of entry into their practice, there are other features that also set them apart from *busarā*. While *busarā* knowledge in principle may be obtained by anyone, *fugarā* knowledge is considered by Beja generally to be secret knowledge. Further, while *busarā* practice is largely non-mystical, the majority of *fugarā* employ 'spirit helpers' in their work. Although the help of 'spirit helpers' is considered invaluable by the *fagīr*, the co-operation is not without dangers, as my *fagīr* friend Ahmad explains:

'Being a *fagīr* is harmful to your children. When you are weak or make a mistake, they [the spirits] can harm your children. They once killed one of my children. This happens when your friendship with them is weak. You must have weapons with you like a knife or something similar. Also, when you get rid of spirits from a patient, sometimes these spirits harm you. It can make you a mental case, or put you in a bad mood. I need to take care. This Holy Quran [he shows me one exemplar and holds it firmly] is keeping the spirits away from you.'

In order to get friendly with helping spirits, he had to go though a period of special observances called *etikāf (A)*, Ahmad explained to me:

'During the *etikāf* period, for one year and nine months, you have to abstain from all kinds of animal products, anything which has a soul *(ruḥ)*, including birds. You can never leave your house, never joke, never speak about absent persons, you must eat *balīla* food [beans with water and salt, boiled], no smoking, no snuffing, and your age must be more than forty years. Women can not have spirit servants.'[24]

While *busarā* knowledge in the Red Sea Hills is part of a local tradition, the *fugarā* tradition is part of a wider discourse of the whole Islamic world, although their importance in different societies may vary (Holy 1991). The characteristic features of *fugarā* I encountered in Sinkat do not differ substantially from the *fuqarā* counterparts in other parts of the Muslim world (see, e.g. Eickelman 1981; Holy 1991; Nasr 1972)

Generally, although it is clearly the case that *fugarā* knowledge is a specialized knowledge set apart from ordinary folk-knowledge, Beja people very much live in a world in which spirits are present. Even if they usually will state that all 'spirit matters' belong to *fagīr* knowledge, the folk knowledge concerning spirits is elaborate, as will be demonstrated in Chapter 6. Folk knowledge, as well, expands beyond the limits of *fagīr* knowledge, a fact which is exemplified by the popular *zār* cults and beliefs about *zār* spirits.

4.1.4. The *táflam basīr*

The *táflam basīr* is a specialist in the stomach sickness of *táflam*. While people usually will go to a *fagīr* for sicknesses thought to be caused by spirits and to a *basīr* for most other sicknesses, the sickness of *táflam* is a noteworthy exception. This *basīr* is thought to be capable of dealing even with spirits causing *táflam*. His methods vary from using specific herbs, making burns on the stomach or whispering Quranic verses while performing abdominal massage.

Why do people not consult a *fagīr* for such spirit related complaints? A possible explanation could be that people think about *táflam* spirits as a type of spirit not definable in Muslim terms. They tend to speak about them as small capricious spirits rather than evil spirits *per se*. As in the case of *zār* spirits, as we shall see, people tend not to classify them in a clear way as either Muslim, non-Muslim, good or evil. I even came across cases where Quranic treatment was not considered effective. The patient in one case was told not to say 'bismillah'[25] after eating and to eat with the left hand, both kinds of behavior at odds with Muslim prescriptions. In other instances, instead of reading the Quran, the *basīr* read magic formulas of threat in order to frighten the spirit away.

Similar forms of mixture between Quranic treatment and *busarā'* treatment are employed for breast infection in women, called *toodíh* in Beja language. Whispering threats or Quranic verses in the ears or over the breasts of the patient is the usual treatment, a practice which is somewhat similar to the 'counter-irritation by means of singing' described by Slikkerveer for Cushitic Oromo and Somali general practitioners in Ethiopia (see above). Brandings on or near the breast are often combined with the whispering. Unlike for *táflam*, however, I never came across a *basīr* specialized only in the sickness of *toodíh*.

The *táflam basīr* belongs to the same old local *busarā'* tradition of the Red Sea Hills as outlined above. Although more specialized than an ordinary *basīr*, his knowledge is not exclusive or monopolized. While *fagīr* knowledge is specialized and exclusive knowledge, *basīr* knowledge is, in all cases, folk knowledge of the kind mainly underlying the theories to be discussed in Chapter 6.

4.1.5. The *zār* doctor

While *fugarā'* are able to deal with more easily definable spirits according to a Muslim schema, they are unable to deal with the unpredictable and capricious *zār (A)* spirits. While *fugarā'* are often able to identify a problem as caused by *zār* spirits, the *zār* spirits are outside their domain of influence. Although, as will be discussed later, the *zār* cult is in some respects at odds with Islamic principles, a *fagīr* may often recommend the treatment of a specific specialist who only deals with *zār* afflictions. Beja people often expressed a rather pragmatic attitude to this: 'Well, *zār* ceremonies are not Islamic, but *zār* spirits are present among us, so what can we do?'

The *zār* doctor, or *sheikh (A)*, will often recommend that a *zār* ceremony be arranged. Although the specialist may be able to identify a sickness as resulting from *zār* during a shorter consultation, the ceremony is seen as necessary in order to identify the type of spirit and its needs. People in the Sinkat region described two types of *zār* ceremonies:

1. The *jallūka* ceremony, where the name *jallūka (A)* refers to the drum used. This is a complete ceremony which may last from three to seven days. Ideally, guests are served meals as long as the treatment lasts. I had the opportunity to be a guest at seven such parties, two in the Red Sea Hills. In both Beja parties a huge sheep was offered in the first day of the ceremony. Both the sheep and the patient were painted with *henna* beforehand, a tradition which is only performed during marriage or for married women, signaling their married status. The patient is referred to as the bride, married to her *zār* spirit. After slaughtering the sheep she is given some of its blood to drink. The further development of the ceremony, which will be discussed later on, is characterized by drumming, singing and violent trance-like dancing where the identity of the spirit is sought as well as its wishes.

2. The *tayyāb* is a smaller party conducted without drum rhythms. There are two variations of this ceremony, one urban type and one rural. The rural one is more simple than the urban in regard to equipment and the food served. Sometimes the treatment consists merely of buying special

items for the sick person. *Ṭayyāb* is also used as a treatment for bad luck and troubles, one of my informants states.

The wishes of the spirits vary according to their ethnic background and sex. The spirit may be a British colonial officer or an Ethiopian prostitute, and both the ceremonial requirements and the gifts will naturally vary accordingly. Aisha, an elderly woman whom we will encounter later on, explained her type of possession by a European spirit: 'My kind of *zār* is *khawája*[26] *zār*. This *zār* spirit wants the equipment of trousers, shirt, necktie, cap, pipe and boots and a black stick.' This equipment represents the kind of clothes and paraphernalia used by male British colonial officers earlier this century.

The *zār* cult is accounted for by various researchers as a predominantly urban phenomenon in all the societies in which it is present, occurring mostly in cities and sometimes in bigger villages. Conceptions about *zār* and *zār* treatment seem, however, to be as common in rural areas as they are in the urban areas of the Red Sea Hills.[27]

There is one clear difference between urban and rural areas, however. Large-scale *zār* parties only take place in the towns. Further there are, to my knowledge, almost never any *zār* doctors visiting patients outside towns. *Ṭayyāb* is performed in urban as well as rural areas, although a simpler treatment is more common in the rural parts. This treatment consists of giving traditional items like a comb, a male dress and a sword with silver to a male or women's clothes, ornaments and jewels in gold, silver or less precious material to a female. This is usually done without any kind of celebration, or alternatively, with a simple meal offered to visiting relatives. Also strikingly, while traditionally *zār* spirits tend to have a different sex from their hosts, the gifts given to patients in rural areas are always in accordance with the sex of the sufferer.

Since *ṭayyāb* and simpler forms of treatment are used for *zār* affliction, sicknesses in general and occurrences of 'bad luck' in rural areas, this simpler tradition of *ṭayyāb* may represent a typical Beja tradition as well as the more widespread *zār* tradition. As I will argue later on, Beja conceptions of fertility and good or bad luck may be incorporated into the quite recent *zār* cult in a way which might explain its success both in Beja rural and urban areas.

After this brief general outline of Beja people and society we might be able to raise some questions regarding their narrative constructions of meaning. For Beja people, as for people in general, the need for constructing meaning arises when the daily flow of life is interrupted in one way or another. The type of interruptions I will focus on, is the occurrence of sickness. In the remaining part of this book I want to explore how Beja's personal and mythical narratives are employed as a cultural means of creating meaning, as well as dealing with the sicknesses themselves in a culturally appropriate manner. Naturally, this will involve exploring the cultural theories and propositions seemingly underlying the stories, or, in other words, the cultural knowledge activated by telling stories.

NOTES

1 Dr. Abu Amne received his basic medical education and training in Germany. He has worked for roughly thirty years in Port Sudan and the surrounding area as a pediatrician.
2 Source: Dr. Mohammad, Sinkat hospital.
3 Lower level traditional Beja leader.
4 *Herár* is a Beja concept similar to the Sudanese Arabic concept of *yeraghān*, both denoting the symptoms of yellowish coloring of the skin and sclera in a broad range of conditions.
5 The words 'cause' and 'causality' are problematic and will be discussed later on.
6 See later discussions on 'Greeco-Islamic medicine'.
7 'Tibb an-nabawi' in Arabic.
8 In the period of 691–751 according to Muslim time reference.
9 Having received a university education in Islamic law from Damascus, his skills in classical Arabic language proved an invaluable help for me in translating this otherwise difficult accessible source. Since there tends to be numerous repetitions of words, expressions and even whole sentences in old Arabic sources, we took the liberty of making some simplifications, as far as possible without altering the meaning of the original text. In case there should be inaccurate instances of translation in my quotations, those should rather be attributed to my lack of time doing the translation than to my research assistant.
10 The Sudanese Arabic term commonly used for the sickness of Malaria.
11 Because the Beja language is an oral language, the users often have much freedom in choosing ways of expression. The sickness may be pronounced 'tesérimt' or 'sérimt.' In both instances the 't' is a marker of femininity, a typical trait of all so-called Cushitic languages. It is interesting to note that most sicknesses have feminine forms in the

Beja language. Only a few, all of them very serious sicknesses, are male, while all minor inflictions, without exception, are female. Some people say thay the word *tesérimt* is a Beja word for a special voice made by animals when sleeping. Others say that *tesérimt* is a special voice from sleeping children when they are affected by this sickness.

12 The rural household typically consists of a single nuclear family of parents and their children.

13 Sudanese Arabic form of Arabic *shaqīqa*.

14 Many young women married at the age of fifteen. The youngest one I heard about was thirteen to fourteen years old (age is mostly approximate in the Red Sea Hills).

15 *Karāma* in Arabic: see later discussion Chapter 6.8.

16 Prof. J. Bell, University of Bergen, personal communication.

17 Pl. of *basīr*.

18 Sharif Harir, University of Bergen, Norway, personal communication (on Western Sudan); Jamal Ghazali, University of Khartoum, Sudan, personal communication (on the Sudan generally).

19 Pl. of *fagīr*, possibly translated as 'Islamic healer by religion': See later discussion in this chapter, part 4.1.4.

20 *Wadie* in Sudanese Arabic.

21 The *fagīr* writes Quranic verses (often seven) on a piece of paper or wood and washes off the writing with water afterwards. This water is carefully collected and given to the patient to drink.

22 Beja word meaning 'blessed,' 'luck-bringing' etc.

23 Plural form of the Arabic word *hejāb*.

24 In practice female as well as male *fugarā'* in Sinkat and surrounding areas generally claim to have spirit helpers.

25 Meaning 'by the name of God' in Arabic.

26 Sudanese Arabic word used for white foreigners.

27 My own data are predominantly from the Sinkat province, although I had the opportunity to meet *zār* doctors in Haya and Derudeb occasionally. According to informants, however, my findings are not untypical of areas closer to Port Sudan or, in the other direction, to Haya and Derudeb.

5

BEJA SICKNESS NARRATIVES AND CULTURE

When thinking about my various meetings with Beja people, so many social gatherings in which I had the privilege to take part, come to my mind. A Beja is seldom alone in complete privacy. Most often he is accompanied by one or more friends or relatives or is engaged in various kinds of gatherings of ceremonial or ordinary kinds. In several of the gatherings in which I took part not much was said. People did not seem to be embarrassed by periods of complete silence during social gatherings. If anybody had a story to tell, however, people were eager to listen and provide commentaries as well as to supply their own stories.

Beja stories are sources of traditional wisdom. They provide insight into how specific people evaluate other people and their actions, how to deal with various threats to people and animals, and what to expect of help or enmity from different groups or persons. Stories are also means of ridicule by which conformity may be obtained. And, finally, storytelling is a source of entertainment breaking up the otherwise monotonous daily routine of life.

Beja society is a predominantly oral society and most people are non-literate. Their oral tradition, however, is very rich. This richness of oral culture Lewis (1968) also comments upon regarding the non-literate Somali nomads. For the Somali, as for the Beja, the world[1] is essentially hostile (ibid., p.268). 'The power of the tongue and of the spoken word in spreading hostility and enmity, in countering it, or in broadcasting conciliatory messages, in ruining reputations or praising men to the skies, is very evident in Somali culture.' For this reason skills in oral performance are extremely important for Somali people. The same description could clearly be given of the Beja as well.

What intrigued me more than anything else were the things not told in the stories. Sometimes each statement in a story required an enormous amount of cultural knowledge in order to be understood. Some stories were very short and seemingly uncomplicated, like when Ha'isha, a middle-aged woman, told me about the son of her mother's sister who died two years ago. He was working in the harbor of Port Sudan. Once he went swimming in the sea, he cut his leg. Shortly afterwards he died. His relatives thought that the cut stemmed from an insect. And then, in a matter of fact way, she told that they went to several *fugarā* for treatment. But, why should they seek the treatment of Islamic healers treating by the Quran and Quranic means? Why did not he go to the *busarā* the traditional healers of wounds and broken bones? Quite possibly he tried other kinds of treatment as well. It may be that after trying different means his relatives considered it a case for the *fugarā*. However, Ha'isha did not bother to explain the choice they made. As it will turn out through the presentation of Beja theories of sicknesses, in order to understand the significance of her statement one needs to have extensive knowledge about the way people conceive the spirit world and how to relate to it. At this point it is sufficient to state that the Beja think about the spirit world as a mirror image of the physical world, with spirit humans, animals and plants. A spirit insect, like its physical counterpart, may have the power to sting and to poison people.

Death among the Beja occurs frequently and often after a short time of sickness. A Beja will never ask the question, 'Whose fault was this death?' like people in societies where witchcraft or sorcery are much at stake. Even when people believe that an 'evil eye' caused sickness, a specific person is rarely held responsible. 'Anyone might have done it,' was the most frequent answer I got when asking about who cast the 'evil eye.'[2] After discussing some possible theories of etiology for a while, people will normally conclude that 'it was fate' or that 'it was the will of God.' However, this does not mean that Beja people do not seek explanations or do not seek to make death meaningful. In one instance Aisha, an elderly women living in the rural area of Odrus, told us about one time she lost a newborn child:

'One time I was pregnant and a person who had that kind of camels[3] came and stayed with us over night as a guest.

And then, in the next day he came to me to say "hello." And before he reached his sleeping place, I felt fever and coldness. My family gave me this treatment of *tesérimt* and butter oil, and in that night I delivered a child who began to cry. His stomach was full by air, and immediately he died.'

So many questions are left unanswered in the mind of a foreigner hearing this story, questions which a native Beja would probably not ask. What are the special attributes of the camels of the man visiting? What did the appearance of this man have to do with Ha'isha delivering a sick child? What is the relationship between this man and his camels? As is apparent from the plot of the story, there is obviously a connection between a special kind of camel and one or more types of sickness. However, did the man bring his camels with him? Did his camels effect him in a way which made him effect Ha'isha in a special way, which caused the child to become sick and then die?

None of these questions can be answered in a shorthand way. In supposing some answers to them, I have come to recognize that these answers relate to Beja folk theories of which the researcher has to acquire an understanding. Such an understanding must also be related to a wealth of other cultural theories which I will account for in order to give as complete a picture as possible. This does not mean that all facets of Beja society and culture have to be taken into consideration. I also hold it plausible that there are vast areas of understanding and experience in Beja culture for which I am not able to present any insight.

In the following chapter I will try to elicit as much as possible of the Beja theories which became clear to me as I investigated the implicit theories and assumptions underlying the Beja stories which I heard. I gained insight into some of their cultural understandings by asking the narrators and other informants about how to understand various parts of the narratives. Before proceeding with this task, two important questions have to be asked:

1. How may I know that the stories I present in this book are the same or similar stories as the Hadandowa Beja tell each other without a researcher present?
2. How do I know that my representation of Beja knowledge is adequate?

Concerning the first question, there are several reasons why I do not think that the stories with which I am acquainted differ substantially from stories which are told in more 'natural' settings. Firstly, some narratives I heard several times told by different narrators without big differences in form or content. Secondly, some stories were stories which were retold by my informants, stories which they heard from friends or relatives. Such stories were not qualitatively different from stories which I heard directly from people. Thirdly, I was seldom alone with the narrator. Relatives, neighbors and friends were mostly around and served as a check for the content of the stories.

The second question may be rephrased as follows: how do I know that my interpretation of Beja sickness theories represent the Beja cultural knowledge? No doubt there are some differences between their knowledge and mine. Firstly, their knowledge is acquired through real-life experiences throughout a lifetime. Their knowledge is naturally more practical and extensive than mine. Secondly, throughout my fieldwork I have been equipped with scientific theories which naturally have had a pronounced effect upon the ways in which I organize and think about what I assume to be their knowledge. Nevertheless, the knowledge which I acquired enabled me to understand narratives which I previously was not in a position to understand. That knowledge also gradually increased my ability to understand and appreciate new stories. Moreover, I became increasingly better equipped to explain changes of strategy by sufferers of sickness and their relatives during cases of prolonged sickness. This latter point will be further discussed in Chapter 7. For these reasons I believe that what I as an anthropologist have to know in order to understand their stories is not too different from what Beja people themselves have to know.

At this point we are probably ready for a journey into the wealth of Beja sickness stories and the manifold of cultural theories invoked by them. Instead of first presenting the reader with the stories, I want to begin with presenting some of the cultural richness of sickness theories which an analysis of the stories made me realize. Armed with this background knowledge the reader will more readily be able to appreciate the stories presented in Chapter 8 and to see the relevance of the Beja folk theories for various sequences of each of the stories. I gained insight into some of their cultural understandings by asking the narrators and other informants about how to understand various parts of the narratives. This supplied me with some clues which enabled me to dig further into the 'taken for granted knowledge' by both partaking in informal chattings and conducting open-ended interviews. Further, during this research process, previously acquired knowledge about Beja culture gained new relevance.

NOTES

1 Meaning both the surrounding world and their 'life world'.
2 As argued earlier, Beja theories of 'evil eye' are different from witch-craft theories in that no specific person is thought to be a witch or have 'the power of the evil eye'. The mere utterance to parents of words like 'what a healthy and fat boy you have!' may magically harm the child regardless of whether the person uttering the words is known to be envious or not.
3 Meaning a specific kind of camels which may transfer the severe sickness of *tesérimt* to small children as well as to not-yet-born children.

6

BEJA THEORIES OF SICKNESS IN THE CONTEXT OF ANTHROPOLOGICAL DISCOURSE

6.0. INTRODUCTION

I have not tried to fully account for all Beja theories and propositions of health and sickness. However, I maintain that the limited range of theories I have covered is important to grasp in order to understand Beja narratives about the experience of sickness as well as 'mythical' stories about the merits of healers in former times. My outline should hence be seen as what the anthropologist at least must know in order to understand Beja stories about sickness and misfortune.

Some general aspects of Beja culture and society covered in the third chapter of this book are parts of a general framework to which I will relate all cultural theories of health and sickness to be discussed in this chapter. I will, throughout this analysis, try to draw some lines to different spheres of life experience to which this general framework relates.

It is necessary to make a conceptual clarification at this point. I am using the words 'model,' 'cultural model' and 'schema' interchangeable, although I mostly prefer the concept 'schema.' Both propositions and theories are schemata, although more abstract and less specific in their meaning than lower level schemata.

Formulations in brackets represent my own inferences of higher level schemata, which are instantiated at lower levels by filling out 'open slots.' The formulations which are not in brackets are not in all cases literal translations of what people say. However, in all cases I have tried to remain faithful to the ideas inherent in what people say and have rendered a nearly word-for-word translation wherever possible.

The cultural schemata at the lowest level are most often directly expressed by Beja people. However, the models at higher levels are inferences which can be deduced from statements at a lower level, or, conversely, the models at the lower levels are instances of higher level models. Sometimes informants give expression of schemata at several levels of abstraction. The statements at a higher level, however, are frequently made only by one or few informants, while most informants are probably not conscious about them.

The lowest level statements are often in the form of cultural prescriptions, which sometimes have the form of 'one should or ought to do this or that.' These statements, whether they are clear prescriptions or not, are linked to specific situations. For this reason, they clearly link the grander scale models and the theories to which they pertain to the diagnosis of sickness and to specific forms of treatment. As may be clear already, in my use of the concepts 'theories,' 'propositions,' and 'schemata,' theories are made up by interlinked propositions. The propositions may be seen as interlinked cultural schemata.

As already discussed, trying to define prototype sicknesses or to categorize sicknesses by linking etiologies and kinds of treatments to diagnostic labels, often do not reveal the important cultural theories which people employ when dealing with sicknesses. However, by starting out with an elucidation of important cultural theories and propositions, one is able to explore the links between cultural theories, treatment options and diagnostic labels at the lowest level of theories.

One point concerning the distribution of cultural theories is important to make: not all Beja agree on every single lower level statement. However, most often people express similar thoughts making similar inferences. As an example, people who do not think that sitting in blood is good treatment for *kosúlt*, nevertheless agree that *kosúlt* is caused by internal body heat which may be, for example, extracted by burying the patient in wet sand. In other words, the technique of extraction of body heat is at issue.

This fact has important implications for the potential validity of higher level schemata: if individual variance in a constallation of lowest level schemata exists, but the variance is of a kind which allows for the instigation of the same higher level schemata, this should strengthen rather than weaken the validity of the overall folk theory to which the lowest level schemata pertain. This mostly turned out to be the case.

People's knowledge varied a great deal at the lowest level. Firstly, individual persons differed in the amount of knowledge they possessed. Some people were able to present a range of lowest level schemata, while others had more limited knowledge. Naturally, parents with several children possessed much more detailed knowledge about children's diseases like *hāf masóob* than young parents with one small child. Also, some people were not so interested in the field of health and sickness as others, and hence they paid less attention to it. This does not mean that they were not bothered by the possibility of sicknesses striking themselves and relatives. Rather, they would maintain that there are enough knowledgeable people around who would know what to do. Secondly, the means of treatment employed by people differed somewhat from area to area, and sometimes from *diwáb* to *diwáb*. Those differences most often pertained to the most technical knowledge at the lowest level schemata, but, as already stated, made no difference in their instigation of higher level schemata.

One might expect that people exposed to biomedical health care in urban centers would present knowledge very much at odds with traditional knowledge. However, I was often surprised by urbanized people utilizing biomedicine in a traditional fashion and conceiving of the utility and results of 'modern' medicines within the framework of traditional understanding. I will give a couple of examples to illustrate this point. Painkillers like Aspro[1] were popular in rural as well as urban areas. They were sold outside pharmacies at *tabiliyyas*[2] in the market place. In some instances people would burn them on a fire and inhale the smoke through the nose while covering themselves and the fire under a carpet or a traditional *toob*. This traditional way of administering a 'modern' medicine is consistent with their belief that what enters the nose, directly and instantly affects the whole body. Another example pertains to medical injections. If people conceived they had the sickness of *hāf*, they would be hesitant to agree to take injections of insulin or antibiotics. The injection might 'feed' the *hāf* and make it more complicated. As a third example, people will often avoid drinking red colored drinks like *karkadé*[3] before giving a blood sample at the hospital, because the stomach content is believed to go directly and immediately from the stomach and into the blood. For this reason the laboratory technician will be deceived by the red color of the blood, thinking that all of it is pure blood.

Finally it is important for me to emphasize that I make absolutely no claims that the theoretical structures I outline below are represented in the minds of Beja people generally or in the mind of any single Beja person. It is primarily a device which best simulates, I hope, the way Beja represent their knowledge. At the level of 'theories' in my notational system, theories with different spans of application are presented as being of equal importance. They are, in other words, presented as if they instantiate approximately identical numbers of lower levels of instances and equally many instances at each level. Of course, as will very soon become evident, this is not the case. Some theories explain a lot, others have a more limited application to real-life situations. To the extent that the outline of theories renders the narratives I present meaningful to the readers, however, I am inclined to believe that it accounts to some degree for how Beja people mentally represent their own knowledge.

6.1. GENERAL THEORIES OF HERBS AND HERBAL TREATMENT

'You have to take care when harvesting the herbs, because they have one way in which they are useful but nine ways of doing harm' Hawa Ali

6.1.1. Introduction

In a recent article Pool (1994) takes issue with the position of Foster (1976) and other medical anthropologists (see, e.g. Fortes 1976; Loudon 1976; Yoder 1982) who between the mid-1970s and mid-1980s aimed at recasting or re-evaluating African etiologies. These anthropologists pointed out that earlier anthropologists interested in native explanations of sickness and misfortune generally tended to focus on supernatural causation to the neglect of discussing natural causation. Foster (1976:775) makes the following main points:

'A personalistic medical system is one in which disease is explained as due to the *active and purposeful intervention* of an *agent*, who may be human (a witch or sorcerer), non-human (a ghost, an ancestor, an evil spirit) or supernatural (a deity or other very powerful being). The sick person is literally a victim, the object of aggression or punishment directed specifically against him, for reasons that concern him alone. Personalistic causality allows little room for accident or chance ... naturalistic systems explain illness in impersonal, systemic terms. Disease is thought to stem, not from the machinations of an angry being, but rather from such *natural forces or conditions* as cold, heat, winds, dampness, and, above all, by an upset in the balance of the basic body elements'.

If anthropologists pay more attention to naturalistic systems of explanation of sicknesses, the gap between Western and non-Western medicine will be bridged according to Foster. However, the questions put forward by Pool are: why do we bother at all to identify indigenous 'medical systems'? And why do we make a point out of making such 'systems' compatible with a Western medical system? For Pool, the truest thing one could say about native 'medical systems' is that they do not exist. By trying to extract a 'medical system' from the overall 'complexes of behavior, sets of beliefs and spoken discourses' (p.17), we restrict rather than expand our understanding of how people in different cultures relate to questions of sickness and ill-luck. What we should do instead is to look pragmatically at the knowledge people employ and express when confronted with sickness 'not so much as a medical system but as part of the necessary cultural camouflage, clothing and food, that enables one to survive ...' (Last in Pool 1994:17).

Although I partly agree with the criticism voiced by Pool, I will maintain that the 'cultural camouflage' related to health and sickness in some respects may be said to represent a discrete field. At the level of non-specialists, in Beja culture as well as other Middle-Eastern and African cultures there exist practical areas of knowledge with related 'taskonomies'[4] having primarily to do with restoring health or preventing ill-health. Further, specialists like the Beja *busara'* deal primarily with sicknesses without involving themselves in responding to other kinds of ill-luck. In addition, I think that the claim of Foster that earlier ethnographers tended to focus upon personalistic and super-

84

natural etiologies is defensible. Following Pool, however, I agree that constructing native 'medical systems' which may be made compatible with 'the Western medical system' creates a lot of new problems without solving any old problems.

A main point that I will make in the further discussion is that trying to delineate and define a 'naturalistic' field of knowledge of health and sickness is in itself problematic. As will become clear from the very first outline and discussions of theories and propositions of herbs and herbal treatment, 'naturalistic' and 'personalistic' etiologies seem to intermingle at the level of explaining concrete occurrences of sickness. I do not take the position that one should disregard the very concepts 'naturalistic' and 'personalistic' in relation to folk etiologies. I will maintain, however, that to look for a 'naturalistic field' of native tradition in relation to health and health management is a futile project, at least when dealing with Beja culture. Herbal treatment, although involving concepts of hot and cold as well as other physical properties, also relates to a rich world of supernatural beings.

Even in older Islamic scriptures advocating Quranic medicine and the classical humoral tradition, a clear-cut division between 'naturalistic' and 'personalistic' theories is difficult to make. An example from the 14th century text *The Medicine of the Prophet* illustrates how a 'naturalistic' kind of treatment is advised to relieve a physical sickness caused by supernatural agents:

> 'Magic itself usually stems from effects of bad spirits which influence a particular part of the body. For that reason, if a patient makes *hejāma* (bloodletting by a "bleeding horn") in this place, it is useful' (p.100).

Another conceptual distinction I will only mention briefly, since it will not be employed in this book. The distinction between 'illness' and 'disease' is advised by Kleinman (1978, 1980). By the term 'disease' he denotes 'a malfunctioning of biological and/or psychological processes' while illness 'signifies the *experience* of disease (or perceived disease) and the societal reaction to disease. Illness is the way the sick person, his family and his social network perceive, label, explain, evaluate and respond to disease' (Kleinman 1978:88). However, this view may downplay the cultural forces at work in biomedicine (see, e.g. Stein 1990) as well as the fact that medical practitioners may in some instances view experiential factors as part of the disease itself, like in reactive psychoses. Frankenberg (1980:199) voices a similar critique of Kleinman's distinction:

'The *individual* patient and his/her family are seen as constructing a reality around the disease event out of the cultural material that comes to hand. The physician in contrast constructs his cultural reality which if there is "genuine" disease is likely to be correct. If he detects no "disease," he collects a fee when appropriate and releases the patient to go elsewhere. . . . Social reality is easily reduced to dyadic transaction terms in this way.'

Frankenberg proposes instead to add the term 'sickness' to the terms 'illness' and 'disease.' While 'illness' should denote the 'individual making conscious of the disease' (ibid.), 'sickness' should apply to the totality of social, cultural and historical processes in which context management of 'diseases' takes place. However, by introducing a third concept which also logically presupposes a 'disease' in the way Kleinman perceives it, I feel that nothing else is gained than further conceptual confusion. For the sake of simplicity I prefer solely to use the concept 'sickness' as standing for 'perceived bad physical and/or psychological states' and let it be clear from the context of my discussion whether I am focusing on the non-specialist's, the specialist's, or the sick person's perceptions and interpretations. Since I am primarily focusing non-specialists, sickness conceptions and interpretations which are discussed here will mainly represent a lay perspective.

Making this a point of departure at the outset, I feel it is high time to explore the different theories of sicknesses in Beja culture. By organizing the discussion thematically, I am going to discuss grander theories side by side with smaller-scale cultural propositions.

6.1.2. Outline

Proposition I: 'God made every *hindíib*[5] useful for something'

This is a general proposition which is part of an overarching theory about the relation of God to the world and the things in it which he created. It is outside the scope of this discussion to give an outline of how Beja are influenced in this matter by the Quran and other Islamic scriptures. This proposition has, however, implications for how Beja relate to trees, bushes and herbs in their environment. Also there is no sickness for which God has not foreseen a possible treatment;[6] there is no *hindíib* which is created for no purpose. Hence one should never cease to investigate how different *híndib* can be used to treat different sicknesses.

Proposition II: 'A *hindíib* may be hot or cold'

Proposition III: 'Some *híndib* clean the stomach of poisons and bad substances by causing diarrhea'

Theory A: The propositions IV, V and VI are all expressions of a more general idea which may be represented like this: ['*Híndib* are like humans']

Proposition IV: ['*Híndib* can hear and understand human speech. They have memories and make contracts']

  a: 'You must tell the *hindíib* before harvesting it'
  b: 'By paying *karáma*[7] for the *hindíib* one avoids the harmful effects of it'

Proposition V: ['*Híndib* are conscious agents which have the power to heal and to do harm']

  a: '*Híndib* might provide a cure if one make suitable contracts with them'
Virtually for every state of sickness Beja conceive of there is a herbal treatment, at least as one of the treatment options.
  b: '*Híndib* might protect against sicknesses, spirits, dangerous animals and enemies'
      1: '*Tembláess*[8] hung around the neck of a child protects against whooping cough.'
      2: 'If you have *tílil*[9] in your house, you will never get *táflam*[10] from spirits'
      3: '*Oodʰháu*[11] hanging on the neck of a child protects against whooping cough and fright sickness'
      4: 'Tying *hállig állim*[12] on the arm protects against fright sickness'
      5: 'By a stick from *gána hindíib*[13] one can beat forty

persons in a fight or war if it is not urinated upon by humans or animals'

6: '*Hallig állim* gets rid of spirits'
7: 'Some *hindib* protect against getting bitten by a snake'
c: '*Hindib*, especially powerful ones, may cause illness and misfortune'
   1: 'Powerful *hindib* may harm people's fertility, make them "mental cases" or make people unable to move'
   2: 'Powerful *hindib* may cause eye inflammation'
   3: '*Hindib* may cause blindness'
   4: 'If one sleeps or takes a rest under an *úsher*[14] tree, it may cause *ť'háasimt*'
   5: 'The very powerful *kardáp hindib* may cause infertility in oneself or sicknesses in ones children'

Proposition VI: '*Hindib* eat sicknesses'

1: '*Osár*[15] eats *heminéit*'[16]
2: '*Osár* eats *kosúlt*'
3: '*Dau'há*[17] eats *kosúlt*'
4: '*Osár* sucks the blood out of *hāf*'[18]

The next proposition, proposition VII, concerns other non-animal and non-human traits of herbs:

Proposition VII: ['Some *hindib* are both more useful and more dangerous']

a: 'Powerful *hindib* are dangerous to harvest'
   1: '*Kardáp hindib*[19] are very powerful and should be harvested by slaves, old women or donkeys, since they may cause infertility and health damage for people'
   2: 'Before harvesting a powerful *hindíib* one should tell the *hindíib* that one wants to harvest it and offer *karāma* for it before harvesting it'
b: 'Using a herb for a specific sickness without having it, may cause this sickness'
   1: 'Using a herb for *kardáp* without having the sickness may cause sickness of *kardáp*'
   2: 'Smell of *ool'áu*[20] may cause the sickness of *gúrda*[21] if you do not have *gúrda* beforehand'

6.1.3. Discussion: *híndib* as natural and pseudo-natural kinds

As is illustrated by proposition II, several *híndib* have the physical property of hotness or coldness. Cold *híndib* are used to counteract hot sicknesses, while cold sicknesses are treated by hot herbs, a fact to which I will soon return. Such properties of herbs easily fits into the conception of naturalistic medicine advocated by Foster (1976). Causing diarrhea (proposition III) is another physical attribute having to do with the naturalistic effects of herbs. Beja frequently employ means which cause diarrhea in order to cure stomach sicknesses as well as sicknesses of 'bad blood.'

It may, however, come as a surprise that the bulk of Beja theories of *híndib* concerns personalistic traits. They are described as being able to listen, having memory as well as wanting to make contractual agreements with people. *Híndib* are intentional beings capable of curing sicknesses as well as causing sicknesses and misfortune. In addition, they are sometimes conceived of as curing sicknesses by 'eating' them. Most of those attributes may apply to animals as well. A more human attribute, however, is their ability to make social contracts.

In an unpublished paper, Boyer (1996a) discusses James' (1988) account of 'ebony divination' among the Uduk-speaking people of the Sudan. The people hold the ebony tree to be different from other trees in that it is able to hear. In particular they are able to 'hear signals about what is going on in the human world.' Fortunately they are able to convey their knowledge to humans when branches from the ebony tree are manipulated in a specific way during a ritual of interrogation. The trees are not only passive listeners and recorders, for people who are able to read their signals they convey knowledge about problems in the human world (e.g. witchcraft) as well as propose solutions to those problems.

In addition to the projection of personalistic traits to plants, the projection of personalistic traits to various religious artifacts is common cross-culturally. How might this be explained so as to elucidate facets of human thinking? Is there a process of metaphorization at work? When people conceive of the lion as 'the king of animals,' they may see it as 'moving majestically,' 'being wise' and 'responding in a powerful way' when 'raised to anger.' In the same vein it could be the case that when herbs are conceived of as similar to humans, several human traits become relevant in describing them. Not all human traits are made relevant when Beja speak about herbs, however, as will be discussed for theory B and C, metaphorical structuring is always partial. It is important to note that while the metaphorical structuring for the spirit world, for example, is quite obvious in Beja thinking,[22] conceiving of herbs as 'human-like' is much more implicit in Beja folk theories. While Beja people are quite explicit in stating that the spirit world is in many respects a mirror image of the human world, I believe it is unlikely that a Beja will ever state that an herb resembles a human. However, when speaking about herbs, human-like traits are constantly evoked.

A note of caution has to be made here. Although metaphorization in some cases is not verbally explicit, this does not preclude metaphoric and metonymic processes. However, deeper mental and cognitive mechanisms may possibly underlie metonymic and metaphorical processes, as will be discussed for Theory I in relation to the notions of 'positive' and 'negative' contagion.

Pascal, an anthropologist who worked among the Fang of Cameroon, supposes a different explanation (Boyer 1993, 1996a, 1996b). His theory of 'pseudo-natural kinds' represents an extension of the notion of essence and natural kinds discussed earlier in Chapter 2. He presents the hypothesis that humans extend their ideas related to natural kinds like plants, animals, and non-animate substances to areas in which they do not strictly apply. The example from his own ethnographic work concerns the notion of *evur* among the Fang. *Evur* is a mystical inner organ which some humans with particular skills, for example healers, witches and skillful businessmen, have. It is an invisible inner essence making those skillful people what they are. Like the 'goldness' of gold, or the 'giraffeness' of a giraffe, this essence cannot be seen nor defined. However, as will later be discussed in relation to the Beja concept of *héequal* as a luck-bringing internal essence in particular humans, the essence of *evur* is defined by its manifestations *as if* it is a natural kind. Once the manifestations of '*evur*-ness' are present, a person is fully *beyem*, i.e. has an *evur*. There is no way of being half-*beyem*. Either one has an *evur* or one does not.

There seem to be other processes at work as well which relate to this powerful cognitive tool of pseudo-natural reasoning. By making a list of standard default activations of ontological

assumptions to persons, animals, plants, natural objects and artifacts, Boyer (1996a) comes up with the following list of types of
ontological expectations in humans cross-culturally:

1. For persons: psychological, biological and physical.
2. For animals: psychological, biological and physical.
3. For plants: biological and physical.
4. For natural objects: physical.
5. For artifacts: physical.

The argument Boyer makes is that cross-culturally, in all kinds
of religious beliefs, violations of expectations or transfers of
expectations occur. Since the ontological expectations for each
of the five categories can be altered regarding psychological,
biological or physical expectations by violations of expectations
or transfers of expectations, logically 15 basic different constellations are conceivable. An example may be the above mentioned
ebony tree, in which case a transfer of psychological expectations
occurred. The likelihood that such an alteration survives in a
culture is related to two main characteristics of the belief:

a. Its attention grabbing potential, arising from violations of
   intuitive expectations.
b. Its inferential potential provided by the default background
   assumptions.

Beliefs with no violations of intuitive expectations may not be
expected to become central elements in cultural beliefs because
they do not have an attention grabbing potential. Such concepts
also have restricted inferential potential. In addition, beliefs in
intention-less phenomena like invisible rocks or 'soulless'
animals seem not to be widespread. Humans cross-culturally
seem to be primarily interested in having beliefs and assumptions related to intentional beings like themselves, a topic to
which I will return.

Counter-intuitive assumptions do not require elaborate cultural explanations like the processes of metaphorization do. Once
a clue is given by a specific violation of expectations, a wealth
of inferences may be made *ad infinitum*. Beja transfer of psychological expectations to trees, bushes and herbs has, as we have
seen, a rich inferential potential.

As will be shown later on, the human-ness of *híndib* is often
employed in various explanations of sickness occurrences.

Another counter-intuitive attribute of herbs is an undefined inherent property keeping sicknesses, misfortune or enemies away. On several occasions I heard people referring to a stick from a specific bush keeping policemen away and another one as capable of beating forty people if used as a weapon in war. Specific herbs were said to keep spirits away from one's tent or hut. This kind of magical thought, which is probably widespread across different cultures, is even represented in a traditional saying from the Prophet Mohammad, as referred to in *The Medicine of the Prophet* (p.26): 'Prophet Mohammad [once] said: 'If a person takes honey three times every month, great disasters can not affect him.'

Muslim healers from Western Africa, when they travel through Beja territory, often bring with them charms which are believed to have similar magical effects. Some charms may attract the person with whom one is in love or provide protection from bullets in war. Although Beja may be unique in attributing such powers to unprocessed trees and bushes, they also reckon with the protective power of charms like *hejbāt*[23] or from stones like the red stone of *adal óot*. However, the power of such objects to keep sicknesses away depends, as we shall now see, upon theories related to the nature of sicknesses.

6.2. GENERAL THEORIES OF SICKNESSES

6.2.1. Part a

6.2.1.1. Introduction
In 18th century Northern Africa hot food like ginger and honey were thought to make the blood flow faster while cold food like watermelons and cucumbers were said to make the skin cool and the body and its contents still (Gallagher 1983). Sicknesses were sometimes attributed to collection of blood in a specific body organ (ibid.). These considerations are still valid for present day Beja. Their theory of 'hot' and 'cold' sicknesses, body states and food items turn out to be part of a more complex web of meaning where several substance characteristics seem to be of importance.

6.2.1.2. Outline
Theory B: The Propositions VIII, IX, X, XI, XII and XIII are all

expressions of a more general idea which may be represented like this:
['Sicknesses are substances']

Proposition VIII: ['Sickness substances have constant quantities']

  a: ['If a child gets some sickness through the breast milk of its mother, the mother will have less of it']
    1: 'If a mother with *kosúlt* breastfeeds, she will herself have less *kosúlt*'

  b: ['The healer might gradually receive a sickness from the patient']
    1: 'When a *basīr*[24] treats a person with *táflam*, he may gradually get sick as the person gets better'

  c: ['When a sickness spreads from one body organ to another, there will be less of it in the first organ]'
    1: 'Measles begins in the intestines. When they appear in the skin, there will be less on the intestines'
    2: '*Dérwout*[25] may make the rashes of *tesérimt* go out of the body and appear on the skin, after which the rashes may be destroyed. If they do not appear on the skin, the intestines may be destroyed'

  d: ['A sickness may be let out of the body by cupping, sweating, diarrhea etc.']
    1: ' "Bad blood" may be let out by making cuttings on the body, by cupping or by making *hejāma*'[26]
    2: 'If a person has "night blindness,"[27] it may stem from "hot blood," which one can get rid of by making *hejāma*'
    3: '*Dérwou*[28] may stem from too much blood, in which case *hejāma* may cure'
    4: 'The sickness of *dalil óob*[29] may be cured by letting out "bad blood" by *hejāma*'
    5: 'If a person has *háf*, one may make cuttings on his stomach so as to let out the "bad blood" "
    6: 'The "bad blood" of *watáb*[30] can be let out by making cuttings on the legs of the sick person'
    7: 'A "common cold" may be let out of the body through sweating by taking smoke baths'
    8: 'The sickness of *berudéit*[31] may be let out of the body

by taking a smoke bath in order to sweat out the coldness of the bones'

9: 'If a child has *hāf masóob*,[32] one may give it butter to cause diarrhea'

10: 'If one has *gúrda*, one can drink sea water in order to have diarrhea'

11: 'If one has "bad" *heminéit*, one may get rid of it by drinking sour milk or by boiling *hallig állim* in water to cause diarrhea'

12: 'If one has the sickness of *gúrda*, one can drink butter oil to cause diarrhea so as to clean the stomach'

13: '*Kalendóy*[33] cleans the stomach and gets rid of *heminéit*'

14: 'If a person is bitten by a scorpion, he should drink a tea of ginger, *togarár*[34] and *sinaáb*[35] in order to cause diarrhea and vomiting'

15: 'If a person is bitten by a scorpion or a snake, he should eat butter or drink camel's milk to cause vomiting and diarrhea to get rid of the poison'

16: 'If a person has malaria, he should eat butter so as to get rid of the *heminéit*'

17: 'If one has *kosúlt*, one should try to let out the *heminéit* [by diarrhea or vomiting']

e: ['A sickness may be let out of the body by sneezing'][36]

1: 'The sickness of *khoof*[37] in a child may be let out by getting it to sneeze by applying black pepper, ginger, snuff or *kamūn aswad*[38] near its nose. When the child sneezes, the fright might go out of it'

2: 'If a child has *na'éh*[39] caused by fright, sneezing will make it get rid of the sickness'

3: 'Sicknesses resulting from *zār* may be expelled by applying black pepper near the nose of the sick person'

Proposition IX: ['The sickness substances may be hot or cold and treated by substances of opposite temperature']

a: ['Hot sicknesses may stem from hot substances, hot body states, or other hot sicknesses and may be treated by cold substances and food'][40]

1: '*Kosúlt* is like a fire within the body'

2: 'Hot and tasty food like food with red pepper and very sour milk should not be given to a patient with *kosúlt*'

3: '*Kosúlt* is heat going inside the body'

4: 'The hotness of *kosúlt* may create the hot sickness of *koléit*[41] in women'

5: 'The *ool áu* is cold. For this reason it treats the hot sickness of *gúrda*'

6: 'The cold *ool áu* treats every kind of fever'

7: 'Walking in the sun may cause *kosúlt* in women'

8: 'If a woman walks in the sun and breastfeeds her child, the hotness will transfer to her child and make *kosúlt* or diarrhea'

9: 'Boiling *heminéit* creates hot blood'

b: ['Cold sicknesses may stem from cold substances, cold body states, or other cold sicknesses and be treated by hot substances and food'][42]

1: 'Cold water[43] on an empty stomach causes cold blood and the cold sickness of *watáb*'

2: 'The [cold] sickness of *herár*[44] may stem from having the cold sickness of *watáb* for a long time'

3: 'The cold sickness of *watáb* may be treated by making cuttings on the legs in order to let out the cold blood'

4: 'The cold sickness of *watáb* may be treated by burnings on all the finger and toe nails'

5: 'Hot *madída* [sorghum porridge] and "hot" [spicy or tasty] food with red pepper and salt are good food for persons with the cold sickness of *watáb*'

6: 'The cold sickness of *watáb* may stem from postponement of breakfast'

7: '*Hérjal*[45] is a hot herb. For this reason it is good for the cold sickness of *yambírir*'

8: 'The cold sickness of *shagīga*[46] may be treated by holding a warm stone against the affected side of the head'

Proposition X: ['Sickness substances can be solid, fluid or vapor']

Proposition XI: ['Sicknesses with a solid substance and/or darker color are more cold than sicknesses with less solid substance and/or lighter color']

a: 'The cold blood of [the cold sickness of] *hāf* is black and solid'

b: 'The cold blood of *hāf masóob* is black and solid'

c: 'When making cuttings on the legs to let out the cold blood of *watáb*, the blood will be black'

d: 'The blood in the hot sicknesses of *kosúlt* is red, fluid and hot'

Proposition XII: ['A sickness may spread through contamination'][47]

a: ['A sickness may spread through sexual contact']
  1: 'The hot sickness of *kosúlt* transfers to other persons through sexual relationships by transferring the hot substance'
  2: 'The hot sicknesses of *koléit*[48] and *bájal*[49] are spread through sexual relationships'
  3: '*Hallíg*[50] may spread through sexual contact'

b: ['A sickness may spread through handshaking or through contaminated objects like a water pipe or clothes']
  1: '*Kosúlt* may spread through smoking the same water pipe'
  2: '*Koléit* [gonorrhea] may spread through handshaking, clothes and bedclothes'
  3: '*Hallíg* [syphilis] may be spread through handshaking, clothes and bedclothes'

Proposition XIII: ['Hotness makes hot sicknesses worse and coldness makes cold sicknesses worse']

a: ['Hot treatment makes a hot sickness more hot and hence worse']
  1: 'Giving a person with the hot sickness of *kosúlt* hot,[51] tasty or spicy food[52]makes the *kosúlt* worse'
b: ['Cold treatment makes a cold sickness more cold and hence worse']
  1: 'The cold sickness of *áfram* is sometimes mistaken for the hot sickness of *kosúlt*. If cold treatment is given for *áfram*, however, the sickness becomes more serious and complicated'

6.2.1.3. Discussion: the substanceness of sicknesses

The theme of hot and cold substances connected to hot and cold sickness states is a very old one in the so-called Greco-Islamic medicine[53] (Bastien 1989, Foster 1984, 1987), South Asian traditions (Nichter 1989, 1992) and Chinese Medicine (Leslie & Young 1992). The concepts of hot and cold substances and sicknesses are sometimes, as in the classical humoral tradition, combined with concepts of wet and dry in several contemporary societies (Bastien 1989). However, as Foster (1984, 1987) has demonstrated, this is not always the case.

Although some influence from Greco-Islamic humoral medicine is unquestionable in many present day societies in the New World as well as in the Middle East, Indonesia and Malaysia, one may question the extent to which it has really spread as an ideational system or whether it only slightly transformed an already existing healing tradition. Laderman (1981, 1992) admits that the Greco-Islamic medical tradition spread to the Malay peninsula with the spread of Islam and to some extent transformed the existing traditions. However, some significant aspects of the greater tradition were omitted and others were transformed, like Malay people supposedly striving towards 'coldness' rather than balance in food matters, perceived body state and temperament. Bastien (1989) in his study of an Andean society, questions whether both pre-Spanish Kallawaya Andeans and Classical Greeks shared a 'humoral epistemology based on analogic thinking and systems of correspondence' (p.45) which facilitated the spread of some concepts and treatment options from the classical humoral theory, but without really profoundly changing the existing Kallawa tradition.

In present day Beja societies, old scriptures from the Greco-Islamic tradition are still read by literate Islamic healers and still have significance. For many of the ideas contained within such books one may find equivalents within the local *busarā'* tradition. However, the *busarā'* tradition is very much a 'tradition of the people' where it is often difficult to draw the line between specialists and non-specialists. It is a tradition constituted and maintained primarily by people who, unlike the literate *fugarā'*, are not able to read those old scriptures. The *busarā'* tradition clearly has absorbed both ideas, concepts and treatment techniques from this larger tradition, but it is not clear that this really has transformed the local system of treatment.

The *busarā'* tradition in the Red Sea Hills may clearly be seen as a tradition in its own right, although it shares some important traits of Greco-Islamic medicine. As will be demonstrated, several aspects of the *busarā'* tradition are important aspects of other spheres of Beja experience not having to do with health and sickness *per se,* like religious offerings or efforts to increase the fertility of animals.

What seems striking when one focuses on the hotness/coldness dimension of body states, sicknesses and foodstuffs, is not the significance of this dimension in itself. Rather, it is the way this dimension links on to other dimensions having to do with the 'substanceness' of sicknesses that is striking. Like physical substances generally encountered by Beja, they give sicknesses several substance-like attributes such as color, temperature and fluidness/solidness. Further, they make connections between those attributes which may possibly be derived from daily life experiences with different substances. The hot substance of *kosúlt* is red and fluid, while the cold substance of *hāf* or *watáb* is black and solid.

The blood itself is also described by Beja people as either 'red,' 'fluid' and 'hot' or 'black,' 'cold' and 'solid.' In the first case it is often talked about as 'awake,' while in the second case people say it is 'sleeping.' Those attributes may be paradigmatically represented as four sets of contrasting attributes:

'Red' vs. 'black,' 'fluid' vs. 'solid,' 'hot' vs. 'cold' and 'awake' vs. 'sleeping.' These contrast sets typically combine in syntagmatic associations.

Table 1: *Physical qualities of human blood*

Paradigmatic dimension	'Red'	'Fluid'	'Hot'	'Awake'
	'Black'	'Solid'	'Cold'	'Sleeping'

Syntagmatic dimension→

How can such a deep-structural grammar of Beja sickness understanding possibly be explained? It is difficult to see how it might relate to old Greco-Islamic medicine. Although in this classical humoral tradition a connection is made between the fluidity of the blood and body heat, the traditional connection is inverse, as is illustrated in Ullmann's seminal work *Islamic Medicine* (1978:58):

'Blood is produced in the liver from the juice of the digested food. The blood in the arteries is of fine consistency, it is pure red with sometimes a tendency to reddish-yellow. The blood in the veins holds the balance between fine and coarse;

it is dark red, has a sweet taste and quickly coagulates when it comes out. This blood is produced when the heat of the liver is lessened. If there is too great degree of heat and dryness in the liver, the blood becomes muddy and coarse; if there is too much wet and cold, the blood becomes thin and watery.'

There may well be elaborate cultural explanations for the different constellations of physical attributes made by Beja. However, one may as well pose a simple one having to do with their daily life experience.

A possible simple explanation could be that Beja people, when fulfilling daily tasks like cooking food, make the experience that very hot things like charcoal burning or a piece of metal held in fire may become red and that solid things may melt or become more fluid when heated. When the charcoal or the piece of metal cools down, it will become more black. When the porridge or stew cools down, it will become more solid. For this reason, linking red color and fluidness to hot substances and black color and solidness to cold substances may well have an experiential basis. Similarly, Beja, like all humans, observe that cold substances are heated by hot substances and that hot substances are made colder by cold substances. Since sicknesses have the qualities of substances with temperatures, they logically follow the same laws. In line with this, hot treatment may make an already hot sickness even hotter and a cold sickness may become even colder by cold treatment. The connections Beja make between qualities of sicknesses, causality and optimal forms of treatment may be illustrated the following way as contrast sets which combine in syntagmatic associations:

Table 2: *Substance qualities of sicknesses*

	'Hot'	'Fluid'	From 'hot' food or 'hot' substances	Treated by 'cold' food or 'cold' substances
Paradigmatic dimension	'Cold'	'Solid'	From 'cold' food or 'cold' substances	Treated by 'hot' food or making brandings

Syntagmatic dimension→

In the first syntagmatic dimension 'hot sicknesses' are related to fluidity, as well as to optimal forms of treatment like giving 'cold food' or treating by 'cold substances.' In the second syntagmatic dimension 'cold sicknesses' are related to 'solidness,' as well as to optimal forms of treatment like 'hot food' and 'brandings.' The treatment options for each kind of sickness are often combined, like giving a person with a 'cold' sickness both 'hot food' and brandings.

The concept of 'hotness' is metaphorically expanded by Beja to include spicy, tasty as well as very sour tasting food as 'hot.' The concept of 'coldness' is expanded so as to cover 'food which has lasted overnight' as well as 'fresh' and not boiled milk. One may speculate why such metaphorical extensions of these concepts occur. The feeling of body hotness after eating very spicy food may possibly explain why spicy food is considered 'hot,' while the other metaphorical extensions of 'hot' and 'cold' are not as easily explained in this manner. However, once a particular food or sickness is defined as 'cold' or 'hot,' it easily fits into the schemata for 'hotness' and 'coldness' and comes to bear the same implications in their models as hot and cold temperature states.

Since sicknesses are discrete substances, it is quite reasonable to assume that they have constant quantities like other substances which are visible and encountered in daily life, like food and water. Just as when some of the water in a jug is poured out and less remains in the container, if sicknesses are such substances, it makes sense to think that they may spread within the boundaries of the body and when some of it spreads from one body organ to another less of it will remain in the first organ. It is also logical to think that such substances can be let out of the body and that the more that is let out, the less will remain within the body. It is also conceivable that the sickness substances may spread through mother's milk or by sexual contacts between individuals. As an example, people think that *kosúlt* is usually more hot in women without children, because the heat produced in their bodies finds no outlet through the mother's milk. These women are, in line with this thought, seen as more likely to pass on *kosúlt* or the hot substance of gonorrhea to men through sexual relationships.

A second explanation has to do with the 'deep-structural' conceptions of 'essence' and 'spread of essence' already introduced.

To conceive of sicknesses as physical substances with physical substance qualities fits the general 'essence' notions which I find so central to Beja reasoning about sickness and health.

However, regardless whether the proposed explanations are valid or not, what evidence may be mounted to render it plausible that most Hadandowa Beja people think of sicknesses according to the contrast sets presented in Table 1 and Table 2? Of course, I have no direct evidence for this explanation being plausible. There is also no real evidence of when substance thinking of sicknesses first occurred among Beja people or whether such ideas were introduced from outside Beja society. Given the severe lack of written historical sources on the Beja, such evidence is not very likely to be mounted in future either. Further, if one conceives of the 'sickness substance' constellation of schemata as originally Beja, there is no evidence of the cultural idea from which such a constellation might stem.

In order to give some substance to my claims regarding the substance dimensions in Beja reasoning about sicknesses, I want to present some rough statistics from my initial interview. In those interviews, in contrast with later interviews, I gave my respondents no clues as to what I was looking for, but asked them to freely make associations about symptoms, etiology and treatment forms for different sicknesses. Here are some of the results:

Kosúlt. **40 respondents**

Table 3: *Symptoms of kosúlt*[54]

Symptoms	Increasing thinness	Hotness of the body	Loss of appetite	Diarrhea	General weakness
Number of responses	18	5	5	15	11

Table 4: *Causes of kosúlt*[55]

Causes	Unsuitable food	Unsuitable earth or air	Weakness and lack of food during pregnancy	Through sex with men	Child gets it through breastmilk
Number of responses	12	5	6	7	14

Table 5: *Treatment of kosúlt*[56]

Treatment	Give herbs	Sit in hot blood	Wrap in goatskin	Change food, water, or residence	Give nutritious food
Number of responses	15	16	20	16	18

For each of the tables the five most frequent answers are given. The less frequent answers are given in the footnotes. Since respondents were asked to give free associations, each respondent could possibly recognize all the different forms of treatment, symptoms and etiologies. For this reason the results should not be interpreted as exhausting the knowledge of the respondents. As an example, I am absolutely sure that all Beja know about the treatment of wrapping a patient in goatskin as a means of extracting heat from *kosúlt*. However, by asking people to associate freely, I consider the results to have a greater psychological validity. It allows for people to give unexpected answers at odds with general models of a given sickness.

As is evident from the range of answers concerning symptoms, thinness and body hotness are among the most frequent answers, while no respondent (including less frequent answers given in the footnotes) mentioned for example coldness or 'solid parts' in the body. Regarding causes, sexual transmission and transmission through breastmilk are among the most frequently perceived etiologies, together with unsuitable food or place of living. Hotness and *heminéit* are less frequently mentioned as causes (see footnotes), while nobody mentioned coldness as a possible source. Among treatment options, means of heat extraction by herbs, by sitting in blood or wrapping in goatskin are among the most frequently mentioned, together with searching for suitable food, water and place of living. Burying in wet sand, which is quite frequently conducted in some rural areas, was provided as an answer by one respondent only. No respondents mentioned forms of 'hot' treatments.

All in all this clearly points in the direction that the Beja, when conceiving a sickness as 'hot,' are consistent in their conceptions of symptoms, etiology and forms of treatment. Turning to the prototype 'cold' sickness of *hāf*, we get the same clear picture:

Hāf. **26 respondents.**

Table 6: *Symptoms of hāf*[57]

Symptoms	Large stomach	Weakness	One side of abdomen larger	General thinness of the body	Increased appetite
Number of respondents	14	5	6	10	4

Table 7: *Causes of hāf*[58]

Causes	'Cold food'	From *Hāf Masóob*	'Cold milk'	Falling down	Carrying heavy things
Number of respondents	7	5	4	4	3

Table 8: *Treatment of hāf*[59]

Treatment	Burning by *Basīr*	Cutting by *Basīr*	Avoid nutritious food or take medicines	Eat *Dúkhun*	Cupping
Number of respondents	23	7	6	4	3

Like for *kosúlt*, the five most frequent answers are given for each of the tables. The less frequent are accounted for in the footnotes. Regarding the symptoms, big swollen stomach is most frequently given. At the same time ten of the respondents mentioned general body thinness, except for the stomach. Six people reported that unilateral swollenness of the stomach is usual, while three explicitly stated that solid bodies can be palpated on the stomach. None of the respondents mention 'body hotness,' like several did for *kosúlt*.

Regarding causes, 'cold food' and 'cold milk' are among the most frequent, while no respondent mentions 'hot food,' 'spicy food' or 'hotness' in more general terms. Regarding treatment options, burning by hot iron is mentioned by most of the respondents. Four persons responded that eating the hot grain of *dúkhun* is good. Nobody mentioned 'cold' kinds of treatment. In short,

Hadandowa people seem consistent in their descriptions of symptoms, etiologies and treatment options with regard to the 'cold' sickness of *hāf*. More statistic examples are given in Appendix 3. So far in the discussion, however, enough evidence may be mounted to support the view that most Beja are relatively consistent in their usage of models of 'hotness' and 'coldness' in relation to diseases and body states.

For some of the dimensions of substance-ness of sicknesses, like proposition XIII: ['Hotness makes hot sicknesses worse and coldness makes cold sicknesses worse.'] I have not been able to find more than a couple of instances which instantiate this schema. Even if those dimensions are left out, however, this does not change the overall picture of the perception of sicknesses as substances. Furthermore, if those dimensions are taken into consideration, they strengthen rather than weaken the general argument.

The state of the stomach is interlinked with the state of the blood, a facet which will be more fully discussed together with theory E: ['There is a direct pathway between stomach and blood.'] If the stomach is 'boiling,' it creates hotness and hot sicknesses in the body. In this case Beja will also say that the stomach is in 'unrest' or 'awake.' Such a state of the stomach makes the blood 'awake' and also makes the sickness of *kosúlt* 'awake.'

Are the metaphors 'awake' and 'sleeping' just apt metaphors which are 'good to think with' or are they expressions of other important constellations of ideas? In order to answer this question I will turn to a discussion of theory C: ['Sicknesses are like humans']. Here another and quite astonishing picture of Beja perception of sicknesses will emerge.

6.2.2. Part b

6.2.2.1. Introduction
When speaking with Beja people about incidences of sickness, they often used expressions like 'his *kosúlt* came to him.' On some occasions I asked informants what they meant by such a phrase, only to get the answer that 'we do not know. It's just an expression.' As will be demonstrated in the outline below, however, when this and similar phrases are placed in the context of the schemata of the theory 'sicknesses are like humans,' it is rendered more understandable and meaningful.

6.2.2.2. *Outline*

Theory C: The propositions XIV, XV, XVI, XVII and XVIII are all expressions of a more general idea which may be represented by the following theory:
['Sicknesses are like humans']

Proposition XIV: ['When you mention the name of a sickness, it may come to you']

   1: 'If you mention the name *"hāf"* you may get the sickness of *hāf'*

   2: 'If you speak about *tesérimt,* you may get this sickness in yourself or your children'

   3: 'If you speak about *toordíp* [epilepsy], the sickness may come to you'

Proposition XV: ['You may speak to a sickness present in a patient, and it will listen to you']

   1: 'One may speak to *toodíh* by whispering over the sick breast or in the ear of the sick woman'

   2: 'One may whisper Quranic verses [or other formulas] over the stomach of a person with *táflam'*

Proposition XVI: ['A sickness may think and speak']

   1. 'I used to hear that *annáp*[60] says:– I have to come to a person who has no butter oil'[61]

Proposition XVII: ['A sickness may be surprised and jump out of the body of a patient']

   1: 'If one gives a child with whooping cough donkey's milk without telling that it is donkey's milk, and afterwards reveal the truth, the sickness will jump out of the body by surprise'

   2: 'If one throws donkey's milk on a child with whooping cough, the sickness will be surprised, startle and jump out of the body'

Proposition XVIII: ['Sicknesses eat']

   a: ['Sicknesses are fed by body tissue']

      1: 'Rashes of *t'háasimt* may go inside the body and eat the liver'

    2: *'Kosúlt* eats the ribs and the spine and causes the sickness of *kássar'*
b: ['Sicknesses may want particular food']
    1: *'Kosúlt* may want particular food like wild rabbit meat, *gabāt*[62] fruits or water from another place'
    2: 'If an adult person has *kosúlt,* one might ask him what food he will like, and this food will be the best food for the *kosúlt'*
    3: *'Hāf* is fed by rich food like meat, milk and butter oil'
c: 'Sicknesses are fed by *heminéit'*
    1: 'All sicknesses are fed by *heminéit'*
    2: *'Kosúlt* is fed by *heminéit'*

6.2.2.3. Discussion: the personality of sicknesses

Trees, bushes and herbs are tangible and visible objects in the world. Sicknesses are not. In contrast to phenomena like humans, animals and natural objects, beliefs about sicknesses naturally involve greater reliance on inferences made from other spheres of experience. Since a sickness is not per definition a natural kind, violations of natural ontological assumptions are not in question. Even a person with the mystical and invisible internal substance of *evur*, is, after all, a tangible concrete human being to which people tend to have primarily natural ontological expectations. For this reason, Boyer's 'theory of essences' seem not to bring much light into the present discussion about the nature of sicknesses.

When speaking about the 'personality' of sicknesses, one may easily infer that Beja people automatically attribute intentionality to sicknesses. This may not be true, or, at least, not always true. Although a sickness may arrive to afflict a person mentioning its name, there is no evidence of people attributing intentionality to sicknesses. The arrival of a sickness in response to hearing its name may be perceived by Beja people as an automatic response, if they are holding a theory of it at all. Also, jumping out of the body in surprise may not be seen by Beja people as involving conscious reasoning by the sickness or sickness causing agent. In other words, even if a sickness may come when its name is mentioned, may act from surprise or may want to eat particular food, the sickness may be metaphorically more equal to an animal with no ability of reflexive thoughts and intentionality.

However, that a sickness may be able to listen to speech, to understand, remember and respond to it, is a clear indicator that Hadandowa people at least sometimes think of sicknesses as intentional and reflective beings. The utterance 'I used to hear that *annáp* says: – I have to come to a person who has no butter oil' clearly shows that Beja people have cultural resources for thinking about sicknesses as intentional. For this reason it seems like one does justice, at least in part, to Hadandowa culture when describing one theory of sickness as 'sicknesses are like humans.'

Not all dimensions of human-ness are relevant in describing sicknesses. Beja never speak about sicknesses as 'growing old,' as 'wanting to learn something new' or 'having fun.' However, such limitations on how metaphors are realized are typical of the way metaphorization works. Metaphorization is usually partial in the way it works. In the words of Lakoff and Johnson (1980) this partial metaphorical structuring 'highlights and make coherent certain aspects of our experience' (p.156). If, for example, a sickness is able to hear and understand speech, speaking to it may become part of the treatment. Whether it 'is having fun' does not have implications for how the patient experiences the sickness nor for how one might go about treating it. Hence, this latter ability is not a relevant feature in how Beja people reason about sicknesses.

As is well known from various researchers working on meta-phorization of health and illness, imbuing sicknesses with personality-like traits seems to be quite widespread within Western thinking as well, both within 'folk perceptions' and professional biomedicine (see, e.g. Sontag 1988, 1989; Stein 1990). Until recently military-like metaphorization of sickness and treatment made viruses and bacterias into soldiers fighting on a battlefield. As usual, the metaphorization is partial, but all the same, it has seemingly been very influential on the thinking of both lay persons and professionals.

In older Norwegian tradition the 'magic of words' connected to names of sicknesses made people avoid mentioning dangerous sicknesses or speaking about them in a very circumscribed way (Alver 1971). 'If you mention the name of a sickness, you may get it,' people used to say.

It may seem strange that Beja sometimes speak about sick-nesses as substance-like and sometimes as human-like. Two of the most frequent diagnoses Hadandowa Beja make, *kosúlt* and

107

hāf, or the less serious variant *hāf masóob,* are sicknesses with most of the substance-like qualities Beja people describe for sicknesses in general. However, these two sicknesses are also described as human-like in some situations. *Hāf* may come to a person mentioning its name and is fed with rich food. *Kosúlt* often wants particular kinds of food. If it gets the right food, it will be quiet, and the blood as a consequence will become more quiet and less hot.[63] The way Beja speak about *kosúlt* also indicates that the sickness moves toward specific people as if with intention: 'His *kosúlt* came to him' is a very usual expression when a person gets sick from *kosúlt.*

Since metaphorization is always partial and different metaphorizations highlight different aspects of phenomena and hence 'do different jobs,' it is not unexpected that the same phenomenon may be highlighted by very different and incommensurable metaphors. This, in my experience, occurs in Western biomedical settings as well. In line with recent research on cancer cells, researchers and biomedical practitioners may speak of 'treating and healing sick body cells.' One may speak of facilitating and strengthening naturally occurring curing processes within the body in order to achieve improvement in cancer patients. At the same time the older military metaphor of killing 'invading' cancer cells persists. Obviously, these different metaphorical means are employed in different contexts where different forms of treatment are at stake. So far 'treating and healing sick body cells,' either by gene manipulation or by 'facilitating processes already existent in the body' is successful only in regard to limited forms of cancer. And, not surprisingly, each of the two different approaches may be employed in different periods of treatment for the same cancer patient. Although the models are incommensurable, the combination of them in treatment situations may do a good job.

With regard to *hāf,* the substance qualities of the sickness are relevant to diagnosis. When 'solid parts' can be palpated on the surface of the stomach, this is an indicator of 'solid blood' in the sickness of *hāf.* Since it is a substance which may be removed from the body, it makes sense to make cuttings on the surface of the stomach in order to let out the cold blood. However, since the sickness is fed on rich food, part of the treatment should be to persuade the patient to avoid fat and nutritious food.

Since the sickness of *hāf* may afflict a person mentioning its name, part of the prophylaxis will be to either avoid mentioning it or, when mentioning it, to employ means of protection. When doing interviews or chatting with people about the sickness they usually chose the latter strategy. When mentioning the name they always muttered a protective formula like 'may God protect people from getting this sickness.' Quite often they turned their head away from me and spat on the ground. It was explained to me that spitting was a way of barring the sickness from coming. By showing unfriendliness towards the sickness it does not feel welcome and will turn away. In short, both types of metaphorization have to be understood in order to capture the Beja understanding of *hāf* and *kosúlt*. The two types are, however, employed in different situations.

6.2.3. Part c

6.2.3.1. Introduction
Sweets of shapes and colors designed to invoke disgust have been popular kinds of sales items among Norwegian children and children in other Western societies over the last few years. They carry provocative names like 'doggie-doo' and 'ear wax' and look quite similar to the items the names represent. While they are popular among children, especially young boys, grown ups find them disgusting and certainly never buy them. Obviously, our sweets industry plays with a cultural conception that things that look similar have similar qualities.

In a series of experiments, Rozin & Fallon (1987) and Rozin & Nemeroff (1990, 1994) explored the emotion of disgust in Americans related to what they call 'revulsion at the prospect of oral incorporation of an offensive substance' (p.205). In addition to noting that contact with offensive objects like cockroaches rendered otherwise edible food inedible even in absence of sensory trace of the contact, they discovered that their subjects tended to refuse to eat things like candies shaped like a realistic fly or animal or human excrement. Inspired by Frazer's *The Golden Bough* ((1890), 1951) and works by Tylor ((1871), 1924) and Mauss ((1902), 1972), they continued a systematic investigation on a type of magical reasoning apparently occurring in the United States as well as in less complex societies. This type of reasoning seemingly follows two laws which Frazer named 'the laws of sympathetic magic.' The first one concerns contagion and the second similarity.

The law of contagion holds that 'things that have once been in contact... may influence or change each other for a period that extends well past the termination of contact, perhaps permanently' (Rozin & Nemeroff 1990:206). Contagion is here used in the broad sense of having good as well as bad effects on the persons or objects with which the contagious objects come in contact. The law of similarity holds that 'things that resemble one another share fundamental properties... or that superficial resemblance indicates deep resemblance or identity' (ibid.). As we shall see, although those two 'laws' may seem similar in some senses, they are also in a fundamental sense very different from each other. To name both of them 'magic' or 'sympathetic magic' may rather be confusing than illuminating.

6.2.3.2. Outline

Theory D: The Propositions XIX, XX, XXI, XXII, XXIII and XXIV can all be regarded as expressions of the following general theory:
['Things causing sicknesses or things similar to them or to a sick body organ may also be used for destroying sicknesses']

Proposition XIX: ['Manipulating or destroying objects causing sicknesses, or pieces of such objects, can heal them']

- **a:** ['If an internal substance or force in a domestic animal causes sickness, a part or product of any domestic animal may heal that sickness']
    - **1:** 'A crushed cow intestine may treat *tesérimt* from [domestic] animals'
    - **2:** 'Eating dry camel stools may treat *tesérimt* from [domestic] animals'
- **b:** ['Destroying an agent that causes a sickness to worsen may make that sickness less severe']
    - **1:** 'If worsening of *t'háasimt* stems from fried meat, fried meat should be burned in fire and destroyed as treatment'
    - **2:** 'If *kayyán* of *t'háasimt* is caused by perfume, then a bottle of perfume should be destroyed as treatment'

110

c: ['A herb used for inflicting sickness upon others, may also be used for treating that sickness']

    1: *'Kardáp* may be caused by using a piece of *ábil gábil* [a bush], but it is also treated by it'

    2: *'Gúrda* may be caused by *ool áu* (a bush), but it is also treated by it'

Proposition XX: ['Destroying a sickness causing object may protect against this sickness']

  a: ['Destroying a herb causing sickness may protect against this sickness']

    1: 'Burning *shaushót*[64] with *abebaníb*[65] may protect against sickness from *shaushót* spirits'

Proposition XXI: ['A thing of the same kind as a sickness causing agent may protect against this sickness']

  a: ['A characteristic of a sickness causing agent may be used to gain protection against this sickness']

    1: 'If people know that a particular [domestic] animal is dangerous, they will make the same tribal mark as the mark of this animal on newly-wed women as protection against sickness from this [domestic] animal'

Proposition XXII: ['Objects similar to a sick internal body organ or constituent may heal the sickness of it']

  a: ['If a body organ is sick, it will be treated by keeping the equivalent body organ from an animal over the place of the sick human body organ']

    1: 'The liver of a sheep placed over the sick liver of a child may heal the sick liver, which is causing *eratiót*'

  b: 'Blood sicknesses may be treated by blood or other red substances used in religious offerings'

    1: 'Red things or blood can treat sicknesses of "bad blood" '

    2: *'Dalil óob,* a sickness in the ears caused by "bad blood," may be treated by smearing blood from the ear of a sheep on the sick ear'

    3: 'Powder from the red stone of *adal óot* can treat any kind of bleeding'

Proposition XXIII: ['Procedures similar to treatment procedures for a sickness may relieve or treat this sickness']

    a: 'If a child has the sickness of *kusháabe*,[66] blood from a wild goat on the outer sexual organs of the child will relieve the symptoms from sickness caused by lack of circumcision'

Proposition XXIV: ['Hidden things can treat hidden things']

    a: 'Hidden sand from under a stone treats *táflam* from *íwhib* [underground, 'hidden' spirits]

    b: 'Thing out of sight for humans, like dust hidden under a stone, may be smeared on the forehead of a child with *khoof* as treatment'

    c: 'Dust hidden under a stone may be mixed with water and given to drink for a child with *khoof*'

6.2.3.3. Discussion: 'laws of sympathetic magic' and principles of resemblance in Beja sickness theories

There seem to be at least two main kinds of ideas related to theory D. One idea has to do with the duality of sickness causing agents. A source of sickness may also be a source of treatment. The other idea has to do with symbolic links Beja people make between objects of treatment and the sickness condition. In some cases, as we shall see, this symbolic connection involves iconic resemblance. An object resembling a sick body organ or bodily fluid or resembling a symptom of a given sickness may cure that very sickness.

In his outline of sicknesses and treatment among the Ndembu of Zambia, Victor Turner (1989) mainly explores metonymic and metaphoric extensions of concepts like the colors of white, red and black, where 'white' may symbolize life, purity etc., 'black' sickness, impurity, death etc. and 'red' blood, life, war, danger etc. Some other examples Turner mentions in an extensive list of relationships between sicknesses and forms of treatment among the Ndembu seem to illustrate an iconic principle. A type of bush tree is considered 'stiff to bend,' and for this reason a piece of it is used against 'stiff neck.' A bush or tree with 'mottled bark like leper's skin is used against leprosy. A couple of trees have white sap 'resembling the pus of gonorrhea' and are hence used against gonorrhea. A tree with red gum like 'the blood of bilharziasis' is used to treat this sickness. The fruits of one tree 'resembles testicles,' while the fruits of another 'resembles swollen testicles.' Both of them are used for elephantiasis of the scrotum.

An Beja example of an iconic image schema from the outline above is the belief that 'hidden things treat hidden things.' A similar iconic principle seems to be present among the Berti people of the Western Sudan when a branch of a specific tree which is different from others because it remains green throughout the whole year is used in various rituals in order to obtain fecundity of people as well as general prosperity (Holy 1991). It is also used as medicine against a range of different sicknesses. However, an iconic kind of symbolism also seems prominent from Turner's (ibid.) discussion, although he only makes a short commentary upon it.

Frazer ((1890), 1951) gave an account of a similar principle working in a native treatment tradition among 19th century peasants in France:

'... The peasants of Perche, in France, labour under the impression that a prolonged fit of vomiting is brought about by the patient's stomach becoming unhooked, as they call it, and so falling down. Accordingly, a practitioner is called in to restore the organ to its proper place. After hearing the symptoms he at once throws himself into the most horrible contortions, for the purpose of unhooking his own stomach. Having succeeded in the effort, he next hooks it up again in another series of contortions and grimaces, while the patient experiences a corresponding relief' (p.19).

His story illustrates the 'law of similarity' mentioned above. This principle seems to underlie several of the different schemata presented in Theory D, like 'objects similar to a sick internal body organ or constituent may heal the sickness of it' (Proposition XXII), 'procedures similar to treatment procedures for a sickness may relieve or treat this sickness' (Proposition XXIII) and 'hidden things can treat hidden things' (Proposition XXIV). The last schema is more complicated, since it involves an iconic principle of resemblance as well as a metaphorical expanding of the 'hidden underground spirits' to 'hidden dust under a stone.'

Another peculiar instance of the 'law of similarity' is represented by the schema 'a characteristic of a sickness causing agent may be used to gain protection against this sickness' (Proposition

XXI, part a), exemplified by the Hadandowa habit of making the same tribal mark as the mark of sickness causing animals on newly-wed women, in order to avoid *tesérimt* in their offspring (see Proposition LVII, Theory L). The same principle of manipulating a characteristic or part metonymically standing for the sickness causing agent, is invoked when Beja destroy a piece of a herb or tree thought to cause a particular sickness. Destroying this 'exemplifying object' is believed to protect against this sickness (Proposition XX). This last schema exemplifies what Frazer ((1890), 1951:42) calls 'homeopathic or imitative magic [employed] to annul an evil omen by accomplishing it in mimicry.' He illustrates this principle by accounting for the practice in 19th century Madagascar of burning down a small shelter set up at the birthday of a baby born on an unlucky date. Being born on such a date means that one's house or hut will burn down in adult age. By setting the shelter on fire the destiny is circumvented.

The 'theory of similarity' involves both 'forward' and 'backward' principles of causation. Forward causation may be described as 'satisfaction or discomfort, potential benefit or harm, resulting from intimacy with a replica of valued or offensive entity' (Rozin & Nemeroff 1990:224). This idea is not 'magical' in the sense that operation on an object causes things to happen at a distance. Rather, this idea concerns the spread of 'substance' or 'essence,' which is basically a theory of 'contagion.' Backward causation 'describes feelings that sources will be influenced if action is taken on their images' (ibid.), of which techniques of sorcery is a primary example. This is 'magic proper,' which, as will later be discussed, can be of basically two types: iconic causality, where two objects with an iconic remblance are as though to share the same essence and operating on one of them will influence the other, and metonymic, where a part of an object, like human hair in sorcery, is operated on in order to influence its source at a distance. The Beja schemata of treatment presented above mainly represent the backward principle of the 'theory of similarity.'

As has been discussed for the theories of 'essence' and 'natural kinds' (Chapter 2), in Western thought and possibly worldwide, a notion that things are what they are because of an invisible, undefinable inner essence seems profoundly to influence the way we perceive animate and inanimate objects in the world (Boyer

1993, 1996a, 1996b; D'Andrade 1995). Indeed different theories of essences seem to have been prominent in the works of various Western philosophers, as noted by D'Andrade (1995:176):

'It is a common belief, found in many Western cultures, that certain things are the way they are because of some essence . . . Slightly differing doctrines of essence have been propounded by Aristotle, Aquinas, and various Scholastics: the general doctrine has been attacked by Locke and other empiricists, as Bertand Russell outlines in his *History of Western Philosophy.*'

When Americans in an experiment of Rozin *et al.* (1986) refused to hold a rubber replica of vomit between their lips, their reaction may illustrate the same principle in that an inner essence normally inferred from the color and shape of the rubber replica is perceived as being part of the object although the subjects know this to be 'logically false.'

That people perceive such an 'inner essence' as transferable in some instances may be a phenomenon occurring cross-culturally. Such a transference seemingly underlie conceptions of positive and negative contagion worldwide, as exemplified by Tylor's account from classical Greece:

' . . . The citizens of Ephesus carried a rope seven furlongs from their walls to the temple of Artemis, thus to place themselves under her safeguard against the attack of Craesus; and in the yet more striking story of the Kylonians, [they] tied a cord to the statue of the goddess when they quitted asylum, and clung to it for protection as they crossed the unhallowed ground . . .' (Tylor 1924:117).

A transference of an invisible beneficial substance from the two Greek gods was perceived by the ancient Greeks to spread to them through contagion. When Beja people place the liver of a sheep over the sick liver of a child (Proposition XXII, part a.1) or smear blood from the ear of a sheep on a sick ear of a child (Proposition XXII, part b.2, from 'bad blood' in the ear), both a principle of contagiousness with transfer of a beneficial substance and a principle of similarity of iconic kind seems to be involved.

A notion of positive and beneficial contagiousness is not unknown in modern Western societies. A chair owned by Elvis Presley may be sold at an exceedingly high price to an Elvis fan

115

at an auction. The item is treated as if the previous contact of the rock-and-roll star with the chair transferred an essence of him to the chair. Lovers in some instances deliberately expose each other to mutual contamination, as when they drink from the same cup or feed each other with spoons from the same plate of food. A more dramatic instance of a similar habit from the Ilahita Arapesh of the East Sepik Province of Papua New Guinea is presented by Donald Tuzin (1980, in Tuzin 1986:6): ' . . . during the ritual cleansing following a couple's honeymoon seclusion, the bride eats some of the blood which the groom lets from his penis.' The smell of the husband is thought by this and similar means to be transferred to the wife so that the yams spirits of his 'ancestral yams' will recognize her as familiar when she works in the yam garden of his ancestors.

Examples of negative contagiousness are not difficult to find. People may refuse to move into a house in which a murder is known to have taken place. Even if very few people actually believe that the house is haunted by ghosts or evil spirits, most people seem to act as if the house inherited some malicious substance from the murderer. Another example is given by Rozin & Nemeroff (1990). When they presented the question to Americans whether they were willing to wear a sweater previously worn by a 'street person' or a person they disliked, 90% of them were reluctant to do so, even when it was stated that the item was thoroughly washed and clean.

Several examples illustrating the 'laws of sympathetic magic' will be discussed throughout the presentation of Beja theories of sickness. As it will turn out, such ideas seem to be pervasive in Beja thought as well as occurring worldwide.

6.3. THEORIES OF HUMAN PHYSIOLOGY AND SICKNESSES

'There are two main reasons for all body sicknesses: bad stomach and hot blood' Hussain Barakwin

6.3.1. Part a

6.3.1.1. Introduction

The brain and nerves are noteworthily absent from Beja thoughts about human physiology and sicknesses. Although they have a

116

word for brain, *hūm*,[67] sickness states are to my knowledge never related to it. Human knowledge is supposed to be in the head (Beja do not specify 'brain'), while thinking (see below) is attributed to the heart. The word *ináwa* means 'nerves.' When a neck of an animal is cut during slaughtering, people say that the nerves of the animal are cut. Nerves are, however, never related to human health conditions. One informant suggested that the Beja word for blood vessels covering both veins and arteries, *imérar*, sometimes may include 'nerves' when people speak about sicknesses and treatment. However, I never got any evidence of this.

The heart, *óogna*,[68] is for Beja as it is for Iranians 'a highly polysemous symbol, linked to domains of personal meanings as well as socially organized and value-laden domains of public experience' (Good 1992). In all kinds of psychological disturbances Beja use the expression 'the heart moved from its place' (*óogna ehét*). A similar saying is used when people get bad news and become sad, for example when they hear about the death of a parent: 'The happening caused the heart to remove from its place (*óogna hő'ishat*). As for Iranians, the heart for Beja people is the seat of thoughts as well as for emotions like love, anger and sadness. Hurting peoples feelings may cause physiological sickness in them by hurting the heart, captured in the common expression 'do not make his heart sick' (*óogna baa l'hássa*), which may be interpreted as 'do not make him sad.' According to an informant who used to travel in northern and central parts of the Sudan, the same conceptions are widespread in all the Muslim societies in the Sudan.

Physiological sicknesses are, however, seldom attributed to the heart as an organ. In these matters the stomach is much more important. When speaking about sicknesses, Beja often do not distinguish between different parts of the stomach. The word *kalawáb* in Beja literally means the 'inside' of anything, like the inside of a cup. It is also used to denote the stomach in a broad sense, the 'belly,' referring to the stomach, intestines, the liver, spleen and kidneys. Although they have separate words for all those inner organs,[69] the general collective notion of *kalawáb* is most frequently in use when speaking about health and sicknesses.

While the heart is the center of emotions and psychological sicknesses and disturbances, the stomach (broadly) may be seen as the center and origin of the bulk of physiological sicknesses in Beja theories. And, at least for rural Hadandowa, the stomach content of *heminéit*[70] is seen as the 'fuel' for the body without which it is impossible to live. When once asking a Beja with experience in harbor work about what would happen if one lacks *heminéit*, he answered: 'This is impossible. Can you conceive of a ship moving forward without any fuel?' However, as we shall see, when the stomach contains too much *heminéit* or *heminéit* of poor quality, it may cause many kinds of sicknesses.

6.3.1.2. Outline

Theory E: The Propositions XXII, XXIII, XXIV, XXV and XXVI are all expressions of a more general idea which may be represented like this:

['There is a direct pathway between stomach and blood']

Proposition XXII: 'Things eaten go into the blood immediately'

> **a:** 'If one takes a blood sample after drinking red *karkadé*,[71] much of the blood will consist of *karkadé*, and the measurements from the blood sample will be wrong'
> **b:** 'Drinking *karkadé* makes the blood quiet'

Proposition XXIII: ['Food not compatible with a person may cause bad *heminéit*, which in turn may cause "bad blood," which causes sicknesses in the whole body']

> **a:** 'Unsuitable food may cause stomach *heminéit* which will make *kosúlt*'
> **b:** 'If the stomach *heminéit* is quiet, the *kosúlt* will be quiet'
> **c:** '*Heminéit* may cause every kind of sickness'
> **d:** 'Suitable food makes the *heminéit* quiet'
> **e:** 'Suitable food makes the *kosúlt* quiet'
> **f:** ' "Bad stomach" may cause *ogwéb*'[72]
> **g:** '*Ool áu* is good for *gúrda* because it makes the *heminéit* quiet'

Proposition XXIV: 'Causing diarrhea cleans the whole body from dirt and bad substances'

Proposition XXV: 'By causing diarrhea one might get rid of "bad blood" as well as sicknesses' a: *'Hāf masóob* can be treated by swallowing butter to make diarrhea'

b: 'If one has *gúrda*, one can drink sea water in order to have diarrhea'

c: 'If one has "bad" *heminéit*, one may get rid of it by drinking sour milk or by boiling *hallig állim* in water to cause diarrhea'

d: 'If one has the sickness of *gúrda*, one can drink butter oil to cause diarrhea so as to clean the stomach'

e: *'Kalendóy*[73] cleans the stomach and gets rid of *heminéit'*

f: 'If a person is bitten by a scorpion, he should drink a tea of ginger, *togarár*[74] and *sinaáb*[75] in order to cause diarrhea and vomiting'

g: 'If a person is bitten by a scorpion or a snake, he should eat butter or drink camel's milk to cause vomiting and diarrhea to get rid of the poison'

h: 'If a person has malaria, he should eat butter so as to get rid of the *heminéit'*

i: 'If one has *kosúlt*, one should try to let out the *heminéit* [by diarrhea or vomiting]'

A last proposition is not part of the general theory above:

Proposition XXVI: ['Stomach *heminéit* is necessary, but it can cause sicknesses directly or indirectly']

6.3.1.3. Discussion: from boiling stomach to hot blood

'Cold water is bad for the blood. It makes it solid and then corrupted'[76] Umar Okir

'The only cure attempting to correct the cause of sickness is mending broken bones,' Ausenda (1987:424) states when describing the native healing traditions among Beja people. This is more than an oversimplification. Whether he is alluding to causes as seen by biomedical practitioners or as seen by Beja with no biomedical background, his description does not do justice to their traditions.

Several Beja attempts at addressing the perceived causes of sicknesses are directed towards the stomach. Since Beja people conceive of a direct and immediate pathway from the stomach to the blood, 'bad blood' and sicknesses resulting from 'bad blood' may instantly result from a 'bad stomach.' As is evident from the outline above, many treatment efforts seek to correct the cause of those sicknesses by means like causing diarrhea in order to get rid of 'bad' or superfluent *heminéit*.

While classical humoral medicine contained the notion of four bodily fluids (see, e.g. Good 1992; Laderman 1992; Ullmann 1978), the Beja people generally only reckon with two in their practical reasoning about sicknesses and health: the blood and the stomach fluid of *heminéit*. The blood, as has been discussed, may have different qualities. The stomach fluid can also have different attributes, which are illustrated by table 9 below:

Table 9: *States of the stomach heminéit*

Paradigmatic dimension	Strongly acidic	In 'unrest'	In excess
	Less acidic	In 'rest'	Normal amount

Syntagmatic dimension→

The qualities of *heminéit* are represented paradigmatically as three sets of contrast. It can be more or less acidic, of normal or increased quantity and at 'rest' or 'boiling.' The last attribute is often expressed as the state of 'sleep' in contrast to 'awake.' In the second syntagmatic dimension normal quantity of *heminéit* is connected to less acidic and 'sleeping' *heminéit*. This is the healthy state of the stomach fluid. In the first syntagmatic dimension strongly acidic *heminéit* is connected to too much and 'boiling' *heminéit*, which is an unhealthy state causing a range of physical sicknesses.

Although the qualities of the stomach fluid are most often verbally expressed in absolute terms by Beja people, the dimensions may to some degree also be seen as continuing scales. Individual Hadandowa people may differ in how fine of discriminations they make. Some informants distinguished between four different colors of the *heminéit*, yellow, white, black and red. The different colors often correspond to different degrees of 'awake-ness' of the stomach fluid. Other informants made rougher distinctions.

The stomach fluid of *heminéit* cannot be translated as 'gastric juices' for two reasons. Firstly, Beja people in general do not share the biomedical models to which the concept 'gastric juices' belongs. Secondly, the *heminéit* is not confined to the stomach as the container of food *per se*. Rather, the fluid of *heminéit* circulates within the greater abdomen and possibly the rest of the body. This is in line with the account given by Evelyn A. Early (1988) from her fieldwork among working-class Muslim women in Cairo:

'Baladi ["native"][77] women are acquainted with basic physiology; womb, liver, stomach, colon, and tonsils are part of everyday parlance. They do not, however, think of these units as discrete, but rather as overlapping much like the conjunction sets in mathematics ... Easy circulation means parts adjacent to a diseased organ are vulnerable' (p.73).

While 'the heart is what matters' in some Middle Eastern healing traditions (Good 1994; Morsy 1980), for Beja people 'the stomach is what matters' in the majority of physical sicknesses. After engaging in several discussions with Hadandowa people concerning various physical sicknesses, I clearly have the impression that the stomach (or, broadly, the abdomen) is the center of their universe of physical sickness conceptions.

6.3.2. Part b

6.3.2.1. Introduction
The ancient Greco-Islamic medicine was divided into theoretical and practical branches. The first category contained among other things the knowledge of the six common principles determining the health condition of humans. The first principle has to do with the quality of the air people breathe[78] (Abdallah, in Feierman & Janzen 1992; Ullman 1978). It is not surprising that good and bad smells are linked to health and sickness in the classical humoral tradition, since the nostrils were considered continuous with the brain. Galen (A.D. 129–200), the most prominent Greek proponent of the classical theory, considered there to be a separate olfactory part of the brain. 'Odor particles' were transferred directly through pores in the nasal cavity to the olfactory brain. The whole brain pulsated by contracting and expanding independent of the pulsation of the heart. When the brain contracted, air is 'sucked in' through the nostrils, while air and secretions excreted by the brain are expelled when it is

expanding (Siegel 1970). Personal hygiene with removal of bad-smelling secretions as well as surrounding oneself with good-smelling items like perfumes naturally became important for his theories of health and etiology of sicknesses. Surrounding oneself with good-smelling substances has also been looked upon as means of counteracting the effects of plagues within the Greco-Islamic tradition, as accounted for by Classen *et al.* (1994) in *Aroma. The Cultural History of Smell*:

'Scents, either inhaled through the nose or absorbed directly by the body, were regarded as important healing agents in antiquity. The ancient custom of applying perfumes to the head and chest, consequently, was not simply an aesthetic practice but also a means of promoting well-being' (p.40).

This is also exemplified by Gallagher (1983) in a later historical period, from 18th and 19th Tunisia:

'Aromatic substances such as bitter oranges, mint, vinegar, and apples placed in the sickroom were also beneficial. Burning of musk of amber or tar was similarly helpful. Ointments of bitter orange, sandalwood, vinegar, and camphor were rubbed on the body' (p.27).

A preoccupation with smells in relation to human health has been a prominent feature in Europe since the time of Galen and until the growth of biomedicine from the end of the 19th century. Corbin (1986, in Rozin & Nemeroff 1990) comments upon Western Europe in the 18th century:

'Odor became an important, and highly threatening, carrier of personal properties and disease in the beliefs of 18th-century Western Europeans, leading to a great interest in masking with pleasant odors, disinfection, and ventilation by the end of the 18th century and a tendency to rid oneself of odor-retaining things' (p.212).

In the same light that saw odors of decay emanating from the earth and making agriculture a dangerous enterprise a century earlier, in the 18th century the perceived abundance of patho-logical odors in the towns created panic among the social elite:

'Excrement, mud, ooze, and corpses provoked panic. This anxiety, flowing from the peak of the social pyramid, sharp-

ened intolerance of stench ... Contemporary scientists ...
offered a fragmented, olfactory image of the town ... To
escape this swamp of effluvia, the elite fled from social
emanations and took refuge in fragrant meadows' (Corbin
1986:230).

In deodorized and sterile environments of present-day Western
societies we like to think of ourselves as having sickness explanations more in line with science. The removing of 'natural'
odors from our surroundings is seen as a secondary result of
cleanliness and removal of microbes and substances which
contain microbes. However, there is a growing market in Western
Europe and the USA for so-called 'aroma-therapy,' a non-
biomedical form of treatment where positive stimulation of the
senses, first and foremost the olfactory one, is believed to be
facilitate good health.

The Beja, like people in many other Middle Eastern societies,
explicitly link good odors to good health and bad smells to
various sicknesses. They have, however, no theory of odors
linked to the function of the brain. Although they have to some
degree been influenced by the Greco-Islamic tradition and continue to be so through Beja literate religious men, most of the
anatomical notions developed in this tradition do not belong to
Beja folk knowledge. As we will see, Beja conceive of the nostrils
as immediately continuous with the rest of the body through the
blood vessels of the head instead of being in direct communication with the brain.

6.3.2.2. Outline
Theory F: The Propositions XXVII, XXVIII, XXIX and XXX can all
be represented as instantiations of the following general theory:
['Things entering the nose directly influence the whole body']

Proposition XXVII: 'Butter oil, the best human food, is more
healthy if taken in by the nose'

Proposition XXVIII: 'Medicines work best when inhaled through
the nose'

Proposition XXIX: ['Smells cause or worsen sicknesses in
humans']

a: ' "Bad smells" may cause sicknesses in humans'
   1: ' "Bad smells" may cause the "common cold" '
   2: ' "Bad smells" from dead animals or excrement may cause eye inflammation'
   3: ' "Bad smells" may cause *shagīga*'[79]
   4: 'Lung inflammation may be caused by "bad smells" of excrement, long-stored sorghum and the like'
   5: '*Woréeb*[80] [smallpox] may be caused by "bad smells" '
   6: 'Nowadays many sicknesses are caused by "bad smell" from dirt in the roads'

b: [' "Nice smells" may complicate sicknesses']
   1: ' "Nice smells" like the smell of good perfume may complicate the sickness of *herár*'
   2: ' "Nice smells" may make the sickness of measles worse'
   3: ' "Nice smells" may complicate the sickness of *t'háasimt*'[81]
   4: 'The smell of perfume may make the sickness of *boyée*[82] worse'

c: 'The smell of green autumn grass after rain causes sickness in humans'
   1: 'The smell of green autumn grass may cause the sickness of *gúrda*'
   2: 'The smell of green autumn grass may cause the sickness of malaria'

d: ['The smell of a healing herb may cause the same sickness as it is supposed to heal']
   1: 'The smell of *ool áu* may cause *gúrda* if you do not have this sickness on beforehand'

e: ' "Nice smells" may be made by spirits in order to attract humans. If one smells them, one will get sick'

Proposition XXX: ['Smells may promote health and counteract sicknesses in humans']

   a: 'Smell of perfumes and other nice smells have a healing effect on humans'
      1: 'The smell of perfume treats the sickness of *shagīga*'
      2: 'The smell of nice perfume treats *mírquay*[83] ['fright sickness']
      3: 'Nice smells make the blood better'

4: ' "Bad smells" from spirits cause sicknesses in humans, sicknesses which may be treated by "nice smells" '

5: 'If a person is fainting, nice smells will do him good'

6: 'Nice smells from herbs or perfume kept in a pillow or tied in a small skin bag tied around the neck of a child are making its health stronger'

b: 'The smell of some herbs is treatment'

    1: 'The smell of *kamūn aswad*[84] is treatment for *shagīga*'

    2: 'The smell of *uhúk*[85] treats headache'

    3: 'Smelling *hallig állim*[86] treats *mírquay*'

    4: 'Smelling *hallig állim* makes spirits go out of the body when the smell goes into the body'

    5: 'The smell of burning *sarrób*[87] helps against *uáy*'[88]

c: 'The smell of powerful herbs or incense help against attacks from spirits'

    1: 'The smell of incense keeps spirits away'

    2: 'The smell of *hallig állim* keeps spirits away'

d: 'Smell of butter oil promotes health and is a treatment for many sicknesses'

    1: 'The smell of butter oil makes the health strong'

    2: 'The smell of butter oil treats the sickness of *saríit*'[89]

e: ['Smell of blood from sacrifice heals sicknesses caused by spirits']

    1: 'The smell of blood from sacrifice treats the sicknesses from *zār*'

f: 'The smell of blood from circumcision heals sicknesses from lack of circumcision'

g: 'The smell of "bad blood" treats sicknesses of "bad blood" '

    1: 'If a person with the sickness of *watáb* smells the blood from cuttings on his own legs, the smell may cure him'

6.3.2.3. Discussion: smells, fumes and health

As most Beja tend to see it, not only odors, but everything which enters the nose has an immediate effect on the state of the whole body. For this reason taking in the health-promoting butter oil through the nose is a highly recommended practice. Some old informants use to take a whole cup of butter oil through the nose at a time.[90] Fumes of medicines and herbs are said to be more effective when inhaled through the nose, a notion which is seemingly shared by Cushitic Oromo and Somali people as described by Slikkerveer (1990) from his fieldwork in Ethiopia.

Beja concepts of smells and fumes and their relation to health clearly have a basis in their notions of physiology, where the nostrils are seen as entering directly into the system of blood circulation. When informants are asked why butter oil is most healthy if consumed through the nose, they usually answer that the butter oil goes directly from the nose into the blood vessels of the head, from which it is easily spread throughout the whole body. For this reason butter oil is inhaled through the nose both as a general health promoting means and as a treatment for the back sickness of *sariit*.

The smell of perfumes makes the quality of the blood better and hence also treats sicknesses of 'bad blood.' Pleasant smelling herbs are often kept in pillows or in small skin bags tied around the neck of children so as to promote good health in them. Bad smells like smells from corrupted food, excrements or long-stored sorghum may cause a range of different sicknesses like migraine headache, lung inflammation and small pox. In towns like Port Sudan I often observed passengers in public buses protecting themselves from bad smelling objects like old and filthy leather bags by covering their noses with a piece of cloth.

However, there is more to Hadandowa concepts of inhalation of smells and nutritients than mere physiological notions. Good and bad smells are also connected to the spirit world and the works of spirits. Bad smells from spirits cause sicknesses in humans. Generally, Hadandowa people tend to think that evil spirits have bad smells. Nice smells like smells of perfumes may treat or relieve sicknesses caused by spirits, like 'fright sickness'[91] in children.

Like 'hot' and 'cold' sicknesses, Beja people tend to think about smells as substance-like. Smells are substances filling the blood vessels of the body. When smelling a powerful bush like *hallig állim*,[92] the smell spreading in the body will make evil spirits within the body leave. In this case, not only the nice smell, but also a powerful substance of the herb is counteracting the spirits (see theory A). Beja people do not speak about 'particles of odor' like people within the classical humoral tradition. Like for all health and sickness promoting agents, however, they seem to speak about smells and relate to them as substances evaporating from health and sickness causing agents and penetrating the body of humans in various ways. The 'hotness' of a mother's breast milk who has walked in the sun before breast-feeding will influence the body of an infant as a 'hotness' substance (theory B).

There may be a principle of contagion at work here. In reviewing a large number of instances of contagion, Crawley (1902, in Rozin & Nemeroff 1990) concludes that there seems to be a widespread belief cross-culturally that one's body odors may contain the properties of the person. Odor seems to be important in identifying the 'essence' and properties of things. If this observation is correct, it may be quite logical if people conceive of bad odor as reflecting a 'bad inner substance' of something, be it spirits or whatever. Since bad substances may be conceived as contaminating by contagion, it is not surprising that in many societies a notion of relationships between qualities of smells and health states are causally connected, like Donald Tuzin (1986) reports for the Ilahita Arapesh of Papua New Guinea:

'Though all objects have essences, only some have a detectable odor, and it is this feature which renders them morally identifiable and problematic . . . the Arapesh understand that smell is the communicable aspect of its source, which is the innermost core of the object emitting it . . . the goodness or badness of a thing is transmitted in its smell, the vapors of everyday life are a constant source of moral contagion' (p.2).

Sometimes the visual and tactile boundaries of a given object do not correspond to the perceived 'essence' boundary. For some objects even approaching them is believed to contaminate. It may be reasonable to think that olfactory experience of objects with strong smells may have led humans to think that an 'essence' can extend beyond the physical boundaries of animate as well as inanimate objects. An example of 'positive contamination' seemingly acting at a distance is the 'blessed' presence of holy men like the Pope, whose shared presence mediates blessings to his audience.

6.3.3. Part c

6.3.3.1. Introduction
Using branding irons has been used in Greco-Islamic medicine for several centuries. According to the author of *The Medicine of*

the Prophet, even Prophet Mohammad himself treated patients by making burnings (p.49). Possibly cautery was primarily a means of treating such bad physical states as skin sicknesses, superficial wounds and infected swellings at the time of the Prophet (Gallagher 1983).

6.3.3.2. Outline

Theory G: The Propositions XXXI, XXXII and XXXIII are all expressions of a more general idea which Beja people express as follows:

'Burning places on the body with hot iron cures a lot of sicknesses [and "bad physical states"]'

Proposition XXXI: 'Burning over broken bones make them heal'

Proposition XXXII: ['Burnings may cure "cold sicknesses" and sicknesses from "bad blood" of a "cold" state']

- **a:** 'Burnings on the finger and toe nails cure the cold sickness of *watáb*'
- **b:** 'The sickness of *herár* is treated by making thirteen burnings on various sites of the body'[93]
- **c:** 'Burnings on the stomach treats the cold sickness of *hǎf*'
- **d:** 'Burnings on the stomach treats the cold sickness of *hǎf masóob*'
- **e:** 'Burnings on the stomach treats the cold sickness of *táflam*'

Proposition XXXIII: ['Burning might frighten spirits and make them go away']

- **a:** 'Burning on the stomach for *táflam* makes spirit causing *táflam* go out of the body by fright'

6.3.3.3. Discussion: branding irons and the local busará' tradition

Burning with branding irons is, to my knowledge, only done by a specialist *basír* in the Red Sea Hills. Indeed, this is one of the few practices which sets the *busará'* apart from non-specialists. The converse; however, is not true: not all *busará'* use cautery in their practice.

When speaking with non-specialists, they mostly were not able to formulate any reasons why using branding irons is an effective form of treatment. However, when asking them what sicknesses should or could be treated by hot irons, all the sickness states mentioned represent 'cold sicknesses,' with the exception of broken bones and joints, and none of them can be considered 'hot sicknesses.' In other words, to some degree the local cautery tradition conforms to the hot-cold schemata discussed for theory B.

When speaking with specialist *busarā'*, they often added another explanation for why using hot irons is effective as a treatment. For both conditions like broken bones and *herár*, stimulation of blood vessels by making brandings on their sites in turn facilitated healing processes in bones and internal organs influenced by those blood vessels. In cases like *saríit* (lower back pain), burning with a hot iron strengthens the weak bones making pain, while in the case of broken bones, it stimulates growth.

A third conception seems to be shared by both specialists and lay persons. Since spirits are able to feel pain and are frightened by the prospect of being burned (see theory J), burning with hot irons on body parts affected by spirits like the stomach in the case of 'dysentery' *(táflam)* or female breasts in cases of 'breast infection' *(toodíh)* may scare the spirits in question and make them disappear.

6.3.4. Part d

6.3.4.1. Introduction
Although cultural principles of contagion may be present in all societies, cultural propositions and theories linking sicknesses to contagion do not seem to be universally occurring. According to Murdock (1980), 49 of the 139 cultures he reviewed made an etiologic connection between contagion and sicknesses. Only 31 of those cultures, however, had notions with some elements similar to elements of the biomedical germ theory.

Theories of contagion, as we shall see, are important in several Beja etiologic explanations. In some cases it may look like they have partly absorbed biomedical theories of sickness, as in the cases of measles and tuberculosis. Their conceptions differ, however, from the biomedical ones in some important regards.

6.3.4.2. Outline

The following three propositions are expressions of Beja conceptions which are important in sickness diagnostization. They are not, at least as far as I have detected, expressions of higher-level ideas.

Proposition XXXIV: 'The sickness of measles makes the intestines soft'

Proposition XXXV: ['Sicknesses may spread to humans from drops of spit in coughing'][94]

a: *'Shisht*[95] [tuberculosis] may spread through drops of spit while coughing'

Proposition XXXVI: ['Falling down makes sickness in the stomach']

a: 'Falling down may make *hāf* in the stomach'
b: 'Falling down make *hāf masóob* in the stomach of a child'

6.3.4.3. Discussion: Western biomedical influence or nativization of biomedical concepts?

Even in Western societies it is not meaningful to speak about non-specialists absorbing whole biomedical theories, or even models (see, e.g. D'Andrade *et al.* 1972; Stein 1990). In societies like the Beja society, where representatives of the biomedical tradition are either absent or have a severely limited sphere of influence, as in Sinkat, there is no reason to assume that the few biomedical concepts used by Beja people have acquired the same meaning for them as for biomedical practitioners.

Beja people are well aware of the sickness of measles. They know the visible skin symptoms as well as the fact that the sickness is contagious. Their concept of contagiousness seems, however, to be substance related rather than related to microbes. Also, the assumed sickness history of a patient with measles differs from the biomedical conceptions. Most Hadandowa tend to believe that the sickness of measles begins as rashes on the intestines. The rashes will make the intestines soft and fragile, for which reason all kinds of solid food should be avoided. As the rashes spread towards the skin and become visible, however, the rashes in the intestines will disappear (see Proposition VIII (part c), Theory B). The child with measles has, however, to avoid solid food for forty days after the onset of the sickness until the quality of the intestines is restored.

It is part of a biomedical understanding of human anatomy and physiology that a severe physical blow to the stomach may result in life-threatening bleedings from damaging internal body organs which are rich in blood supply. Beja people also think that physical trauma from a blow or from falling down may cause serious internal sickness in the stomach. In the traditional understanding of physiology, however, blood 'collecting' in the stomach may result from particular kinds of food or states of food (see Theory B) as well as traumas. The reason for the serious condition of the patient has both to do with the collection of the blood as well as its cold and solid substance. In other words, there is no reason to assume that the connections they make between physical traumas and stomach sicknesses may stem from spread of biomedical models. Even if it should be the case that their thoughts are influenced by the biomedical tradition, the concepts they have acquired are framed within a traditional framework which does not render their concepts meaningful in a biomedical framework.

Some Beja speak about 'small insects' which are spread through drops of spit from persons with tuberculosis to other people. Most informants, however, did not seem to have any concepts similar to bacteria when explaining the spread of this disease. Tuberculosis is greatly feared as well as stigmatized, and people usually avoid any contact with persons sick from tuberculosis. As in the case of measles, however, a general understanding of contagion and contamination similar to this discussed for theory D seem to underlie their conceptions of tuberculosis.

As demonstrated by Evelyn A. Early (1988), even having a notion of microbes does not imply a biomedically inspired understanding of how sicknesses spread. From her fieldwork among working-class women in Cairo, she tells:

' . . . infection is thought to result from a general circulation of *microbs* and, unlike the cosmopolitian conceptions of contagion, not to have any specific vehicle such as the blood. *Microb* is a catchall term . . . to define the etiology of afrangi

131

["non native"][96] disease. *Microbs* are free agents which can "bombard" a patient much as black magic can' (p.73).

Even when lacking concepts of germs, as seems to be the case for most Beja, it is neither just nor scientific to regard theories of contamination as primitive. If this should be the case, young children should tend to hold such theories, and with increasing age and education the importance of theories of contamination should diminish. Psychological research among American middle-class children, however, render the opposite to be most likely (Fallon *et al.* 1984, in Rozin & Nemeroff 1990). Notions of contagion seem to be absent in small children.

6.4. A PRELIMINARY CONCLUSION: BODIES, SOCIETIES AND PROCESSES OF TRANS-SUBSTANSIATION

By way of concluding the section on human physiology and sicknesses, it seems clear that Beja notions of physiology shares the fluidity characteristic of the Greco-Islamic tradition (see, e.g. Good 1992; Laderman 1992; Ullmann 1978). The same observation is made clear by Evelyn A. Early when she states that the

'body is seen as a dynamic organism whose parts are integrally related and through which foreign objects can move following courses other than standard circulatory or alimentary ones . . . [their] notion of fluidity is consonant with the humoral system' (1988:73).

Given the Beja fear of substances like food or other kinds of influences from outside their society (see Theory L), it may be tempting to see their notions of the vulnerability of the human body from penetration of various substances from outside it as a partial reflection of a concern with the vulnerability of their own society and adaptation to various forces from outside. Although this is in many ways a mere speculation, I am inclined to believe that it is a quite plausible speculation given the many linkages Hadandowa people make themselves between encroachment from outside on their society and the health situation of people.

A similar link is posed by several anthropologists for various societies, among others Janice Boddy (1988, 1989) who discussed the intrusion of *zār* spirits (see Theory J) for a village community in Northern Sudan. While various anthropologists have addressed the notion of societies and human bodies as vulnerable to 'trans-substantiation' or intrusion of various substances, however, theories of the nature of such substances have very often not been paid as much attention. If a broader range of characteristics of transgressing substances in native theories are accounted for, intrusive forces may turn out to be of beneficial kinds as well as threatening and damaging. Such a positive side of transgressions is illustrated by the notion 'positive contagion,' a notion which is already introduced and which will be more fully discussed in sections to come (see, e.g. Theory J and L).

6.5. STINGS AND BITES FROM ANIMALS AND INSECTS

6.5.1. Introduction

As will be discussed for Theory J, animals and insects attacking people may often be spirit animals and insects. For this reason, people often go to a *fagīr* as a primary choice after being bitten. Beja theories allow for more 'natural' explanations, however, when ordinary snakes and scorpions poison people. Their physiological explanations of how the poison influences the body of a victim are, however, related to a broader network of theories and conceptions.

6.5.2. Outline:

Proposition XXXVII: ['Stings and bites from animals and insects make humans sick through poisoning']

  a: 'A sting from a scorpion makes hot blood and poisons of the stomach in humans'
  b: 'A bite from a snake makes hot blood and poisoning of the stomach in humans'
  c: 'Bites from spiders make skin rashes through poisoning'

6.5.3. Discussion: poisoning makes hot blood

Whether a person eats unsuitable food, corrupted food or poisonous food or is stung by a poisonous animal or insect, a concept of stomach poisoning and subsequent 'hot blood' is usually involved in Beja folk diagnosization. In other words, the

133

schemata involved in conceptions of poisoning by animals relate to Beja overall conceptions of 'hot' and 'cold' body states and sicknesses as discussed for Theory B.

The same mechanism is involved if the insects or reptiles are spirits. In these cases, however, the symptoms will normally be expected to be worse and the treatment more difficult. A skilled *faqīr* is perceived to be able to localize the poison and by the movement of his fingers combined with prayers and incantations to make the poison move backwards into the affected limb and be led out of it distally through a finger or a toe.

6.6. FOOD, PLACES AND SICKNESSES

'The living conditions have changed now. All sicknesses are increasing, and recovery is decreasing, because the general conditions of people are worse than before. This is because the rain is now less, and we are always dependent on animals and agriculture. But the most useful food for us is from animals. If we for example use sorghum for a long time without animal products, we feel sick.' Hamed Tahir

6.6.1. Part a

6.6.1.1. Introduction
In the classical book *The Medicine of the Prophet* from the 14th century[97] people are strongly advised not to fill their stomach with too much food. When people eat too much, the food will take up too large a proportion of the stomach and 'there will not be enough room for water and breathing, which causes sicknesses' (ibid., p.13). Among Beja, eating too much is seen as both unhealthy and un-Islamic. Since most Beja presently exist near the borderline of starvation, however, this theme is not often discussed. Naturally they are more occupied by sicknesses following from lack of nutritious items, especially from the lack of animal products. It is clearly believed that under some conditions however, rich and fat food may cause or 'feed' certain sicknesses, (see also Theory B).

6.6.1.2. Outline
Theory H: The Propositions XXXVIII, XXXIX, XL and XLI are all

expressions of a more general idea which may be represented like this:
['Too little food supply or eating food with too little fat, as well as eating too much "rich" food cause sicknesses']

Proposition XXXVIII: 'Lack of food facilitates or causes all kinds of sicknesses'

Proposition XXXIX: ['The condition of plenty after much rain may cause sicknesses in humans']

    a: 'The smell of green grass after autumn rain causes *gúrda* in humans'
    b: 'The milk of animals eating much green autumn grass causes *gúrda* and malaria in humans'
    c: 'Rich milk from fat animals may cause *hāf masóob* in children'

Proposition XL: ['Some sicknesses are fed or worsened by rich, fat food or the smell of it']

    a: '*Hāf* is increased by eating rich food, while the rest of the body remains thin'
    b: 'The sickness of *hāf masóob* is fed by rich food'
    c: 'The sickness of *herár* is made worse by eating fat food or by the smell of fried meat'
    d: 'The smell of fried meat makes the sickness of *t'háasimt* more complicated'

Proposition XLI: ' "Dry food" [food without fat] causes sicknesses'

    a: 'Dry food' causes *kosúlt*'
    b: 'The sickness of *eratiót*[98] may be caused by lack of fat in the food'
    c: 'Lack of fat in the food may make *heminéit*'
    d: '*Hereraníb*[99] may be caused by "dry food" '
    e: ' "Dry food" may cause the sickness of *hāf*'[100]

6.6.1.3. Disussion: sicknesses of lack and plenty

Lack of fat in food is seen by Beja as detrimental to the health. There seems, however, to be another idea involved as well. Even if people get enough fat from other food items, items lacking animal fat or fat from animal milk are often seen as causing sicknesses in themselves. A notion of 'essence' which is inherent in the food and makes it both lacking in fat and being unhealthy may explain this observation, a notion which will be further commented upon for Theory I.

Another idea seems to be related to Beja conceptions of people, items and forces which potentially increase fertility and enhance well-being and good health, an idea which will be discussed at length for Theory L. Green grass resulting from plenty of rain and the fat-rich milk of animals eating the nutritious grass may both harm the health of people as if they contain a powerful 'essence' both potentially beneficial and dangerous. These qualities of this 'essence' may be transferred to humans by 'contamination' with direct contact as well as by smells from *oolʔáu* and other green vegetation (see also Theories A, B and D).

6.6.2. Part b

6.6.2.1. Introduction

The theory about the relationship between the state of the stomach and different kinds of sicknesses very much involves Beja concepts of food quality and its connections to human health and well-being. In other words, the Beja preoccupation with health and foodstuffs may be understood as a concern with what enters the bodily orifice of the mouth. This appears not unexpectedly to be a primary concern for humans cross-culturally. As noted by Rozin & Nemeroff (1990):

'Both in terms of psychological reactions and the actual invasion of the body by foreign matter, the oral contact/ingestion route seems most highly charged and potent (leaving aside the one competitor for this dubious honor, the vagina). The mouth accounts for almost all of the overt material transaction between the rest of the world and the self. It is, approximately, THE incorporative organ' (p.214).

Experience of contagion may be seen as involving three levels of 'closeness': from proximity to contact to incorporation. The most acute and intimate type of contamination is by incorporation, of which eating is the most elementary experience. It is perhaps no wonder why people in many societies seem to have the concept that 'one is what one eats.'

6.6.2.2. Outline

Proposition XLII: '1. Animal products, butter oil in particular, are most healthy as food for humans. 2. They also help broken bones grow'

Proposition XLIII: '*Hemiéf* [postponement of breakfast], eating a lot while hungry and drinking cold water on empty stomach all cause sickness [directly and indirectly]'

- **a:** 'Postponement of breakfast may make the sickness of *watáb*'
- **b:** 'Cold water after a long period of thirst may cause *háf masóob* in children'
- **c:** 'If a person has not had rich food for a long time and then suddenly eats a lot of it, this will make *heminéit* for him'
- **d:** 'If one eats very much while hungry one may get the sickness of *táflam*'

Proposition XLIV: 'Unfresh food ["cold food"][101] may cause sicknesses'

- **a:** 'Unfresh food may get corrupted and hence cause sicknesses'
  - **1:** 'Dirty or corrupted food may cause *táflam*'
  - **2:** 'Dirty or corrupted food may cause *háf masóob* in children.
- **b:** 'Unprotected food may get magically changed by spirits and cause sickness'
  - **1:** 'Spirits may cause magic to unprotected food by spitting in it or by looking at it'
  - **2:** 'Food seen by spirits may cause the sickness of *táflam*'
  - **3:** 'Food seen by spirits may cause *háf masóob* in children'
  - **4:** 'Food seen by spirits may cause the sickness of *sírr* in humans'

6.6.2.3. Discussion: 'filling in slots': propositions about relationships between food and well-being as examples of the flexibility of Beja reasoning

The three different propositions dealt with here have few things in common other than the fact that they all deal with relationships between health and food habits. The nutritious content of the food, whether or not it contains butter oil (Proposition XLII), the timeliness of breakfast (Proposition XLIII), and the

137

freshness of food (Proposition XLIV) affect human health and well-being in very different ways. The three propositions are, in other words, very different from one another regarding etiological explanations.

The propositions have in common, however, the fact that they overlap with other theories and propositions in several aspects. The Proposition XLII fits as part of treatment strategies to most sickness conditions, except sicknesses like *hāf*, where the sickness is 'fed' by fat and rich food. Proposition XLIV overlaps with general theories of spirits (Theory J) by involving the works of spirits as 'pseudo-natural' kinds having 'pseudo-natural' essences.

Regarding Proposition XLIII, there is the 'substance' or 'essence' overlap with Theory B: 'Sicknesses are substances.' Postponement of breakfast produces a condition which facilitates the 'cold' sickness of *watáb*, which again by its 'cold' substance may lead to the 'cold' sickness of *herár*. The substance-mediated 'coldness' of cold water on an empty stomach may lead to the 'cold' sickness of *hāf masóob* in children. The proposition also overlaps with the Theory E: 'There is a direct pathway between stomach and blood.' The 'coldness' of the blood in the sickness of *watáb* is caused by emptiness of the stomach.

As will be discussed in a later section of this Chapter (6.13), such kinds of overlap are typical in Beja sickness theories and contribute to their flexibility. The same diagnoses or theories of causality may often 'fill in' the 'slots' of various schemata being part of different theories and propositions. Finally, and interestingly enough, the theories and propositions are not merely linked on a higher level of abstraction. To the contrary, it seems more often likely that they are linked at the lower level of non-conscious 'essence' inferences.

6.6.3. Part c

6.6.3.1. Introduction
In the classic humoral tradition eating and drinking habits as well as the air one breathes are among the six factors seen as vital for human health[102] (Ullmann 1978). However, different individuals had to adapt differently to those principles:

    ' ... these six things must be treated differently and individually. If a body, for example, has a balanced temperament, its owner should follow a balanced way of life. Spring-like air is good for him, he should indulge in exercise in moderation, bath in moderately warm water, should not sleep too little or too much, should only practice coitus when he feels happy and refreshed, when his stomach is not too full or too empty, and when he is neither hot nor cold. In a body which deviates from the right proposition, a way of life must be followed which deviates from the right proportion but in the opposite direction' (Ullmann 1978:97–98).

In principle, the philosophy of adaptation of different individuals to their environment and to optimal lifestyles summarized in this citation is not different from Hadandowa Beja thought in principle. In this way the Beja differ from the Muslim Orang Asli on the Malay Peninsula (Laderman 1992). The Orang Asli are clearly influenced by the Greco-Islamic tradition, and possibly also by Indian and Chinese classical traditions, which all stress the balance of universal and opposing elements as vital for good health. Nevertheless, they seek 'coldness' and 'humidity' as an optimal state of the body rather than balance (ibid.). The Beja, in contrast, seem to value balance in most respects. Although they share a philosophy of balance with the classical humoral tradition, however, the content is different in some regards.

While the four 'temperaments' of humans were important in Greco-Islamic theorizing, Beja people seem to have no similar ideas. As has been discussed for Theory B, they seek to give cold treatment and food for hot sicknesses and body states and hot treatment and food for cold sicknesses and body states in order to keep a balance between hotness and coldness in the body. The quality of bodily fluids is important in Beja cultural models. Ideally they should be in a balanced state with regard to viscosity ('fluidity'), color and temperature. The concern with viscosity may possibly be a transformation of the moist-dry dimension of the classical tradition, but this idea represents only mere speculations.

As in the classical humoral tradition, Beja people are concerned with individual characteristics with regard to their lifestyle and environment. However, it is to my knowledge never made explicit what kind of properties of humans are important in this

139

regard. It is recognized, however, that different individuals may benefit from different environments and lifestyles.

6.6.3.2. Outline
Theory I: The Propositions XLV, XLVI, XLVII and XLVIII can all be seen as instantiations of the following general theory:
['Food not compatible with an individual or his sickness might harm him']

Proposition XLV: 'Food not grown in your area of origin or water from other places might harm you'
This is a general idea which people express in different contexts, but which is not related to concrete sicknesses, as far as I have discovered.

Proposition XLVI: 'Food or water which you are not accustomed to might harm you'

- **a:** 'If one gives a child food which it is not used to having, it may cause diarrhea'
- **b:** 'Food that one is not used to may cause *heminéit*'

Proposition XLVII: ['Food, water or air have to be compatible with specific sicknesses of people']

- **a:** 'If a person has *kosúlt*, one has to try out meat, milk and butter oil from different kinds of animals'
- **b:** 'If one person is sick by *kosúlt*, even if all members of his family benefit from a particular meat, another kind of meat may benefit the sick person'
- **c:** 'If a person with *kosúlt* eats food not compatible with him, his stomach will be in unrest'
- **d:** 'If the treatment of *kosúlt* is not successful, it might be because the earth, the water and the air of the place is not compatible with the person, in that case he should move to another place'
- **e:** 'A person with *hāf* or *hāf masóob* should not eat rich and fat food'
- **f:** 'If a person has measles, he should avoid solid food'

Proposition XLVIII: ['If one part of an animal is good, the rest

140

of it is good, and if one product of a place is good, the whole place is good']

  a: 'If one part of an animal is good for a sick person, then the rest of the animal will be compatible with him and do him good as well'

    1: 'If a person with *kosúlt* gets better by drinking milk from a particular animal, then the meat, butter oil, skin and blood from the animal will be good for him as well'

  b: 'If one product of a place is good for the health of a sick person, then the place as a whole is compatible with him'

    1: 'If the water of a place suits a person, the earth and its products and the air of the place will suit him as well'

6.6.3.3. Discussion: when the place and its products do not do you good

Informants asked about how one is to know what kind of food, water and air is suitable with a given person usually answered that one may only know from experience. 'In a family with five children, one of the siblings may need different food and water from the others,' one of them added. In addition to recognizing that different optimal adaptations exist for different individuals, people recognize that a given optimal adaptation may change for an individual in circumstances of sickness and ill-health.

It is important to make clear that as for other Beja theories of health and sicknesses, the above theory of individual adaptation becomes important when something goes wrong. This is to say, when sickness occurs there is something which needs explanation. When an individual is in good health, people do not seem to speculate much about what specific kinds of food, air, water or earth is good for him or her. While specialists within different ancient or present traditions have enjoyed the luxury of speculating about general principles of bodily functions, health and well-being, non-specialists, like the bulk of the Beja, invoke their cultural resources of sickness theories when things are out of order. As hopefully has been abundantly demonstrated, this does not imply that the theories and propositions are uncomplicated and simple. As will be discussed in the narrative section in Chapter 8 and in the case study section in Chapter 7, however, the broad ideas entailed in the theories as well as their flexible modes of invocations allow for their utilization in real-life situations.

Two schemata clearly support notions about the value of traditional food and food grown locally. The schemata 'food not grown in your area of origin or water from other places might harm you' (Proposition XLV) and 'food or water which you are not accustomed to might harm you' (Proposition XLVI) both support suspiciousness of new and unknown food items as well as food not grown locally. The body is seen by Beja people as slow to adapt to new kinds of nourishment. In addition a notion of contagion seems to be central to these schemata, an idea to which I will soon return.

A principle of metonymy is clearly involved in two instances of Theory I. If a part of an animal, like the milk of it, seems to improve the condition of a sick person, the rest of the animal must be good and compatible with him or her as well (Proposition XLVIII, part a). If one of the products of a place, like the water in local wells, is good for a person, the sorghum grown there, other food items, and the air will be good for this person as well (Proposition XLVIII, part b). In an important way such a metonymic principle often seems to be part of a 'theory of essence' in the form of a notion of contagion:

'There is a close parallel between similarity and contagion. The image equals the object, a shorthand for similarity, can be glossed as a part of the object. . . ., can stand for the whole object, and behaves in significant ways . . . as the real object. The part equals the whole, a gloss of the holographic aspect of contagion, represents basically the same relation. Although these two relations have been distinguished as metaphoric and metonymic . . ., they share the part/whole feature. In other words, both can be thought of as generalizations, or over-generalizations' (Rozin & Nemeroff 1990:228).

Rozin & Nemeroff (ibid.) mention in this context that the widespread notion of 'you are what you eat' may stem from the same kind of generalization or 'over-generalization.' This notion may be rephrased as 'you become what you eat.' However, since 'what you are' at the moment is so important for Beja assumptions about optimal life-styles, one may eat a specific food or change the air which one breathes in order to 'change what one is' in a preferable direction.

The pervasiveness of metaphors and metonyms as argued by various cognitivists (see, e.g. Lakoff 1987; Lakoff & Johnson 1980; Lakoff & Kovecses 1987; Johnson 1987) has been questioned by Naomi Quinn (1991) based on her own research on American middle-class metaphors and models of marriage (see also Holland & Quinn 1987; Quinn 1992a, 1992b). She demonstrates quite convincingly the seeming lack of creativity of her subjects in inventing new metaphors in order to achieve an understanding of the complex experience of marriage. A cultural model, or models, of marriage seem more basic to people's everyday understanding of marriage. The range of metaphors of marriage seems restricted to fit a given model. However, it could well be that in more tangible areas like human health, processes of bodily and spatial metaphorization are more prominent. Moreover, as demonstrated by Rozin & Nemeroff (1990, 1994), even in love relationships a notion of positive contagion may involve metonymic principles in the way people seek to expose themselves to contagion from the beloved one. A piece of hair or a picture of a person with whom one is in love may serve such a purpose. I even came across instances where people kept an item like an unwashed shirt of a beloved one and refused to wash it.

Although such metonymization is abundantly verbalized in poetry, it might well be that most processes of metaphorization and metonymization escape us because we look for their verbal expressions. Indeed this may be a fallacy of research within the linguistically inspired 'metaphors we live by' tradition. By focusing on how people use and relate to various objects related to their assumptions of inherent qualities or 'essences' of those objects, one may get a better understanding of how possibly deeper mental processes may underlie metonymic and metaphoric expressions.

By employing the notions of positive and negative contagion, one's understanding of how the Beja relate to food items or remedies like the red stone of *adal óot*[103] seems to be enhanced. As will further be demonstrated, seeking out kinds of positive contagion and avoiding or counteracting substance mediated contagion believed to be harmful are central themes in Beja theories of health and sickness.

6.7. THEORIES OF SPIRITS AND THE SPIRIT WORLD

6.7.1. Introduction

While evil spirits and their works are greatly feared by all Beja, stories about them are also a source of entertainment. The spirit world as described by Beja people is a culturally rich world which often intermingles and interferes with their own. This is not a unique feature of the Beja. Equally rich descriptions are given from other parts of Muslim Middle East, as the account from Morocco presented by Greenwood (1981:220) demonstrates:

> '[The spirits] are characteristically capricious, vengeful, libidinous, obscene, demanding and violent, and are generally respected and feared. A large body of custom relates to their avoidance and propitiation, and to places and circumstances where they are likely to be encountered. But Moroccans have to live with the problem of sharing their environment with these beings, who, if offended, retaliate by causing illness and madness.'

For the Beja as for the Moroccans their preoccupation with spirits is natural, since they continuously impinge on their lives and well-being. Moreover, since theories of spirit aggression seemingly fit their mode of production and existence (see Chapter 3), the Islamic heritage concerned with spirits is highly developed among Hadandowa Beja.

6.7.2. Outline

Theory J: The Propositions XLIX, L, LI, LII and LIII are all expressions of a more general idea which may be represented like this general theory of spirits, parts of which Beja people explicitly express:
'1. All living things have their counterpart in the spirit world. [2. They have properties similar to their living counterparts, like the ability to feel pain for animals and humans.] 3. Only people with a special blessing from God can deal with them'[104]

Proposition XLIX: 'Spirit humans and spirit human societies are similar to humans and human societies in many, but not all, regards'

144

a: 'Spirit humans are like humans in most respects'
   1: 'Like humans they may be Muslims and non-Muslims'
   2: 'The spirit humans are males and females with spirit children'
   3: 'Like humans they differ in rank'
   4: 'Like humans they have desires, intentions and goals'
   5: 'They may be evil, benevolent or naughty and unpredictable'
   6: 'They try to make contracts with humans, especially *fugarā* and holy men'
   7: 'Like humans they may fall in love, both with spirit humans and humans'
   8: 'They seek marriages, both with spirit humans and humans'
   9: 'They may become jealous and involve themselves in a struggle for a mate'
   10: 'Like humans they eat food'
   11: 'They are able to speak'
   12: 'They are able to listen'
   13: 'Like humans, they speak different languages'
   14: 'They are able to feel pain'
   15: 'They are able to smell bad smells as well as perfumes and other nice smells'
   16: 'Like humans they have blood and may bleed'
b: 'Spirit humans are different from humans in some respects'
   1: 'They may make themselves visible or invisible by their own will'
   2: 'They can move much faster than humans'
   3: 'They can move through physical hindrances like walls or human flesh'
   4: 'They like to dwell in humans'
   5: 'Spirits humans living in humans try to express their wishes through their human hosts'
   6: 'Spirit humans may afflict humans with sicknesses from inside or outside their bodies. They may cause sicknesses like epilepsy, *háale* ["madness"] and *waswás* ["psychological disturbance"]'

Proposition L: 'Zār spirit humans differ from ordinary spirit *junūn*[105] in some respects'

a: *'Zār* spirit humans stay permanently in humans in a lifelong marriage with them'

   1: 'A *zār* spirit can never be expelled from its human host'

   2: 'The human host is forced to adapt as well as possible to the *zār* spirit'

   3: 'Like any other marriage partner the *zār* spirit may become jealous'

   4: ['The *zār* spirit may demand from time to time to be alone with the host']

   5: ['The *zār* as a marriage partner enjoys ceremonies and celebrations similar to marriage ceremonies, which acknowledges and strengthens the bond between the *zār* spirit and its host']¹⁰⁶

b: ['Zār spirits are not very evil nor very good, but simply naughty and unpredictable. For this reason the physical sufferings they inflict in their hosts are seldom serious or life threatening. They may, however, cause severe psychological disturbances.] Besides inflicting humans with sicknesses, they often interfere in matters like marriage relationships and fertility. When their wishes and conditions are met, the host will be left in peace without any bad physical or psychological symptoms'

   1: 'A *zār* spirit may cause a paralysis in a hand or foot'

   2: 'Minor swellings and infections may be caused by *zār* spirits'

   3: '*Zār* spirits may cause *herár*'¹⁰⁷

   4: 'Excessive menstrual bleeding may be due to a *zār* spirit'

   5: '*Zār* spirits can cause depression of the mood'

   6: '*Zār* spirits may cause *waswás*'

   7: 'In bad cases *zār* spirits may cause *háale* [madness]'

   6: 'Infertility may be caused by *zār* spirits'

   7: '*Zār* spirits may create marriage problems'

c: ['They are not strictly Muslim and not strictly non-Muslims. Hence some of their wishes and inclinations may be in accordance with the Quran and some of them not']

   1: 'The prophet Mohammad and his position is acknowledged by *zār* spirits'

   2: '*Zār* spirits acknowledge the Quran and like to hear recitings from it'

   3: 'Zār spirits may demand behavior from humans which is not in accordance with the Quran, like drinking wine and even blood'

   4: 'Zār spirits may prevent people from performing their religious duties like asking them not to do the important Friday mosque prayer'

   5: 'Since they are not strictly Muslim nor evil spirits, fugarā' or holy men using Quranic medicine cannot deal successfully with them'

d: ['Zār spirits communicate with other zār spirits and take commands from zār spirits in a higher position']

   1: 'If a person has been possessed by a zār spirit for a long time and has established good cooperation with his spirit and becomes a zār sheikh, the spirit may help him with getting spirits in other possessed people to tell their wishes'

   2: 'In zār ceremonies, when several zār spirits are present, individual zār spirits are led to identify themselves and their wishes'

   3: 'If a person is possessed by a powerful zār spirit of high rank, he is in a better position to help identifying zār spirits and their wishes in other persons'

e: 'Zār spirits normally want material gain which gives them prestige like nice clothes, jewels and expensive perfume. The wishes are in accordance with the ethnic group and sex of the patient'

   1: 'If the spirit is a Beja, it will want things like a new male dress, a comb and a sword if it is a spirit man, or, if it is a spirit woman, a new dress, gold, jewels or expensive perfume'

   2: 'If the spirit is from another ethnic group it will wish things typically used by people in that ethnic group. If it is a white European spirit, it will want things like European clothes and perfume, horses and for a feast to be arranged with a long table with chairs. Since it is a Christian spirit, it may demand a church and a cross as well'[108]

f: 'Zār spirits always want the blood of sacrificed animals'

g: 'When the demands of the zār spirit are met, the host will recover'

Proposition LI: 'All animals have their spirit counterparts which may cause sicknesses in humans'

- **a:** 'There are spirit spiders which sometimes cause sickness in humans'
- **b:** 'There are spirit snakes which poison just like other snakes, but the poisoning is usually more severe'
- **c:** 'Spirit scorpions may sting humans just as other scorpions'
- **d:** 'Spirit birds may slap the face of humans and cause half-side facial paralysis'
- **e:** 'The spirit bird *guuk* may come and breast-feed infants and hence cause sicknesses in them'

Proposition LII: 'Only *fugarā* and "men of religion" can deal with sicknesses caused by spirits'

- **a:** 'Only *fugarā* can detect whether a sickness is caused by spirits, and only he or she can identify the spirits'
- **b:** 'Only *fugarā* may expel evil spirits'
- **c:** 'Only *fugarā* can provide means of protection against spirits'

Proposition LIII: 'The Quran is a God-given protection against spirits, the most powerful *hejāb*'
Theory K: The Propositions LIV and LV are both instantiations of the following more general idea:
['Some objects attract spirits, while others keep them away']

Proposition LIV: '1. Objects with bad smells, pollution, dirt and leftover food might attract spirits which 2. may cause sicknesses in humans'

- **a:** ['Bodily fluids attract spirits which may cause sicknesses']
    - **1:** 'If a woman's breast milk touches the ground, spirits are attracted to it. If you sit in the place where the milk is spilled, you may get affected by *t'háasimt* from the spirits'
    - **2:** 'When a woman is menstruating, she is in danger of being attacked by spirits'
    - **3:** 'When a newborn is just delivered and covered with blood, the danger of spirit attacks is great'
- **b:** 'Dirt and remains of food on the skin of humans attract spirits'

148

   1: 'One should always carefully clean one's hands and mouth after having a meal in order not to attract spirits'

   2: 'One should always carefully clean ones hands after visiting the restroom/toilet'

c: 'Places with garbage attract spirits'

   1: 'It is dangerous to walk past garbage dumps, especially for menstruating women'

d: 'Bad smelling objects, like toilets[109] and gasoline poured out on the street, attract spirits'

   1: 'One should utter the protective words "*bismíllah*"[110] before entering a toilet'

   2: 'It is dangerous for menstruating women to go to the toilet'

   3: 'One should not walk on oil patches or dirt in the roads since one risks stepping on spirits, which may hurt one'

Proposition LV: 'Some objects keep spirits away and hence protect against sicknesses caused by them'

a: 'Incense of *lubān*[111] and *kamūn aswad*[112] keeps evil spirits away'

   1: 'Incense should be burned near a newborn child for the first forty days after delivery'

   2: 'When a mother has given birth, guests should pass over incense before entering the room of the mother and infant'

   3: 'Burning incense relieves the sickness of persons troubled by spirits'

b: 'The presence of the Quran helps keep the evil spirits at bay'

   1: 'The Quran should always be near a newborn child for the first forty days after birth'

   2: 'Writings from the Quran in an amulet is a powerful protection against spirit attacks'

   3: 'A water solution of ink or ash from Quranic writing keeps spirits away'

c: 'Blood from animals sacrificed as *karāma* and blood from circumcision keep spirits away'

d: 'The presence of a sword helps against spirit attacks'

    1: 'A sword should always be near a newborn child for the first forty days after delivery'

e: ['Powerful herbs keep spirits away']

f: '*Adal óot* keeps spirits away'

    1: 'If you have *adal óot* in your house, spirits will never come to you'

g: '*Otám* [sorghum porridge] on the door posts or roof keeps spirits away'

    1: '*Otám* on the roof prevents the spirit *gūk* [a bird] from breast-feeding and hence harming an infant'

6.7.3. Discussion

6.7.3.1. Living in two worlds

'The jinn abound in our mountains, but nobody but a fellaah [peasant][113] would fear them. Now, wolves are really dangerous.'
Salim Faraj[114]

The above quotation is employed by Trimingham in order to characterize the attitude to the spirit world of Sudanese nomads, 'whether Arab or Beja' (1949:171). This description definitely does not fit the present-day Hadandowa Beja, whether rural or urban. Spirit and spirit attacks are matters of daily conversation and storytelling among the Beja I came to know. The word '*jinn*' or Beja equivalents of it are often avoided, since people fear that the pronunciation of such a word itself may make spirits approach them.

Junūn[115] are said to frequently frighten children and cause sickness by fright in them. When I once asked my informant Hamed about this, he added that '*junūn* sometimes may even steal children.' Since he is a great joker, he continued: 'Maybe parents today would be happy of this, since milk and everything nowadays are so expensive!'

People sometimes said to me that 'white children do not seem afraid of anything.' When I asked them what they meant, they would answer with things like 'just look at your own children. They are running behind the house after dark.' When I asked them why they thought that this was so brave, they said that 'we Bedawiét[116] believe that there are spirits everywhere, especially after dark. We never let our children out of sight.'

Most Beja children I encountered were provided with amulets

150

around their neck or arm as a defense against spirit attack. In addition, people employed a lot of additional means of protection in critical periods like the first forty days after the birth of a child. In rural areas and in the outskirts of the town of Sinkat, a fire[117] often burned in front of the house of a newborn child during the night.

Since both menstrual blood and bleeding from a mother when giving birth are seen as attracting evil spirits, a range of protective means are employed during critical periods of menstruation and childbirth. As in many other Islamic societies, pollution represents the negative side of female procreativity (Bourdieu 1977; Abu-Lughod 1986).[118] The presence of protective means like a sword, a sharp knife, incense, a burning fire and, not least, the Quran, is of upmost importance for Beja people during childbirth and the following forty days.

As already mentioned, Beja usually avoid using the word *'jinn.'* Instead they might say *'ins,'*[119] strictly referring to humans. The proper Beja term for spirits is divided in two: *'Ikwib,* literally meaning 'the overgrounds' and *iwhib,* referring to 'the undergrounds.' Beja people fluent in Arabic often translate *iwhib* as *suflis,* referring to non-Muslim spirits, and *íkwib* to *'ulwis,* referring to Muslim spirits. However, this translation is misleading. While both 'undergrounds' and 'overgrounds' may inflict humans with sicknesses, only non-Muslim *súflis* are capable of such evil acts. The *'ulwis,* by contrast, are often employed as 'helping spirits' by *fugará* in making diagnosis and performing treatment. While 'undergrounds' are seen by some Beja as primarily creating 'hidden' sicknesses like *táflam*[120] and 'overgrounds' as making visible sicknesses like half-side facial paralysis,[121] other Bejas made other inferences or did not bother to distinguish between the acts of different kinds of spirits at all.

Obviously, both a spirit tradition having to do with the spread of Islam and a very local spirit tradition have left their marks on the view present day Beja hold of their spirit world. Rather than trying to distinguish Islamic elements from local and possibly pre-Islamic elements, however, I hold it to be more fair to speak about local or localized Islam. This is in line with the position voiced by Sharif Harir (1995:2–3) when taking issue with anthropologists speaking about 'pre-Islamic survivals' among the Zarawa people of Western Sudan:

151

'The whole notion of "pre-Islamic survival" begs a few questions as to its utility as an explanatory tool for understanding contemporary dualism in religious practices. Given the fact that Islam has been part of Zaghawa life for at least twelve centuries . . ., to describe contemporary practices as pre-Islamic becomes not only problematic sociologically, but pointless epistemologically. Furthermore, the characterization "pre-Islamic survival" is implicitly based upon the notion of checking religious practices in Muslim communities against a theological register which presupposes the existence of an ideal, pure type, and a coherent religion purged of all social influences that come as a result of interaction between religion and practice.'

How can we best grasp the significance of the Beja spirit world in its own right as it currently presents itself? People are clear in their view that the spirit world is a world which in many ways functions like the natural world of living humans. The spirit humans are males and females. They have desires, intentions and goals. They fall in love with spirits as well as humans, and they become jealous in matters of love. They marry and beget children. They are internally ranked and struggle for power and influence over humans and spirits. Like for most Beja, however, the rank described is usually not a rank in a stratified hierarchy. They eat, they listen and speak. Like humans, they even speak different languages. They may be Muslim or non-Muslim as well as evil, good or simply naughty and unpredictable. Like humans, they are all subject to the power of the holy Quran.

Even if people describe them as capable of feeling pain and bleeding, there are some clear physiological and physical differences between spirit humans and ordinary humans. They are capable of moving much faster than humans as well as moving through walls and other physical hindrances. They may become visible or invisible by their own will. They like to dwell inside humans and express their wishes through them. Whether inside or outside humans, they may inflict them with sicknesses by mystical means.

Are they then best described as a metaphorical extension of the human world where attributes of humans are metaphorically projected into the perceived spirit world and given new significance? Or, are they rather to be seen as humans who violate some basic physical expectations? Boyer (1996a) proposes that this is an apt description of beliefs of non-human agents world-wide. Among the African people with whom he carried out his fieldwork, the Fang of Cameroon, the spirits represent the immortal souls of dead Fang people. These 'ghosts' violate physical expectations in several ways (p.2):

'They are invisible, probably immaterial, can easily go through physical obstacles and usually move extremely fast. Also, they have powers that set them off from most other kinds of beings. They can throw "darts" at people, which pierce the skin and "thicken" (i.e. poison) the victim's blood. These powers, and notably the physical properties of the ghosts, are clearly and explicitly construed as out of the ordinary . . .'

Although the 'overgrounds' and the 'undergrounds' of the Beja do not represent dead ancestors, at least not among the present day Beja, the description given by Boyer is not dissimilar in character from the notions Beja present about spirit humans. If a 'pseudo-natural' cognitive mechanism is at work in the Beja construction of their spirit world, however, how can the richness of their conceptions possibly be invoked by a mechanism which is, in principle, so simple?

Boyer suggests that once a cognitive clue is given which allows for the thought that humans with violations of physical expectations exist, rich processes of logical inferences will follow. He does not explicitly state, however, the possible nature of such inferences. Given the human mental capacity for metaphorization, I will suggest that the basic cognitive processes which Boyer suggests allow for new ways of metaphorization. I will state my present position by an illustration from old Norse mythology.

In the ancient Norwegian tradition trolls and similar super-natural beings existed side by side with human beings. Although being similar to humans in many respects like having intentions, desires and emotions, they violated some physical expectations. They might have extraordinary strength, make themselves invisible or hide under water in rivers. The way people used to talk about them in the pre-Christian Norwegian tradition has survived in many Norwegian fairy tales. In one of them a troll became very angry and physically burst into pieces and hence,

153

died. The seemingly frequently occurring cross-cultural metaphor of 'anger as pressure in a closed container' (see, e.g. Lakoff 1987; Lakoff & Johnson 1980; Lakoff & Koevecses 1987; Johnson 1987) is extended as an apt metaphor of anger to the mythical and 'pseudo-natural' beings of trolls.

In other words, I do not think that in following Boyer's suggestions one excludes processes of metaphorization from the realm of supernatural beings. To the contrary, I will suggest that in constructing 'pseudo-natural' kinds, humans allow for additional forms and directions of metaphorization, an argument pursued from a different theoretical angle earlier (see Theory I). Another example more in line with Beja thought, is perceiving 'evil spirits' as collecting around dirt and dirty places on the ground, while 'good spirits,' when making their presence known to humans, speak to them from above. A possible spatial metaphorical schema of 'up is good and down is bad' may be operating in Beja thinking as well as in Western thinking (ibid.). By the process of making the pseudo-natural kind of spirits, a transfer of this schema is facilitated to the realm of the spirit world.

The spirit world encountered by the Beja share some traits with conceptions held by other Muslim Sudanese societies (see, e.g. Boddy 1989; Holy 1991) as well as in local Muslim societies worldwide (see, e.g. Nasr 1972; Hunwick 1992). Conceptions about means of counteracting the work of evil spirits are widely shared, of which Holy (1991:25) gives an example:

'The belief in the "magical" efficacy of Quranic verses deriving from the fact that they come from God, as well as the belief in the protective power rendered by the sheer physical presence of the Koran, is widespread throughout the Muslim world.'

The efficacy of a *hejāb* administered by a *fagīr* is a complicated thing to account for. While the Quran is efficient in healing because it is derived from God, the efficacy of a given *hejāb* may be called into question. Since the Quranic verses entailed in the amulet metonymically represents the holy 'essence' of the Quran itself, part of the power of the amulet obviously derives from this. However, the merits of the *fagīr* prescribing them seem as important for Hadandowa people as the Quranic writings themselves.

The *héequal*-ness of the *fagīr* (see Chapter 4 and Theory L) is thought to be transferred to the person wearing it near his or her body. This represents a *triple* instance of 'positive contagion': the contact of the *faqīr* with God has endowed the healer with a 'holy' inner substance, which is made manifest in fortunate experiences of people who encounter him or her. In a second instance of contagion, by being close to the *faqīr* and by the healer's writing of Quranic verses metonymically representing the *faqīr*, the 'blessed substance' of the *faqīr* is magically transferred to his clients by being close to their bodies, which is the third instance of 'positive contagion'.

The apparent theological contradiction between the Islamic belief that healing ultimately derives from God and local conceptions of Beja people that healing derives (at least partially) from the *faqīr* may hence be logically reconciled in a cultural conception of 'trans-substantiation.'

6.7.3.2. The amoral spirit world

Cults of *zār* spirits are possibly as widespread in the Muslim world as beliefs about evil spirits and Quranic means of counteracting them (Boddy 1988, 1989; Cloudsley 1984; Constantinides 1977, 1982; Hall *et al.* 1981; Lewis 1969, 1971, 1986, 1989; Lewis *et al.* 1991; Kenyon 1991; Makris 1991; Natvig 1992; Safa 1988; Schneider 1988). The theories people hold about them do not vary much cross-culturally. As shown in Chapter 3, however, the significance Beja give the spirits as causal agents is at variance with most *zār* cults in other parts of Sudan and the Muslim world. Especially among rural Beja, notions of *zār* spirits are invoked to explain sicknesses in children as well as in men. Generally, *zār* is described cross-culturally by various researchers as a women's cult (ibid.), or in some cases, as a slave cult (see Makris 1991). In addition, Beja people, especially rural Beja, tend to avoid the elaborate kinds of rituals traditionally performed in healing ceremonies.

While the Beja *zār* traditions vary in some regards from other Muslim societies, there are many cross-cultural similarities shared by the Beja. Firstly, *zār* spirits are not seen as immoral. Instead they are amoral in the sense that they have no moral attitude at all and cannot be evaluated according to standards of good or bad actions. They are seen as being simply naughty and unpredictable rather than evil or good. For this reason people seldom attribute severe and life-threatening sicknesses to them. Beja tend to attribute minor ailments like paralysis of an arm, a mood depression or a slight swelling or local infection to *zār* spirits. This is in line with descriptions of *zār* from other parts of the Muslim world as well, as exemplified by Hall *et al.* (1981) in their description from riverain Northern Sudan:

> 'The indications of Zar possession are not specific and may include a variety of ailments such as headaches, pains, flatulence, paralysis of the limbs or a general feeling of malaise' (p.191).

Since the *zār* spirits are neither good nor bad spirits, they do not easily conform to a cultural schema where they can be dealt with by a Muslim holy man or a Muslim healer. Even the Quran itself does not seem an effective means of counteracting their acts. Moreover, one never knows whether the demands of the *zār* spirit will be in accordance with the Quranic commands or not. For these reasons a *zār* doctor, a healer whose practice is not strictly Muslim, has to deal with problems of *zār*. Since a *zār* doctor is possessed by a high-ranking and powerful spirit, his or her spirit will be in a good position for negotiating with the spirit possessing the victim.

Secondly, a *zār* spirit engages in a life-long marriage with its host. For this reason it often interferes with the marriage of a married host out of jealousy. This might result in relational problems, infertility or excessive menstrual bleeding. However, if the spirit is given enough attention and gets the gifts it wants from its host, the *zār* spirit may be able to adapt to the marriage.

Thirdly, the demands of the spirits will be in accordance with its sex and ethnic identity. One of the main purposes of the *zār* ritual is to elucidate the identity of the spirit as well as its specific demands in order to relieve the sickness condition or the social problems of the victim. As already discussed in Chapter 3, however, rural Beja often tend to treat the spirit as a Beja spirit having the same sex as its host. Urban or semi-urban Beja, in contrast, are similar to Muslims in other societies in that the spirit usually has the opposite sex of the host as well as potentially representing a different ethnic group.

While the spirits dealt with by *fugarā* represent spirit aggression of various forms, affliction by *zār* spirits seems to have nothing to do with the theme of aggression. What forms of meaning does this tradition then take among the Beja? Does it have to do with interpersonal problems in unstable Beja marriages? Does it have to do with negotiations of role and identity of individual Beja? Does it have to do with explanation of illnesses and kinds of misfortune which other cultural models do not account for? My preliminary answer is 'Yes, it has to do with all those areas,' as will be demonstrated for the story of Saleimin Umar later on. And, in addition, it very much has to do with the question of personal intentions, questions which Beja people continuously ask about each other, an important theme to which I will return. Although a majority of people in Western societies tend to be skeptical about theories of spirit possession, expressions related to such theories are frequently employed in questioning the intentions of others. In the words of Kinsley (1995:8) ' . . . the idea of spirit intrusion is suggested when we say such things as: "I wonder what got into him?" "She's not herself anymore." "I wonder what possessed him to do that?".'

6.8. SICKNESSES OF INDIRECT INFLUENCES FROM HUMANS AND ANIMALS

6.8.1. Part a

6.8.1.1. Introduction
The concept of *baraka* is widespread throughout the North and Northeastern Africa (see, e.g. Crapanzano 1973; Holy 1991; Geertz 1968; Gellner 1969; Karrar 1992; Trimingham 1949, 1976; Voll 1969; Westermarck 1926) and possibly the wider Middle Eastern region (see, e.g. Lewis *et al.* 1991). As noted earlier (Chapters 3 and 4), *baraka* may be conceived of as a mystical force bringing blessing from God, increased fertility for people and animals, giving prosperity and good luck to people. In general, it can be seen as a non-definable inner quality of some humans.

In addition to the attributes already mentioned, being *baraka* quite often implies inheriting merits from one's forefathers as well. A similar concept is found in Hebrew societies, where 'pious *rabbis* have adorned the family's genealogy for generations, establishing a sense of *zekhut avot* . . . (Hebrew equivalent to *baraka*)[122] . . . *zekhut avot* implies both divine grace and spiritual force' (Bilu & Ben-Ari 1992:674). The Beja, in a similar fashion, tend to think about *baraka* as a inner substance-like quality which is increased by the merits of forefathers which are collectively represented in an individual religious healer or pious man. While the inheritance is usually patrilinear in Northern African and Middle Eastern societies, among Beja we find several female *fugarā* as well who are said to be *héequal (B)* or *baraka (A)*.

Among Beja, the luck-bringing dimension seems culturally more important than it is for the other societies described. Since the Beja are living in a rather unpredictable world where the social and natural environments are always potentially fraught with danger and possible hazard, the concepts of 'good luck' and 'bad luck' are useful for explaining rapidly-changing circumstances and making them culturally meaningful. Indeed, the best proof of a person being *baraka* is that fortunate things happen to people after they meet him or her. Conversely, since *baraka* or *héequal*-ness involves the merits of one's forefathers, people are possibly more likely to pay attention to such coincidences regarding descendants of persons who have already established this reputation.

Baraka, as seen by Hadandowa Beja, is a force residing in particular animals as well as in a special kind of stone. Although Beja people try to obtain a status of *baraka* in animals by various means and place a high value on such a quality in humans, as we will discuss, *baraka* is also a potentially dangerous force as well as a benevolent one.

6.8.1.2. Outline

Theory L: The Propositions LVI and LVII are both expressions of a more general idea which may be represented like this:
['1. *Héequal*-ness in humans or animals brings good luck, health and fertility. 2. However, invisible influences from *héequal* animals or products of animals may decrease fertility in humans and cause sicknesses which threatens the fertility of humans. 3. The *héequal* promoting red *adal óot*[123] stone, butter oil and some herbs may counteract these detrimental effects as well as sicknesses which generally effect the fertility of humans']

Proposition LVI: ['*Héequal*-ness[124] in humans and animals increases fertility and good luck but is also dangerous. This state may be obtained through ritual means in animals and for a limited period in newlyweds. However, only the blessing from God may make humans permanently *héequal*']

- **a:** '*Héequal* persons bring good luck, prosperity and health to other humans. Bad things will happen, however, to people who oppose them or try to harm them'
    - **1:** '*Héequal* persons give the best treatment for sicknesses and misfortune'
    - **2:** 'If person X is trying to harm or oppose a *héequal* person Y, X will be struck by sickness, misfortune or death'
- **b:** 'A newlywed couple may be made temporarily *héequal* by smearing *adal óot* on their hut'
- **c:** ['Animals may be made permanently or temporarily *héequal* through various objects and ritual means in order to make them more healthy and fertile']
    - **1:** '*Héequal* animals are more fertile than other animals'
    - **2:** '*Héequal* animals are protected from sicknesses'
    - **3:** 'Camels may be made *héequal* for a year by smearing them with powdered *adal óot* stone through the annual ritual of *kamtesilélt*.[125]
    - **4:** 'Camels and cows may be made permanently *héequal* by ritually cutting their ears so as to make them appear sharp [making them *t'héelat (B)*]
    - **5:** 'Sicknesses threatening fertility not caused by *héequal*-ness may be healed by the *héequal* promoting agent of *adal óot*.'
- **d:** 'Permanently *héequal* animals are dangerous for the off-spring of people not owning them and may cause sickness in those children'
    - **1:** 'Permanently *héequal* animals may cause *tesérimt* in small infants'
    - **2:** 'Not-yet-born children may be sick or killed by the influence from permanently *héequal* animals'
- **e:** '*Héequal* promoting objects like *adal óot* may both heal sicknesses which threaten fertility caused by people as well as protecting against them'
    - **1:** '*Adal óot* together with *híndib*[126] and butter oil [a mixture called *dérwout*] protects against dangerous effects of *héequal* animals'

2: 'The mixture of *adal óot, híndib* and butter oil treats the sickness of *tesérimt*[127] caused by *héequal* animals'

3: 'All pregnant women and newborn babies should be given *dérwout* [*adal óot, híndib* and butter oil] regularly'

4: 'The red stone of *adal óot* treats breast infections in women[128] [regardless of cause]'

5: '*Adal óot* treats excessive and irregular menstrual bleeding in women [regardless of cause]'

Proposition LVII: '1. All influence from the outside is of no avail or even dangerous. (2. The dangerous effects may be counteracted by using various objects)'

a: 'Food from outside the Beja territory is valueless or even harmful for Beja people in general'

1: 'Animals and animal products from outside are dangerous for human reproduction and the health of children'

2: 'Relief oil and other kinds of new food items from outside are dangerous to the health of Beja, especially creating *tesérimt* for children'

b: 'People coming from far away places often bring with them harmful (mystical) influences. Those bad influences may harm the health of newborn children.'

c: ['Evil substance-mediated forces from outside Beja society and their effects may be counteracted by using various means and objects']

1: 'The red stone of *adal óot*, together with butter oil and *híndib*, may counteract and protect against the effects of animals and animal products from outside'

2: '*Adal óot* mixed with *híndib* and butter oil may protect against and treat the effects of new items of food from outside'

3: 'All pregnant women and newborn babies should be given *dérwout* [*adal óot, híndib* and butter oil] regularly'

4: 'If one lets people visiting a newborn baby pass by smoke from incense of *lubān* and *kamūn aswad*,[129] the bad influences they carry with them may be counteracted'

6.8.1.3. Discussion

6.8.1.3.1. Camels and the uncanny forces of fertility

As may be obvious from this outline, the concept of *héequal*-ness is closely linked with health and fertility, both of animals and humans. For this reason it is no wonder why people seek healers who are considered *karāma* for protection against bad influences, for restoring good health, and when seeking treatment for infertility or recurrent death of children. *Karāma* may be of a specific kind, like when people attribute special skills as *busarā'* to people from the Hamdab tribe. However, *karāma* or *héequal*-ness may be more generalized and powerful, as with specific *fugarā'* and men of religion. In the latter case, the *héequal* persons are both liked and feared. People tend to think that bad things may happen to persons who oppose them, ridicule them, or do them harm in any way. Many stories are told about various kinds of misfortunes striking such persons. Abu Halima, a local merchant and watchman in Sinkat, tells about a famous *fagīr* relative of his, Ahmad Sedna:

> 'Two boys once stole his milk when he was going home from the market. Later on one of them became a criminal, while the other one turned mad.'

'This Ahmad Sedna is very powerful and very much respected,' he continues, and tells another story about him:

> 'One man once threatened the *fagīr* with his fist. The man stood with his back to a well, and he suddenly fell into it.'

The same double theme related to *héequal*-ness occurs when animals are made permanently *héequal* by making ritual cuttings in their ears. When a camel or a cow did not beget offspring or its offspring tended to die shortly after birth, people used to consider the possibility of marking the camels in order to transfer the ownership directly to God. This symbolic transfer of ownership was also traditionally made visible by letting the animal roam around freely in the wilderness for a period.

This habit is not as common nowadays as it was, even in rural areas. Even today, however, rural and semi-urban Beja frequently claim that *héequal* camels and cows cause sicknesses in their children. Unfortunately, the increased fertility of these animals is dangerous for the offspring of people from other *diwábs*. I

161

sometimes asked people whether the frequency of *tesérimt* cases from such animals is lower nowadays since the practice of marking camels and cows *t'héelat* is less usual than before. They usually answered that the question is irrelevant, since *héequal* camels and cows continuously reproduce themselves. 'There will always be offspring of those animals around,' people used to say. When people told about sickness experiences of *tesérimt*, as will be discussed in Chapter 8.2., they sometimes pointed out a specific animal which caused the sickness. Quite frequently, however, they merely assumed that such an animal had been around at the critical time.

The blessings of *héequal* persons and *héequal* animals always seem to involve some kind of danger. The same theme occurs when people talk about powerful herbs, bushes and trees for treatment (see Proposition VII). In many cases, a *hindíib* may create the very sickness it is supposed to heal. When people were asked why those herbs are that dangerous, they gave answers like 'because they are powerful, they are of course dangerous.' *Fugará*, in general, are both admired and sought out for help as well as feared. This is also noted by Holy (1991) for the Berti society in Western Sudan:

> 'The Berti hold ambivalent views about their *fugaraa*. On the one hand the services they provide in divination and in writing amulets and *mihaai* are positively appreciated. . . . On the other hand, the *fugaraa* are treated with suspicion. They know the "secrets" which can be put not only to beneficent but also malevolent use and they are often suspected of helping others to commit adultery, theft, sorcery *(sihir)* or other undesirable or immoral acts, or of helping them to acquire wealth by illegitimate means or even helping them to kill others' (p.36).

Yet another theme appears from the ways in which Hadandowa people relate to *héequal*-ness. It may well be that they do not conceive of this quality as a 'force' or a 'spiritual force' *per se* which radiates like electrical power from a given source. Instead, it may be better to think about *héequal* as a kind of inner substance which allows for certain things to happen, which is more in line with the ways Beja people verbally express the quality and works of *héequal*-ness. Even when they talk about the dangerous effects of this quality, it is always mediated through some kind of substance, like animals or animal products.

If this point of view is correct, it is in line with the treatment of the Melanesian Kwaio *mana* concept by Keesing in his monograph *Kwaio Religion* (1982), a concept which often has been translated as 'blessing.' Western scholars, missionaries and administrators have tended to treat the *mana* concept as expressing a fertility-increasing power similar to the stream of electricity, a concept which was at the time totally unknown to the Kwaio. Instead Keesing proposes, from a background of a careful linguistic analysis, a conception of *mana* as an invisible shield of protection which keeps evil influences away and allows for the natural growth and reproduction of humans, animals and crops. He proposes the use of the static verb *mana*-ization instead of the substantive *mana* in order to capture both the *active* search of Kwaio for this protection as well as their own linguistic expressions.

I think that some of the same considerations should hold for the Beja as well with some modification. Although the 'shield of protection' metaphor captures part of their thinking, they also clearly think of *héequal*-ness as a substance-like thing mediated as a part of other substances. However, it is a quality which mainly allows for the natural state of affairs among humans and animals, namely health, growth and reproduction. The concept 'fertility' captures part of this state. It also involves, however, prosperity and fruitfulness of the work of humans.

The problem of Enshiband, a highly-feared, powerful, female spirit, illustrates this point well. When she strikes, the breast of lactating women may be affected, women may become infertile and children may die. Besides, she also affects the work effort of people. When people are influenced by her, whatever work they do will bring no results. They will be unable to concentrate on one objective at a time, and they will have nothing to show for their efforts. The spirit of Enshiband represents a powerful source of 'bad luck.' By seeking processes of *héequal*-ization Beja people seek 'good luck' and protection against 'bad luck.' As discussed before, their stress on good and bad luck fits into their unpredictable social and natural environment and their precarious pastoral adaptation well.

The substance of *héequal*-ness turns out to be a rather peculiar substance. Like the *evur*-ness described by Boyer (1993) for the Fang people of Cameroon (see theory A), it is an all-or-none

163

quality. This means that it is not possible to have more or less of it. Either one has it or not. It is not possible to detect it in any direct way. It makes itself known, however, by skills possessed by a person, and even more, by fortunate happenings surrounding animals and people possessing *héequal*-ness.

Unlike the *evur*, however, Beja do not think of *héequal*-ness as manifested in the form of a particular inner body organ. The Beja talk about the mystical substance of *héequal*-ness in the same manner as Fang talk about *evur*, however, as an 'as if' natural kind.

A *héequal* person does not strive to do *héequal* things. The happenings surrounding a *héequal* person or the acts he or she performs naturally follow from the very nature of this substance. And, as soon as a person has been identified as *héequal*, people begin to perceive him as an out-of-the-ordinary kind of person. They start to treat him well and to give him gifts, since they know that fortunate things may happen to them when they treat such a person kindly, while misbehaving may result in all kinds of unfortunate circumstances.

Unfortunately, the potential danger of *héequal* animals is much more difficult to avoid. While making animals *héequal* will gain the *diwáb* which owns them by increasing the fertility of its animals, the reproductive capacity of humans in other *diwábs* will be in danger. As will be more thoroughly discussed in Chapter 8.2., small children as well as not-yet-born offspring of people in other *diwábs* may be exposed to the severe skin sickness of *tesérimt*, a sickness from which many children die. Some informants hence stated that the tradition of making animals *héequal* is a bad habit. A mechanism of 'tragedy of the commons' may be involved, however, since regardless of what people in a given *diwáb* may practice themselves, they will nevertheless be in continuous danger from such animals from other *diwábs*.

Even if people should manage to avoid the negative consequences of their own fertility increasing efforts, the danger of bad influences leading to *tesérimt* in children looms large from sources from outside their own society. Following the latest severe droughts and consequent movements of people and animals, the origin of consumed food items is often difficult to keep track of for present day Beja. As well, at a time with severe lack of nutrients, Beja people usually have to eat what is available at the moment. As we shall see, this situation has dangerous effects on their health and well-being, the way the Beja themselves conceive it.

6.8.1.3.2. What is the origin of the milk you drink and the meat you eat?

Distrust toward non-Beja is, as already commented upon, a general characteristic of all Hadandowa. This might have to do with their past history, with their second-class citizenship within the Sudan and several political and military clashes with surrounding groups and with armies of different emperors and colonialists. It may also have to do with their precarious adaptation to a rather rough physical world where the distance between survival and possible starvation is often extremely short.

Together with this distrust, a negative cultural view of cities and urban centers exists. People think that these promote ill health, dirt, an imbalance in social relations and bad moral conduct in general. As an example, many old women told us that several sicknesses striking young children nowadays were not so usual before. They claimed that the altered roles of women linked to urbanization were the reason why children are generally more prone to get sick than before. This, in their view, has to do with the tendency of mothers not to stay in their tents or houses all the time, but to engage themselves more in social life outside their home and outside their *diwâb*. This last point is relevant in understanding some of .the sickness categories people use. Several sickness categories are linked to some loosely perceived cause coming from a distance and striking the health of people.

As discussed for Theory J, in some special situations people are very careful of letting in visitors coming from 'far places,' even when they are close relatives, such as during and immediately after the birth of a child. People are afraid that visitors might bring with them bad spirits, bad influences from the outside or incompatible qualities from the water, air or soil of other places. Therefore, every guest allowed in has to pass over special incense or sit in a room for a while with incense burning.

The recent socio-economic changes related to increased urbanization together with the involvement of relief organizations and government organizations in the Red Sea Hills have, in most Bejas' opinion, contributed to new sources of ill-health. An important aspect of this is the change in food supply and food habits. In some cases, new items of food are seen as either useless or detrimental to human health. In other cases, the source of the food items makes the food have a dangerous effect on humans, especially children. This notion of food-mediated evil influence is not a new one. Hadandowa people have traditionally been reluctant to eat meat or drink milk from Beni Amer animals as well as from animals whose origin is difficult to trace. Products of such animals are still believed to cause *tesérimt* in children. Recently introduced food items, like commercial food oil from relief organizations, are said to cause miscarriages, *tesérimt* in children and skin sicknesses similar to *t'háasimt* in adults.

Since the social and economic involvement with the surrounding world has largely increased in recent years, the task of keeping track of the sources of food items has become increasingly difficult. It should be remembered, however, that explanations for bouts of sickness always are *post hoc* explanations. With increasing child mortality and sickness occurrences in children, including sicknesses with skin manifestations, there is more to explain at present time than before. Hence, one may expect that the 'tesérimt coming from outside' – model is more frequently employed nowadays than before.

The contagion by a food item carrying a *tesérimt* causing substance is dosage independent. This trait seems to be a characteristic of folk etiologies worldwide. Rozin & Nemeroff (1990:222) gives an example of this principle from the Western part of the world:

> 'There is a strong response among many people to *any* contact with AIDS victims, in spite of medical evidence indicating minimal risk. This appears to be a powerful belief, which like other contagion beliefs, is almost dose independent. The current abhorrence of any sugar in foods among some Americans is another possible example of a belief in contagion. The idea seems to be that sugar carries this toxicity (again, the dose-independence principle).'

6.8.2. Part b

6.8.2.1. Introduction

It may seem peculiar to the reader that the notion that 'unfulfilled wishes cause sicknesses' is set apart both from envy and from the notion of 'evil eye.' However, the way Hadandowa Beja seem to think of 'unfulfilled wishes' as a causal mechanism which has nothing to do with illegitimate and unsociable feelings. The person quite possibly may experience a wish for a particular food and a wish to share the eating of this food with others without having envious feelings in the sense of wanting to have the food instead of others or wanting to have a share at the expense of others.

The idiom of sharing is pronounced in the Red Sea Hills. Regarding food habits, one is per definition not supposed to eat or drink anything in front of others without being prepared to share and without inviting others to share. This idea of sharing is first and foremost directed towards members of ones own *diwáb*. Hospitality towards non-*diwáb* guests is also considered very important, however, as discussed in Chapter 3.

When having a meal together, people always eat from the same dishes. The ordinary manner of eating consists of dipping pieces of bread or meat in the same sauce or stew as the others, or, in more common meals, dipping ones right hand in the same pot of sorghum porridge. A Beja person returning home from abroad who starts to use spoons, knives and forks and hence eating in a more individualistic manner, is ridiculed by fellow Beja.

The idea of sharing as part of sociability seems to be at the bottom of the conceptions of some of the sicknesses and etiologies to be discussed below. However, sicknesses and misfortunes resulting from hostile or envious feelings belong to the realm of illegitimate wishes and emotions. As discussed earlier, witchcraft accusations are virtually non-existent among the Beja. A theory of sorcery is present and developed and will be accounted for below. As pointed out in Chapter 3, however, sorcery accusations are seldom invoked in real-life situations. The harmful effects of the 'evil eye,' is a frequent topic for conversation and is very much feared by all Beja people though.

6.8.2.2. Outline
Theory M: The Propositions LVIII, LIX and LX are all instantiations of the following general idea:
['Unfulfilled wishes cause sicknesses']

Proposition LVIII: 'An unfulfilled wish in a pregnant woman may harm the child in her womb'

167

a: 'If a pregnant woman sees or smells fried meat or other kinds of food she wants, but cannot get, the child in her womb may get sick or miscarried'

b: 'If a pregnant woman wants for example liver but cannot get it, her child may be born with wounds on its skin in the form of a liver'

c: 'Pregnant women should have all the food they desire in order for the baby to stay healthy'

Proposition LIX: '1. A not-yet-born child can smell food and have a desire for it. 2. An unfulfilled wish of a not-yet-born child may harm the mother and the child'

a: 'If a child in the mother's womb smells food which it cannot have, this may result in miscarriage'

b: 'If the time of delivery of a child is postponed, frying good meat may get the child to come out'

Proposition LX: ['If X wants to share in the food Y is eating but cannot, the food may harm Y']

a: 'If a person sees another person eating food which he himself wants, but for some reason cannot share, the person eating may get *sirr*'[130]

Theory N: The Propositions LXI, LXII and LXIII are expressions of a general theory, a theory which is explicitly expressed by Hadandowa people:
'Envy and jealousy cause sicknesses. The effects may be counteracted by *fugarā* by different means, for example by providing *hejāb*'

Proposition LXI: 'The envy of a person may harm other persons, their relatives or property'

a: 'Any person may unintentionally cast an "evil eye" when seeing a healthy child of other parents or some kind of desirable property. [Saying "nice words" of appraisal with regard to the child or the object of desire activates the force of the "evil eye"]'

b: 'Some people have "the evil eye" as a constant property harming others'

　　1: 'A person with the power of the "evil eye" may cause sicknesses in people'

2: 'A person with the power of the "evil eye" may cause children to get sick and die'

3: 'Lack of rain and catastrophe may result from the presence of a person with the power of the 'evil eye.''

c: ['A jealous or envious person may manipulate objects signifying others in order to deliberately harm them by sorcery.[131] The person and his condition can be treated only by finding and destroying this object']

1: 'A jealous or envious person may perform sorcery by using a piece of hair or nails from a person'

2: 'A jealous or envious person may practice sorcery by using the written name of a person'

3: 'By using belongings of a person, like a piece of clothing, or by collecting sand from one of his footprints one can do sorcery to this person'

4: 'A person harmed by sorcery cannot be treated unless the object by which sorcery was done is found'

Proposition LXII: '[Only *fugarā* can diagnose, treat and protect against sicknesses resulting from the envy and jealousy of other people]'

a: 'Only *fugarā* can provide amulets which are effective in protecting people against the "evil eye" [and other effects of envy and jealousy from other people]'

1: 'All children should wear amulets from *fugarā* so as to be protected from "the evil eye" of people'

2: 'By providing a person treated for sickness caused by the "evil eye" with an amulet, the *fagīr* helps prevent the sickness from returning'

b: 'Only *fugarā* can treat sicknesses resulting from the 'evil eye'

1: 'By giving *waṣl*[132] to a person who is sick from the "evil eye," the *fagīr* may treat him'

c: 'Only *fugarā* can diagnose and treat sicknesses resulting from sorcery'

1: 'Only *fugarā* can detect whether sorcery has taken place'

2: 'In case of sorcery, only *fugarā* can detect and destroy the means of it'

3: 'Only *fugarā* can detect the person who did sorcery'

4: 'A *fagīr* will provide *waṣl*[133] which treats sickness caused by sorcery'

Proposition LXIII: ['The Quran as well as the name of God are in themselves the most powerful means for protection against the force of envy or jealousy of other people']

1: 'The presence of the Quran protects against "evil eye" and sorcery'

2: 'Incantation of verses of the Quran protects against sorcery and the "evil eye"'

3: 'By adding "by the name of God" or "thanks to God" after praising a good-looking child or a desired object, the power of "the evil eye" will be made ineffective'

6.8.2.3. Discussion: seeking refugee in the Lord of the Daybreak

Say, 'I seek for refugee in the Lord of the Daybreak,
from the evil in what he has created;
from the evil of the moon when it is eclipsed;
from the mischief of women blowing on knots;
from the evil of the envious when he envies'.
From Quran cxiii.

The above passage from the Quran is frequently cited by literate Beja, often by *fugarā* seeking to give treatment for various kinds of sicknesses caused by evil influences. 'The mischief of women blowing on knots' refers to an old form of sorcery among the Bedouins on the Arabic peninsula at the time of the Prophet Mohammad where blowing on a knot while uttering a spell against a person would 'bind' the fertility, prosperity or some capacity of that person (Trimingham 1949). The 'evil of what he (God) has created' naturally captures all the abundant evil and mischievous spirits which are so very much a part of the daily life of Beja people.

The envy of people is greatly feared. As already mentioned (Chapter 3), among Beja envy is usually supposed to take the form of haphazard and involuntary casting of the 'evil eye.' The 'evil eye' may cause or facilitate any kind of sickness, especially in healthy and good-looking children. For this reason most children I encountered wore protective amulets *(hejbāt)* especially designed by *fugarā* to counteract the influence of the 'evil eye.'

The 'evil eye' has relevance for more than the health of people.

170

Some people told me about fat animals dying from its influence or nice cups or plates falling down and breaking into pieces when a person commented positively upon them. It is tempting to think that the fear of the 'evil eye' may represent a kind of social 'leveling mechanism' of which people are not conscious. Since usually no particular person will be identified as having 'the power of the evil eye' or being a witch, the kind of 'leveling mechanism' described for peasant societies (Bailey 1971; Keesing 1977), where a person who is more successful than others in economical terms risks being accused of being a witch, is not present. Since everyone fears the envy of others manifest in the 'evil eye,' however, this fear may support and strengthen the ideal of sharing.

I have not been able to mount any evidence to support this suggestion. Even if there should be some truth to it, the theory of course does not explain the presence of the 'evil eye' theory among the Beja, since it is predominant all over the Middle East (Barth 1961; Holy 1991; Sachs 1983; Wikan 1982) and in the Circum-Mediterranean area (Brøgger 1971, 1989; Migliore 1983; Murdock 1980). Witchcraft proper, however, defined as an involuntary activation of an inner evil force in specific individuals, is definitely absent among the Beja, although they have a conception of it (see Chapter 3).

It seems, from various ethnographic literature, that witchcraft accusations are predominant among peasants in stratified societies (see, e.g. Bailey 1971; Beidelman 1963; Keesing 1977) where such accusations tend to occur between individuals in close social interaction (see Chapter 3). Since Beja society is predominantly an egalitarian and pastoral society, cross-cultural data does not render it likely that witchcraft accusations should be prominent among Beja. In addition, as discussed in Chapter 3, there are structural and social organizational characteristics of Beja society which do not allow for the escalation of such structurally related witchcraft accusations as described by Nadel (1952) for other African societies.

Although present, sorcery accusations are quite rare among Beja. In this regard it is interesting to note that the cultural models of how to do sorcery are quite elaborate. Most of them seem to involve metonymical rather than iconical principles of how to influence persons at a distance, by using items like the written name, sand from the footprints or a piece of hair from the victim. This need not indicate that sorcery and sorcery accusations have been more important among Beja in the past, since schemata for sorcery and how to do sorcery are widespread as part of the Islamic civilization all over the Muslim Sudan (Boddy 1989; Holy 1991; Trimingham 1949) and may quite possibly have spread to the Red Sea Hills through the influence of Sufi orders as well as through general cultural contact.

It is possible that fear of the 'evil eye' may possibly facilitate social sharing of material goods in Beja society. Notions of the 'evil eye', however, are not used as a means of seeking out scapegoats for social evils among the Beja. I never came across one single incident where an explanation for misfortune involving the 'evil eye' was similar to a witch-hunt.

6.9. FRIGHT AND SICKNESSES

6.9.1. Introduction

'Fright illness' is very much feared throughout Latin America (see, e.g. Logan 1993) and beyond (Murdock 1980). In Latin America 'soul loss' (*susto*) is believed to result from a shocking or frightful experience, which in turn causes general fatigue and all kinds of physical sicknesses. People are often reported to die from the consequences. Unni Wikan (1989), in her account of 'fright sickness' (*kesambet*) in North Bali, described this frequent and feared sickness as revealing among other things 'the reality of supernatural spirits' and 'the vulnerability of the soul' (1989:46). Although this sickness, which is often perceived to cause death in children, does not necessarily involve 'soul loss,' it nevertheless always implies some kind of damage to the vulnerable inner spirit of humans.

Beja people do not have a notion of soul loss. They have elaborated ideas about the vulnerability of the human soul, however, which is thought to reside in the heart. Although shocking experiences may cause sickness in Hadandowa adults, the soul of an infant is seen as much more vulnerable to frightful experiences caused by spirits or other beings. Such experiences are thought to cause 'fright sickness' (*mírquay*), which at first presents itself by causing a child to cry continuously for long times at a stretch. If not treated or not given adequate kinds of treatment, various forms of physical symptoms and eventually death will result.

6.9.2. Outline

Theory O: The Propositions LXIV, LXV, LXVI, LXVII, LXVIII and LXIX are all instantiations of the following theory:
'1. Surprises cause fright and sicknesses 2. The surprises may stem from real animals and humans or 3. Spirit animals and humans. 4. Manipulating certain objects may cure or protect against the fright. 5. If the sickness is caused by a spirit animal or human, only *fugarā* can help'

Proposition LXIV: 'Surprise from a sudden appearance of, or loud voice of, an animal, human or spirit may create fright in small children'

Proposition LXV: 'Sickness of fright results in small children crying and crying without stopping'[134]

Proposition LXVI: ['Prolonged fright causes a constellation of bad body states *(alíib)*,[135] which might themselves be cured by physical means']

- **a:** '1. Fright slows down the flow of blood. 2. Massage can increase it again.'
- **b:** 'Fright may cause paleness of skin, especially in the palms and under the feet'
- **c:** 'Fright may cause disfigurement of hands and feet [distal]'
- **d:** 'Fright may cause paralysis in the feet'
- **e:** 'Fright may cause lack of appetite and thinness of the body'
- **f:** 'Fright sickness may finally cause death'

Proposition LXVII: ['Manipulation of certain objects like hair from animals or humans may cure fright sickness']

- **a:** 'Burning hair from the animal or human causing the fright and letting the child inhale the smoke may cure the fright'
- **b:** 'Burning a piece of hair from the mother of the child and letting the child inhale the smoke may cure the fright'
- **c:** 'Burning a piece of hair or a horn of a courageous animal and letting the child inhale it or giving it bile from the animal in its drinking water may cure its fright'

173

Proposition LXVIII: 'In cases of spirit causation, only *fugarā* can heal the fright sickness'

Proposition LXIX: 'Certain objects may protect against "fright sickness"'

- **a:** '*Hejāb* from *fugarā* protects against "fright sickness"'
  - **1:** 'Since all children may be frightened by spirits or living things, they should wear a *hejāb* on their arm or around their neck from birth'
  - **2:** 'If a child has recovered from fright sickness, it should wear a powerful *hejāb* in order not to get sick again'
- **b:** 'Pieces of hair or horn from a courageous animal may be kept together with a *hejāb* to protect against "fright sickness"'
  - **1:** 'A piece of *karái* [striped hyena] or another courageous animal should be kept together with the *hejāb* on children from the time of their birth'
- **c:** 'Since the sea is big and able to resist everything, a fish bone from the sea may protect against "fright sickness"'
  - **1:** 'All children should wear a fish bone around their neck as protection from the time of their birth'

6.9.3. Discussion: surprises and the sickness of fright

The idea of using parts of 'brave' animals to protect against evil influences is not only found among Beja people. Similar means were used to protect animals against the evil influence of envy in old Egyptian folk medicine: 'On the breast of a horse the tooth of a hyena is hung. ... On a donkey a wolf's tooth is hung' (Ismail 1892–94, in Walker 1934:81).

Indeed it seems that ideas related to conceptions of an 'inner essence' are important in understanding various Hadandowa treatment options for 'fright sickness' in children. Part of the essence making wolves, lions and hyenas what they are is braveness. From the Gaash lowlands,[136] where lions and elephants used to be present, I have been told that people used parts of lions for protection against 'fright sickness' as well as spirit affliction in general, while parts of elephants never have been used for the same purposes. This is in line with a general consideration of Frazer (1951, in Rozin & Nemeroff 1990:214–215):

174

'The savage[137] commonly believes that by eating the flesh of an animal or man he acquires not only the physical but even the moral and intellectual qualities which were characteristic of that animal or man.'

Both of the two 'laws of sympathetic magic' discussed earlier seem to be involved here (Rozin & Fallon 1987; Rozin & Nemeroff 1990, 1994; Rozin *et al.* 1986). In using tokens with a metonymic relationship to the brave animal, like a tooth, some hair or bile from it, the principle of similarity is employed. However, by letting the child inhale smoke from burning hair from the animal, drinking its bile or wearing a tooth from it, the 'braveness essence' will transfer to the child by the principle of contagion. In the same manner as *héequal*-ness and protection against dangerous effects of *héequal*-ness are transferred to animals and people through exposing them to contagion from the *héequal* stone of *adal óot*, the braveness transferred to the child both makes it brave and at the same time protects it from braver forces which may cause fright and 'sickness of fright' in it.

6.10. MOTHER'S WORK AND THE HEALTH OF CHILDREN

6.10.1. Introduction

That items connected to the mother and the mother's work or items symbolizing the mother or her daily work are thought to bring health for her household and children is a cultural notion noted by several ethnographers in different societies. Among the Berti of the Western Sudan sorghum porridge is smeared on the huts of newlyweds in order to enhance future childbirths for the new couple (Holy 1991). Milk is smeared on people or animals in rituals seemingly because it symbolizes the 'whiteness of women,' particularly of nursing women (p.82). Similar symbolic links are noted by Haaland (1990) for the Fur people in Darfur, Western Sudan.

6.10.2. Outline

Theory P: The Propositions LXX, LXXI, LXXII and LXXIII are all expressions of a more general idea which may be represented like this:

175

['Objects connected with the mother and her daily work can promote health and counteract sicknesses in her children']

Proposition LXX: ['Parts of the mother's body are health promoting for her children']

a. 'If a child has *khoof*, burning a piece of her hair and letting the child inhale the smoke may cure the fright sickness'

Proposition LXXI: ['The house, hut or shelter in which the mother works is good for her children's health']

a: 'If a child has *khoof*, a piece of wood from the mother's hut may be powdered and mixed with water, and given to the child to drink'

Proposition LXXII: ['The equipment used by the mother in her daily work is health promoting for her children']

a: 'If a child has *haaf masóob*, milk from an *amúl* [container made from *saaf* by women] with smoke from the fire of the house in it may cure the child'

b: 'If the child has *táflam*, the stones of the fireplace can be washed and the washing water given for the child to drink, and this may cure the child'

Proposition LXXIII: ['The food produced by the mother's work may cure sickness in her children, as well as protect them']

a: 'If a child has *t'háasimt*, *aaf* [dry remains from the cooking pot of sorghum porridge] smeared on the skin may treat the sickness'

b: 'Sorghum porridge smeared on the roof of the hut protects a child from being breast-fed by the harmful spirit *guuk*[138] bird'

6.10.3. Discussion: nurturance is health: substance theories revisited

Parts of the mother, like her hair, the house in which she works and moves, the equipment with which she is in daily contact, as well as products she makes like food and containers for food are considered to be health promoting for children and are used in treating various sicknesses in them. This may be where a concept of 'positive contamination' is most pronounced in Beja theories.

While the Western Sudanese Fur people present elaborated color symbolism related to mothers, mothers work, nurturing and female sexuality (Haaland 1990), Beja people seemingly do not use color symbolism much. They live in an environment mostly dominated by colors like brown, brownish yellow and shades of gray, including their building materials for huts and tents as well as traditional crafts. Ausenda (1987:414–415) gives an account of a rich color symbolism among Beja pastoralists in the Gaash area. At least in the mountains of the Red Sea Hills such ideas are not present. When asked, informants univocally denied the alleged meanings attributed to various colors. Another anthropologist who did fieldwork in the mountains in the Sinkat area, Fadlalla (1992), presented another account of color symbolism, related to the three most basic colors of the Beja, white, black and red. While Ausenda attributed symbolic 'openness' to the color of white, Fadlalla (ibid.) maintained that whiteness symbolizes male semen, male sexuality and the domestic milking of animals, in other words a rather 'closed' area. She explained their habit of not letting women milk the animals as stemming from symbolic links made between the white semen of men and the white milk of animals. Since the red menstrual blood of women is considered incompatible with the white semen of men, female milking of animals is seen as shameful by Beja.

When discussing such links with Beja informants, their reaction was mere amusement and nobody was able to recognize such a trait as part of Beja culture. This 'test' does not, of course, exclude a possibility that Beja people make such symbolic links unconsciously. Such links must, in any case, however, be at a different level of consciousness than for example spatial and military metaphorization which seemingly underlie Western discourses on areas like health and emotions (see, e.g. Brandes 1980; Keesing 1991; Lakoff & Johnson 1980; Sontag 1978, 1989), which represent links which people in Western societies are able to recognize more or less when they are spelled out.

Rather than trying to 'stretch' the data in order to fit a presumably hidden symbolic logic, however, I will advocate focusing on more pronounced traits of ideas related to cultural elaborations on concepts such as motherhood, nurturance and sexuality. The seemingly most pervasive kinds of thoughts present in Beja thinking about health, reproduction (of their society as well as of individual humans) and nourishment relate to 'substance' and 'essence' theories, as has been the most recurrent theme in this theory chapter. The 'positive contamination' of the children by the mother and everything with which she is in contact represents an instance of this. Conversely, frequent absences of Beja mothers from their children as part of their modified life in urban and semi-urban environments is often said to be a cause of increased ill-health in children.

6.11. SINS, FAILURES AND SICKNESSES

6.11.1. Introduction

Sins and failures of religious observances are seldom invoked by Beja people as explanations for specific instances of sicknesses. Although people state that a 'bad life' or moral transgressions may lead to many sicknesses, in actual cases of sickness such explanations are seldom invoked. However, the quality of people's overall relation to God as well as their social relationships to each other is always commented upon during times of catastrophes and general deteriorating living conditions.

The tradition of circumcision represents an exception to this overall picture though. Lack of circumcision is widely recognized by Beja people as causing specific kinds of sickness in children, both boys and girls.

6.11.2. Outline

Proposition LXXIV: 'Sins and bad motives of men cause disasters, which leads to increase in all sicknesses. By offering *karāma* the relationship between the people and God may be restored'

Proposition LXXV: '1. Lack of circumcision may cause sicknesses. 2. Uncircumcised infants are especially vulnerable to spirit attacks'

6.11.3. Discussion: human conduct and health

For the Berti society in the Western Sudan, 'Any disaster is a sign that God is angry with the people and must be placated by an offering. *Karāmas* are made in order to bring about rain, to ensure a good harvest, to avoid illness etc.' (Holy 1991:36). In addition to making offerings, however, it is important for people to correct sinful behavior and to observe their religious duties.

Although circumcision is regarded as a prominent duty by Muslims worldwide, nothing is mentioned about this operation in the Quran (Holy 1991). Among the Beja, as among most Muslim Sudanese, both males and females are circumcised. According to information from a female medical doctor in Port Sudan, possibly as many as 95 to 100% of Beja women are circumcised. Asma El-Dareer (1982) mentions three main reasons why Sudanese people circumcise girls. Firstly, most people state that it is a 'good tradition.' Secondly, it is believed to be according to the religion of Islam. Thirdly, people think that it enhances both cleanliness and beauty. Lastly, people tend to think that a circumcised wife gives the husband greater sexual pleasure (see also Vågenes 1990). Beja people seem unique among the Sudanese in allowing female circumcision as early as from the seventh day after birth (ibid.).

An additional reason for circumcising girls as well as boys among the Beja is that it promotes good health. Uncircumcised children are seen as particularly vulnerable to spirit attacks. For this reason, following this 'religious prescription' helps people avoid some possible health hazard. In my experience, Hadandowa people seem to think of circumcision as a kind of *karāma* or offering to God as well. For this reason it is possible that people think of circumcision as health promoting because it enhances blessing from God. All the same, childhood sicknesses are now and then explained as resulting from lack of circumcision, as illustrated by a story told by a mother from a nearby rural area of Sinkat:

'A child once was weeping and weeping. Then one woman said it needed *kusháabe*.[139] They called for a woman who did the operation and smeared the blood from it on the lips of the child. After this, *xalās*,[140] the child was fine.'

6.12. TRADITIONAL KNOWLEDGE AND TREATMENT

6.12.1. Introduction

Most Beja highly respect Islamic written sources dealing with health and sickness. People with whom I discussed this written tradition generally held the view that all prescriptions given in books of 'prophetic medicine' are useful means treatment for present day sickness conditions. If a particular prescription does not solve an actual health problem, this does not invalidate the prescription itself. Instead the unsuccessful result will be attributed to other circumstances, an attitude Ibn Qayan al-Juwsiyya attributes to the Prophet himself, as the following amusing story illustrates (p.25):

'A man came to Prophet Mohammad and said to him: my brother is complaining about his stomach. Prophet Mohammad said to him: "Give him honey!" This man went to his brother and gave him the honey. After this he came back to Prophet Mohammad and said: "I gave him honey, but his diarrhea did not stop." He [the Prophet] then said to him: "Give him honey again." He then came back to Prophet Mohammad two times more in the same way, and he still got the same device. After that, when he came back the last time, Prophet Mohammad said to him: "The speech of God is truth, but the stomach of your brother is a liar!" '

Religious men well versed in old Islamic scriptures enjoy more respect from Beja people than the traditional *busarā*. All the same, in most practical situations Beja people tend to refer to their own tradition, which is not a 'tradition of the books.' The practical knowledge, wisdom and wit of their forefathers is a source of relevant daily life knowledge as well as a source of Beja identity management.

6.12.2. Outline

Proposition LXXVI: 'Our knowledge in our head and in our experience is often superior to knowledge in the books'

Proposition LXXVII: 'Most of our sicknesses are traditional and require traditional knowledge and treatment'

6.12.3. Discussion: the ways of our grandfathers

The Beja knowledge is seen by Beja people as distributed among Beja individuals as well as constituting traditional knowledge and experience from their grandfathers. In contrast to the knowledge of the 'complicated' townspeople and knowledge in the written literature, Beja knowledge is simple knowledge. Numerous stories are told about how individual Bejas in former times solved complex problems in genial as well as simple ways by simple means and modes of reasoning.

The stories of traditional healers, as will be discussed in Chapter 8, represent such heroic stories. In many of them a representative of higher-level national authorities is contrasted with a practical minded and intelligent Beja. This representative may be a British colonial medical officer who, although pictured as competent within his own field of knowledge, is incapable of dealing with some instances of sicknesses and injuries without the help of a clever *basīr*. Sometimes the ethnic contrast becomes as important a theme as the wisdom of traditional healers, as when colonial representatives are ridiculed in the stories for being unmanly or having strange manners.

6.13. SOME CONCLUSIONS

Researchers who may be critical of the approach I have followed in this theoretical outline may argue that I have imposed a Western linear type of thinking and a hierarchical way of organizing knowledge on a non-Western society where such thinking may not be prominent or typical. I will argue, however, that Beja sickness knowledge is not characterized by linear causal reasoning of the *modus ponens* or *modus tollens* type when they employ it in real-life situations or in performing narratives. By the concept *modus ponens* I refer to the following kind of reasoning:

Premise:
If he is a soldier, then he always obeys orders.
(If P then Q)
William is a soldier.
(P)
Conclusion:

181

Therefore, William always obeys orders.
(*Therefore, Q*)

By the concept *modus tollens* I mean the following kind of reasoning:

Premise:
If he is a cowboy, then he is a chair.
(*If P then Q*)
Bill is not a chair. (*not Q*)
Conclusion:
Therefore, Bill is not a cowboy.
(*not P*)

Rather than following such strict types of logics, Beja people seem mostly to allow for more flexibility by use of *plausible inference*[141] of the form:

Premise:
If a person has *hāf*, then he or she will have 'solid bodies' in the stomach.
(*If P then Q*)
Ibrahim has solid parts in his stomach.
(*Q*)
Conclusion:
Therefore, it is likely that Ibrahim has *hāf*.
(*P is likely*)

Another example goes like this:

Premise:
The sickness of *kosúlt* causes body thinness.
(*If P then Q*)
Amna has recently become very thin.
(*Q*)
Conclusion:
It is therefore likely that Amna has *kosúlt*.
(*P is likely*).

The conclusion that 'Therefore Amna has *kosúlt* ' will be a logical fallacy. This logical form is similar to what D'Andrade (1995) calls 'affirmation of the consequent.' and finally 'denial of the antecedent,' which has the form

Premise:
If *P* then *Q*
Not *P*
Conclusion:
Therefore maybe *Q* and maybe not *Q*.

The 'denial of the antecedent' was a kind of logic I frequently encountered in narratives as well as in concrete sickness situations. A typical example is this:

Premise:
If a person has 'hot blood,' he or she will have a 'dirty stomach.'
(If P then Q)
Mohammad does not have 'hot blood.'[142]
(Not P)
Conclusion:
Mohammad may or may not have a 'dirty stomach.'

An 'unclean' stomach, as we have seen, is a health problem in itself regardless of whether it has caused 'hot blood.' Even if sicknesses of 'hot blood' are excluded, a prevailing sickness problem may stem from a 'dirty' or 'boiling' stomach, which may be relieved by causing diarrhea by various means. Causing diarrhea is also a frequently employed means in order to 'clean' the blood of substances which makes it 'hot.'

These kinds of logic, *plausible inference* and *denial of the antecedent,* render the theoretical inferences in Beja sickness reasoning more flexible than its hierarchical organization should suggest. Several other characteristics of Beja sickness theories as well further accounts for flexible and non-linear kinds of reasoning. Before proceeding further with this task, however, I would like to place schema theories within broader frameworks as developed in various interdisciplinary cognitive approaches.

Classical behavioral psychology presented a stimulus centered approach to mental processing, where the brain was treated as a 'black box' and culture, individual prejudices, expectations and tastes were considered irrelevant. Such an approach, which is nowadays rarely found among scientist in a 'pure' form, is often called a 'bottom-up' perspective (Eysenck & Keane 1995). By contrast, a 'top-down' perspective focuses on what an individual brings to a stimulus situation (ibid.). Schema theorists clearly pay more attention to the latter perspective.

Schemata like the restaurant schema presented by Schank & Abelson (see Chapter 2) represents a special instance of schema often called a script. Scripts may be defined as ' . . . knowledge structures that encode the stereotypical sequence of actions in everyday happening' (Eysenck & Keane 1995:263). Such schemata provide us with standardized and inflexible forms of expectations to frequently occurring situations. Since Schank & Abelson's initial experiments, several psychological experiments have supported the existence of mental scripts. Some of those experiments have been performed in more applied contexts like people giving eyewitness testimony for robberies (Eysenck & Keane 1995:264.265). As will be argued in Chapter 8.3, such standardized schemata may underlie mythical narratives like morality tales and 'what it was like a long time ago tales.

The problem with inflexible scripts is precisely that they are inflexible. They explain how we deal with stereotypical situations well, but they fail to account for how we deal with unexpected happenings like a bank robbery or the sudden onset of an unknown or unrecognizable sickness. Schank (1982) came to recognize this problem himself as well as a problem with people mixing up presumed scripts like a script for visiting a doctor with a script for visiting a dentist. In an attempt to provide a solution he proposed that people's memories are organized around clusters of events which he called scenes. Such clusters partly overlap in that some elements are part of two or more scenes, like 'making an appointment' is part of both a 'contract script' and a 'professional-office-visit script.' Such an organization of knowledge allows for flexible adaptations to novel and unexpected situations by allowing for combinations of established scripts in new ways.

The schemata described as making up the theories and propositions discussed in this chapter have several important features. First of all, they are organized in hierarchies at different levels of generalization. The higher levels are more abstract and less bound to concrete situations than the lower levels. Such a hierarchical organization of schemata with varying degrees of abstractness is part of the new suggestions proposed by Schank

(1982) in order to render his script approach more flexible and compatible with the complexities of real-life situations.

Secondly, the schemata consist of fixed postulated relationships between various phenomena, like 'by causing diarrhea one may get rid of "bad blood" and sicknesses resulting from it' (Proposition XXV, Theory E). This schema postulates a causal relationship between causing diarrhea and getting rid of 'bad blood' and the sicknesses it causes. At the same time, the hierarchies of schemata have 'open slots' to be filled in. Several possible sicknesses of 'bad blood' may be accounted for as well as several means of bringing on diarrhea. If one moves up one level of abstraction, the schema 'there is a direct pathway between stomach and blood' (Theory E) consists of even more 'open slots,' since a lot of lower-level schemata like 'things eaten immediately go into the blood' (Proposition XXII, Theory E) and 'suitable food makes the *kosúlt* quiet' (Proposition XXIII (part 5), Theory E) all instantiate the initial schema.

My proposition is therefore a simple-minded one: the higher the level of a schema is and the more abstract the schema, the more 'open slots' it entails and the more flexible it is in accounting for real-life situations. In addition, the same concepts and items may be 'filled in' in different schemata being part of different theories. *Kosúlt*, for example, may be made quiet by eating compatible food. It may also be relieved by taking a diarrhetic, however, which will remove 'bad substance' from the stomach, which again cleans the 'hot' blood and removes its 'hotness' and hence relieves the 'hot' *kosúlt*. Wrapping the person with *kosúlt* in goatskin may extract the 'hotness' of the blood and hence cure or relieve the patient. Finally, giving the sick person herbs which 'eats the *kosúlt*' may also treat the condition. In this case, then, four different theories account for the treatment of one type of condition. At the same time the same 'deep-structural' 'essence' derived notions pervade all these theories. The fluidity, in other words, pertain to 'surface-structural' cultural theories.

When one adds to these mechanisms of fluidity, the open-endedness of the logic of *plausible inference* with which I began, the apparent fixedness of the theories and propositions of Beja culture appears not to be in opposition to their pragmatic kinds of invocation in daily life situations and in storytelling. While I recognize that the danger of imposing Western ideas and kinds of logic on other cultures is of course real, it is possible, that like Edwin Hutchins did for Trobiand land litigation (1978, 1980), one might often make the discovery that types of reasoning which are present in Western societies are also present in non-Western societies.

Sometimes it may be a question of degree in how much people in a given culture stress different kinds of logic. In some fields of experience, Beja people turn to *modus ponens* and *modus tollens* logics as much as we do, like when discussing inheritance conflicts or when inferring ownership of animals by their tribal marks. In an area like the sphere of experience concerned with health and sickness, however, they seem to me to be much less inclined than non-specialists in Norway, for example, to employ the logics of *modus ponens* and *modus tollens*.

Although it is outside my field of study, it also seems that their kind of religious understanding (with the possible exception of educated people in towns) is more 'open-ended' than religious understanding and reasoning among people such as the agriculturalists in the Northern riverain Sudan. As argued in Chapter 3, this unwillingness to state things dogmatically may be a feature related to the precariousness of a pastoralist adaptation in general and the precariousness of the Beja adaptation in particular.

So far it may seem from my conclusion that all Beja reasoning about sickness and health involves some type of logic, conscious or not. Of course this is not the case. By trying on a 'deep-structural' level to explore how the Hadandowa Beja seem to make instant inferences on basis of 'essence' conceptions, I have tried to account for some of the 'taken for granted' perceptions they make, perceptions which probably make up a significant part of their non-logical basis for understanding.

'Essence' reasoning seems to account for their conceptions of substances in general and 'sickness substances' in particular. Notions of 'contagion' may account for how 'sickness essences,' whether 'natural' or 'mystical,' may spread from a body organ to another, from a person to another, from a lactating mother to a child, from an animal to a human and so forth. 'Contagion' may probably account for how people may acquire God-like properties by 'holy contagion' and how valuable animals may become less susceptible to sicknesses, infertility and death by processes of 'trans-substantiation' or *héequal* 'contagion.'

186

Perception of things being like members of natural categories except for some attributes, as 'pseudo-natural' things, may account for the perception of spirits and for other mystical forces influencing human health and well-being. All those 'essence' related conceptions further enhance a richness of metaphoric and metonymic conception, which are also not 'logical' in the inferences they lead to or are shaped by. This is, however, a theme to which I will return in the last section of this chapter.

By way of preliminary conclusion, although Beja theories and proposition seemingly proceed in a linear fashion by successive instantiations of schemata as we have seen, linearity is not their primary property. I will also propose that they are non-linear in an even more fundamental sense: in the way they are interlinked by cross-cutting theories of 'essences' and different perceptions deriving from them. Instead of proposing in the manner of Schank (1982) that they are interlinked at a higher level of abstraction, I will suggest that they are overlapping and related to each other at a most basic and non-conscious level of reasoning, the level of 'essences' of 'natural' and 'pseudo-natural' kinds and 'contagion' by those 'essences.'

The bulk of the examples discussed in this chapter seem to support this suggestion. Olfaction influences the blood and the stomach via substances passing through the nose. Things eaten influence the stomach through various substances of different temperatures and other qualities. The substances are further spread to the blood, which in turn transfers the properties of the substances to the whole body. Mystical 'pseudo-natural' substances spread through contamination or direct possession and transfer substances and related properties to humans and animals. Sometimes such influences are positive and sometimes they are detrimental to human health, fertility and well-being.

The danger of imposing linear types of reasoning and linear types of causation uncritically on non-Western societies should of course be taken seriously. However, linearity, linear time and linear forms of causation may not be as prominent even in Western societies as we like to think. Anders Johansen's (1984) study of the concept of time in the Western tradition illustrates this point. While we clearly think of time as progressing linearly, we also think of time as circular and 'ceremonial' as when we think of spring time as approaching recurrently, celebrate birthdays and annual holidays and voice expressions like 'history is repeating itself' or 'there is nothing new under the sun.' Time also sometimes appears as punctuated; when we are bored we tend to think that time has 'stopped,' or when several important and exciting things happened to us, we tend to represent the time span of those events as longer than the time it represents linearly. Similar conclusions may be drawn about the Hadandowa Beja. Although they all have clear linear conceptions of time, however, it can hardly be denied that linear time is a more prominent feature of time conceptions in Western societies than among Beja pastoralists.

Experiments by psychologists like Rozin & Nemeroff (1990, 1994) show us that non-scientific ideas of contagion may thrive side by side with scientific ones in Western societies. Scientific progress and educational progress do not preclude 'essence' derived conceptions. As I will argue in the next section of this chapter, scientific theories and 'essence' derived theories explain very different things. However, 'essence' related thinking is probably much more prominent among Beja than among people in Western societies. Thus far it seems to be *the* prominent feature characterizing Beja theories of sickness and health.

In conclusion, Beja cultural theories of health and sickness may be considered 'vertically' as interlinked cultural schemata. A more generalized schema is followed by a more specific one, which is an instantiation of the first. By successive steps of instantiations one finally arrives at situation specific schemata which are similar to cultural prescripts or cultural 'recipes' in form. They may also be seen as 'horizontally' interlinked, but not at a high and abstract level. Rather, they can be viewed as linked by basic and lower level theories and conceptions of 'essence' and 'trans-substantiation.' I suggest that the flexibility in the invocation of Beja cultural theories of sickness and health, in storytelling as well as in concrete sickness situations, may stem from this fact. Different theories and propositions sharing the same underlying basic and spontaneously invoked conceptions allow for the fact that a given sickness label, a treatment option or an etiologic conception may be filled into 'slots' of schemata which are part of different theories.

6.14. A FURTHER DISCUSSION: METAPHORS, METONYMS AND THEORIES OF ESSENCE

After this extensive discussion about Beja folk theories, two important questions are left unanswered. Firstly, in what sense are the 'laws of sympathetic magic' as encountered in Beja folk theories really magic? Secondly, how may spontaneously invoked 'essence' conceptions be conceptually related to processes of metonymization and metaphorization? Before trying to answer these questions, I want briefly to review a contribution by Edmund Leach ((1976) 1981) on magic and sorcery.

In a chapter on 'Theories of magic and sorcery' Leach (ibid.) revisits Frazer's theories of sympathetic magic. While Frazer viewed such theories as 'bastard science' and an 'erroneous belief about cause and effect,' Leach voiced the opinion that Frazer mistakenly confused expressive acts involving interpreting an index as a signal with 'pure' technical acts. In line with Jakobson and Halle (1956), he maintains that the 'distinction between homeopathic and contagious magic is essentially the same as that between metaphoric and metonymic association' (p.29). In his view, performing a magical spell at a distance is similar in form to giving verbal instructions to someone, the verbal instruction being indexes which in given contexts get interpreted as signs upon which the receiver of the instructions will act. Further, the process can be likened to the switch on the wall which is taken to be indexical to a system of electricity present in a room and hence interpreted as possible to manipulate in order to switch on the lights.

His argument seems convincing enough. However, does he not himself commit the same kind of mistaken comparison which he accuses Frazer of performing, of comparing the wrong elements and processes cross-culturally? More fundamentally, does he not mistakenly compare non-scientific theories of homeopathic and contagious magic with Western scientific understanding?

As an example in order to illustrate the problem, even educated Beja in Sinkat refused to use 'relief oil' in their food out of fear of a *tesérimt* causing 'essence' inherent in the oil. At the same time, they tried to convince fellow Beja of the necessity of using anti-microbial medicines against sicknesses which in the biomedical tradition are seen as caused by microbes. They were,

189

of course, convinced by the scientific explanations for why flipping a light switch turns the light on. At the same time, they were equally convinced that pronouncing quotations from the Holy Quran has the magical effect of driving away evil spirits.

It is not more difficult to find similar examples from Western societies, as with racial thinking as a 'pseudo-natural' kind of 'essence' reasoning (Boyer 1993, 1996a). The experiments by Rozin & Fallon (1987) and Rozin & Nemeroff (1990, 1994) clearly demonstrate that even when respondents in the United States scientifically preclude a possibility of contamination, like when wearing a T-shirt of a disliked person or eating a candy shaped as 'doggie-doo,' they act as if an inherent essence of those objects is contaminating them.

Instead of stating in the vein of Leach ((1976), 1981) that homeopathic magic relates to contagious magic as metaphors to metonyms, I will suggest that conceptions of 'essence' and spread of 'essence' by contagion may be more basic to human reasoning than metaphors and metonyms. While verbal expressions of metonyms and metaphors require both developed language capacity and a model of mind, conceptions of 'essence,' similarity and contagion may be language independent.

I propound that conceptions of similarity and contamination, both based on a notion of 'essence,' constitute a rich source for notions and verbal expressions of metonymy and metaphory. Metonymy's 'the part stands for the whole' reasoning may rely both on the 'essences are equally distributed throughout the form which they occupy' assumption and an idea of 'contamination by spread of essences.' Metaphors, by contrast, may be a result of an inversion of a theory of essence, where similar properties imply a similarity of essence, as when a man is called a 'male cat' in Norwegian when he behaves indiscriminately toward women in sexual matters. Types of essence reasoning are probably not the only sources of metonyms and metaphors though.

Cognitive linguists and philosophers (Lakoff 1987, Lakoff & Johnson 1980, Lakoff & Kovecses 1987, Johnson 1987) have convincingly argued that human bodily experiences give rise to spatial metaphorization as well as other physically based metaphors, like 'anger is pressure in a closed container.' They all stress the seeming creativity in inventions of new metaphors as well as the impact of established metaphors on the way humans think. Naomi Quinn (1991), by contrast, maintains that humans are not that creative in their inventions of metaphors but rather employ a restricted range of them. Based on her research on American models of marriage, she argues that more fundamental cultural models render some metaphors salient and others not. In the marriage field of experience she concluded that over a range of American subjects only a restricted range of eight metaphors were commonly in use.

My stance is a relatively eclectic one, recognizing bodily experiences, cultural models and 'theories of essences' as possible sources of metaphorical and metonymical conceptions and expressions. While cultural models clearly are complex sources of metaphorization, bodily experiences and conceptions of similarity and contagion are probably more basic and phylogenetically more ancient in human development.

That bodily experiences like walking upright, having the eyes placed in the front of the head instead of its sides, anger increasing the blood pressure and so on give rise to a richness of metaphors expressing basic human experience seems convincing enough. It can hardly be argued, however, that metaphorization based on such all-human experiences have been pivotal for human adaptation and survival. By contrast, a notion of essence may have had a highly adaptive significance. As discussed earlier, a concept of essence involves a double principle which states that objects with a similar form and appearance share the same basic essence, and this essence accounts for many of the properties of the objects. In other words, sharing the same form implies sharing many of the same properties. Even if not always applicable to the real world, which is sometimes deceptive, this 'principle of similarity' may by and large have served human adaptation well. As noted by Rozin and Nemeroff (1990:225),

'Similarity can be viewed as an overextension of a useful principle. Surely, sometimes appearances are deceiving. But, as a general rule or heuristic, the principle that if X looks like a Y, it is a Y, is a good one. Indeed, it is wise to operate on the principle that what looks like a tiger is a tiger. The problem arises when this heuristic has major influences on behavior in situations where appearances are deceiving. There is mimicry in the natural world.'

At this point I should like to reformulate the above citation from

Leach (ibid.) as 'notions of contagion are a source of metonymy while notions of similarity give rise to metaphors.' As has been repeatedly demonstrated in this work, theories of 'essences' as well as their transferability and modes of manipulating them, greatly enhance rich areas of metaphorization and metonymization. In this manner metaphors and metonyms become less linguistic and more a type of analytical terms which may throw additional light on parts of basic human reasoning.

The 'law of similarity' is depicted by both Frazer ((1890), 1951) and Rozin & Nemeroff (1990, 1994) as a 'law of sympathetic magic.' However, what is really magical about it? And moreover, is there something magical in a notion of contagion? Folk theories of pollution have rarely, if ever, been labeled 'magical' in the anthropological literature. Although neither ideas of pollution nor notions of contagion equal scientific ideas regarding spread of sicknesses in form or content, they are similar in assuming spread of a 'substance' from one object to another by direct close contact or by indirect close contact where the substance is carried by a intermediate object. An example of the latter form is seen in the instance where a Beja touches the rope of a camel with *tesérimt* or when a man sits in a place where female breast milk or menstrual blood has been spilled.

Although the notion of 'magic' may have acquired a rather broad usage in anthropological literature, in most practical examples it involves an idea of a force mystically acting at a distance. In this manner Evans-Pritchard ((1937), 1985) viewed witchcraft as a form of magic, where a mystical inner substance in envious humans involuntarily acted on other people at a distance. The notion of 'the evil eye' may be called magic in the same manner. Sorcery, as observed by Rozin & Nemeroff (1990) represents a form of magic where a force is acting via a mechanism of 'backward causation.' An object seen as sharing the same essence as another by originally being a part of it, like a piece of hair from a person, may be manipulated so as to harm its source at a distance. When Rozin & Nemeroff (ibid.) try to point to similar forms of reasoning in present Western societies, however, they use examples which may also be explained as expressing general notions of essence.

Sometimes, as when people refuse to hold for example an apparently clean rubber replica of vomit between their teeth, an activation of a 'theory of essence' and transferability of essences may explain their reaction rather than a 'magic of similarity.' When people prove poorer at throwing darts at a target between the eyes of a picture of a face of a revered or beloved person than at a disliked one, I am inclined to suppose that none of the subjects really believed or even had an unconscious feeling that they were acting on the sources of the pictures (if the opposite was true for some of the subjects, it would be somewhat surprising that all of them were willing to partake in the experiment). I will rather suggest that an invocation of a general principle of essence, that they acted 'as if' the picture had the same essence as the source, is a more likely explanation.[143]

Two different notions of similarity may explain the way people react to and have feelings towards a picture of a person. Firstly, one may react as if the picture is a part of the person. In such a case the reactions have a similar basis as when a fan of a particular football player greatly values an object like a handkerchief used by the adored athlete. Secondly, one may react on the basis of an overgeneralization of the principle of similarity, that sharing the same form and visible features implies sharing the same essence. None of those reactions implies magic in a strict sense. The first type of reaction is based on a notion that essences are distributed throughout the form which they occupy, which gives rise to metonymical reasoning. When Beja parents think that a mountain hyena is a courageous animal, any part of this animal has an essence with a courageous property. For this reason children with 'fright sickness' may be given a tooth of a hyena to wear close to their bodies as part of a necklace. Alternatively, parents may mix a portion of bile from a hyena in water and give children for the same reason.

The amount of bile is never stated and seems to be unimportant. This seems to stem both from the 'logic of equal distribution' as well as a principle of dosage independence. As noted by Donald Tuzin (1986:2), 'ordinarily, one is able to control what one eats – the nose guides us in this matter – but the contagion requires only a small, perhaps undetectable amount slipped into one's food.' Even a microscopic amount of sewage in a food item makes a whole lot of difference! And, as well, only a very small amount of hyena bile may transfer courageousness to a child suffering from fright by a process of positive contamination.

Notions of things having essences, similar forms having the

same essence and similar essences having similar properties all seem to be notions which are very much part of ordinary daily life for people in Western societies as well as for people in non-Western societies like Ilahita Arapesh of Papua New Guinea or Beja pastoralists in Northern Sudan. When adding the possibilities for 'pseudo-natural' reasoning and spread of essence by contagion, such notions may account for a range of human experiences from believing oneself to be surrounded by spirits to being poisoned by contaminated food. Magical reasoning, however much attention has been paid to it in anthropological literature, may restrict itself to out-of-the-ordinary human spheres of experience where people feel a lack of control.

Probably Erving Goffman (1972) is correct in assessing that human lives in general and human interaction in particular are predictable and routine. In a few areas, like in gambling or sports in Western societies, types of magic are performed in order to effect future events. George Gmelch (1996:197) gives a vivid report of magic among American baseball players as a participant observer:

> 'A seventeen-game winner in the Texas Rangers organization, Mike Griffin begins his ritual preparation a full day before he pitches, by washing his hair. The next day, although he does not consider himself superstitious, he eats bacon for lunch. When Griffin dresses for the game he puts on his clothes in the same order, making certain that he puts the slightly longer of his two outer, or 'stirrup,' socks on his right leg ... He always wears the same shirt under his uniform on the day he pitches. During the game he takes off his cap after each pitch, and between innings he sits in the same place on the dugout bench.'

While some of these and other rituals Gmelch records for baseball players may partly serve as 'setting the stage' for future events, rituals like wearing the same T-shirt night and day for two months before an important baseball competition belongs to a more clear-cut category of magic acts. Quite probably, Mike Griffin and other baseball players will probably not perform similar rituals before going to the hairdresser or driving their cars. Even if driving a car, for example, involves some possible hazards, most of the time the majority of us rightly reason that accidents are exceptions. In baseball, by contrast, the average batter approximately hits safely one quarter of the time (ibid.) Among Beja, prototypical magical acts are performed in life areas with a realistically calculated high risk, as the risk of sickness or death in newborn or not-yet-born children.

In addition to gaining the sense of achieving control, magic may be used to throw light upon and shape order in what seems messy and disorderly. On the basis of her recent fieldwork among magicians in England, T. Luhrmann states that 'the magician is able to give a rich distinction-filled description of the events which surrounds his rituals, and it gives complex structure to life's disordered whole' (1989:117). England, in contrast to Beja society, has a large group of professional magicians.

The bulk of magical acts among Beja people are metaphorical in their nature. As discussed earlier, by metaphory I imply that similar properties in two or more objects are thought to reflect that the objects share the same essence. A sword or a knife has a property of 'dangerousness' as well as 'protectiveness.' For this reason a knife or a sword is always kept near a woman in the process of giving birth. The object is thought to drive away evil spirits, which may harm the woman and the child or substitute an ugly spirit child for the child.

Warfare and violent confrontations, which are not usual parts of Beja lives and have perhaps never been, are also occasions for extensive use of magic of 'forward causality.' Certain trees and bushes are said to be particularly dangerous as well as potentially protective. Even a small branch of such a tree or bush may protect against or kill a lot of enemies.

The concept of the 'evil eye' is most often related to sudden and unexpected serious sickness or death. As a magical theory of forward causation it is employed *post hoc* to account for such events seemingly not influenced by conscious human actions or by human control. Sorcery, as a magical theory of backward causation, is also employed *post hoc* when serious incidents or interpersonal problems between close relatives arise. As earlier accounted for, however, the potential social costs of using such explanations in the ecologically and socially circumscribed small Beja groups may explain the fact that sorcery accusations are seldom invoked in real-life situations.

Sometimes Beja people may refuse to even approach a potentially polluting object like an item with bad smell, a fact which seemingly implies that they conceive that the object is affecting

195

them at a distance. However, Gell (in Tuzin 1986:1) observes that 'smell-signs are semiologically ambiguous, in that they are not fully detached from the world of objects to which they refer.' It may be reasonable to suggest that people learn from olfactory experiences that an essence can extend beyond the physical boundaries. For this reason, a notion of contagion signified by smell may be as direct and non-magical as an idea of contagion in which two objects are in direct contact with each other.

In conclusion, the principle of similarity and the principle of contagion are both by and large not magical in Beja reasoning. By this I mean to imply that causation at a distance, with no mediating objects or substances, is an exception in both metonymical, similarity derived and metaphorical reasoning. At this point it may be appropriate to take a look at how Beja cultural theories and propositions are reflexively and flexibly invoked at different times during the sickness histories of two Hadandowa children.

NOTES

1 Synonymic preparate to Aspirin, contains acetylsalicylic acid.
2 Sudanese Arabic word for small mobile shops selling household items like matches, soap, biscuits etc.
3 Herbal tea with strong red color, believed to be very nutritious.
4 Referring to the notion that cultural knowledge may fruitfully be seen as organized around practical tasks rather than in the form of taxonomies. The concept was developed in cognitive anthropology by Dougherty and Keller (1982) and later employed in a study of folk knowledge of sicknesses Chand et al (1994).
5 Pl.*hindib*. The word has a broad meaning covering trees and bushes as well as herbs.
6 This seems to be a prominent thought within Islamic medicine. The expression is used frequently in an old book of Islamic medicine widely distributed among literate Islamic healers in the Northern Sudan, the book *The Medicine of the Prophet* by the author Shams ad-Din Mohd. Ibrahim Abi Bakri, published at some time during the period 691–751 (Muslim time reference).
7 Arabic word meaning both 'a sacrifice,' 'alms to the poor' and 'an offering to God.' Here it refers to making a sacrifice to the spirits who guard the *hindiib*.
8 Beja vernacular name for a bush occurring in the Sinkat region and some other places in the Sudan, *Rinicus communis*. There are subtypes; but there is only one species present in the Sudan.
9 Beja vernacular word for a herb for which I unfortunately have not been able to identify the Latin name.

10 *Táflam* is a Beja word for a stomach sickness usually described with symptoms like stomach pain with a 'knocking' sensation and severe diarrhea which often contains blood. It may stem from spirits as well as from things like corrupted food or drinking cold water on an empty stomach.

11 Beja vernacular name for a bush occurring in the Sinkat region, *Aspargus africanus*.

12 Beja vernacular name for a bush occurring in the Sinkat region and possibly beyond. I have unfortunately not been able to identify the Latin name of it.

13 Beja vernacular name for a bush occurring in the Sinkat region and possibly in a wider area. I have not yet been able to identify the Latin name of it.

14 *'Usher* is Beja name for a very widespread and frequent occurring tree/big bush used, among other things, as building material for local huts.

15 Beja vernacular name for widespread and common bush in the Red Sea Hills, also called *nawiatéb (B)*, *Fagonia cretica*.

16 See Chapter 4.

17 Also *oodʰháu*, Beja vernacular names for bush occurring in the Sinkat region, *Aspargus africanus*.

18 Beja think of *háf* as a very dangerous 'cold' sickness which often may kill the patient. See earlier description Chapter 4.

19 More than one *hindíib* are used against *kardáp*.

20 *Ooľáu* is a Beja vernacular name for a bush which is common in the Sinkat region and, possibly, beyond, *Acasia tortilis*. It has three subtypes, however, and I am uncertain which subtype is present in the Sinkat region in the Sudan.

21 See Chapter 4.

22 See discussion Chapter 6.7.

23 Plural form of the Arabic word *hejáb*.

24 Pl. *busará*, Sudanese Arabic word designating the 'bone setter' type of specialist, primarily mending broken bones and joints. However, the local *busará* in the Red Sea Hills are also specialists in local herbs and animal products used for treating a wide range of sicknesses. See earlier description in Chapter 4.

25 This is a Beja name for a mixture of *adal óot*, a red stone which is believed to have healing as well as supernatural qualities, *híndib* and butter oil.

26 Induce bleeding and use a 'bleeding horn' to let out blood, for example from the neck of a patient.

27 *Gusháash* in Beja language.

28 Beja word for 'fainting'

29 Beja name for sickness characterized by ear infection.

30 *Watáb* is, as described in Chapter 4, a Beja word for a non-serious condition characterized by headache, tiredness and lethargy.

31 Beja word, same as *rutúba*, a Sudanese Arabic word used in Beja language as well, possibly translated by 'rheumatism' in English.

32 As described in Chapter 4, *háf masóob* is a children's sickness which

is less severe than *hāf*, but can proceed to *hāf* if it is not treated. Like *hāf* it is a cold sickness, but one cannot always feel any 'solid parts' on the stomach. The child will typically have swollen stomach and diarrhea.

33 Beja vernacular name for succulent frequently occurring in the Sinkat district, *Aloe sinkantana*.

34 A spice.

35 Beja vernacular name for a local bush, possibly the same as *Citrullus colocynthis*

36 I have no evidence that Beja generally are conscious of such a broad theory. However, one of my informants in Odrus stated that 'One can get rid of every sickness by sneezing.' It is interesting to note the custom many Beja use when the afterbirth does not come out after a woman has given birth: Some black pepper is smeared under the nose of the woman. When she sneezes, the afterbirth will be expelled. It might be tempting to speculate whether such a physiological experience might have facilitated a theory that sicknesses can be expelled by getting the patient to sneeze.

37 Literally meaning 'fright' in Arabic. As discussed in Chapter 4, *khoof* or *mírquay* (B) is also the name of a childhood sickness resulting from a frightening experience, like seeing a spirit in sleep or while awake, being surprised by a dog suddenly barking behind you etc. See also later discussions.

38 Sudanese Arabic name for type of cumin spice widely used in the Middle East.

39 Infectious swelling in the umbilicus is the main symptom of *na'ēh*.

40 Not temperature only.

41 The most commonly used Beja name for gonorrhea.

42 Not only temperature.

43 The cooling effect of water is generally noted by Holy (1991) for the Berti people in the Western Sudan as well. Water is frequently used by Berti to cool hot body states and sicknesses.

44 *Herár* is a Beja concept similar to the Sudanese Arabic concept of *yeraghān*. As described in Chapter 4, both concepts are denoting the symptoms of yellowish coloring of the skin and sclera in a broad range of conditions.

45 Beja vernacular name (possibly from Sudanese Arabic *'hargal'*) for a widespread and frequently occurring bush in the Sudan, *Solostemma argel*.

46 Sudanese Arabic word for half-side severe headache with light intolerance and nausea. See Chapter 4.

47 Microbes are most often not part of Beja people's concepts of contamination.

48 Beja name for gonorrhea. See Chapter 4.

49 Seems to me to be a later stage of gonorrhea. See Chapter 4.

50 Beja word for syphilis.

51 Meaning hot temperature.

52 This is an extension of the concept of 'hotness,' and when speaking

about hot or cold sicknesses, people often use the concepts 'hot' and 'spicy' or 'tasty' interchangeable.

53 The term 'Islamic' in Greco-Islamic refers to Islamic civilization rather than religion. The early practitioners were of course Jewish and Christian as well as Muslim. In addition, to my knowledge, treatment traditions with roots in Greco-Islamic medicine are present in non-Islamic as well as Islamic groups in the Circum-Mediterranean and Middle-Eastern areas today. Other terms used in literature for the classical humoral tradition like 'Arabic medicine', 'Tibb Unani' or 'Islamic medicine' are for obvious reasons not better substitutes for the term 'Greco-Islamic medicine.'

54 Three respondents mentioned 'vomiting,' 3 'wounds in the mouth,' 3 'dry mouth,' 3 'coughing,' 2 'swollen stomach' and 1 'pain in the bones.'

55 Six respondents mentioned 'lack of milk and fat in the food,' 3 'heminéit,', 3 'from clothes, waterpipe or breath of people,' 2 'if mother walks in hot sun and then breast-feeds a baby,' 1 'tiredness,' 1 'if mother eats bad food and then breast-feeds,' 1 'if mother is hungry and then breast-feeds' and 1 'hotness' (in general).

56 Four proposed 'smearing the body with blood,' 3 answered that 'the mother should stop breast-feeding a child with kosúlt,' 2 'give butter' (in order to cause diarrhea), 2 'smear animal fat on the body,' 1 'wash the body by milk,' 1 'avoid hot or spicy food,' 1 'bury in wet sand' and 1 'cause diarrhea in order to let out heminéit.'

57 Four respondents mentioned that 'the upper part of the stomach will be wider,' 3 mentioned that 'if you make a cutting on a solid part of the stomach, black blood will come out,' 3 mentioned a 'solid body in the abdomen,' 2 'air in the stomach,' 2 'loss of appetite,' 2 'pain in the abdomen', 1 'headache' and 1 'no blood in the soles of the feet, in the palms or under the eyelids.' Regarding prospects for recovery, 6 respondents added that the sickness often leads to death of the patient.

58 Two responded 'from cold water after fasting or while hungry,' 2 'from "sleeping blood" collecting in the stomach,' 1 'from poison,' 1 'from heminéit,' 1 'from drinking very cold water,' 1 'from problems of umbilicus,' 1 'from hard work,' 1 'from being hit by a stick' and 1 'from sicknesses in general.' A very young respondent thought that also very sour food could cause háf.

59 Three responded 'herbal treatment,' 2 'using no salt in the food,' 2 'basíir touching the stomach (i.e. making massage), 2 making hejáma, 1 'eat otám' and 1 'drink as little as possible.'

60 A kind of severe skin infection with swelling and pus.

61 As is evident from the form of the statement, this is a statement from just one informant. I chose to present it word by word as stated by the informant because of its very richness.

62 Sud.Arabic nábak, Zizipus mucronata or, possibly, Zizipus spina-christi. The fruits from it taste sweet and are popular to eat as well because they are available all over and can be bought for a cheap price at market places.

63 See later discussion about the connection between the stomach and the blood.

64 *Shaushót* is a Beja vernacular name for a widespread and common bush in the Red Sea Hills, in Sud. Arabic *heg léeg*, *Balanites aegyptiaca*.

65 *Abebaníb (B)*, *Cadaba farinose*, is a herb sometimes clinging to the *shaushót*. Many Beja believe this to be an indicator of the presence of spirits.

66 *Kusháabe* is both a Beja word for circumcision and for sickness resulting from lack of circumcision.

67 The word *hūm* is in indefinite form. The definite form is *uhūm*, showing that it is a masculine word (u- is the masculinum prefix, whilst tu- is the femininum prefix).

68 This Beja word has the indefinite form *gínea*.

69 *Mánab* means intestines, covering both the small and big bowels. The word *tunquiláat* means kidneys as well as 'sickness of kidneys,' a condition very seldom referred to. Spleen is *shinkída*. This is an internal organ of animals which some subsections of Beja (like the Hakwolab sub-tribe of Kolit) have a taboo against eating. The liver is called *se*.

70 *Hemineít* is, as discussed in Chapter 4, a substance with sour taste present in the stomach of all humans. However, if it is too much *hemineít*, or if it is not quiet, is boiling, has the wrong quality and color, this may cause a lot of health problems.

71 Herbal tea with strong red color, believed to be very nutritious.

72 *Rámal* in Sudanese Arabic, a kind of eye inflammation.

73 Beja vernacular name for succulent frequently occurring in the Sinkat district, *Aloe sinkantana*.

74 A spice.

75 Beja vernacular name for a local bush, possibly the same as *Citrullus colocynthis*.

76 *Ademidíin (B)*: 'to be solid,' in Arabic: *jijmat* ('becomes solid'). *U'bóy fasíid*: 'The blood becomes corrupted' ('blood' is masculine).

77 My own rough and inaccurate translation of a concept with a rich fan of connotations, a concept used in opposition to *afrangi* ('native') in Sudanese Arabic as well.

78 The five other principles concerned: 2. Movement and rest, 3. eating and drinking, 4. sleep and lack of sleep, 5. the natural excretion and retention (included bathing and coitus) and 6. the moods of the soul, like anger etc.

79 *Shagīga* is a Sudanese Arabic word denoting a sickness with a hemispheric headache with symptoms similar to migraine. See Chapter 4 for a description.

80 Beja name for 'small pox,' *jédari* in Sudanese Arabic.

81 See Chapter 4.

82 *Boyée* is a Beja word for a sickness with infected wounds in the mouth. I am not sure whether those wounds may be fungus infected as well as bacterial.

83 See Chapter 4.

84 Sudanese Arabic name for type of cumin spice widely used in the Middle East.

85 Beja vernacular name for a tree occurring in the Sinkat region.

86 Beja vernacular name for a bush occurring in the Sinkat region.

87 *Túndup* in Sudanese Arabic, Beja vernacular name for a widespread and frequent occurring bush in the Red Sea Hills, *Capparis decidua*

88 Beja word for mouth blisters.

89 Beja word for a condition characterized by severe backache in the lumbaric region.

90 The practice is not as usual nowadays as before. Whether this is due to severe lack of butter oil under present-day conditions or whether this is part of a cultural change, I am not in position to say.

91 See Theory O.

92 See Proposition V (part b.4+6), Theory A.

93 Most Beja tend to think that if the cold sickness of *watáb* lasts for a long time, *herár (B)*, a condition of yellow discoloring of the skin and sclera, may follow. However, although Hadandowa informants in many situations treated *herár* as a 'cold' sickness, some of the food restrictions like avoiding giving the patient meat and fat food is not entirely consistent with treating the sickness as a 'cold sickness.' Although I am somewhat inaccurate in classifying the sickness unanimously as a 'cold' disease, I do not think that this represents a grave distortion though.

94 So far I know only of one sickness where I am absolutely sure some Beja (not all) make clear that drops of spit may spread the disease, namely tuberculosis. For whooping cough, I think it is possible that some people may hold this belief, but I am not sure.

95 Beja word used for tuberculosis.

96 My translation.

97 See Chapter 4 for further reference to this influential book.

98 Beja term for a sickness characterized by fatigue, bloatedness and paleness.

99 Beja word for a pronounced swelling with pus in the face.

100 I only heard one informant state this as a cause behind *háf*. It seems consistent with the idea that the quality of the food has implications for the quality of the blood, however, which, if it is 'bad', may cause different kinds of sicknesses.

101 The expression 'cold food' is often used by Beja for unfresh food.

102 See also introduction to Theory D.

103 Red stone believed to enhance fertility, good luck and prosperity as well as avoiding or counteracting sickness from substance mediated evil influences (see Theory L).

104 Exceptions: *Zār*-spirits (see Proposition L, part c) and also *táflam* spirits, which are not serious, but may pose some non-Muslim conditions for the healer and his patient.

105 Plural form of the Arabic word *jinn*.

106 As discussed in Chapter 4, people use several items, ritual elements

and expressions in *zār* rituals which else are used solely in marriage ceremonies.

107 *Herár*, the general Beja term for the condition of yellow coloring of the skin, may be caused by *zār* spirits. However, if the patient dies, people tend to question this diagnosis.

108 It seems impossible for most Beja to think about Europeans as something other than Christians, let alone to be without religion.

109 A toilet is of course a special instance, since it contains expelled fluids and digested food from inside of the human body, and hence the precautions also pertain to bodily fluids attracting spirits.

110 Meaning 'by the name of Allah' in classical Arabic.

111 *Commiphora pedunculata*.

112 Sudanese Arabic name for spice used all over the Sudan, *Caminum cyminum*.

113 My translation.

114 Ma'aza *sheikh*, quoted by G. W. Murray, in: Trimingham (1949:171).

115 Plural form of *jinn*.

116 The word local people use instead of the term 'Beja'.

117 Called *midrát* in Beja language.

118 The Muslim Berti people of the Western Sudan seem to be a noteworthy exception in this regard (Holy 1991). Among them 'female symbolism (is) exclusively beneficient' (p.101).

119 From Arabic *insān(un)*, which may be translated 'a human being' (Catafago 1975).

120 Stomach sickness with symptoms similar to dysentery (see earlier description).

121 Called *kilay t'át* (B), *kilay* meaning 'bird' and *t'át* possibly referring to a slap by a wing of the spirit bird. See Chapter 4.

122 Commentary in brackets represents my own addition.

123 A soft, red stone found in a specific reddish mountain in the area. According to what I have heard, there are only two such mountains in the Red Sea Hills. This stone is only used for healing purposes and for making humans and animals *héequal*. Some people, when they dig out the stone, offer *karāma* to God by slaughtering an animal and smearing the blood on the spot where they dug out the stones. Others maintain that this habit is superstition, but all the same use the stone for the same purposes.

124 As discussed in Chapter 4, *héequal* is a concept denoting both good luck, luck-bringing and holiness. It is associated with fertility and growth, good health, prospering, and generally, with the blessing of God.

125 Related to the word *t'héelat* below (4). *Kām* is the Beja word for camel (indefinite sense). They word *t'héelat* or *telt* only occurs in one other connection, as part of the concept for old, pre-Islamic square graves, called *acrathél*. However, no evidence exists which points to this being a salient connection.

126 A Beja concept covering both herbs, bushes and trees (see Theory A).

127 Skin disease, see Chapter 4.

128 Called *toodíh* in Beja language, see Chapter 4.
129 Imported spices used for incense all over the Northern Sudan (see Theory J).
130 Beja word for sickness characterized by severe vomiting: See earlier description in Chapter 4.
131 Called *kardáp* in the Beja language or *'amal* in Sudanese Arabic.
132 Meaning making the patient 'drink the Quran': See Chapter 3 for explanation.
133 See above.
134 The converse is not true, since continuous crying in small children may indicate other etiologic possibilities for Beja as well.
135 See Chapter 4.
136 The lowlands around Kassala, to the west of the Red Sea Hills.
137 Needless to say, his concept 'savage' represents the spirit of his time, the early infancy of Anthropology as a discipline.
138 A big bird which is said to exist in the real world as well, but which I have not been able to identify.
139 The Beja word for circumcision. This word is as well sometimes used for particular sickness resulting from lack of circumcision.
140 A Sudanese Arabic expression having a broad range of meanings like 'everything is ready,' 'the problem is solved', 'the condition has come to an end' or 'now we can go.'
141 Same in form as affirmation of the consequence: *If P then Q. Q. Therefore P* (see, e.g. Eysenck & Keane 1995), which is strictly invalid in its conclusion *therefore P*. If instead concluding that therefore *perhaps P and perhaps not P*, the logic gets a more valid form (see f.ex. D'Andrade 1995) and approaches the *plausible inference* logic (see f.ex. Hutchins 1978, 1980).
142 Disconfirmed if various kinds of 'cold treatment' seem to make his sickness worse.
143 Alternatively, the subjects may interpret the act as a symbolic act (like burning a flag) which they feel reluctant to perform.

7

TWO CASE STUDIES

7.0. INTRODUCTION

So far various characteristics of Beja cultural knowledge have been considered. Non-verbalized conceptions of 'essence' and 'trans-substantiation' have been demonstrated to be interlinked with and inseparable from explicit Beja theories and propositions of health and sickness. At this point the pragmatics of sickness negotiation will be a major concern. The following discussions mainly serve two aims. Firstly, by demonstrating the relevance for real-life situations of the sickness theories and propositions presented in Chapter 6, I aim at demonstrating their validity. Secondly, various manners by which this knowledge is a cultural resource in real-life situations will be explored.

As shown earlier, there is no neat correspondence between Beja sickness labels and descriptions of symptoms or between sickness labels and choice of treatment options. If one instead chooses to focus on theories of sicknesses, a pattern of correspondence between any given theory of sickness and perceived symptoms, etiology and forms of treatment will emerge. However, a given theory may pertain to several sickness labels rather than one sickness label. As an example, taking a rest under the powerful *úsher* tree may lead to the skin sickness of *t'háasimt* as well as eye inflammation or blindness. Conversely, several mutually exclusive theories may be relevant in linking causality to one given Beja sickness label. This was demonstrated earlier for the sickness of *táflam* ('dysentery'), which may result from spirits in the stomach, from the glance or spittle of a spirit magically altering the food one eats, from corrupted food or from cold food.

204

As shown in Chapter 6, a given theory employed in an instance of sickness does not accurately predict the symptoms which people will highlight and stress or the specific treatment they will choose. As we will see in Chapter 8.2., sicknesses resulting from *héequal*[1] camels is a good example of this. Once Beja people invoke a theory, however, the theory will clearly render a more limited range of symptoms plausible as well as make the range of possible choices for treatment narrower.

When looking at real sickness cases, some additional interesting features become clear. Firstly, in a real sickness case there may be several sickness labels which cover the constellation of symptoms people perceive. As an example, a distended stomach in an otherwise thin child may be diagnosed *hāf masóob, hāf, tesérimt* (if newborn) or as resulting from prolonged 'fright sickness.' Additional symptoms or sickness history may make it easier for people to decide on the diagnosis. If, for example, a child is known to have 'fright sickness,' the sickness of *alíb*[2] is more likely to be the problem. If 'solid bodies' may be palpated on the stomach, the dreadful sickness of *hāf* may be suspected. If it is known that a camel race took place nearby and there is a chance that a *t'héelat* camel was present, the sickness of *tesérimt* may seem likely and so on.

A second interesting feature relates to the fact that people often alternate between different theories of explanation at different points of time during the development of a sickness case. There may be several reasons for such changes in perspective. In many instances, the inefficiency of one kind of treatment which relates to a specific theory of causality may lead people to seek for other explanations. A trial and error strategy may lead people in the same instance of sickness to seek a *basīr*, then a medical doctor, then another *basīr*, then a *fagīr* and finally a *zār* doctor. As we will see from the discussion of the empirical example below, such trial and error strategy is not haphazard. People make decisions about which specialist to seek for help or whether to try out home remedies based on theories of explanations. By trying to apply a given cultural model, people open up specific possible courses of action.

7.1. THE CASE OF MUSA OSMAN[3]

Musa Osman is a boy who is about four years old. He lives with his parents, three brothers and three sisters in Dinayet, a suburb in the western outskirts of Sinkat. Except for his brother Eisa, who is less than two years old, his other siblings are all older than him. Both his parents arrived in recent years from rural areas west of Sinkat, belonging to the Musa Atman branch of the Rabba Maq tribe. They now live among relatives in a Rabba Maq part of Dinayet, the wife's mother living together with them.

The parents of Musa Osman, Todis and her husband Osman, married about thirteen years ago, when she was seventeen years old. Typically, her husband is ten years older than she. Osman married his father's brother's daughter, which is the culturally most favorable way of marrying.

Figure 1: *The family of Musa Osman*

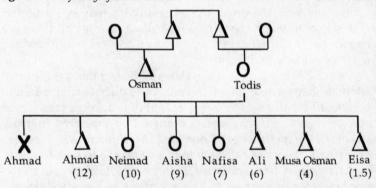

Explanation of symbols: 'O' means female, a triangle means male, 'X' means deceased, lower horizontal lines stands for marriage bond while higher horizontal lines symbolize sibling bonds. The numbers in brackets represent age.

The first-born child, Ahmad died after naming day. According to custom, the next son, who is now twelve years, was named after him. Since the death of their first child, sickness and poverty have been part of daily life for the family. While some people from their tribe maintain a source of income in rural areas while living in Dinayet, the family of Musa Osman depends solely on the urban occupation of the father. He is presently working as a guard in the local hospital, work which provides him with the total monthly salary of 4,000 Sudanese pounds. According to my own estimation, this sum could cover about eight single meals at the local truck stop.

When talking to neighbors and other people who know the family, they acknowledge that this family is in a terrible economic situation. Although their income cannot be considered exceptionally low in present-day Sinkat, their number of children is far above average (see Appendix 7). People who know Osman, the father, describe him as having 'a hot stomach,' meaning that he is easily raised to anger. He often quarrels with his wife, children and relatives and, now and then, yells at people. Some people think that his problems stem from 'reading the Quran too much,' an exceptional attribute, since nearly 100% of the people in Dinayet are illiterate. Other people describe him as a 'hero of everyday life,' mastering the feeding of many children under very extreme conditions. They tend to see his 'hot stomach' as natural in the given circumstances.

Both Musa Osman and his brother Eisa suffer from severe sickness. Neither of them are able to walk or talk. Musa Osman is very thin and his stomach is blown up. He looks very weak and seems uninterested in what goes on around him. Todis, his mother, states that this condition has prevailed since his birth. She twice brought him to the feeding centers of two locally represented relief agencies during his first year of life. She thinks that this did not do him good, however, but instead caused a more severe sickness which now prevails in the child. 'The relief food, their oil, wheat and milk made him sick,' she states.

For this reason they made *dérwout* for him, a home-made remedy consisting of *adal óot, inkúffid* and butter oil. My female research assistant who is from Hamdab, the tribe famous for its *busarā*, asked the grandmother (MoMo) why they did not consult Hamdab healers for the condition. She answered, 'We took him to one professional from Hamdab, and he prescribed a mixture of *dérwout* which is containing *adal óot, gána hindíib,*[4] *inkúffid*[5] and butter oil. We bought those things, but we did not give it to the child.' She added later on: 'There is no need for a *basīr* to make the *dérwout*, Beja people used to make it themselves in their own houses.' She then complains about food oil from abroad:

207

'Some time ago there was a butter oil available here imported from Holland. It had the same color as the goat butter oil, but when you threw it on the ground, and it went into the ground, it went even faster than water. I once tasted this butter oil, and it gave me a headache and wounds in my head. Even now there is some itching in the skin of my head. The mother of those children, my daughter, has been regularly sick until now, and this Eisa (the youngest child) once felt fever, and after this fever, he got leg paralysis.'

The theory invoked by the parents and the grandmother at the time after they visited the feeding centers, is the theory of *tesérimt* as a mystical influence through food items from outside their society (see Theory L). The treatment discussed, giving *dérwout*, is the prototypical treatment for this condition. At the time of our contact, they have all returned to this explanation. In the meantime, however, they have tried out several other options.

At various points of time they have tried out the treatment and advice of several *busará*. Since giving *dérwout* did not prove efficient, the parents sought to explore another type of explanation. Given that 'fright sickness' may result in the sickness of *alíib*, which may have a similar constellation of symptoms as described for Musa Osman, this theory provided the parents with another cultural resource which allowed them to follow another course of action (see Proposition LXIV, Theory O). A 'sickness of fright' which is serious and persistent enough to cause *alíib* naturally must stem from evil spirits. Since only *fugará* and holy men are able to deal with spirits, consulting a *fagīr* is a logical solution (see Proposition LXVI, Theory O). It is, however, an economically costly solution, since, in the best case, one single *fagīr* consultation will cost at least one-eighth of the monthly pay of Osman. The fact that they consulted many *fugará* over the last three years suggests that they held this explanation to be the most plausible for a long time.

When the treatment from various *fugará* proved inefficient, they paid a couple of visits to the local hospital. Possibly this was purely trial and error. All they are able to state from the treatment is that 'he got a kind of syrup from them.' In other cases I encountered, however, parents of children suspected to have *tesérimt* sought the help of biomedical practitioners, since

'Western medicine' may have solutions for *tesérimt* resulting from influences of food items from the West.

Recently the parents visited a female *fagīr* from the Marafadit suburb of Sinkat. She gave them *mihaya*,[6] but with no results. They still have some *mihaya* left, but they do not think that it is of any help to continue. During the five months we stayed in contact with them, they did not take any steps to try out new solutions. They seemed somehow apathetic and told us that they were tired of seeking new specialists for treatment. During our contact they returned to the theory of foreign food items causing *tesérimt*. They considered seeking the help of a professional *basīr* from the Hamdab, in case a specialist would be able to advise a better *dérwout*. Butter oil, however, an important part of the contents of *dérwout*, is not as abundant as before. When women make butter oil in their homes, it is solely meant for sale in order to get additional income for the household. The grandmother expresses this problem in the following way:

> In former times we used to give pregnant women this *dérwout* so as to avoid *tesérimt* for the child. We also gave it to women giving breast. But now the situation of people has changed and the butter oil is rare and people ignore this custom. For this reason children now begin to be affected by *tesérimt*. When the mother knows several options in front of her, she has to eat the available food.'

The case of Musa Osman illustrates well the point that several diagnostic labels may be applied to a specific physical sickness. Obviously this has to be so, as long as different theories may render the same sickness culturally meaningful. When different cultural theories are invoked, however, different symptoms seem to be stressed. This will be more clearly demonstrated in the next case study, the case of Ahmad. In the case of Ahmad, the diagnostic label for his condition is unchanged although the theories applied by his parents changed from time to time. While the story of Musa Osman showed how the same problem could be given different Beja folk diagnostic labels as the understanding of the problem changed, the next story shows us that a shift in cultural theory does not necessarily result in changes in the diagnostic label.

209

7.2. THE CASE OF AHMAD

Ahmad is a fourteen-year-old youngster who is still living with his parents and one younger sister of seven, Katonab. They live in a remote rural settlement in Odrus, where his father Hamed tries to make a living out of a rather small animal herd combined with seasonal cultivation of sorghum. An older sister, Nafisa, is married with two small children. They live next door to the tent of her parents. Another sister, a twin of Katonab, died shortly after birth. She died from *tesérimt* after a camel race was arranged to celebrate her birthday, her mother Amna tells us.

Amna herself is a talkative and friendly woman in her early fifties with a bright outlook on life. She has not, however, gone through life without any troubles or hardship. Two of her four sisters died from sickness, the last one seven years ago. One of her living sisters lost six of her seven children following the droughts in 1984 and 1991, while the other sister lost her only son. Her own child Katonab has been sick with 'fright sickness' from time to time. At the present time she is well, however, thanks to successful treatment by a local *fagīr*. She still wears an amulet *(hejāb)* from the *fagīr* in order to keep her from relapses or further spirit attacks. Amna, as well as her two grandchildren, Umar (3) and Ali (1), have all been sick from *t'háasimt* for a couple of months. Both 'underground' and 'overground' spirits caused sickness for them, she states. Fortunately, they all recovered shortly before I left the field, after being treated by different *fugarā*.

Her son Ahmad, however, has been sick since he was a small child. After he was born, 'he got sick with fever for nine months. However, he has been a "mental case" *(háale)* since he recovered.' He has to be looked after, dressed and given food. He seldom speaks, and he only stares in front of him when guests arrive. During bad periods, his family has to go and look for him when he walks around, since he is not able to find his own way back to his home. We asked her what she thinks caused his condition. 'It seems that his condition stems from envy *(hassād),*' she states, and continues:

> 'When we were in Port Sudan, we tried to gain a piece of land. Then, in the same day as I bought this piece of land, I bore this son, and women came to congratulate me. Then one of them said to me: "You are lucky. You gained a nice

piece of land and a son." From this day, I assume, his sickness began.'

They went to several *fugarā* in order to relieve his condition, but without any success. After this they tried to consult the hospital. Since the treatment of various Islamic healers proved unsuccessful, his parents allowed for the possibility that his 'madness' may have a physical cause which the hospital could deal with. However, it turned out that the hospital staff could do nothing for him, and Amna goes on:

'Then some people said to us that he may have *zār*. We took him to one *zār sheikh*, Saleh in Port Sudan, from Beni Amer. He said to us: "He has had *zār* for a long time." He tied a rope on his neck and then he gave him *bakhūr*,[7] and he recovered a little bit. 'He managed to request food and also to feed himself. In past time, if he went from our house, he was not able to return, unless we looked for him. Now he began to return to our house and make his own *jábana*.[8] But Saleh said to us that his treatment will be completed by a big *zār* party, which requires slaughtering seven sheep. We do not have the ability to fulfill this.'

Amna and her family used to be in a far better economic situation. Her efforts to treat Ahmad, however, were a severe drain on their resources. At the present time, they find themselves unable to pursue any further treatment efforts. She repeats this sad state of affairs to us:

'We took him to several *fugarā* and *zār* sheiks. We lost all our money, sheep and gold. And at last one *fagīr* said to me: "You should go to this Saleh." And then, when I went to Saleh, he said to me that "the treatment of your son requires a big party, which needs seven sheep for slaughtering." This is outside our possibilities.'

The story Amna tells about her son comes in bits and pieces. Like any story concerning a serious health problem yet unsolved, her story is only partly coherent. What caused the sickness, is explained in two very different ways, as a severe infection and as resulting from the 'evil eye' of a woman who commented upon their success in both having a son and gaining access to a piece of land at the same time (see Proposition LXI, Theory N).

The two explanations are not necessarily incompatible. It is quite possible to imagine the power of the 'evil eye' causing an infection which again caused his present mental state. However, after several social gatherings with Amna, it became clear to us that she did not combine these points.

Another point is also difficult to grasp. When Amna sought the help of various *fugarā'*, she seemed to stress the problem as a problem of spirit affliction and not as envy. The *fugarā'*, as well, treated his problem as a problem of spirits (see Propositions XLIX (part a.6) and LII, Theory J), though it is conceivable that the 'evil eye' facilitated both the infection and later the spirit affliction. As will become clear when personal narratives are discussed in more detail, however, people often do not make such explicit connections.

When some relatives of Ahmad suggested that his condition may be due to *zār* spirits, another cultural resource was invoked. As we will see in Chapter 8.1, theories of *zār* possession may very well explain his condition as well as the lack of success in the previous efforts of his family. For example his impaired ability to communicate may be due to the *zār* spirit wanting more attention from its host and, as in any marriage, wanting him now and then to be totally alone with it (see Proposition XLIX, Theory J). Regarding the treatment, the sphere of action of religious healers does not, for religious reasons, include *zār* spirits (see Proposition XLIX, part c). Since part of the *zār* treatment for economic reasons is not complete, his family is still left with some hope that he may recover.

The bits and pieces of Amna's story seemingly serve yet another purpose. Amna and her husband are portrayed in her stories as parents who did everything they could in order to seek out the available opportunities for treatment of Ahmad. Although, as in all Beja stories, the cultural logic and the cultural theories underlying the treatment options chosen are not accounted for, the stories are told in such a way that every Hadandowa Beja hearing the story will understand the cultural logic behind their choices. At this point in the discussion it may be worthwhile to turn to take a closer look at Beja narratives.

NOTES

1 Camels treated in a special manner in order to make them more fertile: See earlier discussion Chapter 4.

2 The label indicates a sickness resulting from 'fright sickness' which is not treated or not adequately treated. Typical symptoms are general weakness, thinness, reduced strength in the feet and, possibly, a distended stomach. See earlier discussions.

3 The names here, as elsewhere in the thesis, are not the real names. All other information, like names of tribes and subtribes, is factual information.

4 Beja vernacular word for a local bush. See Chapter 4.

5 Beja vernacular word for a widespread bush in the Red Sea Hills used to treat several different sickness conditions.

6 A water solution of ink from a Quranic writing on a piece of wood or paper: See Chapter 4.

7 Sudansese Arabic for 'incense.' See Chapter 4 and Chapter 6.

8 Traditional Beja coffee.

8

RETURN TO THE STORIES

8.0. INTRODUCTION

At this point in the analysis I want to turn to a detailed sequence by sequence analysis of some Beja narratives. Like for the previous chapter my aim is twofold. Firstly, I want to demonstrate the necessity of various folk theories presented in Chapter 4 for understanding those stories. By filling in the many 'open slots' in the stories I want to demonstrate how a broad range of cultural knowledge is implicitly a part of them.

Secondly, I want to elucidate how narrators invoke folk theories in specific narrative contexts. In other words, the pragmatics of Beja narrating will be considered. By pragmatics I mean how the narrators link their cultural resources to real-life situations and give Beja folk theories explanatory force.

The Beja are people who to a great degree place weight on the history of particular individuals and happenings, whether it be the history of persons and their conduct, their *diwáb*, their tribe, or, generally, the history of the Beja people. In their narratives, as we have seen, they draw very much upon past experience and the significance of past episodes. The Beja narratives, whether personal narratives or mythical stories about healers in the past, generally have short, condensed and complex sequences. They are condensed and complex in the sense that much cultural knowledge is taken for granted. The mythical stories are, I will argue, nevertheless easier to grasp because they are more structured and more directed by narrative means than personal narratives. The personal stories are hence more flexible and open to possible interpretations than are the mythical stories.

Statements in Beja narratives allude to cultural and historical

214

knowledge as well as taking this knowledge for granted. Sometimes the background knowledge evoked is clear to the audience. In personal narratives it is sometimes unclear what knowledge is underlying a statement, a feature which renders the statement ambiguous. This ambiguity may sometimes be more or less consciously employed as a means of seeking the participation of the audience in the unfolding of the story. The stories where the uncertainty is presented at most are of three main kinds. In the first type of story seemingly new sickness experiences are accounted for. In the second type, a case of ill-health is still unsolved. Thirdly, there are cases of sicknesses resulting in death in the past where the narrator seeks support for his or her ways of finding a possible solution for the suffering family member or relative.

The Beja narratives are full of suspense. The historical stories of *busarâ* unfold gradually toward an often surprising solution. Usually no indications are given of what is going to happen before the tension is relieved when the solution is presented at the very end of the narrative. The personal narratives often entail several moments of tension relief, as several sub-stories within the narrative are presented like a record over several attempts to solve a problem and, finally, the outcome of those attempts.

I have stated that most of the relevant information needed in order to understand the stories is left out of them. It is worth noting that one of the important elements seemingly lacking in the stories, is making clear the intentions of the characters. At first sight this seems to be in contrast to Beja people's constant preoccupation with the motives of each other. I will come to argue that one of the most prominent features of their stories is that they are very much about the motives of people. However, by letting those motives be implicit in the stories, the motives come to the foreground in the minds of the audience. There might be a sociological explanation for this, an explanation to which I will return later on. Before doing this, I want to present the rich personal narrative of Halima Umar.

8.1. PERSONAL NARRATIVES: THE STORY OF HALIMA UMAR

'It is the uniquely self-reflexive paradox of the self that it comes into existence only to the extent that it can be re-collected out of the past . . .

The present is the pivotal point out of which the "I" who recollects retrieves its own self. But the present is not a static point, or some measurable duration. Presence is always leaning into that vast unknown that we call the future, projecting itself into the future, and that project in which it is engaged determines the way it is present.'

S. Crites 1986[1]

8.1.1. Introduction

This is an attempt at presenting the story of Halima Umar as she tells it herself about her experiences with being possessed by a *zār* spirit for many years. It is about experiencing having a spirit 'self' within the boundaries of her own body, a spirit 'self' which is seemingly heavily intermingled with her own 'self.' When first getting acquainted with her story, I had a confusing feeling of not being able to distinguish in different parts of the story which thoughts, feelings, intentions and actions had her own 'self' or the *zār* spirit 'self' as their source. Indeed, parts of her narrative seemingly give the impression that, in the words of Spiro (1993), ' . . . an individual's other-representations are included within [her] self representation,' which is 'a sign of rather severe psychopathology.'[2] From her mere words one easily gets the impression that Halima confuses her inner representation of herself and those of her *zār* spirit when telling her own story.

Through subsequent reviews of her story, however, I came to view it as in many ways a typical story of *zār* possession described by Sudanese psychiatrists (Ahmad al-Safi 1970; Rahim 1991) as well as anthropologists (Boddy 1988, 1989; Constantinides 1977, 1982; Kenyon 1991; Makris 1991; Schneider 1988) in different parts of the Sudan. None of the psychiatrists described the belief of being possessed by a *zār* spirit as a sign of serious psychopathology, and none of the anthropologists described *zār* cults as a fringe phenomenon primarily attracting people with psychological disturbances or people with special problems involving social adaptation.[3] Halima's story, I will maintain, turns out to be a culturally well framed and appropriate story when the listener or reader is supplied with sufficient cultural background knowledge. Before presenting her story, however, I will give a brief presentation of the woman Halima Umar to the reader.

216

8.1.2. Halima Umar

Halima is a friendly and talkative woman living in Dinayet, an area on the outskirts of the small mountain town of Sinkat. This area is considered an 'illegal' part of the town because it has not undergone proper official registrations of houses and properties and has as yet no plan for regulated water supply and renovation. Most huts have no type of toilet, and water has to be carried from nearby wells. The area is located in the lower part of a steep, barren hill. This fact creates considerable problems for the inhabitants during heavy rainfalls, since their wooden huts are simply raised on mud ground without any kind of foundation. Halima lives in a small hut made of a skeleton of branches from a local bush and covered by *burūsh*,[4] the dried leaves from the *doom*[5] palm. Many of her close relatives live nearby, some of them sharing the same yard as Halima.

Dinayet is situated west of the town center. Most of its inhabitants have moved from rural western areas of Sinkat province since the severe drought in 1984,[6] most of them from Odrus or Agwamt. Halima and her relatives came from Agwamt earlier, about twenty years ago.

The inhabitants still have considerable interests in the rural areas from which they originate. First and foremost, many of their relatives are still living in those rural areas. Some inhabitants of Dinayet still have animals and grazing areas there and others seasonally go to Odrus or Agwamt for the cultivation of sorghum.

Halima herself is a widow. Her husband, Bakash, died a few years ago in a car accident. Her age is not easy to determine. She might be between 50 and 55 years old. Beja people do not keep records of their age since they are normally non-literate. She is, however, the mother of five and grandmother of seven children. Unfortunately one of her children, Hussain, died shortly after his naming day.[7] One of her grandchildren, Hamed, died 9 months ago. He was about 9 days old and died after complications resulting from what his relatives regarded as a 'common cold.' However, compared to many other families around her, the mortality in her family is low.

Halima is poor, but not worse off than most of her relatives and neighbors. She has a few goats, maybe three or four.[8] This is enough to supply her with milk daily, but not enough to survive on. For this reason she is dependent upon help from her close relatives.

Halima has outlived her two sisters. One of them, Saleimin, recently[9] died from malaria. Halima is a woman of strong will and is influential in health matters among her relatives, as is also evident in the story. When sickness occurs among her relatives, she often takes a different position regarding diagnosis and treatment options from those of her relatives. She is regarded as an experienced women in health matters, especially in problems related to zār-spirits. For this reason, while she is not always capable of influencing the choice for treatment among her relatives, people always listen to her when she voices opinions about diagnoses or treatment options. Such discussions in difficult sickness cases typically never end, even after the death of the afflicted person.

Halima is a woman of strong will, but she is also well known for changing her mind quickly, something we experienced several times when arranging to meet her. This is clearly reflected in the very large number and broad range of healers she involved in her own experience of sickness as well as sudden changes in health-seeking strategies. However, involving different kinds of specialists or healers in one instance of sickness is not itself untypical in the Red Sea Hills.

The settlement in Dinayet Halima lives in is a settlement of Hamdab people, the subtribe of Hadandowa Beja famous for having great traditional healers. My female research assistant, Aisha, is herself from the Hamdab subtribe and has known Halima for a long time. She and my wife Janike paid her several visits during the spring of 1995. One such occasion Halima explained to Janike about different kinds of zār, since Halima herself has arranged for several zār parties over the years in her home area.

8.1.3. The story

After chatting for a while, Aisha asked her to tell Janike about the background for her own zār possession, and she gave a quite extended narrative in response, without any interference from Aisha or Janike:

'At first I felt pain in one of my thighs like after an injection. It

218

made a terrible pain so that I couldn't sleep for 3 months. After that I called for my sister Saleimin from Agwamt to come and stay with me. Then I decided to destroy this swelling which was painful, and to do it myself. I destroyed it with my hands and it bled a lot. After that I decided to go to rural areas with my sister. When we reached Hilayet on our way to Agwamt, we stayed over night there. And then one **fagīr** *from Ashraf who is living in Agwamt came, passing by Hilayet. Then I went to this* **fagīr,** *and he said to me: "Bring a white goat. Before slaughtering it, you must move around this goat seven times." Then he slaughtered it near my feet, then when this blood came on my feet, I put some of this blood on my mouth.*

Always I used to feel tension, for this reason I always wanted to be alone. Then after the slaughtering I went so as to stay alone by myself. Then after that he gave me **hejbāt,**[10] *and he advised me to go to a particular* **zār sheikh**[11] *in Port Sudan. Then I proceeded to Agwamt, took some goats and sold them after which I went on to Port Sudan.*

Then I met Saleh, from Beni Amer. My relatives there took me to him, but I refused, because I thought I looked strange. Also I heard that he was preparing for **zār,** *so there were other people with him, and I did not want to meet them. But my family forced me to meet him. Then, when I met him, he took some ash from a fire, mixed some of it with charcoal and water and gave it to me to drink. And after I drank it, I felt as if nothing had happened to me and I felt very well. And then he asked me to bring two goats, one kid and one grown up goat, and one camel. I found no camel, so I was to pay the cost of it. Also I should bring perfumes and* **bakhūr.**[12] *Then he made for me a* **taljāb.**[13]

After that this **sheikh** *gave me a kind of wood for* **bakhūr** *and also* **mihaya**[14] *so as to mix it with washing water in order to wash myself in the morning and evening for forty days.*

And after this I returned to my house in Port Sudan. I used the water until I completed it. I did not feel anything wrong in this period. And after 40 days those disturbances came to me again. Then I decided by my own will to go to a doctor, Jirihi[15], *and he gave me five injections. I think he knew nothing. After that I became pregnant with my first son. Then also this disturbance did not leave me. Then I secretly sold some of my gold so as to have treatment by* **fugarā´**; *and I went to several* **fugarā´**, *any* **fagīr,**

219

*in Sinkat and Kassala. Also no successful results, and my situation
became more complicated.*

*And one night I dreamt that a man with a spear was threatening
me so I would give him my son and my gold. And I forced my
sister to wake up that night and give me my gold which I kept
with her. And she said to me: "Why do you want this gold from
me now in the middle of the night?" And I answered: "I want to
wear it." And I also bought animals, because I thought that my
family ignored me and was not feeding me properly. And after
that my desire for food was less. My family used to force me to
eat. One guy, who is the husband of my sister, whom I respect,
he used to force me to eat the food. But he has a beard, and just
to avoid seeing his beard, I used to take the dishes of food quickly
from him. And after that my family and relatives said to me: "This
is your **zār**. And you have to fulfill your promise quickly and
make a big **zār** party."*

*Then suddenly my sister [Saleimin] felt sick by false pregnancy,
and we took her to a **fagīr** from Samarai Diwab. Then this **fagīr**
said to my sister: "If you promised to fulfill this **zār** party for
your sister, you have to do it." Then he gave her **mihaya**. Then
also, after this, my sister was affected by a bleeding problem. The
fagīr said to me and my sister: "You have to fulfill your promise."*

*And then we made preparations for the **zār** party, which
included a cow, three sheep and one goat. We also prepared kinds
of sweets, vegetables like olives, raisins and canned food. Then I
bought a **toob**,[16] an 'imma[17] a **gurbāb**,[18] a **sidderiyya**[19] and also
shoes.[20] This was the preparation for a Moroccan party. We
also brought some chairs. All of this was for the first night of the
party.*

*The second afternoon I was given Beja clothes like **sirwāl**,[21]
sidderiyya, a comb and **shayyeet**.[22] This **zār** was a **jubāli zār**.[23]
This proceeded until the third day, Sunday. Then there was no
celebration on Monday.[24] It went on Tuesday afternoon with a
new uniform, **kastāni**. We took Wednesday off, and on Thursday
we first prepared for this banquet with a long table, took a sheep,
filled it with rice and baked it. Then they gave me a full suitcase
which contained skirt, trousers, jacket, necktie and a black stick,
and they brought a horse to ride on. This **zār** is **khawāja zār**,
injilīzi.[25]*

After this I recovered. At first my husband refused parties of zār, but after that he himself became possessed and made seven zār parties.'

8.1.4. Analysis

As stated previously, her story like all Beja narratives requires extensive cultural background knowledge in order to be understood. By going through it line by line, I hope to make explicit what one at least needs to know in order to understand her story. Throughout my analysis I will make commentaries in brackets for the corresponding theories and propositions discussed in Chapter 6.

1.a. *At first I felt pain in one of my thighs like after an injection.*
She begins her story without stating when and where the happening described began. It is obvious from the story, however, that the sickness began as she was staying in Dinayet, an 'illegal' *hay*[26] in the outskirts of Sinkat town. Usually in Beja narratives about personal experiences the setting is either obvious from the story and the context of its performance or it is explicitly made clear.

The time reference for the beginning of the story, however, is typically more imprecise. Sometimes the narrative is initiated by statements like 'when I was young' or 'once upon a time.' Even, as here, it might not be commented upon at all.

The story begins with stating the problem, which is not unexpected, since the story was provoked by Aisha asking about her story related to her *zār*.

1.b. *It made a terrible pain so that I couldn't sleep for three months.*
Most narratives about one's own sickness experience or that of close relatives typically involves evaluation and specification of the problem. Sometimes, like here, the duration of the problem is approximately accounted for.

2. *After that I called for my sister Saleimin from Agwamt to come and stay with me.*
This is an appropriate and expected action. In cases of sickness or when about to give birth, a relative will usually be there to guard and to take care of the person's needs. The guarding often involves helping to protect against spirit attacks (see Proposition LIV (part a.3), Theory K).

3.a. *Then I decided to destroy this swelling which was painful, and to do it myself.*

221

She did not state before this that it was a swelling. Obviously this swelling was a kind of big fistula containing some pus.

Beja seem to show much more indifference to pain than Europeans do. Even youngsters may be seen burning themselves with hot irons as treatment for different sicknesses, without any overt show of pain.

3.b. *I destroyed it with my hands and it bled a lot.*
This statement is intensifying the active 'I decided to . . .' in the previous sentence, underlining the agency of the narrator.

She states that '*it bled a lot,*' a further description and evaluation of the problem.

4. *After that I decided to go to rural areas with my sister.*
This utterance represents quite a quick move from the previous sentences telling about her self-treatment. Obviously, her treatment was unsuccessful or only partially successful, but this is for the listener to infer. It might well be that the story is not strictly chronologically ordered, which is not untypical in Beja narratives concerned with personal experiences. I suspect that the sentence 1b: '*It made a terrible pain so that I couldn't sleep for three months*' is extending in time into the story, and that the continuing of this terrible pain made her go to rural areas in order to pursue further treatment.

The 'I decided to . . .' is repeated again, by which Halima is presenting herself as an able and autonomous woman who 'takes her destiny into her own hands.'

Since many of her relatives are still living in Agwamt, it is an understandable decision from her to go there for many reasons. Her relatives there may help her with useful advices and establish economic support for further treatment. In some cases, like Halima's, the economic costs may be considerable.

The people who still manage to stay in rural areas are supposed by more urban Beja to live a healthier life away from the dirt, immorality and unhealthy food of the towns (Ausenda 1987, Dahl, *et al.* 1991). For this reason it may be considered wise for people to return to their rural areas in cases of sickness. In some cases I encountered people who brought water and sorghum to sick persons from their home area, because water from a strange well and food grown on unfamiliar soil were considered possible sources of ill-health (see Propositions XLV and XLVI, Theory A, and Propositions LVI and LVII, Theory L).

The change of place of living may itself be health promoting in case of *kosúlt*.[27] In another place the water, air and food grown might be more compatible with the sick person (see Propositions XLVII and XLVIII, Theory I).

5.a. *When we reached Hilayet on our way to Agwamt, we stayed over night there.*

This sentence is functionally only a bridge to a new development in her story. It represents a kind of shortcut device, in which both her preparations for traveling, her negotiations with her sister in order to join her to Agwamt and the journey itself are rendered unimportant for the plot of the story.

5.b. *And then one fagīr from Ashraf who lives in Agwamt, came passing by Hilayet.*

The Ashraf tribe is considered its own subtribe (non-Hadendowa) of the Beja tribe. The people in this subtribe are believed to be directly descended from the prophet Mohammad (Ausenda 1987). For this reason the *fugarā'* and holy men in that tribe are expected to be especially powerful.

6.a. *Then I went to this fagīr, and he said to me: 'Bring a white goat. Before slaughtering it, you must circle around this goat seven times.'*

'Then I went to this *fagīr* . . .' is stated in a 'matter of fact' way. Given that it is quite possible that spirits may cause sicknesses in people (see Theory J), Halima does not have to justify her decision to contact a *fagīr*. Moreover, women are especially susceptible to spirit afflictions and spirit attacks, since they often are in a state of pollution because of menstruating, giving birth and lactating (see Proposition LIV, Theory K).

Based on the tacit knowledge that he as Ashraf is expected to be a powerful healer and that, since he is from her home area, and hence is known by her and can be trusted, it logically follows that she seeks his advice.

The treatment itself is usually described in great detail in stories people tell about their own health-seeking career. A greater part of the stories, like here, is usually made up by accounting for practical intervention in the sickness case.

A white goat or a white sheep is very often used as *karāma*[28] in simple offerings concerning supernatural powers, whether those powers are considered Muslim proper by people or not (see Proposition IV (part b), Theory A, and Proposition XLIX (part a.6), Theory J). More elaborate rituals might for example involve a white and a black goat, seven white goats or sheep, etc.

The number seven often recurs in treatment procedures, especially when the direct intervention of God or spirits is sought. People might be advised to drink *mihaya* or take a bath by it seven times or for seven days, a treatment may be recommended on the first, third, fifth and seventh day or the first, third, fifth or seventh month, like using *dérwout*[29] during pregnancy to prevent the sickness of *tesérimt*. Seven verses from the Quran are used in *hejbāt* as protection from the attacks of *junūn* (see Proposition LV (part b), Theory K).

6.b. *Then he slaughtered it near my feet.*

By this utterance she takes a big jump from the previous sentence where she tells about the prescription of the healer. The whole story in between, her acceptance of his prescription and how she went about finding the goat and bringing it to the *fagīr*, is not told, but again it is left to the listener to make inferences about.

While paying attention to what she omits, it is even more interesting to focus what she mentions. It is important for her to tell, not only that the healer slaughtered the goat, but that he slaughtered it 'near my feet.' The blood coming from the sacrifice is considered to be both holy and health bringing (see Proposition LV (part c), Theory K). This is a theme recurrent in both Islamic and *zār* rituals in the Red Sea Hills. This may also be the case in other societies in a wider region.[30]

6.c. *When this blood came on my feet, I put some of this blood on my mouth.*

She elaborates on the same theme, stating that while the *fagīr* is slaughtering the goat, some of its blood comes on her feet. She even helps herself in order to render the treatment even more efficient, by applying some of the blood to her mouth. She states this without giving any kind of explanation. In fact, there is a complicated 'taken for granted' knowledge underlying her act and her retelling of this act.

As in 'religious' rituals described from many societies,[31] the orifices of the body are given a special significance in Beja healing rituals as limits between the outside and inside of the body. But there is more to Halima's act than that. The smells of things are considered an important source of health and ill-health among Beja[32] (see Theory F). This is also a recurrent theme in old Greco-Islamic medicine.[33] Blood from sacrifice or from circumcision is considered especially health bringing. Smelling blood from sacrifice is for those reasons considered healthy (see Proposition

XXX (part e), Theory F). Just as when the substance of 'blessing' positively contaminates people wearing an amulet from a *héequal fagīr* or when animals are smeared with the powdered stone of *adal óot*, contact with blood from sacrifice acts on people through a process of 'sympathetic magic.'

Many Beja in the Sinkat area speak about a sickness stemming from not having been circumcised. Some even call it *kusháabe*, meaning circumcision in Tu Bedawie (see Proposition LV (part c), Theory K, and Proposition LXXV). As treatment it is usual, after performing the circumcision, to smear some of the blood from it on the mouth or under the nose of the patient in order for him/her to smell the blood of circumcision (see Proposition XXX (part f), Theory F).

6.d. *Always I used to feel tension, for this reason I always wanted to be alone.*

At this part of the story, this sudden jump in the theme is not easy to explain. So many things are left unsaid in her narrative. Why is it important for her at this point in the story to tell about her psychological tension and wish to be alone?

6.e. *Hence, after the slaughtering I went so as to stay alone by myself.*

Because she repeats the same point by stating that she actually went to be alone after the slaughtering, this narrative clause is evidently important for the story.

Beja people are virtually almost never alone. A common feature in different kinds of psychological problems as Beja see them, is the wish of the sick person to be alone and the tendency to isolate oneself from relatives, friends and neighbors. People are simply expected to be sociable, and when they are not, this is seen as a serious problem.

6.f. *Then after that he gave me **hejbāt**, and he advised me to go to a particular **zār sheikh** in Port Sudan.*

Amulets *(hejbāt)*, mostly containing verses from the Quran, are protective means against spirit attacks. Very often *fugarā* give *hejbāt* in order for the patient not to relapse into sickness again after treatment (see Proposition LV (part b), Theory K). Depending on the *héequal*-ness of the *fagīr*, a positive contamination affects the carrier of this sacred object.

It is very interesting that she tells in such a matter-of-fact way that he advised her to seek *zār* treatment without telling anything about the results of his treatment. Also, the *zār sheikh* and the *fagīr* are supposed to belong to different worlds of discourse, since the former is involved in a supposedly non-Islamic practice and the latter is considered by people to be a proper Islamic healer, depending first and foremost upon his closeness to God for his success in healing (see Theory J). For this reason it may seem quite surprising that a *fagīr* would recommend a non-Islamic practitioner.

People I spoke to seem to have a quite pragmatic approach to this puzzle. They state views like 'There are both *junūn* with which the *fagīr* can deal and *zār* spirits in the world. The *fagīr* cannot deal with the *zār* spirits, so what can we do?' Sometimes *fugarā* are reported to make deals with *zār* spirits in order for those spirits to stay away from them and not interfere in their practice.[34] The requests of the *zār* spirits may be quite un-Islamic, however, like even staying away from the Friday prayer, which is considered an enormously important duty of a Muslim (see Proposition L (part c), Theory J).

In other words, the recommendation of the *fagīr* to go and see a *zār sheikh* may be seen as a way of stating that he has done what is within his power as a *fagīr*, but since it is a *zār* spirit, she has to involve a different healer for treatment (see Proposition L (part c.5), Theory J). Whether Halima really feels better, we are not told. But, since the *fagīr* gives her a *hejāb* for further protection, he seemingly wants to show that his treatment is not in vain, but has its limits in this case.

There is also a second possible explanation, which does not rule out the first one. As made clear earlier, the role of the *fagīr* is not only to heal, but also to reveal the truth to people about different matters.[35] After making *karāma* to the *fagīr*,[36] he may reveal where stolen gold is to be found, what kind of spirits are inflicted upon you, whom to seek for further treatment etc. (see Proposition LII, Theory J). Since this *fagīr* is beginning to talk about *zār* and a particular *zār sheikh* after the offerings, this might be seen as a revelation he got during the treatment process.

7. *After this I proceeded to Agwamt, took some goats and sold them after which I went on to Port Sudan.*
She finally went to her home area and sold some goats in order to pay for expected future treatment expenses. Whether those goats were strictly her own, herded by relatives, or belonging to one or several close relatives, she does not tell us. Strictly there is no need for her to tell this, since family members and relatives

are expected to help in case of sicknesses. As discussed earlier, the ethos of sharing is very strong among the Beja, and especially in cases of need like when natural disasters or instances of sickness occur.[37]

8.a. *Then I met Saleh, from Beni Amer.*

It is clear from the previous sentences that Saleh is the *zār sheikh* and that she met him in Port Sudan. His tribal affiliation is important, so she makes this clear. The time, however, is unimportant or at best of subordinate importance, so she does not state it.

8.b. *My relatives there took me to him, but I refused, because I thought I looked strange.*

I do not know the full significance of this utterance. However, it seems to be a further characterization of her symptoms, involving the pain in her thigh and her wish to be alone. Typically *zār* spirits are said not to make life-threatening sicknesses,[38] but to cause 'minor inflictions' like paralysis in a limb, fainting, unusual menstrual bleeding and infertility etc. All her complaints are examples of such uncomfortable, but not very serious symptoms (see Proposition L (part b), Theory J).

8.c. *Also I heard that he was preparing for zār, for which reason there were other people with him, and I did not want to meet them.*

The picture she gives of her symptoms is dramatized by her account of how her sickness made her refuse to meet the *sheikh* and the people staying together with him.

8.d. *But my family forced me to meet him.*

In addition to intensify the dramatism of her story, this utterance clearly shows the strong belief in her relatives that she really was affected by *zār*. This gives us a reason to believe that they conceived of her case as typical rather than unusual.

8.e. *Then, when I met him, he took some ash from a fire, mixed some of it with charcoal and water and gave it to me to drink.*

Stuff related to women's work like ash from the cooking place, dry leftovers of *otâm* porridge[39] from cooking utensils or even the stones from the cooking place are considered by Beja to be health bringing (see Theory P). In some cases I encountered parents who gave sick children water to drink after using it for washing the stones of the fireplace. Ash from the fireplace is used as a health bringing device also by *fugarā'*.

8.f. *And after I drank it, I felt as if nothing had happened to me and I felt very well.*

227

This is the first time she is stating that she felt improvement. When telling about earlier treatments, she did not bother to tell whether she experienced some improvement, partial improvement or no improvement at all. This might be because what is really important for her in this story, is the confirmations she got for having *zār* and the utility of continuously making *zār* ceremonies.

8.g. *And after this he asked me to bring two goats, one kid and one adult goat, and one camel.*

8.h. *I found no camel, so I was to pay the cost of it.*

The cost of this single treatment is enormous, considering the economic situation of Halima and her family. Even before the devastating drought in 1984 she would need the economic support of many relatives to be able to undergo this treatment. That she herself, her family and relatives are willing to invest so much in treatment of a non-life threatening sickness like her's is clearly showing how much value they put upon being in good health and in doing as much as is within human power so as to achieve good health. I came across several instances in which parents with only three or four goats to their name offered one of them to a *fagīr* in order to treat diarrhea in one of their children.

There is a point about these high costs of treatment. When someone, particularly your wife, has a wish, you do your best as a Beja to fulfill it. Unfulfilled wishes, especially in pregnant women, may cause sicknesses both in the mother and the fetus (see Theory M). If for example a pregnant woman wishes fried sheep liver, and she is for one reason or another not able to get it, the child may be born with skin wounds with the shape of sheep liver.[40] The story about the wife who found the spleen missing in the animal which her husband slaughtered for her (Chapter 3) highlights this point. A Beja husband ideally will do everything in his power in order to fulfill the wishes of his wife. Paying for treatment expenses for his sick wife is clearly expected of him.

8.i. *Also I was to bring perfumes and* **bakhūr**.

Perfumes are considered important in many types of treatment. Perfumes might, by their pleasant smell, promote good health in the sufferer. Bad smells, in contrast, may cause many kind of sicknesses (see Theory F). In some instances, however, perfumes are supposed to have a harmful effect. This is for instance the case with the skin disease of *t'hâasimt*,[41] which is caused by spirits. Those spirits might be attracted by the nice smell of perfumes or frying meat, and the sickness may appear again in the patient.

Spirits have human-like faculties like the ability to smell (see Proposition XLIX (part a.15), Theory J). In the case of *zār*, the perfumes are supposed to please the spirits (see Proposition L (part e), Theory J). Indeed, during the treatment or ceremony, the spirit may explicitly ask through its host for expensive perfumes. The perfumes will hence indirectly benefit the patient.

The burning of *bakhūr*, however, is a more complicated topic. *Bakhūr* is used, as a rule, in every kind of *fagīr* treatment. Some *fugarā'* I talked with believed the *bakhūr* to drive spirits away. In the case of *zār* spirits, this explanation of course does not fit, since the aim of the treatment is not to drive the spirits away. Most people I talked with, however, told me that they do not know why this *bakhūr* is effective, but that they have experienced the usefulness of it through using it.

8.j. *Then he made for me a taljāb.*

I am not sure, but this is most probably a type of *hejāb*, an amulet usually containing a piece of paper with written verses of the Quran. This is thought to prevent the patient from relapsing into sickness again by keeping the spirits at bay. The word *taljāb* stems from the Arabic root *lajab*, which as a noun means 'a huge powerful or noisy army,'[42] a fact which might support my hypothesis.

8.k. *After that this sheikh gave me a kind of wood for bakhūr and also mihaya so as to mix it with washing water in order to wash myself in the morning and evening for forty days.*

The force of *mihaya* as protection stems from the power of the holy Quran itself, which in Aisha's words 'is itself the most powerful *hejāb*.' But, like amulets, the power of the *mihaya* derives from another source as well, the charisma or the *hēequal*-ness of the *fagīr* and *sheikh* (see Proposition LVI, Theory L). This is a complicated theological theme, however, since healing is thought to stem directly from God alone.[43] However, a theory of 'transsubstantiation' where a positive contamination of the *fagīr* by God in turn contaminating the *mihaya* which further endows the patient with a sacred substance may, as discussed earlier, partially resolves this theological puzzle.

The *bakhūr* is widely used by people for many purposes. Mostly it is not prescribed by a healer, but bought in a market or shop and administered by the people themselves. After the birth of a child, people will usually burn *bakhūr* continuously for 40 days. All visitors to the mother and child, including relatives, are supposed to pass by this incense in order not to bring spirits or other harmful influences with them into the house (see Proposition L (part a), Theory J).

9. *And after this I returned to my house in Port Sudan.*

This means that she was staying with relatives in Port Sudan. Such kind of lodging is an obvious duty of relatives. Even when not in any kind of need, friends and relatives may without sending a word in advance stay in the house of their host for at least three days.

10.a. *I used the water until I completed it.*

10.b. *I did not feel anything wrong in this period.*

This seems to confirm for her that her problem is *zār*. At this point in the story it may be appropriate for us to dwell on some properties of personal narratives in general. There has been much discussion among analysts of narratives regarding the extent to which the story told really temporally reflects the temporality of the events told about.[44] There seems to be some cross-cultural variation in this respect, however (see, e.g. Good 1994). Beja stories often do not stress a linear temporality as much as is seen in modern European narratives. In general, the persons involved, their reputation and tribal affiliation, and the places where things happened are obviously more important.

All the same, as might be expected, the reflexive character of personal narratives is a profound trait cross-culturally (See, e.g. Bruner 1990). This reflexivity involves two distinct processes: (1.) The narrator is foreshadowing what is going to happen later in the narrative in her present formulations and (2.) The narrator is encapsulating what has already been told in her present formulations. For this reason the things told about at a later stage in a story is naturally strongly colored by things told about earlier in the story and at the same time are colored by what she anticipates is going to happen.[45]

At this stage, it may be easier to find some plausible explanations for utterances earlier in this story, which seemed difficult to account for. In sentence 6.d. she states that *'Always I used to feel tension, for this reason I always wanted to be alone'* at a point in the story where it seems natural to expect that Halima will carry on with her retelling of the treatment itself. However, one of the symptoms of *zār* affliction and other spirit afflictions often reported, is the wish of the sufferer to be alone. The bond between the spirit and the human is supposed to be strong, and the spirit is conceived of as jealously wanting the attention of its host (see Proposition L (part a), Theory J). Many stories are told for example about how spirits may create problems for a host who wants to marry. In other words, the social isolation of the sufferer might be the wish of the spirit. In sentence 6.e. Halima goes on to state that after the offering, she actually went away so as to be alone. This might be interpreted as a result of the spirit's reaction to the *fagīr* trying to fight it.

When describing the offering itself in line 6.b. and 6.c. she is stressing that the animal was slaughtered near her feet and that blood fell upon her feet. In addition, she took some of it and smeared it around her mouth. In the case of *zār* this may be significant. Blood is considered of primary importance in healing *zār* afflictions. As discussed before, a person who is host to a *zār* spirit will never get rid of it (see Proposition L (part a), Theory J). However, the spirit may be silenced when its needs are fulfilled (see Proposition L (part g), Theory J). First and foremost the red *zār* spirit wants blood. As we have seen, a *zār* ritual ideally involves even drinking of sacrificial blood by the sufferer. In a case of *zār* the blood at the feet and around the mouth of Halima will be a significant event to report (see Proposition L (part f), Theory J).

In this way it seems that the elements of the story point not only backward toward the history of the sufferer, but also forward giving signals about what is to come. What is said in the beginning of the story is rendered understandable or at least interpretable by what comes later in the story.

11.a. *After forty days [however] those disturbances came to me again.*

Things happening during those forty days are not commented upon, obviously since they have no relevance for her narrative. Forty days is a period of religious significance in some Quranic stories. Forty days is often the recommended period by *fugarā'* for treatment. Forty days is also the period for which the newborn and its mother should be closely guarded against harmful spirits by a close relative. People, as we have seen, usually only make approximate time estimations, when they make them at all. Forty days seems a good cultural estimation 'to think with' whether or not this precise time period has passed.

In Halima's case, the period of use of *mihaya* came to an end after forty days. Obviously, in her experience, the spirit then plagued her again after she stopped using this protecting means (see Proposition LV (part b), Theory K).

11.b. *Then I decided by my own will to go to a doctor, Jirihi,*[46] *and he gave me five injections.*

The 'I decided' from the sentences 3.a. and 4. here reoccurs, even strengthened by the words 'by my own will.' Beja people are expected to do something about sickness and, in some cases seek any kind of treatment, in order to show their responsibility for their own and other family members' health. People continuously evaluate demonstrations of responsibility in other people. As an example, one of Halima's sisters grandchildren, Osman (17), is sick with *toordíp*,[47] fainting with convulsions from time to time. Halima comments upon this with the following narrative:

> 'At first Osman was affected by *mírquay*. They first went to *fugará*, then doctors, but neglected him a lot. I advised them to treat him for *ablága*,[48] but they did not follow my advice, and after a while it developed into *toordíp*. They tried to treat him for the *toordíp* several times, but the situation remained the same.'

In telling her own story about what she thinks is a case of developed 'fright sickness' (see Theory O), she underlines several times that she is active in seeking a solution to her own case and has done what can be done. When people have, according to other's perception done everything they can do in a case of sickness and the patient does not improve, gets worse or dies, they will state that 'God's will happened,' and, according to my field assistants 'this ends all further discussion.'

Her shift in treatment strategies is noteworthy, however. Medical doctors are not supposed to know anything about *zār* possession or to be able to do anything in cases of *zār*. Her shift of strategy clearly demonstrates that she opens up her world to other kinds of possible explanations than *zār*, even though she experienced relief during *zār* treatment in the past. She offers no rationalization or explanation for her change in treatment option. Obviously she takes for granted that the listeners will not expect it.

Such changes in strategy open up other possible diagnoses, hence other possible theories of etiology and another possible range of treatment options. This is a normal feature in stories people tell about their own sickness experiences or in such stories about relatives and friends. Sometimes they will state that additional knowledge or the appearance of additional symptoms made them change strategies. Usually, however, the change in treatment is not explained in any way.

Beja people seem to be involved in a life world where discussions almost never end, and where additional explanations nearly always seem possible. Such features are described as typical for nomadic societies (Lewis 1981; Storås 1996) and oral societies (Goody 1968, 1977; Ong 1990).

11.c. *I think he knew nothing.*

It is interesting that she does not elaborate at all on this theme, but finds it sufficient to only make this short statement. There is obviously a lot of tacit knowledge underlying this utterance. Since she does not expand on this theme, one might logically infer that she does not expect the listeners to demand it.

As has been shown earlier, most sicknesses that occur among Beja they themselves classify as traditional, non-modern, sicknesses. For most of these sicknesses traditional treatment is assumed to be more appropriate that modern biomedical treatment in hospitals or health centers (see Proposition LXXVI and Proposition LXXVII). Regarding *kosúlt*, for example, many people have told me that it is one of the most frequently occurring sicknesses, but 'doctors seem to know nothing about it.' Biomedical types of treatment might be less widespread and less recognized among Beja than reported in most other African societies.[49] Old stories are sometimes invoked to show the superiority of their own traditional healer, the *basīr*. Such mythical stories will be presented in Chapter 8.2.

12.a. *After that I became pregnant with my first son.*

12.b. *Then also this disturbance did not leave me.*

The birth of a child, especially a son, is an important and reportable event, the sort people relate when framing their narratives in time. Otherwise, as discussed earlier, the location of stories in time is not very important to Beja people.

12.c. *Then I secretly sold some of my gold so as to have treatment by fugarā', and I went to several fugarā', any fagīr, in Sinkat and Kassala.*

Her desperate situation once again made her follow her own plans without consulting her husband or other family members.

To show how desperate she felt her situation was, she stressed that she did not only go to several *fugarā'*, but to '*any fagīr*,' with stress and high intonation on 'any.' It is not unusual among Beja to try several specialists of the same kind. It might be that one of them is especially *héequal*, meaning both luck-bringing and holy, or that one of them has got special knowledge from God relevant to their case (see proposition LVI, theory L). The speed of change in strategies in Halima's case is however unusual, and fits into a broader picture of her as a woman who quickly changes her mind.

12d. *Also after this there were no successful results, and my situation became more complicated.*

She does not state in what way her situation became more complicated. This sentence both functions as a summarizing device and as a dramatic building up towards the latter part of the story.

13.a. *And one night I dreamt that a man with a spear was threatening me so as to give him my son and my gold.*

13.b. *And I forced my sister to wake up that night and give me my gold which I kept with her.*

13.c. *And she said to me: 'Why do you want this gold from me now in the middle of the night?'*

13.d. *And I answered: 'I want to wear it.'*

This is a very mysterious exerpt which is difficult to interpret as part of the overall story. Obviously, the dream was interpreted by her as a warning, since she woke up her sister in order to wear the gold on her body. But what about her son? Did she take any protective actions in order to make him safe? If she did, why does she not mention it when she tells about her act to secure her gold?

Her answer 'I want to wear it' is also a strange answer to the sister who wonders why Halima was in hurry to get her gold in the middle of the night. Clearly, this section represents a very open-ended part of the story with many unanswered questions on behalf of the listeners. There are at least two possible interpretations:

1. It could be that she was ashamed of her fright and did not want to tell her sister about it. For this reason she used the typical Beja woman's wish of wanting to wear gold and jewels as an excuse for waking her sister up.

But still this does not explain why she takes precautions about her gold but not her son. For this reason the other interpretation might be more plausible:

2. The *zār* spirit wants the gold, which is a typical *zār* wish (see Proposition L (part e), Theory J). It might inflict her son with illness if the mother does not fulfill her promise to make a *zār* party, but it is not interested in the son *per se*. When it makes Halima wear the gold close to her body, the spirit is pleased. This interpretation might explain why Halima tells this peculiar story within her overall narrative: this story underpins the *zār* diagnosis and is an instance of how this spirit works within her and takes command of her desires (see Proposition XLIX (part b.5), Theory J).

I think the second explanation most plausible. Hence, the reason why Halima did not explain to her sister that her wish for the gold stemmed from her *zār* spirit is that there was no need for it. Halima knew that she and her sister shared a common understanding regarding Halima's sickness. Moreover, as Beja women both of them shared common cultural models regarding how *zār* spirits manifest themselves. Every Beja knows, for example, that *zār* spirits generally appreciate gold. In other words, Halima did not explain anything to her sister simply because there was nothing to explain.

14.a. *And I bought animals, because I thought that my family ignored me and was not feeding me properly.*

She does not directly state that her family really ignored her, only that she at that time thought that they did not feed her properly. In other words, it is left for the listeners to make up their minds as to whether she really was badly treated or whether her thoughts had something to do with her sickness.

14.b. *And after that also my desire in food was less.*

14.c. *My family used to force me to eat.*

Those statements supports the second interpretation in line 14.a., that her sickness made her think she was badly treated and not given proper food.

14.d. *One guy, who is the husband of my sister, whom I respect, he used to force me to eat the food.*

14.e. *But he has a beard, and just to avoid seeing his beard, I used to take the dishes of food quickly from him.*

In a way, she sometimes portrays her own acts and thoughts as strange and unusual. This is particularly evident in the last passage. It seems that she both in this part 13 and 14 of the story keeps a distance to her own acts and thoughts, like saying 'under those conditions and with my sickness developed that far, I behaved thus and said such and such.' This might to some extent explain her unexpected sub-story in part 13, as given as an example to show how her life was dominated by her state of sickness. It might be reasonable, however, to think also in terms of her personality and the personality of the *zār* spirit, which both worked through her and were influencing her thoughts and behavior.

15. *And after that my family and relatives said to me: 'This is your* **zār** *and you have to fulfill your promise quickly and make a big* **zār** *party.*

Zār parties represent the most elaborated and complicated type of *zār* treatment. They usually go on for three days and up to a week. The way the party is organized depends on what spirits are involved, whether a British military commander from the colonial times, an Ethiopian prostitute or a hardworking woman from Western Sudan (see Proposition L (part e), Theory J). Halima gave Janike a brief account of what may be involved:

'There are several kinds of *zār*. My kind of *zār* is *khawāja zār*.' For this *zār* the equipment is trousers, shirt, necktie, cap, pipe and boots and a black stick.[50] Usually, when making *zār* for a person, the special clothes have to be saved till the death of that person. We believe that if the clothes are destroyed or lost, if she then gets sick, it might be because the clothes are lacking. In *khawāja zār* we use a special kind of drum rhythm, also special food, canned food, spoons, knives and forks. We use fruit, chairs, long tables, done the European way and we are also riding horses.'

Zār treatment may also be of a more simple kind, called *ṭayyāb*, Halima explains:

'In *ṭayyāb* they cut the neck of two animals, a black goat and any kind of animal. The black goat will get rid of spirits, and people will not eat it. The patient will wear a black *toob* and *sideriyya* and also a long, black Indian skirt. The other animal they will eat in a normal way, drink coffee, use *bakhūr* and perfume. If they want, they can have rice with black pepper and *girfa*.[51] After the party of *ṭayyāb* [done Tuesday or Wednesday, during the day], a week later they invite the patient for a meal containing *o'tám* with milk and butter oil, some friends of the patient are invited. After this, she takes a bath, and wears ordinary clothes [she has been wearing black for a week]. She must avoid leaving one room of her house for another week. Then she can, during the third week, move inside her house, but not out of it. After three weeks, the whole procedure of *ṭayyāb* is finished. *ṭayyāb* means 'to get a person well'.

Sometimes *ṭayyāb* is a preliminary stage for a big party of *zār*. If the patient does not get well, then they will make a big party. Halima herself recently took part in a *ṭayyāb* ceremony. She has been wearing black clothes for a week at the time of Janike and Aisha's visit.

If the patient promises to make a *zār* party and delays his or her promise, the sickness may get more severe or more complicated. Even children of the afflicted person may get sick.

16.a. *Then suddenly my sister [Saleimin] felt sick with a false pregnancy, and we took her to a* **fagīr** *from Samarai Diwab.*

16.b. *Then this* **fagīr** *said to my sister: 'If you promised to fulfill this* **zār** *party for your sister, you have to do it.'*

Sicknesses occur constantly under the harsh environmental conditions in the Red Sea Hills. The reason why the sickness of Saleimin is focused on in particular and made part of Halima's story, however, is evident from the evaluation of the *fagīr*: Saleimin promised to help Halima with arranging for a *zār* party, and since she delayed her promise, the spirit is afflicting her as well.

16.c. *Then he gave her* **mihaya**.

Treatment by *mihaya* belongs to popular Islamic discourse. Although the treatment of *zār* spirits does not belong to the same discourse, the *fagīr* obviously sees no contradiction in administering this treatment with Quranic verses for her sickness. Halima also makes no comments about the peculiar mixture of Islamic and non-Islamic traditions.

16.d. *Then also, after this, my sister was affected by a bleeding problem.*

16.e. *The* **fagīr** *said to me and my sister: 'You have to fulfill your promise.'*

It seems clear from what she says that they both went to the same *fagīr* again. The *fagīr* sees her problem as an additional symptom resulting from their delay in making the *zār* party. This time the *fagīr* speaks to both of them, seeing their different constellations of symptoms as part of the same overall problem involving the same etiology. Halima retells this in a matter-of-fact way, obviously perceiving this explanation as self-evident.

17.a. *And then we made preparations for the* **zār** *party, which included a cow, three sheep and one goat.*

17.b. *We also prepared kinds of sweets, vegetables like olives, raisins and canned food.*

This is typical preparation for a party which extends over one week. I attended another party in Dinayet which was much more modest economically. At that party two sheep were slaughtered. Even so, the costs of it was 90,000 SD, at that time equivalent to half the cost of a brand new Mercedes!

Lewis (1971, 1989) holds the position that *zār* is a 'marginal' cult involving politically marginalized groups of people in the societies in which it occurs. Among Beja this is at best a truth with modifications. Although women are more frequently seen as possessed by *zār*, men and children are often afflicted as well.[52] In addition, the costs of preparing for such parties pose a considerable economic strain on the relatives of the patients. In the cases I observed, virtually all relatives shared the costs. However, the closest relatives naturally made the biggest contribution. All this indicates that *zār* as a phenomenon has a wide acceptance among Beja in the Sinkat district and that most of them recognize the necessity of performing *zār* rituals.

17.c. *Then I bought a* **toob**, *an* **'imma**, *a* **gurbāb**, *a* **sidderiyya** *and also shoes.*

Several of these items are parts of men's clothes. In *zār* events the women typically dress in male clothes, perform male behaviors like smoking, drinking and leading prayers, and move around with rough, male movements. Typically, this reflects the gender of the spirit. The *zār* leader addresses the spirit directly rather than its female host. In *zār* parties I have observed, female patients are continuously addressed with masculine grammatical forms. That bonds between humans and spirits may have an erotic component is explicit in many Beja stories about spirit possession. In *zār* possession, however, the marriage bond between the spirit and its host is always pronounced, as accounted for by Proposition L, Theory J. The demands of the *zār* spirit, the way it afflicts its host and its jealousy and other emotional reactions all fit metaphorically nicely into a Beja model of a marriage.

17.d. *This was the preparation for a Moroccan party.*

17.e. *We also brought some chairs. Everything was for the first night of the party.*

17.f. *The second afternoon I was given Beja clothes like* **sirwāl,** **sidderiyya,** *comb and* **shayyeet.** *This* **zār** *is* **jubāli zār.**

17.g. *This proceeded until the third day, Sunday.*

The same celebration usually will address several kinds of spirits with different ethnic backgrounds, since the women present host many different spirits.

17.h. *Then there was no celebration on Monday.*

Mondays and Wednesdays are usually days off during *zār* celebrations in the Sudan. When I tried to ask people about the reason for this, they were only able to state that 'this is our tradition' and 'it is important to avoid *zār* parties on those days.'

17.i. *It went on Tuesday afternoon with a new uniform,* **kastāni.**

17.j. *We took Wednesday off, and on Thursday we first prepared for this banquet with a long table.*

17.k. *We took a sheep, filled it with rice and baked it.*

17.l. *Then they gave me a full suitcase which contained a shirt, trousers, a jacket, a necktie and a black stick, and they brought a horse to ride on.*

All the features described in line 17.j-l. reflect positions held by Beja about the customs of the colonial British: they baked stuffed sheep and sat down at long tables for celebrations. They used equipment like a necktie and walking sticks and rode horses. Arrangements like this make the *khawāja* spirit feel comfortable and at home.

Halima's *zār* spirit is a male spirit demanding male clothes and equipment used by former British colonials. This is very typical in *zār* stories,[53] where the sex of the spirit is usually different from the sex of the host. Female hosts then typically act out very masculine behavior, like rough movements in the ritual dances, dominance displays, smoking in front of men (an inconceivable act in other Sudanese settings) and taking roles of leadership, like leading an imitated Muslim prayer.

17.m. *This* **zār** *is* **khawāja zār, injilīzi**

The term 'khawāja' is commonly used by Sudanese to denote all white foreigners. In *zār*, however, the word is often used

239

synonymically with British people, sometimes limited to British people during colonial times.

18. *After this I recovered*.

After addressing her kind of *zār*, the *khawāja zār*, she finally recovers. She does not have to explain this point or to account extensively for it, since it is culturally well established that once the wishes and needs of the *zār* spirit are met, its host will recover (see Proposition L (part g), Theory J). The *zār* party got the most detailed and extended description in the narrative. Although several spirits are addressed during this ceremony, the most detailed description is reserved for the *khawāja* part of it. This reflects clearly that her later conception of what her problem really was, makes a great impact on how the story is constructed.

19. *At first my husband refused parties of *zār*, but after that he himself became possessed and made seven parties of *zār**.

This is a triumphant end to her story, making a strong claim for *zār* as a possible explanation for occurrence of sickness. Instead of showing how a line of argument might persuade others, she gives a prime example of the *zār* spirit world that existed for her and also impinged on her husband until he was persuaded of its presence. It is a kind of conversion story constituting the end of her powerful personal narrative.

8.1.5. Cultural theories and the presentation of self in Halima's story

Halima's story is very much a story about possession. Another 'self,' the 'self' of the spirit, expresses its wishes through her, influencing her behavior, the choices she makes, and her mobilization of her social network. A key feature of *zār* spirits is that they will remain forever in their hosts. For Halima this means that she will have to live forever with a European spirit inside her, a spirit with aspirations, inclinations and dispositions different from those of ordinary Beja people. In other words, she can never, by any means, separate herself from the spirit and she is also forced to meet the wishes and needs of the spirit in order to stay healthy.

All the same, this is not only a story about possession; it is a strong self presentation as well. Halima is presenting herself as a person with a strong will, decisive and even stubborn in pursuing goals which she thinks are important for her. At the same

240

time as she rids herself of responsibility for actions like isolating herself from people at culturally inappropriate times, she also gives accounts of how she manages to act economically independent in situations where women are supposed to be strictly subordinated to decisions made by the husband and close male relatives. And, not least, she wins a final victory at the end of her story by convincing her skeptical husband about the utility of *zār* parties, and in addition to that, makes him arrange for *zār* parties himself.

However, is there a real contradiction here between describing oneself as subjugated to the wishes of a powerful and unpredictable alien spirit and at the same time as a strong character successful in mobilizing social relationships in an appropriate Beja way? I think the discussion of three general points is necessary in order to answer this question.

Firstly, in *zār* rituals, as already pointed out, women typically display behavior which is strictly reserved for men. In societies like the Beja society women are officially subjected to the wills and supervision of their husbands and close male relatives like fathers, brothers and sons. For women in such societies, they may be said to face what Boddy (1988) calls 'the cultural overdetermination of women's selfhood,' an 'over determination' which finds its physical expression through the Pharaonic circumcision, an operation which nearly all Beja women have experienced.

In Beja society, like other Islamic societies, *zār* rituals provide occasions for alternate discourses contrasted to the discourses pursued in male dominated areas like the mosques or *khalwas*.[54] Although such 'cults of affliction' seldom give rise to active opposition to dominant views and the people holding them (see, e.g. Lewis 1971, 1986, 1989), they may provide occasions for alternate discourses in which Beja women can contribute in defining their own selfhood.

By performing typically male acts and displays, women are able to define themselves and their roles relative to men. By acting out the male identity of their spirits, they are at the same time making it clear how their own roles and identities differ from those of men and how they are intertwined in relationships with them where men dominate them in different ways. In other words, their male spirits constitute a kind of mirror through

241

which the women may look at themselves, making explicit the ways their lives differ from lives of men.

Secondly, since the spirits often have a different ethnic identity from the host, the *zār* spirits provide a background for perceiving how Beja women and their situation may look in the view of people from other ethnic groups. If, for example, the spirit happens to be a female spirit, she is typically very different from Beja women. She may be from Western Sudan, where the women are much more economically independent and, even when married, tend to cultivate their own plot for which they themselves are economically responsible. When a host is possessed by a female spirit from Western Sudan, she displays rough movements as if working very hard cultivating land.

Thirdly, the *zār* spirits are demanding spirits, demanding expensive perfumes, clothes and jewels. Since meeting their demands is important for the health and well-being of the host, the possession provides the host with powerful influence over male relatives.

Halima is possessed by a male high-ranking British colonial officer.[55] This *zār* spirit gives her the opportunity for self expression and self reflection which she cannot find in any other situations her culture provides her. In addition, being dominated by her spirit gives her unique opportunities for adapting to her husband and relatives in non-standard ways without threatening the overall system of power relations. Indeed, this is a culturally correct way of escaping the seemingly severe constraints on power of women as well as escaping their self-hood being exclusively prescribed by men.

Halima is using the cultural resources at hand creatively. She, at several points in the story, presents an unclear picture of whether she is talking about her own wishes and inclinations or these of her *zār* spirit. But, as may now seem plausible, this is, in some respects, what *zār* is about. She is perceived by herself, her relatives and healers she encountered as 'married'[56] to the *zār* spirit and behaves in culturally appropriate ways given this situation. This is precisely what gives her additional opportunities for self expression and for being in position to influence social relationships in ways which would otherwise not be possible for her.

Halima is successful in relating to the spirit and to her relatives at the same time. She is also successful in creating a coherent narrative which is open-ended and suggestive enough for other people to put their own experiences into it and to make use of their own tacit knowledge, their own cultural resources, in order to understand her story. The story is open-ended enough for others to pose questions or make remarks, so it facilitates others taking part in her story performance. Her version of her sickness story has become well recognized by her relatives, and thus provides her a reputation and opportunities for pursuing further goals through arranging *zār* ceremonies for other people. Her 'self' as presented in the story is not a disintegrated self, crippled and disempowered, making her socially marginal as a Beja woman. On the contrary, it may be plausible to say that her involvement in *zār* cults makes her as powerful and capable of self expressions as her culture allows her to, and these self expressions are conveyed to others by narrative means. As Miller *et al.* (1990) notes:

'Because personal storytelling is characterized by a unique three-way intersection of self, narrative, and face-to-face interaction, it provides an optimal site for exploring processes of self-construction' (p.305).

Halima's narrative does not suggest in any way whether Halima really experienced the spirit within her or whether she now and then experiences states of trance where she feels her behavior is temporarily under the full control of the spirit. Unfortunately I was not present in the field any of the times that she was the focus of attention in a *zār* ceremony. Last time I left the field she was about to raise money for a ceremony. I have been present at several other ceremonies, however, including one held for a close relative of Halima who lives in her neighborhood. Typically in such ceremonies the patient and other *zār* adherents present get into states of trance. They get beaten with a leather whip by the *sheikh* or other people present without experiencing pain. I have observed people in *zār* trances banging their heads against a concrete wall, and telling me afterwards that they did not feel any pain.

Nonetheless, there are still clear limits on what behavior women in trance are allowed to exhibit. They are, as Muslim women, never allowed to show their hair or body parts like naked shoulders. During their violent movements, however, their veils may occasionally fall off, in which case other women immediately help to put them into place again. It happens also that a woman loses her veil, corrects it herself, and then continues in being whipped without showing any signs of pain.[57]

So the cultural shaping of trance expressions is, I think, unquestionable. However, it works both ways: once in Khartoum I was present at a *zār* ceremony where an elderly woman started crying violently to such a degree that other participants were disturbed and felt ill at ease. She made very violent movements, and after a while the *sheikha* diagnosed her as possessed by a Hadandowa Beja spirit. They are conceived of, by other Sudanese, as being especially 'wild' and warlike. After getting the diagnosis, the woman started to herd imagined animals with a whip with violent movements, consistent with the belief that a male Hadandowa (women do not herd) possessed her. In other words, the unexpected behavior of the woman was diagnosed in a way which was culturally acceptable, and the woman herself channeled her outburst according to the expectations of people present.

As pointed out in my discussion, it seems that the cult of *zār* is not a cult of psychologically disturbed people or socially marginalized people. On the contrary, it seems that people in Khartoum and the Red Sea Hills are able to distinguish people whom they simply consider 'mad' and people possessed by *zār*. As the example of the possessed by the Hadandowa spirit above indicates, however, *zār* culture even seems to have the flexibility of coping with unexpected behavior and possibly psychologically disturbed patients by defining and channeling the sickness in a culturally appropriate way.

As may be clear, the extent to which possession is a psychological reality for patients of *zār*, is a very complicated question. At the very least, it seems like it does not *have to* be. All the same, from an outsider's point of view there seems to be a lot to gain for women[58] engaging in such cults:

1. They have the opportunity to express themselves in ways which are not possible in any other setting.
2. They may achieve considerable material gain through relatives collecting for new items like clothes, jewels, perfume etc. which is 'demanded by the spirit.'
3. They may, at least temporarily, achieve relief from their responsibilities for family members.

4. The occasions of *zār* ceremonies give them opportunities for self reflexivity, for defining themselves in opposition to others, and get approval from other women of their ways of defining themselves.

5. They may sometimes experience real relief from their physical and/or psychological complaints.

However convincing such functionalistic or utilitarian points may seem, I want to be careful with stating them in a dogmatic way. Depending on the aims of analysis, one might attribute a lot of contradictory 'functions' of *zār* ceremonies in the Sudan serving one's own research interests and aims. The fact that not only women, but also men and even children may become sick by *zār* in the Red Sea Hills should lead the researcher to be careful in creating and presenting neat pictures which seemingly present holistic data.

What I feel more confident about, however, is what more clearly is present in Halima's story: her self presentation is strengthened, not weakened, by her accounting for the *zār* spirit within her and how this spirit influences her thoughts, feelings and inclinations as well as her relationships with significant others. Her presentation of the *zār* spirit as part of her story helps us as an audience to get a clearer picture of who Halima is and some of her ways of exploring the possibilities for her as a Beja woman to express herself as an individual within a culture which seemingly insist women act within so many limitations and constraints.

8.1.6. Conclusion

In this section it has been demonstrated how physical and psychological complaints may be rendered both understandable and meaningful by implicitly invoking Beja cultural knowledge by narrative means. The flexibility of such a personal narrative renders it possible for the audience to fill in various cultural schemata in each of its 'open slots.' This means that the narrator adapts to real-life problems in a flexible way which makes explanation possible, although the theories which are invoked are inflexible in their inherent logic and structure.

The analysis of Amna's story has demonstrated that Beja narration is a powerful means for mobilization of relevant cultural knowledge in real-life situations. By narrative means Amna has made her complaints culturally understandable and acceptable. Moreover, her way of narrating her experiences of suffering has proved helpful for managing a positive identity as a Beja woman.

In the next section of this chapter, stories of severe child sickness and death of children will be presented. The pragmatics of narration will still be the main concern. Like for Amna's story I will look at how parents and close relatives of the sick or deceased children present condensed stories where vast areas of knowledge may be flexibly 'filled in.' In addition I will take a closer look at how the use of language expressions in the narratives facilitates their 'open-ended' character and makes them apt as means for engaging the audience in discussions. I argue that the flexibility of the narrated texts with regard to their interpretation serves as a means of engaging the audience in the cultural process of making traumatic experiences like child death culturally meaningful.

8.2. THE POLITICS OF LANGUAGE AND THE STRATEGY OF OPEN-ENDEDNESS

8.2.1. Introduction

In this section I will largely focus on how rural Beja people relate to severe sickness and sudden death in small children. Personal narratives about the mystical sickness of *tesérimt* will be the main material for discussion, although I will touch upon spirit affliction as well. In addition to showing how the many 'open slots' in the stories contributes to their flexibility as means of interpreting real-life problems, I will, as already mentioned, also demonstrate how use of a special linguistic style may contribute to the 'open-ended' character of the narratives. The analysis of the pragmatics of narration will, in other words, be extended to cover a broader range of pragmatic means. A comparative perspective on such traits in Beja narration will be provided by presenting some cross-cultural findings in narrative studies.

The Hadandowa experience of the particular childhood sickness of *tesérimt* can be seen as interwoven in a larger web of meaning and in other fields of experience related to their historical, social, economic and ecological setting. I will argue that this mode of analysis can be achieved by looking at how they create stories about themselves and their family members and how they invoke and retell older stories. I want to give some possible explanations as to how the characteristics of narration mentioned above may make an instance of sickness meaningful by Beja narrators drawing upon different and sometimes conflicting cultural models. In other words, I will focus on how storytelling renders particular instances of sickness meaningful rather than look at sickness categorization *per se*, which would be part of a much more complex discussion.

Beja people translate past experiences into expectations about the future. Their expectations about the future color their view of the past as they present the past in personal narratives. I hold it plausible that such ways of narrating contribute to creating a sense of continuity in people living in a rapidly changing world like the Beja do.

Storytelling and story creating is perhaps the most genuinely human of all projects in which human beings involve themselves. Narratives, as part of conversation, are available to children early in childhood and these stories make a huge impact on later personal development in every culture and play an important role in socialization (Bruner 1990; Miller and Moore 1989; Miller *et al.* 1990). My own children have been engaged in telling stories, primarily about themselves, since they learned to make simple sentences. Bedtime is a very intense story-producing phase. A typical story from our eldest daughter, Sofie (5), after she had been put to bed one day, went like this: 'Today I drew the day (she pulled off a piece of paper from the calendar with the actual date, as if 'drawing lots') in the kindergarten. Lisa wanted to, but Aunt Sigrid did not allow her. I drew it, and afterwards we went out and looked at some chickens [they made a visit to a nearby farm]. When I am big, and I have a girl [baby], I can decide what she shall do. I can decide what I can do, also. This is true, isn't it, papa?' Then she went on talking about what sort of games she played with other children. One important dimension of narration is present in her story: her thoughts about future [when I am big] throws light upon her past experience of her day in kindergarten, at the same time as the act of 'drawing the day' points to increased autonomy in the future, and thereby shapes her experience 'here and now.' A sense of continuity of self and of experiences is shaped by projecting the past into the future. This prominent feature of telling stories, which will be the main theme of this outline, is evident in many Beja stories about sickness and health as well.

8.2.2. A comparative point

As a point of departure I will present a few general theoretical points based on cross-cultural research on narration which may explain how narration functions as a device for negotiation and pragmatism in situations where people try to link cultural resources to the solution of a perceived problem and at the same time manage to maintain their own sense of cultural identity and cultural continuity. This is based, of course, on an *a priori* assumption that people really are trying to maintain a sense of continuity of self and society through storytelling. However, a wealth of studies of narration do lend support to such an assumption (Bruner 1990).

This general insight drawn from worldwide studies of narration will supply the basis for more substantial discussions about relevant features in Hadandowa storytelling. I will argue that what gives the Hadandowa way of narrating its special character is not primarily that it has features other than these reported from cross-cultural studies or lacks any of them. Instead, I suggest, the Beja narrative style places special emphasis on some of these particular features.

My aim here in focusing on the style of narration in relation to sickness stories is to detect some ways in which Hadandowa people engage in a meaning-making project in their narration. For this reason, I will focus more on questions related to 'why me, why us, why now?' than how possible explanations relate to a 'factual' world, whether the 'social world' at large or the so-called 'clinical reality' specifically. On a larger scale, I will discuss how sickness episodes offer opportunity for a discourse about much more than sickness *per se*.

8.2.3. Stories of *tesérimt* and the intrusion of evil

Cross-disciplinary studies of narratives worldwide has as yet a rather short history. Many important descriptions from recent studies, like the inherent sequentiality of events composing the plot of the story (Bruner 1990, Good 1994), and, related to this plot, what Bruner (op.cit., following Burke) calls the 'pentad of an Actor, an Action, a Goal, a Scene, and an Instrument – plus trouble,' might beneficially be drawn into my discussion of sickness narratives. For the clarity of my argument, however, I will discuss only a few relevant traits and functions of storytelling, leaving out many important cross-cultural findings. I will mainly be concerned with different aspects of what I call *irrealis* or 'uncertainty makers.'

As a point of departure I want to look at a story concerning the sickness of *tesérimt*. This case shows how people in a small nomadic settlement present a new skin sickness attacking small children as well as some adults. This case history provides an entry into this field of investigation.

'*One day my interpreter and I stayed in a camp in Herétri, quite far away from the urban center of Sinkat. The inhabitants very seldom receive visitors from outside, since they have no road connections with any other settlements. It is sometimes visited by Red Crescent staff, who once made a hut called a **khalwa**[59] in the middle of the settlement for the Islamic education of women.*

*After reaching the **khalwa**, we saw some women gathered together inside. Since I am a man, I had to wait outside for a while until my interpreter told me that they accepted my entrance. After a while some of their husbands arrived, and we started to ask about their situation in general, leading into questions about the health of their children. They told me that some of their children, and even some adult children, have a terrible sickness for which there seems to be no cure. They added that they were afraid to speak about the sickness. Quite typically they thought that mere talk might cause them to get the sickness.*

*When my interpreter told them that I was a health worker and that I was collaborating with Red Crescent and Red Cross, they brought a child to me so that I could see the skin marks and give some advice. The marks looked circular with a slight depression, and some waterpapillons around some of their borders. They described to me that "the sickness always starts with rashes filled with water, which were emptied and then black, after this the skin gets discolored around this black center." When we asked them about the treatment they had tried to seek, they told us that "we have tried everything, and now we are very tired of trying one thing after another without any help. Our own **fugará**[60] and* *busarā'*[61] *do not know themselves . . . they are trying and trying just like we do."*

They first went to *fugarā'* who were unable to do anything. *Busarā'* supplied them with different kinds of medicines. The most important of these was *dérwout*, which can be either a herbal mixture or part of a mashed duodenum of a cow. This *dérwout* is believed to be helpful against the sickness of *tesérimt* resulting from a mystical bad influence stemming from meat, milk or butter from animals from other tribes.

The people themselves seemed to believe that such a mystical influence from the outside was the most probable. For this reason I asked them what particular influence they were afraid of, and they told me that "this sickness is new, the first time we encountered it was two years ago. We think it might stem from the vegetable oil we got in the last relief distribution. Perhaps you will know a medicine for this sickness . . ." I had heard several times before that many Hadandowa people were skeptical about the oil and said that it had a smell of fish.[62] Fish is not considered food for humans at all by Hadandowa pastoralists. I asked them if the oil has a smell of fish, and they answered "no, it smells like locusts."

When we tried to ask them more about what kind of treatment the different healers had prescribed, they were unwilling to say more than that they got some *dérwout* from the *busarā'*. What this *dérwout* consisted of, "only the *busarā'* know." – We do not like to talk about it, not even now . . . Previously our local *busarā'* were able to help us with everything. They were even more clever than doctors.

To underpin this last point, they told us the following story about the cleverness of one of their local *busarā'* during the colonial times: 'Once a lizard managed to go inside a head of a person and sitting on his brain and clung to it. – We do not know how it entered, only God knows. When doctors tried to do operations on him, they were not able to do so, because it clung so strongly to the brain that they could not remove it without removing part of the brain. Because the English people of that time knew that the Hamdab were very experienced people, they asked for them. A Hamdab person came, and he brought three things: a piece of fire [metal heated in fire], a piece of cotton with butter and a metal tool to hold the heated piece of metal. First he took the heated material and moved it near the brain after the doctor opened the skull, and he then put the metal closer and *closer to the lizard. It retracted its legs, and he applied cotton under them one by one, repeating the procedure four times for each leg. After this it was easy to remove the lizard, because it could not manage to cling to the brain any longer. Sometimes the Yudia people[63] know even more than the doctors.*

After we chatted with the people for a while, asking general questions concerning native diagnoses, they asked me to go to a hut where a small baby had the same skin lesions, but on the palms, under the feet and around the mouth. The mother told me that "we have tried every traditional treatment. In addition, we have tried some Tetracycline-powder directly on the wounds with some improvement." People said to me that "we are sure that there are many other incidents. We do not know how many because people do not speak about it." I asked, 'Because they are afraid of getting it themselves?' "Yes, they are afraid because they do not know the reason for it."

When back in Sinkat, I asked some health workers about the cases, and they told me that recently syphilis has been introduced into the area and several cases has been reported. I asked the medical doctor in Sinkat about the symptoms, and he confirmed that at least the case with lesions in the palms and under the feet certainly must be syphilis.[64] He had himself never visited any rural areas because, as he conceives it, his car is not a proper car for such trips into the wilderness.'

This case is somewhat complicated because it contains both a full mythical story (which will be analyzed line by line in section 8.3. of this chapter) and bits and pieces of personal stories, interrupted by me and other people present. How are we to grasp the cultural meaning and social situatedness of such a complicated meeting? The presentations given to us contain so many subjunctive[65] elements with so many possible interpretations. The presentations are subjunctive in several ways. First of all, people are reckoning with a mystical influence. Secondly, the character of this mystical influence is not absolutely fixed in the minds of people. It might be *junūn*, the probable reason why they first went to the *fagīr*. It might be supernatural influences from food of strange animals, the reason why they went to *busarā'* for *dérwout*. Thirdly, this influence might have something to do with recent material and social changes, changes of which they do not know the consequences. This may be why they wanted me and

251

the Red Crescent members to give them biomedical advice to cope with this new sickness. In other words, if the sickness was transferred to them from the Western world, it can only be cured by Western medicines.

8.2.4. Narratives as negotiation

The subjunctive characteristics of their presentation are typical elements in all the stories people told about their own sicknesses or misfortunes[66] or from stories about others' experience, some of them retellings of stories I had heard before. I will contend that such elements are necessary traits of all stories, whether told by adults or small children: they represent perhaps the most fundamental way humans involve themselves in social inter-action with others.

The folk model of a story in Western societies is a story pre-sented wholly and uninterrupted by a narrator to a reader or a listener. The story, whether written or oral, is seen as shaped only by the narrator. I suggest that a story, when verbally presented, is a more complex affair. First of all, a story told is most often interrupted several times by listeners. In this respect the case study above is somewhat simplified, since much of what is told represents bits and pieces of personal stories interrupted by ques-tions from me, my field assistant and several other people sitting around. For instance, when one person vaguely talked about a mystical influence similar to *tesérimt*, she mentioned several pos-sible food items, but without specifying what kind of new element could have caused the new skin sickness. When I and others asked about the particular new intrusion she was afraid of, she began to talk about the relief oil from abroad. In answering this, she added a new subjunctive opening: since the sickness probably stems from abroad, perhaps I, as a foreigner, am in a position to find a cure.

Evelyn Early observed from her fieldwork among working-class women in Cairo that a story often was interrupted after only three or four sentences by other listening women (Early 1985). They play an active part by questioning 'what really hap-pened' or whether the characters' behavior in the story was morally acceptable or not. The listeners may offer alternative interpretations (Gaik, in Duranti & Goodwin 1992) from the narrator or may add elements of personal experience (Early 1985). They may also urge the narrator to expand on certain details. In addition, as an obvious fact, the narrator will present the story with the listeners and the immediate context in mind.

8.2.5. Subjunctive stories, *irrealis* and possible worlds

Most often the narrator will be part of the story, and sometimes it may be his or her explicit goal to elicit support for a certain kind of behavior or the choice of a certain solution (Berentzen, in Grønhaug *et al.* 1991). Sometimes listeners are openly requested to comment on a certain act, but more often stories contain 'built in' devices encouraging conversation between narrator and listeners. Such devices could be expressions like 'it could be that . . ., but it seems to me that . . .' or 'it is unbelievable, but . . .,' or it could be words like 'possible,' 'probable,' 'if' etc.

Such words and expressions are called *irrealis* within science of literature (Lyons 1977, Quirk *et al.* 1972). These words do not imply people's judgment of what is likely to happen. They only point to possibilities and open up what Gaik (see Duranti & Goodwin 1992) in his analysis of 'clinical conversations' between psychiatrists and patients calls 'possible worlds' (see, e.g. on philosophy: Elster 1978; on linguistics and science of literature: Lewis 1973). Initially in such conversations the patient is encouraged to present a personal story about his or her problems, while the psychiatrist interrupts with sentences like '**Do you think** this is your real problem?' or 'It **seems to me** that your relationship with your mother is quite strained . . .' After this collaborative phase, the psychiatrist changes his strategy in what Gaik calls 'the therapeutic part' of the conversation and goes on telling the patient in an authoritative way what he perceived the problems to be and how they should be solved. In this last section, after gaining the confidence of the patient, he could not afford to open up for 'possible worlds,' otherwise the patient would lose faith in his professional abilities as a therapist with a therapeutic solution.

The American psychologist Jerome Bruner (1990) makes it a general point that the subjunctivity of personal narratives makes it easier for others to enter into them and to identify with them. Typically narrators employ 'subjunctivizing transformations' which are 'lexical and grammatical usages that highlight subjective states, attenuating circumstances, alternative possibilities' (p.53). Byron Good makes similar inferences based on studies of narratives of epilepsy in Turkey (Good 1994).

In the stories of Beja parents and Beja people in general, people never totally leave the subjunctive phase of their discussions. Even in meetings between healers and patients I observed, the talk of the healer was seldom authoritative. The story of Saleimin, a rural woman who gave birth to seven children and lost six of them, shows this point:

> 'Also, once upon a time, I delivered a girl. And fourteen days after the delivery, it seemed to me a black ghost passed by us. In the morning after that night I woke up with the neck of my child quite stiff. I took this baby to several *fugarā*, who gave **mihaya**, but unfortunately with no successful result. And the girl lived for 3 years in this position without walking, speaking or having sufficient food. And, also I myself did not have sufficient food in those years because of this. And afterwards I took my baby to a *fagīr* in Sa'átim. He gave her **mihaya** and said: 'It might be this **mihaya** treats the girl, and it might be not. I will try, and if your girl recovers, I will ask you for a lot of money. The result of this treatment should appear after one week.' But, unfortunately, after use of this **mihaya** for three days, the girl passed away. People said that it might be that **alíib** killed her.'

In this story the healer, the *fagīr*, states that he is not sure whether his cure will help or not. The story is full of other uncertain elements as well: it **may be** that a black ghost passed by. If it passed by, it **may be** that it caused the sickness. After the death, some people thought that **perhaps** *alíib* killed her. *Alíib* often involves symptoms like thinness and paralysis. It is conceived of as resulting from 'fright sickness' (see Proposition LXVI, Theory O). The fright may be caused by sudden strange sounds, animals or spirits (see Proposition LXIV, Theory O), and the primary symptom is ceaseless crying (see Proposition L, Theory J). In other words, if a black ghost passed by the child, it most probably caused fright in the child, causing sickness in the child which, if not treated, could lead on to the more serious sickness of *alíib*, which in turn might cause death (see Proposition LXVI (part f), Theory O).

In many cultures this openness of stories seems to be a most prominent feature (Bruner 1990). The telling of a personal story usually is a cooperative project. This is no less the case when people in the Red Sea Hills tell stories about sickness in their children, where so much is at stake for the parents. Since the fertility rate is comparatively low in nomadic populations,[67] and since the mortality rate is rather high in the drought-ridden Eastern Sudan, it is reasonable to assume that people have quite an acute preoccupation with the health of children.

Every story I heard about personal sickness and their children's sicknesses is filled with subjunctivizing elements like 'may be,' 'if . . . then' and 'probably' in addition to expressions like 'it might be something from Allah,' 'it might have to do with *hamashragadíd* (meaning unseen creatures), 'if this (remedy) does not help, it might be something else' (another sickness) and 'hopefully Allah will grant health.' These subjunctive elements were present regardless of whether the story told was about present or past conditions.

The telling of Beja sickness stories seems to me to be a typical creative project where the narrator and listeners create the story together. In the present case, for example, where people knew that both my interpreter and I were health workers, the narrators of the story added new subjunctive elements to the story like the apparently underlying proposition that *if* the sickness comes from the outside world, then outsiders might be in a position to offer the cure.

In the case presented regarding *tesérimt*, people tell that *fugará*, *busará* and biomedical staff have been consulted, in addition to their own efforts and home remedies. This is consistent with what I generally found for the Red Sea Hills, which supports the view of Boddy (1988, 1989), that people are quite eclectic with regard to what kind of specialist they seek for treatment. And, very often they do not go to a specialist before they themselves have tried out a lot of home remedies, supporting the view of Kleinman (1980) that in every society most treatment is practiced at home by parents, relatives, neighbors and friends. In addition, at the level of lay-persons it is quite clear that people do not share completely the paradigms of any one specialist (Good 1994, Kleinman 1980, Nichter 1989). In many cases, what the specialist prescribes as a treatment is not the treatment the patient gets. It often happens, for example, that when a biomedical practitioner prescribes Aspirin to a child with a chronic headache, the mother will burn the Aspirin and let the child inhale the smoke under her *toob*. The opening up for possible worlds in stories finds its practical counterpart in people's health-seeking career where they involve healers from different traditions in the same instance of sickness, as demonstrated for the case studies in Chapter 7.

8.2.6. Giving meaning to sickness and death of children

Many writers have stressed one pronounced cultural dimension among Bejas in general: their resistance to any kind of social, cultural or economic change (see, e.g. Bonsaksen 1991, Paul 1954, Trimingham 1949, Vågenes 1990, 1995). This is especially the case among the Hadandowa people, who throughout recorded history have offered strong resistance to such change, often with violent means. When I once went through old literature describing native medical practice among Hadandowa, I was struck by the similarities between practices I myself encountered and the ones described up to 200 years ago.

Social and economic changes are, however, occurring more and more frequently among the present-day Beja (Bonsaksen 1991, 1993; Vågenes 1990; see also Chapter 3). Nevertheless, as will be discussed for *tesérimt*, recent changes, like changes in sickness occurrences and food items, tend to be interpreted within a traditional cultural framework.

Hadandowa Beja people have kept a strict distance from surrounding groups like the Beni Amer. The Beni Amer are to some extent social and culturally different from other Bejas and many of them speak a totally different language as mother tongue. Hence, those differences have been kept alive in spite of the Hadandowa and Beni Amer being territorially close neighbors. Sometimes animals or animal products which stem from Beni Amer are distributed among Hadandowa, in which case people often will relate the sickness of *tesérimt* to these 'strange' animals.

As discussed in Chapter 4, *tesérimt* is a sickness of the unborn child. The pregnant woman will feel pain in her stomach and sometimes have bleeding. In the worst cases this will lead to miscarriage or death a short time after birth. If not, the child will remain very weak for a long time and be covered by particular skin marks and sores. Most people I interviewed in a more extensive mapping project were very aware of this possibility, and most of them tried to prevent the onset of such a sickness by getting the special medicine of *dérwout* from *busarǎ*. As discussed in Chapter 6, this medicine should be given to the mother in the first, third, fifth and seventh month of pregnancy and immediately after the birth to both mother and child.

Before arriving at the camp of Heretri I heard that a camel recently died. People were mostly happy about this, since they considered the animal a cause of *tesérimt*. They told me that even if a pregnant woman crossed the trail of that camel, she could get the sickness. But still other large animals in the area are thought of as capable of causing *tesérimt*.

In any Beja *diwáb* people are afraid of all kinds of intrusion or any kind of change stemming from outside. As I have already discussed, this fact is related to several different cultural and social factors. When my interpreter and I arrived in the camp in Heretri, people took great pains to prevent their children from getting into close physical contact with us. If we tried to smile at any of them, they showed obvious fear.

In the present situation where sudden changes have made a huge impact even in remote places like Heretri, people seem to be aware of new possibilities of influences causing sickness in their children. From my initial story, we get the idea that both their perceived causes and categories might be very flexible. The new skin sickness was, after a lot of failed healing attempts, conceived of as probably stemming from relief engagement in general and relief oil in particular. At the present time they therefore try to give sick children *dérwout*. But this choice of treatment clearly shows that the old category of *tesérimt* had taken on a new meaning for them, opening up the possibility of mystical substance mediated contagious influence through Western relief food. Also, the skin symptoms have, in some respects, a different appearance than the ones usually attributed to *tesérimt*. Because of this, the possibility that a new type of Western *dérwout* was necessary to cure the sickness was recognized.

In other words, the content of the category of *tesérimt* seems to be subject to the broader and more extensive cultural models accounted for in Theory L. I learned, through asking about particular sickness cases in a small village (near Heretri), that on average one child in every household died of what people conceived of as *tesérimt*. The symptoms described in each case varied; sometimes people stressed particular skin lesions as characteristic and maintained that this symptom always occurred when a child is sick from *tesérimt*. Others mentioned different symptoms like crying without stopping or a distended stomach, in addition to skin lesions.

In several cases people thought the sickness was transferred to the child through the mother, mostly before birth. The mother herself will usually experience no sickness, although sometimes she will sporadically feel a pain in her stomach. The *dérwout*, which is both treatment and prophylaxis, always contained powder of a stone called *adal óot* (see Proposition LVI (part e), Theory L). As mentioned earlier, people get this stone from a particular 'red' mountain, one of two such mountains in the whole area. Some people make a sacrifice of a sheep or goat when digging out stones and smear the blood on the place from which they dig. In addition, as earlier discussed, it contains butter oil from animal milk[68] and a herb, or sometimes, part of a cow's duodenum.

It might be revealing to look at different contexts in which this *'dal óot* is used: it is smeared together with animal milk on camels during a 'camel festival' once a year. This is done to increase the fertility of the camel and to protect it against sicknesses. It is ritually smeared on the bed, door frame and door of the house of a newlywed couple. This is to ensure the happiness and fertility of the couple. *'dal óot* is not only used against *tesérimt*, but against many other sicknesses as well.

When trying to look at the causal explanations people gave in several actual sickness cases perceived of as *tesérimt*, a different explanation turned out to be dominant. As discussed earlier, if a camel turns out to be infertile or its offspring die a short time after birth, people may make special cuttings in its ears and let it move freely around in the terrain for some time. This camel is then considered *héequal*. Unfortunately, as explained previously, this camel is a danger to pregnant women, except women from the household which has ownership of the camel. Even the visit of an owner of such a camel might lead to miscarriage or giving birth to a sick child, which the following story reflects, told by a woman in her sixties:

'One time I was pregnant and one person who had this kind of camels came and stayed with us overnight as a guest. Then, the

next day he came to me to say "hello." And before he reached his
sleeping place, I felt fever and coldness. My family gave me this
*treatment for **tesérimt** and butter oil, and in that night I delivered*
a boy. He cried and cried, and also his stomach was full by air,
and immediately he died.'

Yet another old woman, who lives alone without any living
children, told a similar story:

'Once I had a baby, a boy, with Ahmad Musa. The boy died two
days after birth. In the second day of his life we made a camel
race for him to celebrate his birth. Then a man came with a
t'héelat[69] camel. This man ran towards our house with his camel,
*and when he reached our house, the child got affected by **tesérimt**.*
*We gave him a herb for **tesérimt**, but all the same he died. After*
this I never bore a child again. Problems arose between me and
my husband, and he divorced me.'

This *tesérimt*, as discussed in Chapter 6, sometimes represents an
intrusion of dangerous influence from outside the settlement. In
other cases it turns out to be conceived of as part of a problem
inside the settlement. Several people spoke to me about how
recent droughts and threats to the fertility of people, animals
and crops are results of God's punishment for people having
evil thoughts against each other. By offering *karāma*, involving
animal blood, or an apparent equivalent, the red stone of *adal*
óot, fertility might be regained. The cutting of the ears of the
infertile camel is, according to informants, conceived of as a
mark showing that the camel 'belongs to God' and is *héequal*.
But, unfortunately, the 'holy' and 'luck-bringing' camel is
bringing luck and fortune only to its owner, while its holiness
poses dangers to others. *Tesémint* turns out to be part of a cultural
discourse about fertility, in which two different cultural models
or schemata seem to be invoked, the first one presented as Proposition LVI, part of the general Theory L:

['1. *Héequal*-ness in humans or animals brings good luck, health
and fertility. 2. However, invisible influences from *héequal*
animals or products of animals may decrease fertility in humans
and cause sicknesses which threaten the fertility of humans. 3.
The *héequal* promoting red *adal óot* stone, butter oil and some
herbs may counteract those detrimental effects as well as sicknesses which generally effect the fertility of humans']

The first part of this theory, Proposition LVI, is concerned with forces of fertility inside a given Beja locality and is presented here for the second time in order to help the reader:

Proposition LVI: ['*Héequal*-ness in humans and animals increases fertility and good luck but is also dangerous. This state may be obtained through ritual means in animals and for a limited period in newlyweds. However, only the blessing from God may make humans permanently *héequal*']

  a: '*Héequal* persons bring good luck, prosperity and health to other humans. However, bad things will happen to people who oppose them or try to harm them'

    1: *Héequal* persons give the best treatment of sicknesses and misfortune'

    2: 'If person X is trying to harm or oppose a *héequal* person, Y, X will be struck by sickness, misfortune or death'

  b: 'A newlywed couple may be made temporarily *héequal* by smearing *adal óot* on their hut'

  c: ['Animals may be made permanently or temporarily *héequal* by various objects and ritual means in order to make them more healthy and fertile']

    1: '*Héequal* animals are more fertile than other animals'

    2: '*Héequal* animals are protected from sicknesses'

    3: 'Camels may be made *héequal* for a year by smearing them with powdered *adal óot* stone through the annual ritual of *kamtesilélt*,[70]

    4: 'Camels and cows may be made permanently *héequal* by ritually cutting their ears so as to make them appear sharp [making them *t'héelat (B)*]

    5: 'Sicknesses threatening fertility not caused by *héequal*-ness may be healed by the *héequal* promoting agent of *adal óot*'

  d: 'Permanently *héequal* animals are dangerous to the offspring of people not owning them and may cause sickness in those children'

    1: 'Permanently *héequal* animals may cause *tesérimt* in small infants'

    2: 'Not-yet-born children may be sickened or killed by the influence from permanently *héequal* animals'

e: *'Héequal* promoting objects like *adal óot* may both heal sicknesses which threaten fertility caused of people as well as
protecting against them'

    1: *'Adal óot* together with *híndib* and butter oil [mixture
called *dérwout]* protects against dangerous effects of
héequal animals'

    2: 'The mixture of *adal óot, híndib* and butter oil treats the
sickness of *tesérimt* caused by *héequal* animals'

    3: 'All pregnant women and newborn babies should be
given *dérwout [adal óot, híndib* and butter oil] regularly'

    4: 'The red stone of *adal óot* treats breast infections in
women[71] [regardless of cause]'

    5: *'Adal óot* treats excessive and irregular menstrual
bleeding in women [regardless of cause]'

The second model represents part B in the same Theory XII
(also presented before):

Proposition LVII: '1. All influence from the outside is of no avail
or even dangerous. [2. The dangerous effects may be counteracted by using various objects]'

a: 'Food from outside the Beja territory is valueless or even
harmful for Beja people in general'

    1: 'Animals and animal products from outside are
dangerous for human reproduction and health of
children'

    2: 'Relief oil and other kinds of new food items from
outside are dangerous for the health of Beja, especially
creating *tesérimt* for children'

b: 'People coming from far away places often bring with them
harmful [mystical] influences. Those bad influences may
harm the health of newborn children.'

c: ['Evil substance-mediated forces from outside Beja society
and their effects may be counteracted by using various
means and objects']

    1: 'The red stone of *adal óot*, together with butter oil and
híndib, may counteract and protect against the effects
of animals and animal products from ouside'

    2: *'Adal óot* mixed with *híndib* and butter oil may protect
against and treat the effects of new items of food from
outside'

3: 'All pregnant women and newborn babies should be given *dérwout [adal óot, híndib* and butter oil] regularly'

4: 'If one lets people visiting a newborn baby pass by smoke from incense of *lubān* and *kamūn aswad*, the bad influences they carry with them may be counteracted'

Those two propositions, cultural models which Schneider might have called complex symbols (see D'Andrade 1995), represent two very different modes of understanding of what is involved in the causation of *tesérimt*. All the same, the openness and subjunctiveness of narration make it possible to invoke the one which has the best explanatory power for people in a given situation. If for example a man with a *t'héelat*[72] camel passed by a pregnant woman and she miscarried or gave birth to a sick baby, the second model may *post hoc* render the experience culturally meaningful. Although strictly Muslim, Beja people are very pragmatic in many regards. A more dramatic example may illustrate this. If a woman or a child is possessed by a *zār*-spirit, conceived of as a non-Muslim spirit, healing often will involve negotiation with the spirit. The spirit might impose restrictions on praying on Fridays for a period of time. The importance of the duty of Friday prayers for Muslims should be well known. 'But,' people will argue, 'what can we do? There are Muslim and non-Muslim spirits, and we have to relate to both of them. If a person is sick, we have to do something.'

In neither of these two stories about sick children does the narrator make explicitly clear that assumptions linked to what I call 'the second model of *tesérimt*' explain the causality behind the sickness. It is left open to the active audience to make the right inference, which makes other people co-narrators. The power of the sequentiality of presentation indirectly invoke a cultural model which fits and at the same time imbues the experience with meaning and offers an explanation. In both cases the child died after getting *dérwout*, but none of the narrators bothers to ask 'why.' This is unnecessary for three reasons:

1. It might well be that the herbal contents of *dérwout* were not appropriate for the *tesérimt*.[73]
2. It might be that none of the models of understanding outlined above fit. This represents an open third alternative to the two models outlined above. In several chats with people about specific sickness cases people say that 'we have tried

everything' and that 'only God knows' what sickness it might be. At the same time they continue to seek treatment, thereby opening up unexplored explanations.

3. In every instance, life and death are finally submitted to the will of God. Nobody can question the will of God.

The loose and open-ended conclusions of the stories contribute to their subjunctiveness. They are not performances, but contributions in a continuous negotiation of life, death, health and sickness. In narrating, Beja people not only point to different 'possible worlds,' but they are also obviously involved in a process of 'possibilization.' Beja narrators tell personal stories in such a way that more questions are asked than answers given. It is as if the narrators are inviting people to join in organizing an unfinished jig-saw puzzle. This, which obviously is a trait in storytelling worldwide (Bruner 1990, Good 1994), is seemingly a more profound feature in Beja stories than in stories in literate societies.

However, there seems to be an underlying ethos of Beja making this uncertainty of presentation something more than just an invitation for others to participate in the creation of the story. The Beja seem to me simply less willing to state the truth about things than many others, as for example people in Khartoum. It looks like they are to a greater degree 'picking their way through as they go along.' When stating this, I know that I have deliberately walked out on thin ice! But, although I have severe difficulties in mounting any kind of evidence for this point, I have a strong feeling that this is one of the most central cultural traits I can present about the Beja. For this reason I will try shortly to defend this position.

Several times when I asked people about a specific kind of treatment, they answered that 'I have heard about it.' Later in conversations it often turned out that they sometimes had witnessed it or even tried the treatment themselves. This shy and careful style of presentation is the rule rather than the exception. But, much more than a style this seems to be a way of thinking. As an example, when Beja speak Arabic they use uncertainty markers like 'insha Allah,'[74] 'mumkin' and 'yimkin'[75] much more than Arabic speaking people from Khartoum or Northern Sudan. In this way every 'truth' presented by central politicians gets a certain twist when retold by a Beja. In addition to being representative of Beja ethos this might also be a device of speech used by the powerless (Professor Roy Wagner, personal communication).

This ethos of uncertainty seemed most profound when speaking with some of the few English speaking Beja who have read some of the scarce academic material presented on the Beja. For them, most of the points made in scientific books and papers are open to debate. The most positive commentaries might sound like 'It was nicely written, and there might be some truth in it.' The objectivizing danger of making truths by writing things down is seemingly more a danger for a Western academic than for a Beja!

One might say that for Beja people joining in solving the jig-saw puzzle of narration is as important as participating in a process of rendering experiences meaningful is in our society. However, they are apparently less occupied with ending up with a final completion of the puzzle than we are. Both in narration and other daily speech their statements are more open-ended than in Western society. Their mode of speaking also seems more open-ended than among settled people in Northern and Central Sudan.

Much more seems at stake in narration concerning sickness occurrences than the instances of sicknesses themselves. The intrusion of evil from outside is more than the intrusion of sick-ness-provoking forces; it relates to the intrusion of foreign juridical judgment outside the tribal traditional legal system, to intrusion of railway and roads, alien types of health care and to relief help, only to mention a few. I deliberately use 'relates to,' because the new factors are not unambiguously negative or evil. Rather, changes which many Bejas might favor, all the same to some extent have consequences which seem out of the control of the Beja themselves. In addition, the exact character of changes that Beja conceive of as evil is often difficult to make explicit. For this reason, the open-endedness of their narratives fits the overall discourse of their society very well (see Chapter 3).

The 'evil from inside' their society is difficult to grasp as a topic for continuous narration, whether related to sicknesses or other 'out of the ordinary' happenings. When individual Beja households try to counteract bad effects of droughts, for example, by reducing economic expenditure on social occasions, they at the same time undermine traditional ways of relating to other households. The habit of *t'héelat* may serve as an apt metaphor for this. Although this tradition has almost vanished and it is difficult to find animals with such ear-cuttings, people continuously discuss this practice and the evil consequenses of it. Restoring the fertility of the herd of one household is potentially dangerous for all others. At the same time, lack of sociability might also harm the unsociable himself as well. The frequent sickness of *sirr* illustrates this point. As discussed for Theory M, the sickness is caused by a person looking at the other eating. If this person wants this particular food but for one reason or another cannot join in the meal, the food itself will be transformed in a mysterious way by his glance, and it will cause severe vomiting and stomach trouble for the person eating. Lack of social sharing of resources is, in other words, related to sickness.

However, more is at stake than sociability, health and fertility. The sense of continuity of self and society through pronounced changes in Beja society seems to be a primary concern of the Hadandowa people I know. In the case of the skin sickness in Heretri, the dimension of cultural continuity is prominent. Since it is a 'new edition' of an old plague, they asked me about a kind of foreign *dérwout* for curing the sickness. In this way they are pointing to a possible future by invoking elements of the past. This point is underscored by the retelling of an old story about a *basīr* in colonial times. The point is thereby indirectly made that traditional wisdom of *busarā'* still fits the situation of people better than the knowledge of medical doctors. At the same time, by telling this story the narrator invokes the perception of continuity in people in two ways:

1. It points to a continuous indigenous healing tradition that reaches far back in history; and,
2. It points to the relevance of *basīr* treatment for a new sickness. Hence the new sickness will not be experienced as a break with past experiences.

As we have seen, at a 'deep-structural' level, Beja conceptions of sympathetic magic are applied to new as well as old kinds of experiences. A concern with 'essences' and their spread is a main characteristic of the *busarā'* tradition, which renders this tradition meaningful in a changing world where Beja people still are very much concerned with spread of and intrusion of various substances and influences.

265

8.2.7. Conclusion: the past in the future and the future in the past

In Beja narration of sickness experiences both the here and now and the future are rendered meaningful, in terms of the past. Increased child mortality combined with manifestations of a new type of skin sickness is related to the old diagnosis of *tesérimt*. As we have seen, the diagnosis of *tesérimt* may involve one of two very different cultural models, making the diagnosis fit a broad range of experiences in their life-world. Through use of *irrealis* or subjunctive words and expressions the opening up of possible worlds makes the narration a pragmatic enterprise where experiences of sickness and ill-luck might be rendered meaningful and where actions in the world are made possible.

The subjunctive characteristics of storytelling reported from cross-cultural studies seems more prominent in Hadandowa storytelling than what have been shown for most other societies. This might not be a surprise out of two reasons:

1. The Beja have no written tradition which might act as a source for the perception of continuity of their society.
2. The adaptation of Beja to their natural environment is extremely precarious, a fact that makes their life-world full of uncertainties.

The subjunctiveness of storytelling as shown for Hadandowa narration makes storytelling a creative process where shared cultural resources can be made relevant under new circumstances. Both Bloch (1986) and Keesing (1982) have made this point relevant to rituals and myth. In societies like the pastoral and non-literate Beja society the sharing of storytelling in everyday life may have an even more important function related to the cultural adaptations to new experiences in a rapidly changing world.

I have been occupied with a few aspects of the 'meaning-making project' of Beja related to experiences of sickness and bad luck. The possible explanations provided in Beja narratives are not parallel to scientific explanations (see Chapter 6.14.). For this reason my use in this discussion of the concept of 'possible worlds' has differed from the way the philosopher Elster (1978) uses it, where 'possible worlds' pre-suppose and relate to an 'actual world.' In Beja narration the border between 'what really happened' and 'what might have happened' is constantly blurred. This is not only part of the Beja ethos, although I will argue that subjunctivity and an unwillingness to state things absolutely are very pronounced among Beja people. In general, however, subjunctivity tends to be a trait occurring cross-culturally in personal narratives. As Bruner (1990) remarks, a personal story typically can be 'real' or 'imaginary' without loss of its power as a story.

8.3. A DIFFERENT STORY: *BUSARĀ'* STORIES AND OTHER MYTHICAL[76] STORIES

8.3.1. Introduction

In this last section of Chapter 8 I will look at stories which are substantially different from personal narratives both in style, structure and use of language. Although like for personal narratives much knowledge is tacit in mythical narratives, their style and structure make them less 'open-ended' and flexible than personal stories.

All the stories I will present here are stories about experiences of health problems and the way traditional healers deal with them. They are in some respects very different from the kind of narration of personal sickness experiences which I have dealt with up to now, a fact which I will come back to after going through these stories in some detail. Most of the stories, with the exception of story IV, 'The lizard which clung to the brain,' were told by Hussain Barakwin,[77] an old Beja man from the Agwamt area near Odrus. He is a man of extensive knowledge, wisdom and refined sense of humor with whom I had the pleasure of staying in contact throughout most of my fieldwork.

A short technical note: it is often difficult, both in Tu Bedawie and Arabic (even written Arabic) to know exactly where one sentence ends and where a new one begins. In both languages, connective words like 'and' blur the sense of delineated and discrete sentences. However, in this discussion, the written form of the sentences is not important; rather, the meanings of utterances and their functions are the important aspects. For this reason, it may often seem like I have cut a 'natural' sentence into two or more pieces by my way of numbering.

8.3.2. The stories

Story I: The basīr and the surgeon

'Once during the colonial times, a person was hit by a stick or a stone on his head. This blow broke the bones of the head, and some pieces of the skull lay on the brain. The man then began to speak gibberish. No modern doctor could help him. One *basīr* named Shegelab from the Hamdab when he saw this man, touched his body on the arms and eyes just like a doctor. When he got to know about the brain problems, he made a cut in the place. He removed the pieces of bones from the vessels of the brain and covered the place with skin. The person then began to eat and speak normally again. One of the doctors in the Hospital of Port Sudan then said to him [the *basīr*]: "Please stay with us and assist us," but he refused.'

Analysis of story I
'1. *Once during the colonial times,*
   This is a typical beginning in Beja stories from "former times" in that the time is loosely given, the setting is implicitly "somewhere within the Beja territory."
   2. *a person was hit by a stick or a stone on his head.*
   In *busarāʾ* stories, naturally, the stories center around problems to be solved. Like most such frequently retold stories, *busarāʾ* stories tend to be more fixed in their structure than recent stories people tell out of their own experiences. In this story, the problem "a person was hit by a stone on his head" is given early in the story, here even within the first utterance.
   3. *This blow broke the bones of the head, and some pieces of the skull lay on the brain.*
   This is about as far as many Beja stories go in describing the initial problem to be solved.
   4. *The man then began to speak gibberish.*
   This further characterization of how the initial problem was manifest in the behavior or experience of the sick person is often left out in *busarāʾ* stories, demonstrating that they are not strictly necessary to the structure of those stories, as is clearly demonstrated in story IV below, which in many respects is the same kind of story.

5. No modern doctor could help him.

This is a common theme of all Beja stories I have heard about merits of *busarā* in former times.

6. One basīr named Shegelab, from the Hamdab, when he saw this man.

In contrast to the looseness of place and time in such stories, the tribal background of the main characters is mostly explicit, and often detailed. While time and space is not important in most Beja stories, who the characters are with regard to tribal relations make them real and makes the story a 'real' story with which Beja listeners can identify themselves.

7. Touched his body on the arms and eyes just like a doctor.

The characterization of the diagnostic touch by the *basīr* of the body of his patient, 'just like a doctor,' is situating him on the same level as a medical doctor. This is done in the careful Beja way, without making a direct comparison between the skill of a Beja *basīr* and a foreign doctor.

8. When he got to know about the brain problems.

9. He made a cut in the place.

10. He removed the pieces of bones from the vessels of the brain and covered the place by skin.

The procedures of the *busarā* are always given in great detail in the stories, contributing to the credibility of the story. At the same time, the *basīr* is always portrayed as very practical. Since so many details are left out in Beja stories generally, this exception is noteworthy.

11. The person then began to eat and speak normally again.

This outcome is given as a 'dry matter of fact' without any appraisals of the hero or any kind of explanation. It is as if the narrator wants to say: 'This is not something extraordinary. This is the typical outcome of the work of clever *busarā*.'

12. One of the doctors in the Hospital of Port Sudan then said to him:[78] *'Please stay with us and assist us.'*

13. But he refused.'

Beja *basīr* stories often, but not always, end with a conclusion drawing on the following themes:

a. Beja knowledge is not written in books.

b. Beja knowledge is often superior to the knowledge of the books.

c. Beja *busarā* draw upon the common Beja knowledge, which Beja people say is 'in our heads and in our tradition.'

d. Beja *busarā'* draw both on knowledge concerned with healing and general wisdom of life, 'from our experience,' as they frame it.

Story II: The **basīr** *and the Egyptian officer*

'In the colonial period one of the Hamdab *sheikhs* followed an Egyptian officer to collect taxes from the nomads. It was far away from the towns, so they used camels. The Egyptian officer had swollen testicles. When they rode his camel, the swelling was painful. He could not eat or drink, and he was crying. When the Beja *sheikh* saw his situation, he said to him: "I will take you to a *basīr* who can treat you." Then, when they reached a settlement, he [the *sheikh*] told one man to pretend that he was a *basīr*. The man [pretending to be a *basīr*] said to him: "I want to burn you as treatment." Then the *sheikh* said to him: "I will call for four strong guys to hold your arms and legs." He did so, and they held his arms and legs. Then they began to heat a piece of metal in fire. The Egyptian began to cry loudly, and the swelling went back into the body and disappeared due to his fright. Then the man pretending to be the *basīr* said to the four men: "Leave him." The Egyptian then was well. He began to eat and drink tea, because you know, those Egyptians they love tea!'

Analysis of story II

'1. *In the colonial period one of the Hamdab* **sheikhs**[79] *followed an Egyptian officer to collect taxes from the nomads.*

Like the first story, this story also begins with a rather loose account of time, with the setting implicitly being 'somewhere in the Red Sea Hills.'

2. *It was far away from the towns, so they used camels.*

This is a rather unusual explication of space, and is obviously done because it is important to the story and its credibility. Even in colonial times, camels were not used by officers in the urban areas in Eastern Sudan.

3. *The Egyptian officer had swollen testicles.*

This story is a more complicated one than story I (above) in having two main themes to convey.

270

Normally, problems related to the sexual organs are not openly spoken about among the Beja. In this case, when it is done regarding a foreign, unpopular Egyptian officer, it gives the story a rather humorous touch, denigrating the power of a representative of the powerful Egyptian army. In addition to making the story extraordinary and giving the audience a reason to laugh, or at least smile, it underpins the *de facto* cultural superiority of the Beja to the military and administratively superior Egyptian. This again, as we will see, underpins the main point of the story. At this point, the problem to be solved is outlined.

4. *When he rode his camel, the swelling was painful.*

5. *He could not eat or drink, and he was crying.*

These elements, recounting the consequences of the problem for the sufferer, is, as in the story above, not strictly necessary for the plot. However, they contribute to the further desacralization of the Egyptian and to an additional smile from the audience.

6. *When the Beja **sheikh** saw his situation,*

7. *he said to him: 'I will take you to a **basīr** who can treat you.'*

The *basīr* is such an obvious solution that this is given as a 'matter of fact' solution to the problem.

8. *Then, when they reached a settlement, he[80] told one man to pretend that he was a **basīr**.*

The Beja simply expected the Egyptian to be easily tricked, so they did not even bother about finding a skilled *basīr*.

9. *The man[81] said to him: 'I want to burn you as treatment.'*

10. *After this the **sheikh** said to him: 'I will call for four strong guys to hold your arms and legs.*

11. *He did so,*

12. *and they held his arms and legs.*

13. *Then they began to heat a piece of metal in fire.*

As is usual in Beja *busarā* stories, the procedural parts constitute a large proportion of the story (see the other stories as well). The cleverness and practical wisdom of Beja in general and *busarā* in particular is the main point of the stories. For this reason it is natural that this practical part is given particular consideration.

14. *The Egyptian began to cry loudly,*

15. *and the swelling went back into the body and disappeared due to his fright.*

Braveness and hiding feelings of pain are important expectations for men related to the Beja concepts of manliness and honor. The Egyptian, the unwelcome intruder into Beja territory, is highlighting this constellation of concepts by acting out the opposite.

16. *Then the man pretending to be the **basīr** said to the four men: 'Leave him.'*

17. *The Egyptian then was well again.*

18. *He began to eat and drink tea,*

19. *because you know, those Egyptians they love tea!'*

The cleverness of Beja people is again underlined, in contrast to the Egyptian who was tricked by the Beja pretending *basīr*. This double theme is followed to its very end by commenting upon the tea drinking of Egyptians, in contrast to the coffee drinking Beja.[82]

*Another version of 'The **basīr** and the Egyptian officer':*

19. 'A person once had a big swelling in his testicles. Then one *basīr* made a kind of treatment for him: he called for four persons to hold this man by the arms and the legs. Then he put a piece of iron in the fire, and said to him: "I will burn you with this iron." He [the suffering man] became very frightened. They said to him: "We will burn you when the iron is hot." Then the fright made the swelling shrink and shrink until it disappeared.'

Analysis of the second version
'1. A person once

In contrast with the similar story about the Egyptian officer, there is no mentioning of ethnic identity, position and mission of the sick person. There is also no description of the physical and geographical setting.

2. *had a big swelling in his testicles.*

The problem is simply stated without any elaborations upon symptoms or the reactions of the sufferer, in sharp contrast to the story above

3. *Then one **basīr** made a kind of treatment for him:*

4. *he called for four persons to hold this man,*

5. *by the arms and the legs.*

6. *Then he put a piece of iron in the fire,*

7. *and said to him: 'I will burn you with this iron.'*

The treatment section is as usual the most extensive and

detailed part of the story. The same procedure is followed as for the Egyptian officer.

8. They said to him: 'We will burn you when the iron is hot.

9. He [the suffering man] became very frightened.

While the Egyptian officer was portrayed as 'crying loudly' from fright in an unmanly fashion, the anonymous sufferer in this story is merely said to have become frightened.

10. Then the fright made the swelling shrink and shrink

11. until it disappeared.'

The clever application of commonsense psychology by the experienced *basīr* solved the complicated problem. As usual in *busarā* stories, the healing was achieved immediately without complicated means or actions.

While in all *busarā* stories the 'down-to-earth' wisdom and cleverness of the traditional healer is stressed, the story about the Egyptian officer seems to convey a double set of messages. The wisdom of the *basīr* is contrasted with the foolish behavior of the foreign intruder. The lack of manliness of the Egyptian is implicitly contrasted with the manly and honorable conduct of Beja men. Finally, his habit of drinking tea serves as a metonymical sign of his 'inner essence' of Egyptian-ness, in contrast to the *jábana* drinking Beja.

Indeed, in the *'Busarā* and the Egyptian officer,' the story about the traditional healer seemingly serves a double purpose. Firstly, like all such stories, it both serves the aim of showing the practical wisdom of the *busarā* and the relevance of the tradition they represent for Beja people at the present time as well as in earlier historical times. Secondly, the *busarā* tradition serves as a marker of Beja ethnic identity. While people from agricultural societies are seen as more complicated than the Beja and as organizing themselves in more complicated ways, Beja people like to think of themselves as living a simple life and having a practical wisdom which often supersedes the 'wisdom of books' in real-life situations (see Chapter 3 and Propositions LXXVI and LXXVII).

*Story III: The **basīr** and the child who lacked a mouth*

'A child was once born without any opening for a mouth. Then the family called for a Hamdab *basīr*. He made a mark on the place of the mouth and opened it with a knife. After this he put a stick between the gums. And they fed the child

273

by butter for a long time and gave it milk through a pipe in the mouth for a long time until the child recovered.'

Analysis of story III
'1. *A child was once*
2. *born without any opening for a mouth.*
Here the narrator does not even bother to give a loose statement of time, and as usual, the place is implicit.
3. *Then the family called for a Hamdab basīr.*
As in the other stories, the *basīr* is called for as a obvious solution. And again, his tribal background is accounted for.
4. *He made a mark on the place of the mouth*
5. *and opened it with a knife.*
6. *After this he put a stick between the gums.*
7. *They fed the child by butter for a long time and gave it milk through a pipe in the mouth for a long time*
8. *until the child recovered.'*
The procedures makes up the bulk of the narrative in this case. Of course, since being born without a mouth has such obvious consequences, it is not necessary to go into any detail about what problems it causes.

That the child did recover, is expected to such a degree that the short final 'until the child recovered' is enough to show the outcome of the treatment.

Story IV: The lizard who clung to the brain

'This happened during colonial times. Once a lizard managed to get inside a person's head and sat on his brain and clung to it. – We do not know how it entered, only God knows. When doctors tried to do operations on him, they were not able to do so, because it clung so strongly to the brain that they could not remove it without removing part of the brain. Because the English people of that time knew that the Hamdab were very experienced people, they asked for them. A Hamdab person came, and he brought three things: a piece of fire [metal heated in fire], a piece of cotton with butter and a metal tool to hold the heated piece of metal. First he took the heated material and moved it near the brain after the doctor opened the skull, and he then put the metal closer and closer to the lizard. It retracted its legs, and he applied cotton under them one by one, repeating the procedure four times for each leg. After this it was easy to remove the lizard, because it could not manage to cling to the brain any longer. Sometimes the Yudia people[83] know even more than the doctors.'

Analysis of story IV
'*1. This happened during colonial times.*

Like in the above stories, loose time reference and implicit, loose understanding of setting.

2. Once a lizard managed to get inside a person's head and sat on his brain and clung to it.

3. We do not know how it entered, only God knows.

In a way, it seems like the narrator with this statement in line three anticipates critical thoughts or remarks from her audience, admitting that this cause behind the problem may seem incredible. In addition, this way of formulating uncertainty about the ontology of things is typical to Beja discourse in general.[84]

4. When doctors tried to do operations on him,

5. they were not able to do so, because it clung so strongly to the brain that they could not remove it without removing part of the brain.

In some stories, like story II or III, the doctor is not even mentioned. When the doctor's help is sought, like here, he is incapable of solving the problem. At most, they co-operate with the Beja traditional healer.

6. Because the English people at that time knew that the Hamdab were very experienced people,

7. they asked for them.

The expression 'at that time' indirectly tells that this is how it used to be, but that the times have changed. Now people tend not to consult biomedical health workers at all, and biomedical staff usually ignore the skills of traditional healers.

8. A Hamdab person came,

9. and he brought three things: a piece of fire [metal heated in fire], a piece of cotton with butter and a metal tool to hold the heated piece of metal.

10. First he took the heated material and moved it near the brain after the doctor opened the skull, and he then put the metal closer and closer to the lizard.

275

11. It retracted its legs, and he applied cotton under them one by one, repeating the procedure four times for each leg.

12. After this it was easy to remove the lizard, because it could not manage to cling to the brain any longer.

As in the three stories above, the outline of the procedure is very detailed. However, just like in the other stories, the solution is convincingly simple in its 'down to earth' practicality.

13. Sometimes the Yudia people know even more than the doctors.'

This seems to be the same kind of conclusion which is drawn in the first story, regarding the superiority of Beja knowledge over written knowledge, and the higher value of experience over knowledge from books. However, the conclusion is carefully drawn, not stating directly that Beja knowledge is superior, but with the careful statement that '**sometimes** the Yudia people know **even** more the doctors.' This is typical in Beja stories, where fixed statements are seldom made. Many times those statements have an even weaker claim by using uncertainty markers like 'it seems like,' 'I think,' 'maybe' etc.

Like in the story about the Egyptian colonial officer, a foreigner is contrasted with a Beja and the tradition he represents. While the Egyptian officer was portrayed as a ridiculous figure, however, the British colonial officer[85] is treated with more respect. Nevertheless, although the crafts and skills of Western trained medical officers are recognized, part of the message seems to be that they lack the 'down-to-earth' practical sense and wisdom which so often has proven to provide solutions to seemingly complicated problems.

8.3.3. Stories compared

The five mythical stories represent a very different type of story both in structure and content from personal narratives. Stories from 'former times,' like the stories about the wit, success and wisdom of traditional healers, are different in many regards.

Firstly, the mythical narratives are not somebody's stories. The narrator is in no way part of the stories told. Amna's story, in contrast, is a strong **personal** narrative. As personal stories told in an environment where such narratives are frequently told, they represent accounts with which listeners may to a lesser or greater degree identify themselves. As Miller *et al.* (1990:306) notes, 'the power of stories to amuse or frighten, anger or excite, rests on a felt overlap with the narrator's recounted experience.' Regarding socialization of children, she adds that 'when [they] inhabit environments rich in personal storytelling, they encounter again and again such moments of personal extension' (ibid.). As I see it, *zār* rituals and stories told about *zār* experience may also be seen as supplying adult Bejas with 'personal extension' and enriched self-understanding. This is also in line with how Janice Boddy (1988, 1989) came to view *zār* cults in riverain Northern Sudan.

Secondly, mythical *busarā'* stories have a more well-defined structure than personal Beja narratives tend to have. As will soon be demonstrated, this is a structure which fits into the a seemingly universal type of narrative structure described by Jean M. Mandler in her 'Stories, Scripts and Scenes ' (1984) quite well.

Busarā' stories are all well structured temporally in regard to the events which make up the plot of the narratives, although the broader historical context may be lacking or loose. Amna's story, by contrast, contains 'asides' as well as reflective elements which refer to earlier parts of her story.

Mythical stories are also well structured in the sense that the stories have an intrinsic order of presenting their elements:

a. If they have a time reference, or a spatial reference, it will be given in the very first utterance.
b. After this, the problem to be solved is stated. How the problem came about or-how it is experienced by the sufferer or people around him/her, is sometimes made clear, but not always.
c. Next, an account of the search for a solution is presented. It may have two possible forms: Firstly, seeking a non-traditional and non-successful solution, and then a traditional solution with a successful outcome, or, secondly, directly seeking a traditional solution with a successful outcome.
d. After the positive outcome is made clear, an additional 'moral of the story' might be added, like 'sometimes the Yudia people know even more than the doctors.'

Thirdly, the *busarā'* stories have some message to get through to an audience, in contrast to personal narratives which raise so many questions and give so many loose statements. The cultural knowledge needed in order to understand a *basīr* story seems to

277

be significantly less than the personal narratives, an important fact to which I will return.

The sensual richness present in personal narratives is absent in the mythical stories. While narratives like the story of Halima present the audience with a rich world of smell from incense, sounds from *zār* drums and tangible substances like sacrificial blood, the *busarā* stories are 'non sensual' and appeal to a sense of the logical practicality of the Beja tradition of knowledge. Depriving them of all kinds of sensuality contributes to making them canonical contributions with an aura of 'objectivity.'

Fourthly, 'historical' stories are seldom interrupted by the audience when presented, in contrast to personal narratives. Since they are more 'straightforward' and less open to various interpretations and 'readings,' there is not much need for the audience to interrupt. Personal narratives, by presenting many loose statements and *irrealis* like 'could be,' 'maybe,' 'don't you think' etc., are by contrast inviting listeners to voice comments. For all these reasons, the stories of 'how it was in former times' are simpler and require clearly less mental investment on the part of people listening to them.

There are, however, some similar points between Beja personal narratives and the stories about traditional healers. Firstly, in all Beja stories, most things are left unsaid and left open to the imagination of the listeners. In none of them does one get so much detail that 'the pictures are painted before the audience.' Mostly, only information strictly necessary to the plot of the story is given. Secondly, there is a strong element of suspense: the audience is not given any hint in the story of what is to appear at a later stage.

Although both kinds of stories leave most things unsaid, I will come to argue that there is a basic story structure in Beja mythical stories simulating a 'model of mind' which directs the interpretation by the listeners and make them more easy for the audience to grasp than personal narratives. These devices support mental processes of inference making as well as giving these stories an aura of authority which the personal narratives lack.

8.3.4. Beja mythical stories in a cross-cultural perspective. In support of a recurring underlying schema

While psychologists like Jerome Bruner (1990) typically draw our attention to personal narratives, the cognitive psychologist Jean M. Mandler (1984) focuses on stories of a more mythical character like mythical tales of various kinds. While it may be the case that such stories have often escaped the attention of personality oriented psychologists, they nevertheless make up a significant part of the cultural environment in which personality develops in most, and possibly all, societies. Mandler's work built upon the early and seminal works of Rumelhart (1975, 1977), a psychologist doing research on story recall and comprehension. Although she disagrees with some of his claims,[86] she has basically adopted his ideas and simplified them.

Since one of the stories Mandler adopts illustrates her mode of analysis very well, I will take the liberty to present it without abbreviation. The story represents an adapted version from *The Tales of the Dervishes* by Idries Shah (1970, in Mandler 1984) and has the title 'How knowledge was earned.' The number of each sentence corresponds to a structure of connected schemata presented in the figure 2.

'1. Once upon a time there was a man who was tired of his uninformed life. 2. He decided that he needed knowledge. 3. He went to a Sufi and said, "Sufi, you are a wise man! Let me have a mite of your knowledge, so that I may become worthwhile." 4. The Sufi said, "I can give you knowledge in exchange for something which I myself need. Bring me a small carpet, for I have to give it to someone who will then further our holy word."

5. So the man set off to a carpet shop and said to the owner, "Give me a small carpet, so that I can give it to a Sufi, who will then give me knowledge." 6. The carpet dealer said, "That is what you and the Sufi want. But *I* want thread for weaving carpets. Bring me some goathair to make thread and I will help you." 7. So the man went off to a goatherd and told him his needs. 8. The goatherd said, "What do I care about knowledge or thread or carpets. *I* need a pen to keep my goats in at night because they are straying all over the place. Bring me a pen and then we'll talk about goathair."

9. So the man went to a carpenter and asked him to make a pen. 10. The carpenter said, "Yes, I could make a pen, but I am not interested in carpets or knowledge and the like. However, *I* have a desire; I want to get married. See whether you can arrange a wife for me." 11. So the man went off once more and approached a woman who knew a marriageable girl. 12. But the woman said, "What about me? Everyone wants what he wants but nobody has yet said anything about *my* needs. What I need is something I have wanted all my life. Get this for me and I will help you. The thing I want is . . . knowledge!" 13. "Knowledge!," yelped the man, "but we can't have knowledge without a carpet." 14. "Well, that's the silliest thing I ever heard," replied the woman. "I don't know what knowledge is but I'm sure it is not a carpet." And she sent him away. 15. The man began to despair of the human race and took to wandering around the streets muttering to himself.

16. One day, a certain merchant heard the man muttering about the carpet and holy work, and recognized that he was a wandering dervish. 17. The merchant said to him, "Wandering dervish, I don't understand what you are saying, but I see that you are a seeker of truth. Perhaps you can help me." 18. The man answered, "I understand that you are in trouble, but I have nothing. I can't even get a piece of thread when I need it. However, ask me, and I will see what I can do." 19. The merchant told him that his only daughter was suffering from an sickness that was causing her great anguish. 20. The girl confessed to the wanderer that she was in love with the man whom the wanderer had asked to make the goatpen. The wanderer told the merchant that his daughter would be cured if she could marry a certain carpenter. The merchant was so relieved that he agreed.

21. So the man told the carpenter, who immediately built the pen for the goats. 22. He took the pen to the goatherd who gave him the goathair for thread. 23. He gave the goathair to the carpet maker who gave him a carpet. 24. He gave the carpet to the Sufi, who said, "Now I can give you knowledge. 25. You could not have brought this carpet unless you had worked for *it* and not for yourself."

Jean Mandler's attempt at elucidating an underlying story schema is presented in a modified version in Figure 2.

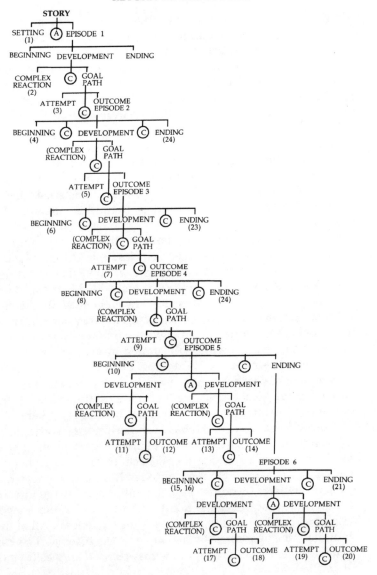

Figure 2: *The structure of 'The Story of the Wandering Dervish' (Modified after Mandler (1984))*

Additional symbols which she has utilized elsewhere are added to her outline. 'A' symbolizes 'and,' 'T' symbolize 'then' and hence a temporal relationship, while 'C' symbolizes a causal relationship. The concept 'cause' is of course used in the broad sense it is employed in folk philosophy, or in a 'folk model of mind.'[87] The same conventions which she uses in this figure will be employed by me for Beja mythical narratives.

Basically, a first episode follows a description of the setting. Each episode is marked as consisting of a beginning, development and ending. The development stage consists of a complex reaction (emotional and/or intellectual) which motivates a pursuit of a goal path. The goal path is characterized by an attempt and the outcome resulting from this attempt. The outcome may further initiate the beginning of a subsequent episode. 'Complex reaction' implies that a 'thought,' an 'emotion,' or both causes a 'wish' or 'desire' in the character.

This story represents what she terms an 'outcome-embedded' story. The outcome of each episode is embedded in the next one, and the outcomes of all episodes are embedded in the final episode and its outcome. Other possible story structures are 'then-connected' stories where two separate episodes are temporally connected, as will be illustrated in my next example of Beja mythical stories. A third type of story structure is the 'ending-embedded' narrative, where two separate episodes with two separate 'goal-paths' are related and unified in a final outcome. This third alternative will not be discussed here.

A broad range of research has been performed in order to test the validity of underlying story schemata. Experiments of story-recalling as well as asking the subjects to group together sentences and separate different episodes has been conducted for dyslexic readers, reading disabled adults, language-impaired children, learning disabled adults, elderly adults and congenitally deaf children (see Mandler 1984 for references). All of them indicated the workings of the same story schema. The same conclusion has been drawn from cross-cultural studies (Mandler et al. 1980).[88]

The story presented by Mandler is quite an extensive mythical tale. Although the narrative could in this case be heavily influenced by a literary tradition, an oral tradition does not preclude a similarly long and complex story. Given that an underlying story structure facilitates the memory of it, a story like the 'wandering dervish' story above may well function within an oral tradition. The Beja story below told by Hussain Barakwin illustrates this quite well (see figure 3), as well as illustrating the deference paid by Beja to the richness of their traditional knowledge.

'1. A man once had three sons, one with one woman and two with another one. 2. He gave the judgment before his death that the two latter sons should inherit from him and the first one not. 3. Because of this problem, the sons went to a judge. 4. The judge was living far away from them, so they traveled to him to settle this problem.

5. On their way to this judge they met a man who had lost his camel. 6. He asked them whether they had seen his camel or not. 7. They said to him: "We haven't seen him, but we saw his footprints. And we know that his tail is cut, one of his eyes is blind and he is sick." 8. Then the man said: "You have accurately described my camel and you know where it is. I want to search for it, and if I can't find it, I will complain to the judge, because you know the place of my camel."

9. Then they proceeded to the judge, and he proceeded on his way. 10. When they reached this judge, he welcomed them and put cooked meat and breads in front of them. However, they refused to eat. Then he asked them: "Why do you refuse to eat this food?" 11. And they answered that "this meat is dog's meat, and the woman who made this bread and the other food has menstruation. And you are the illegitimate son of your father!"

12. He then became angry 13. and tried to pick a fight with them. 14. They said to him: "You can ask your family about those points." 15. Then he went to his wife and asked about the bleeding, 16. and she said: "Yes, this is truth, I am tired and bleeding, but when the guests suddenly came to you, I was forced to move and cook."

17. Then he went to the person responsible for the animals, and he asked him about the slaughtered animal for the guests. 18. And he said: "Yes, this sheep used to nurse at the breasts of our dogs." 19. Lastly he went to his mother and asked if he was his father's legitimate son or not, 20. and she said: "Once upon a time my husband was very rich, and he had a lot of animals. But, unfortunately, he had no children. For that reason I hid myself from him, and I made love with one person who is your real father and who is not the person from whom you inherit. The person from whom you inherit, however, is infertile."

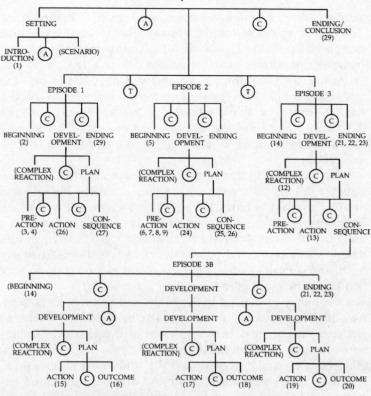

Figure 3: *The structure of 'The three sons and the inheritance problem'*

21. Then he returned to those guests, and he asked them: "How did you know those points?" 22. They said: "It is quite evident. Regarding your illegitimacy, because you gave us bad food, which is the manner of illegitimate persons. Regarding the bleeding of your wife, because the breads are not baked well, which reflects that the person who made those breads is tired and made them without having any desire in them. Regarding the meat you gave us, we know that it is meat of dogs because it is full of veins, which confirms that this is dog's meat." 23. He was surprised by their wisdom.

24. Then suddenly that man whom they met on the way came and talked to the judge about his complaint. 25. Then the judge asked them about this problem, and they replied: "We haven't seen this camel, but we saw some indicators of it. We said it is

blind in one eye because its legs on one side have been making heavier steps. We said that it is without a tail because the camels with tails usually separate their stools as they moves along. But this camel put all its stools in one place, not separating them. And we said that it is sick because its steps were fixed in the sand."

26. The judge then was satisfied in this point. 27. After that they began to speak with the judge about the inheritance problem, 28. and the judge said to them: "Because you are legitimate sons of your father, all three of you must inherit him." 29. Then they were satisfied with his judgment.

This story represents a complex narrative where three incidents are related in narrative, linear time and at the same time are separate stories. Like the *busarâ* stories, the story is simpler than personal narratives in the sense that it requires less cultural knowledge in order to understand it. Like the *busarâ* stories, there is no subjunctiveness about it so it, in the words of Jerome Bruner (1990:54), 'can be tried on for psychological size, accepted if [it] fit[s], rejected if [it] pinch[es] identity or compete[s] with established commitments.' However, it is structurally very complex in that it entails two sub-narratives which are seemingly not necessary elements to the main narrative.

The story about the inheritance problem and the two connected stories are apparently related as what Mandler (1984) describes as then-connected episodes of a story, or alternatively, as then-connected sub-stories temporally co-inciding with the main narrative and the main plot. The outcome of each of the three stories is made clear at the end of the main narrative. The overall narrative represents what Mandler (1984:48) calls 'inter-leafed,' where the first unit of the first episode is followed by the first unit of the second episode and so on. The third story, initiated by the problem caused by the guests refusing to eat the food offered by the judge, is the most complex part in terms of structure. It consists internally of two episodes, the second one organized around a triple problem solved in parallel; that of the origin of the meat, the legitimacy of his birth and the monthly menstrual cycle of his wife. Interestingly enough, Mandler and DeForest (1979) found that when subjects were asked to recall a 'canonical' then-connected story and other subjects were asked to recall the same story in an 'inter-leafed' form, the average score for recall was the same for the 'inter-leafed' form as for the canonical type. This finding clearly supports the psychological validity of the notion of an underlying 'idealized' schema of this type of narrative.

As a then-connected story, the story about the inheritance problem may be represented as suggested in Figure 3. The setting in sequence 1 provides the point of entry for three separate episodes. The outcome for each of them is to be found in the final sequences 22-28. Seemingly the outcome of one episode has no influence over the outcome of the others. The different problems of each episode all find their solution at the end of the narrative seemingly by coincidence.

Nevertheless, when the judge learns about the intelligent and logical explanations of the three brothers for both the food problem and the problem of the lost camel, he is impressed by their wisdom. Nothing is said that directly points to the judge's favorable impression leading him to provide the brothers with a fair and practical judgment. However, when the judge cites his judgment, he clothes it in the expression 'because you are legitimate sons of your father . . .,' an expression which clearly alludes to his own illegitimate status as a son, and hence to what the three brothers revealed about him. Clearly, it is not unthinkable that the obvious wisdom and cleverness of the brothers impressed him in such a way as to pass a favorable judgment on to them. If this interpretation is correct, the story is not really a 'then-connected' story, but rather possibly an 'outcome-embedded' story where the solution of the initial problem depended on the solution of two intermediate problems.

The story may, in other words, be somewhat deceptive. Whatever kind of story it is and in whatever way the three different episodes are related, however, the main theme of it is not open to interpretations or various readings. The moral of the story as partly expressed line 22 ('he [the judge] was impressed by the wisdom') is that Beja traditional knowledge and wisdom is simple, logical, practical and relevant to many real-life situations. It is the kind of knowledge which makes the most out of few facts by adhering to 'down-to-earth' common sense as developed in a pastoral and nomadic adaptation. Although the main theme seemingly is a complicated question of inheritance and its solution, neither I nor my Beja assistant, who together served as audience, saw this as really important to the story.

While some of the *busarā* stories contain a *coda* in the form of a moral or punchline, as in the story about the Egyptian colonial officer, the story about the three brothers ends with finding a solution to their problem of inheritance. As we have seen, however, the final solution coincides with the demonstration of Beja wisdom by the three men. The way the story is constructed facilitates a process of inference in the audience which guides them to the conclusion about the hidden moral of the myth.

As may be evident from Figure 3, the story about the inheritance problem represents an 'inter-leafed' story. Given that it does not break structurally with the 'then-connected' story schema proposed by Mandler (ibid.), the story may be retold in an oral tradition without losing its richness of details. As in the story about the 'wandering dervish,' there is one kind of element which is either omitted or loosely pointed to for each episode. The complex reaction (CR) of the story characters is usually not accounted for.

In episodes 1 and 2 of the inheritance story, nothing is said explicitly about how the man who lost his camel or the three brothers who inherited a problem as well as wealth thought or felt. In sequence 12 of episode 3 it is stated that the judge became angry and wanted to start a fight with the brothers, which is an exceptional display of emotion in a Beja mythical story. However, the narrative does not make it clear whether or how his emotion may relate to the actions the judge later pursues, since he does not try to investigate the claims of the brothers before they suggest this solution to him. As will become clear from a closer look at the *busarā́* stories, this is a characteristic trait of Beja mythical narratives.

The morality tales from the rural and agricultural Oaxacan community presented by Holly F. Mathews (1992) are very different from Beja narratives in this respect. The *La Llorona* morality tales she presents all provide a clear picture of complex reactions in their main characters. A typical *La Llorona* mythical tale goes like this (132–133, all remarks in brackets represent my additions):

[Setting:]

1. '*La Llorona* was married to a hard-working man.
2. They had many children and worked hard to get ahead. All was well.

[Episode 1, beginning:]

3. But one day she began to walk the streets and everyone knew, but her husband did not know.
4. When he found out,

[Complex reaction:]

5. he had much *pena* ['shame'].
6. And he wanted to chastise her.

[Plan:]

7. So he beat her and cursed her
8. and told her that her actions had caused him much *pena* ['shame'].

[Consequence, episode 2: Beginning: Same as above, line 7 and 8]
[Complex reaction:]

9. But the beating gave her *pena*.

[Plan:]

10. And late that night she walked into the river
11. and killed herself [consequence].

[Ending/moral:]

12. And now she knows no rest and must forever wander as a wailing spirit,
13. and all because she was a bad wife.

In sharp contrast to the Beja mythical narratives presented, the emotional reactions are made very explicit in the Mexican morality mythical tales. The emotional reaction, that of feeling *pena* ('shame'), is closely tied up to the moral in the ending of the story, a moral which is always stated as a conclusion in this type of narrative.

In Beja morality tales humans are mostly represented by animals and birds, as in 'The crane who married the crow' (see Chapter 3). Even in this and many other Beja morality stories, both the moral and the emotional reactions of the characters are implicit. As the above outline of the *La Llorona* tale exemplifies, however, the basic structure of such a Mexican morality tale and Beja mythical tales is not different. In both kind of narratives this underlying structure contributes to the directive force of the narrative.

8.3.5. Beja *busarā* stories revisited

At this point of the discussion it may be appropriate to subject the *busarā* stories to a closer analysis in the same vein as that applied to the story about the inheritance problem. For each of the narratives the numbers of the sequences corresponds to the structural diagrams (Figures 4–7). The only story omitted is the second story about the man with swollen testicles, since this story represents a simplified version of the story about the Egyptian officer without deviating structurally from it.

*Story I: The **basīr** and the surgeon*

1. *Once during the colonial times,*
2. *a person was hit by a stick or a stone on his head.*
3. *This blow broke the bones of the head, and some pieces of the skull lay on the brain.*
4. *The man then began to speak gibberish.*
5. *No modern doctor could help him.*
6. *One **basīr** named Shegelab, from the Hamdab, when he saw this man,*
7. *touched his body on the arms and eyes just like a doctor.*
8. *When he got to know about the brain problems,*
9. *he made a cut in the place.*
10. *He removed the pieces of bones from the vessels of the brain and covered the place with skin.*
11. *The person then began to eat and speak normally again.*
12. *One of the doctors in the Hospital of Port Sudan then said to him:[89] 'Please stay with us and assist us,'*
13. *but he refused.'*

This story represents an 'outcome-embedded' narrative, as is demonstrated by Figure 4. The problem of episode 1 causes someone, probably his relatives, to seek out various solutions, including biomedical doctors. Finally they seek the help of a *basīr*. Who the actors are as well as how they came in contact with the *basīr* is implicit in the story. Whatever is inferred by the potential listeners, it is not important for the overall story or for

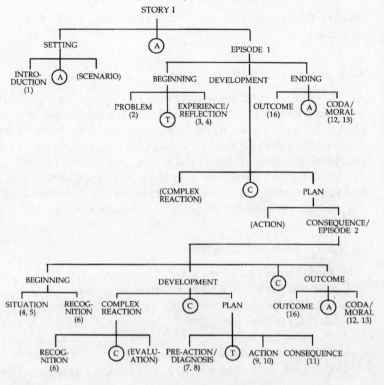

Figure 4: *The structure of 'The* **basīr** *and the surgeon'*

its moral, as made explicit in sequences 12 and 13. The efforts pursued in episode 1 result in a *basīr* following a goal-path in episode 2, which results in an outcome (sequence 11) which represents a solution to both episodes 1 and 2.

The complex reaction in episode 1 is tacit. In episode 2 it is stated that the *basīr* acted in a particular way 'when he saw this man.' This is the closest we get to an account of a complex reaction. However, nothing is said about the emotions or reflections of the traditional healer.

Story II: The **basīr** *and the Egyptian officer*

1. *In the colonial period one of the Hamdab* **sheikhs**[90] *followed an Egyptian officer to collect taxes from the nomads.*
2. *It was far away from the towns, so they used camels.*

3. *The Egyptian officer had swollen testicles.*
4. *When he rode his camel, the swelling was painful.*
5. *He couldn't eat or drink, and he was crying.*
6. *When the Beja **sheikh** saw his situation,*
7. *he said to him: 'I will take you to a **basīr** who can treat you.'*
8. *Then, when they reached a settlement, he[91] told one man to pretend that he was a **basīr**.*
9. *The man[92] said to him: 'I want to burn you as treatment.'*
10. *After this the **sheikh** said to him: 'I will call for four strong guys to hold your arms and legs.*
11. *He did so,*
12. *and they held his arms and legs.*
13. *Then they began to heat a piece of metal in fire.*
14. *The Egyptian began to cry loudly,*
15. *and the swelling went back into the body and disappeared as a result of his fright.*
16. *Then the man pretending to be **basīr** said to the four men: 'Leave him.'*
17. *The Egyptian then was well again.*
18. *He began to eat and drink tea,*
19. *because you know, those Egyptians they love tea!'*

This 'outcome-embedded' story is structurally accounted for in Figure 5. The account in sequences 6 and 7 is not truly a description of a complex reaction, since both thoughts and emotions are absent from it. However, a decision is made clear in sequence 7, a decision which tacitly presupposes motivation. More typically, a description of a complex reaction is omitted for episode 2.

This story is a more complex one than the previous one, since it has both an overt and a hidden message. The overt part has to do with the efficacy of the simple and proven traditional Beja wisdom. The hidden message is that Beja conduct and traditions are superior to foreign ones, here exemplified by a ludicrous Egyptian character. While emotional signs usually are given little or no place in mythical narratives, Story II violates the norm abundantly by both describing the Egyptian as crying from pain and later on as crying from fright. In accordance with this line of thought the story ends with a humorous consideration instead of a general moral in sequence 19.

STORY II

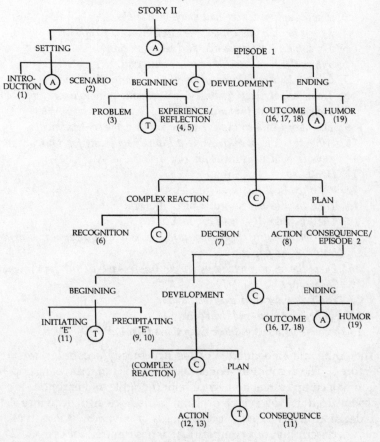

Figure 5: *The structure of 'The* **basīr** *and the Egyptian officer'*

Story III: The **basīr** *and the child who lacked a mouth*

1. *A child was once*
2. *born without any opening for a mouth.*
3. *Then the family called for one Hamdab* **basīr**.
4. *He made a mark on the place of the mouth*
5. *and opened it with a knife.*
6. *After this he put a stick between the gums.*
7. *They fed the child by butter for a long time and gave it milk through a pipe in the mouth for a long time*
8. *until the child recovered.'*

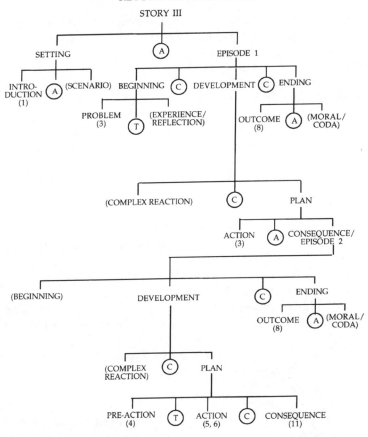

Figure 6: *The structure of 'The basīr and the child who lacked a mouth'*

The Story III is yet another example of an 'outcome-embedded' story, with a structural 'backbone' as presented in Figure 6. The setting and problem are made clear in the briefest possible way. The outcome is inferable from the last sequence 'until the child recovered.' The complex reactions are as usual omitted. Even the beginning of episode two has to be inferred by the audience. This is probably as short and condensed as it is possible to make a narrative and still capture the interest of a general Beja public.

Mandler (1984) concludes from her experiments that one element, such as complex reaction, may be absent from a story without rendering it incomprehensible or contributing to people losing interest in it. However, if two or more core elements are missing in a story version, she predicts that it will not survive. Given this background it is somewhat surprising that a Beja public could be content with stories so devoid of details as to approach the limit of what is understandable. As demonstrated abundantly for personal narratives, the implicitness of Beja narratives may be a special cultural trait in Beja storytelling. Indeed, this trait places the Beja tradition on the opposite end of classical Greek narrative tradition on a tentative scale of 'immediateness'[93] vs. 'implicitness.'

Story IV: The lizard who clung to the brain

1. *This happened during colonial times.*
2. *Once a lizard managed to get inside a person's head and sat on his brain and clung to it.*
3. *We do not know how it entered, only God knows.*
4. *When doctors tried to do operations on him,*
5. *they were not able to do so, because it clung so strongly to the brain that they could not remove it without removing part of the brain.*
6. *Because the English people at that time knew that the Hamdab were very experienced people,*
7. *they asked for them.*
8. *A Hamdab person came,*
9. *and he brought three things: a piece of fire [metal heated in fire], a piece of cotton with butter and a metal tool to hold the heated piece of metal.*
10. *First he took the heated material and moved it near the brain after the doctor opened the skull, and he then put the metal closer and closer to the lizard.*
11. *It retracted its legs, and he applied cotton under them one by one, repeating the procedure four times for each leg.*
12. *After this it was easy to remove the lizard, because it could not manage to cling to the brain any longer.*
13. *Sometimes the Yudia people know even more than the doctors.'*

A structural outline of this story is given in Figure 7. This fourth 'outcome-embedded' story is more complex than the others in that it consists of three episodes. Like the previous ones, however, the complex reactions are systematically omitted.

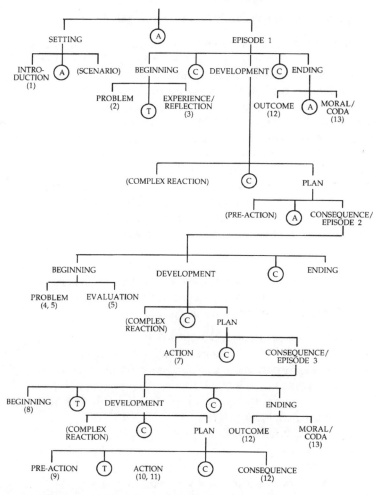

Figure 7: *The structure of 'The lizard who clung to the brain'*

As in the three other *busará* stories the actions and the consequences of the actions occupy most of the sequences of the story. This trait makes such mythical narratives appear condensed. In other words, their content may be said to exceed their basic form.

8.3.6. Story grammars and the 'model of mind'

All the *busará* stories presented in this section demonstrate the
recurrent underlying story structure proposed by Mandler. Basically, this structure represents more than just a device for easy
memorization that occurs cross-culturally. Interestingly enough,
it reflects parts of a typical 'folk model of the mind' as accounted
for by Roy D'Andrade (1995:161–162). In such a model an 'event'
is 'perceived,' which again leads to 'thoughts' in the perceiving
individual. The thoughts evoke 'feelings', 'feelings' further shape
'wishes,' and both 'feelings' and 'wishes' in turn influence the
'thoughts.' The 'feelings' may have an overt manifestation in
'expressive' or 'reflexive acts,' while 'wishes' create 'intentions'
which motivate 'acts.' This 'folk model of the mind' gives a
generalized schema for accounting for why other people react
and act in the way they do. As brilliantly demonstrated by
William Labov (1982), one of the most disturbing experiences
humans can make is when they are part of or observe events
which seemingly do not fit such a folk model. The story of an
American sailor exemplifies this (p.221):

1. Oh I w's settin' at a table drinkin'.
2. And – uh – this Norwegian sailor come over
3. an' kep' givin' me a bunch o' junk about I was sittin' with
   his woman.
4. An' everybody sittin' at the table with me were my
   shipmates.
5. So I jus' turn aroun'
6. an' shoved 'im,
7. an' told 'im, I said, 'Go away,
8. I don't even wanna fool with ya.'
9. An' next thing I know I'm layin' on the floor, blood all
   over me,
10. an' a guy told me, says, 'Don't move your head.
11. Your throat's cut.'

The gap between sequences 8 and 9 is typical in such violent
stories where the narrator is unable to apply a 'model of mind'
to the aggressive part in the encounter. This gap represents a
'blank' in the mind of the narrator. Moreover, for the American
sailor this 'blank' was present before his violent encounter with
the Norwegian. Indeed, as Labov sees it, being denied having a

personal worth and having a 'model of mind' partly explain the violent reaction of the Norwegian. The Norwegian sailor was reduced to a 'non-person.'

Similar points can be made from stories told by torture victims (Bruner 1990, Rack 1986). From what they tell, the most significant part of post-traumatic stress seems to be the inability of the sufferer to create meaning, to render his or her experiences meaningful. Victims of torture often seem unable to apply a 'model of mind' to the torturers. Stories like the sailor's story above or stories from torture victims are never popular or frequently retold stories, but stories which tend to be part of a particular individuals private and painful experience, stories which, as a rule, never transcend this private realm of agony except in very special circumstances like therapeutic encounters.

In contrast to the sailor's story, the *busará* stories, as well as the Oaxacan morality tales (Mathews 1992), exemplify stories where the basic underlying structure fits a prototypical 'folk model of mind.' The model is never really fully represented by the story's structure. 'Feelings,' 'thoughts,' 'wishes' and 'intentions' do not need to be accounted for in presentations of complex reactions in order to render a story meaningful. Moreover, the whole complex reactions may be tacit, left to the audience to infer. However, as we have seen, even when descriptions of complex reactions are missing, the continuity of the stories is not broken. Quite the contrary, as I will argue, the intentions and wishes of the actors in the stories are brought more sharply to the audience's attention by leaving them unstated.

While a folk model of mind is explicit in Oaxaca morality tales, in Beja narratives all the elements of a model of mind are rarely provided. In order to grasp the content of the Beja stories, however, a complete model of mind must be inferred by the listeners. The elements which are most often lacking are 'wishes' and 'intentions.' By contrast, 'perception' of an 'event' or a 'state of affairs' is often mentioned, and a description of 'thoughts' or 'emotional reactions' is sometimes present. I will argue that a Beja model of mind is a model where personal intentions are highlighted by leaving them out of the stories. The listeners attention is drawn towards what is present in the stories even though it is not stated.

Beja people are very much preoccupied by questions related to the intentions and inclinations of other people. Since people in every society naturally have this preoccupation this may sound like a commonplace statement. As discussed earlier, however, the Beja society is an acephalous society where there are no traditional judicial organs which can force a solution on parties in conflict and where people are reluctant to co-operate with non-relatives, whom are looked upon by fellow Beja as competitors for scarce resources and potential enemies. For these reasons the question about other people's intentions is a very acute concern for every Beja person.

I will argue that a Beja model of mind is not different from an Oaxaca model or from the American model outlined by D'Andrade (1995) in the sense that it consists of different elements connected by different types of logic. It seems reasonable to infer, however, that it is different in quality by reflecting a more acute concern for personal intentions. Since Beja stories reflect such a 'biased' model of mind, both their credibility, comprehension and popularity are enhanced.

8.3.7. Conclusion

The basic underlying schema present in the *busarã* stories seems to be a directing force in the mere 'naturalness' of the progression of events or episodes presented in these stories. Moreover, it facilitates memorizing them, which again secures their survival as part of an oral tradition. As evidenced by Mandler's (1984) research, stories structured this way are easily remembered, while stories breaking with this pattern are more easily forgotten as well as not having the attention-grabbing potential of proto-typical stories, the last point possibly explained by their seemingly simulation of a folk model of mind.

This model of mind may not be different from any Western model of mind with regard to constituent elements. I will argue, however, that the Beja model of mind in its presentation is different in quality from these by leaving people's intentions not stated but nevertheless easy to infer. In this way Beja people's attention is directed towards what obviously is in the stories, but is consequently left out. The motives and intentions of people are thus highlighted, a trait which render the stories intense and full of suspense. By repeating a given and relatively inflexible narrative structure reflecting a Beja model of mind, a convincing and easily memorable logic gives the stories a cultural directive force.

The stories are given a directional force by other means as well. This last point is best illustrated by contrasting them with personal narratives. While, as we have seen, personal narratives require much cultural understanding and the cultural background required to understand even a seemingly simple sequence may be vast, this is generally not true for mythical stories of the *busarã°* type. For *busarã°* stories, I propose that even non-Beja with no acquaintance with the Beja culture may easily grasp the main message of the stories. Of course certain kinds of knowledge like knowledge of animal husbandry may contribute to a richer understanding of a story like that of the inheritance problem. However, one may still grasp and enjoy the dominant message of the story without such knowledge.

Hence I will propose that the sequences of such stories are usually not open to different possible readings. Since different cultural theories may render parts of personal narratives understandable, personal narratives may usually be seen as uncompleted stories to which new elements may be added each time the stories are told. *Busarã°* stories, by contrast, are 'canonical' stories told to convince people in a certain matter. The *busarã°* narratives support a traditional belief in the efficiacy, wisdom and relevance of traditional medicine and traditional healers.

Beja personal narratives, in contrast to mythical narratives like *busarã°* stories, allow for flexibility as well as reflexivity. Nevertheless, the reflexivity seems to be mostly bound to the interpretation of concrete instances like specific sickness episodes, the sickness histories and fate of specific persons and detectable changes in their living conditions and social and natural environments. The basic assumptions, through which they experience the world, are in general fixed in their form.

I introduced Chapter 8 by stating my twofold aim. Firstly, I wanted to demonstrate the necessity of drawing upon the various Beja folk theories presented in Chapter 4 for understanding Beja narratives. A line-by-line analysis of both personal and mythical stories has shown the presence of such implicit knowledge in all the stories presented. Secondly, I wanted to elucidate the pragmatics of linking folk theories to real-life situations by narrative means. It has been demonstrated in this chapter that Beja stories about sickness and health are of two main types entailing two very different main forms of pragmatics.

NOTES

1 In Sarbin (1986:162–163).
2 Spiro does not relate his statement to possession at all, and he may possibly be reluctant to my usage of his statement. However, his words somehow capture my feeling when I first heard her story.
3 Several of these researchers, however, acknowledge that women attendants tend to dominate the cults. Makris (1991) notes that for a special type of *zār*, *zār tumbura*, many males of slave descent tend to join. See Chapter 4 and Chapter 6.
4 Sudanese Arabic word for leaves from the local doom palm, leaves used as building material for huts and for making different kinds of household utensils, *birish* (sing.), *burūsh* (pl.).
5 Local palm tree, *Hyphaene theabaica*.
6 During that drought, Beja people lost between 75 and 95% of their animals, the most severe blow ever against their nomadic existence.
7 Slightly more than twenty years before we established contact with her.
8 As discussed earlier, one can never ask a Beja any kind of direct or indirect question regarding their economic situation, for this reason one has to make estimations or indirect inferences.
9 Around two to three years before we met her.
10 *Hejāb* is a Sudanese Arabic word for an amulet containing a paper with protective inscriptions from the Quran on it. See Chapter 4.
11 The word *sheikh* has a range of different applications in Sudanese Arabic. It might be a type of political traditional leader, a religious leader or, as here, a leader of *zār* cults (f.*sheikha*). In this latter sense the word designates a type of healer.
12 *Bakhūr* is the most commonly used incense, usually consisting of *lubān* (gum extract of *commiphora pedunculata* (*lat.*), an imported herb) and *kamūn aswad*, *Caminum cyminum*, an imported herb). It is commonly used by Beja both as treatment and to protect themselves against spirit attacks. See Chapter 4.
13 Most probably a kind of amulet.
14 *Mihaya* is a medicine made by *fugarā'* by writing Quranic verses with ink on a sheet of paper or a piece of wood, washing it off by water and using the water solution of ink as medicine for the patient to drink or to smear on his body. See Chapter 4.
15 A general practitioner in Port Sudan who died several years ago.
16 Arabic word for a particular women's dress.
17 Sudanese Arabic word designating a white head cloth for men.
18 Arabic word, meaning a long Indian shirt.
19 Arabic word for a particular Indian jacket, for men.
20 Traditional Beja shoes.

21 Beja word, trousers for men.
22 Long dress used by Beja religious and political *sheikhs*.
23 Meaning 'mountain *zār*,' a Beja version of *zār*.
24 It is usual to avoid celebrations on Mondays and Wednesdays during *zār* ceremonies, at least in the Sudan.
25 Arabic word meaning English or English-like, addressed to Janike. In this connection it points towards the colonial period before 1956, as it usually does in *zār* when connected to *khawāja* ceremonies.
26 *Hay* is an Arabic word designating an administrative subpart of a town. As an administrative part it is supposed to be regulated in regard to placement of house, size of property, water and toilet regulations. However, most of the population of Sinkat are living in unregulated, so-called 'illegal' areas.
27 See Chapter 4 for description.
28 *Karāma* is a Classical Arabic word meaning 'generosity, favor, mercy.' It is used by Sudanese Muslims for denoting giving of alms to poor and needy and for various offerings or gifts of thankfulness to God.
29 Remedy for the child sickness of *tesérimt*: See theory L for discussion.
30 I took part in some *zār*-ceremonies in Khartoum as well where this theme was stressed. In much literature concerning *zār* and as well *fagīr* treatment from different parts of the Muslim world the holiness and potential healing power of sacrifice blood is stressed (see, e.g. Boddy 1989; and Lewis *et al.* 1991).
31 See, e.g. Boddy (1989) for an expansive outline of this theme from her observance of *zār*-ceremonies in Northern Sudan.
32 See Chapter 4 for a wider discussion.
33 See, e.g. *The Medicine of the Prophet*, reference in Chapter 4.
34 Such deals are called *galád* in Beja language. The ability of the *fagīr* to go into such negotiations with spirits is considered important for his success as a healer.
35 See Chapter 4.
36 It may be more correct to say that the *fagīr* is getting the *karāma* on behalf of God, since God is the one that, in the final analysis, is giving treatment.
37 See Chapter 3 and Chapter 6.8. for discussions on this point.
38 In Beja society this is not a rule without exceptions. I came across several stories about women, men and children who died as a result of *zār* spirits. See earlier Chapter 4 for a more lengthy discussion.
39 The real staple food of Beja. It is made of sorghum and water, ideally with milk added to it. During drought it will often be served without milk.
40 See Chapter 6.8. for a broader discussion of this point.
41 Beja word which literally means 'spider,' but denotes also sickness resulting from spider bites, whether ordinary spiders or 'spirit spiders.' See Chapter 4.
42 See Wehr (1961).
43 See Chapter 4 and Chapter 6.7. for discussion.
44 See, e.g. Labov 1982; Labov & Fanshel 1977; Labov & Waletsky 1967; and Sarbin 1986.

45 Both foreshadowing and encapsulating the past often go beyond the narrative time of the story. As an example, what the narrator thinks will happen in the future, may also be part and parcel of her present story.

46 A general medical practitioner in Port Sudan who died around ten years ago.

47 *Sara'a* in Arabic. Usually translated 'epilepsy' by English speaking people. See Chapter 4.

48 Characterized by weakness in the limbs. The child may be unable to walk and his hands or feet may become turned inwards in an awkward position. See Chapter 4.

49 See, e.g. Feierman & Janzen 1992; Loudon 1976; and Slikkerveer 1990.

50 All old colonial paraphernalia.

51 Cinnamon.

52 One of my Beja male informants has been possessed by a *zār* spirit for more than twenty years. He frequently joins *zār* ceremonies and talks easily about his personal experiences, in contrast to most Beja men who have a *zār* diagnosis. Many Beja men feel that being possessed by a *zār* spirit is unmanly, and for this reason it was difficult for me to find out how prevalent *zār* possession is among males. Among married females the occurrence is high, a fact made visible by the high attendance of possessed women in local *zār* ceremonies.

53 In urban and semi-urban areas. In rural areas, as discussed earlier, the sex of the spirit is often the same as that of the host. In rural areas, affliction by *zār* spirits is sometimes indistinguishable from affliction by 'bad luck' from spirits like Enshiband and other causes (see Chapter 6.7.).

54 Centers for basic Islamic education of children.

55 In the seven different *zār* parties in which I had the opportunity to take part, the most frequently occurring *zār* spirits seemed to be connected to the most recent colonizers in the Sudan, the British. It is perhaps no wonder that the British colonizers provide several kinds of mirrors through which Beja and other Sudanese people may continuously reflect on themselves and their own lives.

56 As discussed in Chapter 4, *zār* ceremonies are characterized by a lot of symbolism alluding to marriage, like calling the patient 'bride,' by using carpets strictly reserved for marriage ceremonies, and by painting the patient and the animal to be offered by *henna, Lawsonia inermis*.

57 Such contradictory observances are described by people studying *ngoma* possession cults in Southern Africa as well.

58 Though I recognize these gains for women, I do not think they totally explain why *zār* cults and theories about *zār* spirits are present among the Beja people. For one thing, many men possessed by *zār* do not obtain similar gains, although some may experience economic support. Some of the Beja men possessed by *zār* spirits are socially marginal, but far from all of them. It also is difficult to see what is

302

to be gained by Beja parents from choosing *zār* as a diagnosis for sick children rather than other diagnoses. Finally, and this is an important point, *zār* diagnosis is often used by Beja as a diagnosis for 'bad luck.' In other words, it seems to me that the Beja theories about *héequal*-ness as a contrast to 'bad luck' intermingles with their ideas about *zār*. If I am correct, *zār* as a phenomenon among the Beja is in some respects different from *zār* in other regions of the Middle East. Hence, even if *zār* as a possession cult may be proved to be primarily a cult of socially marginal people in some other societies, this does not necessarily hold for the Beja.

59 A *khalwa* is a Quranic school where the students are taught to memorize the Quran and learn some of the fundamentals of Islamic belief, law and practice.

60 'Islamic Quranic healer,' see Chapter 4.

61 Plural of *basīr*, the local bone-setter and 'general practitioner' (see Chapter 3).

62 As explained for Theory F, smells are in general thought of as causing both health and ill-health by Beja people.

63 *Busarā'* living in a special place called Yudia, from Hamdab subtribe of the Hadandowa tribe.

64 Later on I asked a new medical doctor at the Sinkat hospital with a better local knowledge. In his opinion, very few of the cases could be syphilis. Mostly he suspected different forms of fungus infections. But, this does not totally explain the durability of the lesions and the extent to which some children were born with them.

65 The term is derived from the grammatical concept 'subjunctive mood' in describing how people in narratives open up for imagined and counterfactual worlds (see, e.g. Good 1994). See later discussion in this chapter on the concept of subjunctiveness.

66 Like recorded from many parts of Africa, Beja people do not always distinguish clearly between sicknesses and other misfortunes, which might have the same etiology.

67 Astrid Blystad and Liv Haram, University of Bergen, personal communication.

68 As discussed in Chapter 4, butter oil is in general looked upon as health bringing by the nomadic Beja and used alone or together with other items as medicine against many sicknesses.

69 A camel with special cuttings in the ears: see following discussion.

70 See Chapter 6.

71 Called *toodíh* in Beja language, see Chapter 4.

72 A camel ritually marked by cuttings in its ears to make it *héequal*, see earlier discussions.

73 As discussed earlier, *tesérimt* may stem from camels, cows and wild animals. Some people think that each of the three instances needs for different kinds of herbs.

74 Meaning, 'God willing' or 'according to the will of God.'

75 Both words mean 'maybe' in Sudanese Arabic.

76 The following stories are mythical in the sense that the audience is presented with propositions about how the world is, but without

experiencing them as propositions. By their mere naturalness the narratives supply the listeners with **the** reality.

77 The only 'real name' to occur in this book.
78 The *basīr*.
79 Here meaning 'political leader.'
80 The *sheikh*.
81 The man pretending to be the *basīr*.
82 Strong coffee, served in small cups, often with spices.
83 *Busarā* living in a special place called Yudia, from Hamdab subtribe of the Hadandowa tribe, one of the five Beja tribes. See Chapter 4.
84 See for example Chapter 6.13.
85 During colonial times virtually all medical doctors in the Red Sea Hills were British.
86 As an example, Mandler (1980) disagrees with the claim of Rumelhart (1977) that story episodes at a higher level of generalization are more important than episodes at a lower level.
87 In contrast with its conventional use within the natural sciences.
88 A comparison was made between the recall of stories by Liberian nonschooled children, nonliterate adults, nonschooled literate adults, and schooled literate adults from a Vai-speaking rural and agricultural society on the one side and American adults and children on the other.
89 The *basīr*.
90 Here meaning 'political leader.'
91 The *sheikh*.
92 The man pretending to be a *basīr*.
93 By 'immediateness' I mean that all elements of the Greek stories are explicitly present so as to render only the 'here and now' important. Such a story is like a type of photograph where everything needed in order to grasp the picture is clearly visible in this picture.

9

ARRIVALS

9.1. BASIC ASSUMPTIONS

Regardless of types of logic employed in Beja reasoning about health and sickness at a 'deep-structural' level, basically their folk theories build upon non-testable assumptions about the world. Many of these assumptions seem to link to conceptions of 'substances' and 'inner essences' of both animate and inanimate objects. There are basically three reasons why I have paid so much attention to 'essence' in this book. Firstly, Beja people steadily voice a concern about substances influencing the bodies of humans and animals making them sick or more healthy. Secondly, theories of 'essence' and 'essence-inferences' have a great explanatory potential in accounting for a broad range of Beja folk theories of sickness and health.

Thirdly, the cross-cultural evidence for instant inferences made from conceptions of essence seems compelling. As has been amply demonstrated by several cognitive psychologists, as soon as people make an assumption about a type of natural object, a cognitive limitation seems to operate which severely limits the range of qualities possible for this particular object. As an example provided earlier, even with small children, if a given object is said to be 'sleepy,' it may well be believed to become angry, but not to be easy to fix to the wall.

Instantiations of essentialist kinds of conceptualizing may hence be a pan-human 'trait.' However, even if future research within the human sciences may validate this theoretical stance, there is probably little reason to assume that overt 'surface-structural' patterns like those found for the Hadandowa Beja cultural schemata of sickness and health can be predicted from such insight. Yet, future cross-cultural research into basic forms of human thinking and reasoning will definitely be a contribution to a humanistic endeavor of understanding more about what makes humans human.

That conceptions of 'essence' are transferred to areas where they do not ontologically apply may well account for various forms of religious beliefs, as has been demonstrated by Pascal Boyer (1993, 1996a, 1996b). However, such transfers of reasoning across concept domains are probably abundantly present in non-religious contexts in Western societies as well. As an example, recent research by Lawrence A. Hirschfeld (1995) suggests that children even as young as three years old spontaneously make conceptual representations of race. Moreover, their representations seem more theory-like than researchers previously have tended to believe. The reasoning of the children who took part in his experiments seemingly has a strong element of 'essence'-thinking which closely resembles reasoning for natural ontologies, or in his own words:

> 'Rather than borrowing principles for causal reasoning from naive biology, I propose that young children's racial thinking is organized around the same biases to prefer certain kinds of explanations over others [. . .] that are embodied in naive biology. Thus what naive biology and racial thinking share may not be a commitment to a morphologically derived ontology, but a common instantiation of an essentialist pattern of causal reasoning' (p.247).

The assumptions of 'essence' exemplified by treating different 'races' as 'natural kinds' is one of the modes of inference which seemingly accounts for Beja theories of supernaturally or partly mystically caused sicknesses, such as sicknesses of 'mystical influence' like *tesérimt* or sicknesses caused by spirit affliction. As has been demonstrated, 'essence' derived assumptions also probably account for the success of some healers and the spiritual force of religious people. In addition, it accounts for many of the 'physical' and 'natural' sicknesses like *hāf* and *kosúlt*, where the sicknesses are thought of as 'natural kinds' with physical properties of various inanimate objects encountered in their daily life, like charcoal and metal cooking equipment. The powerful influence in pseudo-natural reasoning upon theories of sicknesses is, however, particularly evident when the same 'natural' sicknesses, like *hāf* and *kosúlt*, are treated as living persons.

The relevance and salience of 'essence' reasoning in Beja conceptions of health and sickness are greatly expanded by various 'essences' conceived of as being able to spread and be partly transferred to other objects. As has been shown, this theory has its counterpart in the perhaps equally important conception of similarity, in which objects which share some features are treated 'as if' they shared the same basic essence. As made clear in the latter section of Chapter 6, theories of 'essences' are likely to be sources of metaphoric and metonymic conceptions. The notion that 'things similar in form share the same essence' probably partly explain processes of metaphorization. The notion that 'essences are equally distributed throughout the form which they occupy' and ideas of 'contamination by the spread of essences' are both probable, although by no means exhaustive, sources of metonymization.

9.2. NARRATIVES, FOLK THEORIES AND THE PRAGMATICS OF SICKNESS NEGOTIATION

By leaving the greater part of narratives not stated, the listeners are engaged in activating various aspects of their cultural knowledge each time a story is told. As has been demonstrated, the things left unsaid are parts of a wide range of cultural theories. Although these theories are logical in their step-by-step inferences at each theoretical level, they basically build upon presumptions about how the world is; presumptions which are, like dogmas in every culture, closed to disconfirmation.

The personal narratives and the mythical narratives engage the audience in quite different ways. Personal sickness narratives clearly leave more cultural knowledge not stated than *busarâ* stories. For this reason they demand a more extensive body of background knowledge in order to be understood. In addition, different mutually exclusive cultural models may render the same story culturally meaningful. Two important features of personal narratives relate to this last point. Firstly, the body of cultural knowledge invoked by the story is further increased. Secondly, the seemingly fixed cultural theories are, by this flexibility, made relevant for real-life situations, situations which are often marked by uncertainties and doubts. Such uncertainties relate to which symptoms to stress and how to interpret them, what measures to take as well as, in case of prolonged sickness or death, whether everything which could or ought to be done was done.

The mythical narratives require less background knowledge. They have, however, much more directive or 'perlocutionary'[1] force. They acquire this force, apparently, through two means. Firstly, by restricting the area of background knowledge needed to understand them, the range of possible interpretations is severely limited. Secondly, by their very structure simulating a 'folk model of mind,' they entail a persuasive logic compelling the audience to think along a given line. Calling this a 'cultural grammar,' though, may be partly misleading, since the term may in present scientific discourses invoke more linguistic than psychological connotations. Such a persuasive logic is, as we have seen, inherent in mythical folktales like 'moral tales' and 'religious' or 'educational' tales in many societies around the world. Since this persuasive logic is hidden, like hidden messages and devices in types of Western mass media commercial advertising, it influences people without usually itself being put into question. By providing the *basīr* tradition with legitimacy, *busarā'* stories also validate the cultural resources which the folk tradition of *busarā'* represents, namely the cultural theories accounted for in Chapter 6.

At this point it may be proper to draw some conclusions about the very cultural theories and models 'celebrated' repeatedly by performance of both personal and mythical narratives. As discussed in Chapter 2, focusing on the classification of symptoms, sickness labels and etiologies alone prove to be insufficient for this analysis. Looking for such classifications does not enhance an understanding of Beja sickness narratives and the various sequences they entail, although it may lead the researcher to ask more important questions. I arrived at a mode of analysis which provided me with data with a higher degree of psychological validity by directing my efforts toward understanding Beja folk explanations. In this manner I obtained data which I could present in discussions with them and which they could voice opinions about. Although the Beja did not necessarily agree with my conclusions, they were mostly able to recognize the matters I was dealing with and the questions I raised as relevant. A last but not least, an 'unraveling' of Beja cultural models made details in their stories both meaningful and contextually logical, which may be the most important test of the validity of the formulations.

As has been made clear in the analysis, even the simplest utterance made in a Beja narrative may presuppose rich cultural theories. This knowledge may be fruitfully conceived of as consisting of cultural schemata connected to each other. It makes sense to look upon one particular schema as instantiating a lower-level schema as well as being instantiated by a higher-level schema. Quite often the schemata of the lowest level contain situationally specific prescripts for how to diagnose a specific sickness as well as how to go about treating it. This means that diagnosis making and treatment are linked to etiology (theories of causation) primarily at this lower level.

As explained in Chapter 6.13., a general characteristic of the manner in which different levels of the same theory relate to each other may be captured by the concept *plausible inference*, a concept developed by Collins and Michalski (1989, in D'Andrade 1995:197) and applied by the anthropologist Edwin Hutchins for Trobiand land litigation (Hutchins 1978, 1980).

The logics of *modus ponens* or *modus tollens* are virtually never employed in Beja sickness narratives or in real-life situations. As discussed in Chapter 8.2., this may be explained by a Beja 'ethos of uncertainty' and an unwillingness to state things absolutely. However, such an explanation does not alone account for the lack of those two kinds of logic in Beja sickness reasoning and the prominence of the two others. The flexibility created in personal narratives as well as in negotiations of concrete sickness instances by both the logics of *plausible inference* and *denial of the antecedent* render the Beja cultural theories of sicknesses and the world at large meaningful in most thinkable real-life situations. This flexibility is further increased by the narrators using several linguistic uncertainty markers (*irrealis*). If their reasoning was to be 'closed' by logics of *modus ponens* or *modus tollens*, the disorders, surprises and messiness of occurrences of sickness and various kinds of misfortune could not be accounted for.

Clearly, the way in which Beja theories and propositions are put into use in daily life situations allows for flexibility as well as reflexivity. Nevertheless, this reflexivity seems to be mostly bound to the interpretation of concrete instances like specific sickness episodes, the sickness histories and fate of specific persons and detectable changes in their living conditions and social and natural environments. The basic assumptions, through which they experience the world are seldom put into question. One possible explanation for this may be found in the manner in which tacit and not communicated assumptions of the world seem to underlie the cultural schemata which they are able to communicate.

These basic assumptions, as we have seen, seem to be derived from notions of 'essence' and the spread of essence by 'contagion' and appear both to underlie most of Beja theories of sickness and health as well as tying them together by serving as a common theme 'cross-cutting' the theories. This does not mean that it is not possible to make them subject to communication. However, this knowledge is as yet not made verbally explicit. Moreover, it is sufficiently removed from the problems and reasoning of daily life so as to expect that even if some Beja get interested in it, it will probably never become a topic for discussion among Beja people in general. Such revelations will probably suffer the same fate as Susan Sontag's (1978, 1989) popular accounts of metaphors and metonyms in modern Western conceptions of tuberculosis and AIDS. People interested in the development of Western cultural traditions found them interesting, while most people remain outside their influence.

9.3. NOTIONS OF 'ESSENCE' AND 'CONTAGION' IN THE CONTEXT OF BEJA CULTURE AND SOCIETY

Ideas of 'contagion' and 'spread of essence' may continue to be predominant among Beja people in times to come, whether some of those ideas will become explicit matters for discussion or not. Most Hadandowa Beja live in a world where one's own *diwáb* is seen as the most important unit of social reference and the primary corporate and co-operative unit and one's own people are the only ones who can be trusted. Lacking higher levels of effective resource management and living in a rather hostile and marginal natural environment, the enormous significance of the small-scale *diwábs* should not be surprising.

The *diwáb* is also perceived by Beja as closely linked to the area which its people inhabit. Food grown in one's own area is the best and healthiest food, while food brought in from outside is potentially harmful. In general, influence from outside, whether political, cultural or mediated by material objects, is potentially harmful and dangerous. In such circumstances, given the importance of notions of 'essence' in Beja cultural theories, their preoccupation with contagion and intrusion of potentially harmful substances makes good sense. Some kinds of intrusion are perceived by Beja as aggressive intrusion by ill-intended spirits. As discussed in Chapters 3 and 4, notions of such kind of encroachment by 'pseudo-natural' objects makes better sense ethnographically than ideas of witchcraft and sorcery, which are virtually absent in Beja lives.

Ideas of 'positive contamination' seem to be linked to, for example, efforts of transferring a luck-bringing 'essence' to valuable domestic animals like camels in order to enhance good health and fertility. However, the benefits achieved by those efforts for one *diwâb* turns out to be of disadvantage for others. Parallel to the mutual spirit of mistrust among the *diwâbs* are ideas that negative influences by 'contaminating spread of essence' from other *diwâbs* are potentially harmful for ones own.

By way of conclusion, ideas of 'contagion' and 'spread of essence' may probably continue to be important to Beja people, since they make sense within their daily life experiences, of which sicknesses and misfortunes are part. Like ideas of 'an invisible hand' in Western economics, they may survive, not primarily because of their inherent logic or lack of it, but because they continue to make sense to Beja people in a given adaptation and prevailing circumstances and continue to render their experiences meaningful. As I have come to argue, these ideas are not parallel to Western scientific ideas. As we have seen, they rather parallel Western thoughts related to different objects as inherently having 'essences,' objects with similar forms having similar 'essences' and 'essences' having particular properties, properties which may spread to other objects or humans by 'positive' or 'negative contagion.'

A last question should perhaps be asked: how does one know when one encounters knowledge which is not communicated, like notions of 'essence'? My own experience throughout this investigation suggests that one has at least to account for as much as possible of what knowledge is made explicit and communicated inter-subjectively. Armed with such knowledge one may fruitfully investigate the 'unsaid.'

NOTE

1 A 'perlocutionary act' is what we bring about or achieve by uttering something. This 'perlocution' is dependent upon the conventional force of the utterance. See Austin 1962 for a further discussion.

APPENDIX 1

LIST OF SUDANESE ARABIC TERMS USED

ʿamal: Sorcery.

bakhūr: Incense.

baraka: Prosperity; blessing; increased fertility.

basīr
(pl.busarāʾ): Literally meaning 'one who can see the unseen.' Used for bone setters in Arabic speaking areas all over the Middle East.

birish
(pl.burūsh): Leaves from the local *doom* palm, *Hyphaene theabaica*, which are used by Beja as material for household utensils, mats as well as for covering the huts.

bismillah: Meaning 'by the name of God.'

dawa: Meaning 'medicine' in general. However, in Beja ordinary usage it most often designates remedies from *fugarāʾ*.

fagīr
(pl.fugarā): The word stems from the classical concept *faqī*, which strictly means 'poor'. It has also acquired the meaning 'holy or religious man' and is often used for a local religious leader in Islamic societies. In present-day Red Sea Hills it is exclusively used for religious healers.

furāsh: Period of mourning after death of a person.

gurbāb: A long Indian shirt.

harām: Ritually (religiously) forbidden.

hay: An administrative sub-part of a town.

hejāb
(pl.hejbāt): An amulet which contains Quranic verses.

hejāma: Bleeding horn.

313

ḥenna: Made from the leaves of an aromatic tree and mixed with Indian oil. Smeared on the hands and feet of newly-wed as well as married women in general.

'imma: Beja pronounciation of Sudanese Arabic ʿ*imma,* a white head cloth for men.

injilīzi: English; from England.

ins: From Arabic *insān(un),* which may be translated 'a human being.' Beja people sometimes use the word for spirits in order not to pronounce the word *jinn.*

jallūka: Refers in a strict sense to the drum used in *zār* ceremony, but the word is also used to denote *zār* parties proper, of 3-7 days duration.

jinn (pl.junūn):   Meaning 'spirits' in general. However, the word is virtually never used for *zār* spirits. It is as well more often employed to denote evil spirits than good spirits.

jubāli: Meaning 'from the mountains,' often used about clothes etc. in the sense of traditional clothes.

karāma: A sacrifice; alms to the poor; an offering to God.

khalwa: A Quranic school.

khawāja: Sudanese Arabic word for white foreigners.

khoor: Seasonal brook appearing in the rainy season.

mihaya: Formulas, usually Quranic, are written on a sheet of paper or a piece of wood and washed away with water. The water is given to the patient to drink or to smear on the body.

omda: A local political leader, which in present-day Sudan may be traditional or recognized by the political authorities. He is ranking above a local political *sheikh* and below the *sheikh al-qat.*

rutūba: Rheumatism.

shagīga: Half-side acute headache.

shayyeet: Long dress used by Beja religious and political *sheikhs.*

sheikh: Political or religious leader.

sidderiyya: An Indian jacket for men frequently worn in the Red Sea Hills.

siḥir: Sorcery; magic

sūg: From Arabic *sūq,* meaning 'market' or the

(commercial) center of a town.

suflis: Benevolent Muslim spirits.

ṭayyāb: A smaller and more limited version of a *zār* party.

toob: Arabic word for a particular women's dress.

'ulwis: Malevolent spirits.

waṣl: A type of Quranic medicine made by writing a formula or Quranic inscription on a piece of paper, burn the paper and solute the ashes in water and give the patient to drink or smear on his or her body.

zār: A possession cult. *Zār* is as well the name of the spirits possessing people.

APPENDIX 2

LIST OF BEJA TERMS USED

Vernacular names of different herbs, bushes and trees does not occur in this list. All of them are explained in the text as they occur.

Adal óot: Strictly meaning 'red girl'. It is used as a name for a red stone deriving from a particular red mountain, which probably was considered to be holy in former times. The stone is used in powdered form to counteract the sickness of *tesérimt* (see below).

Alíib: Sickness resulting from prolonged 'fright sickness'. Typical symptoms are general weakness, thinness, reduced strength in the feet and, possibly, blown up stomach.

Boyée: Sickness with infected wounds in the mouth.

Dérwou: Meaning 'fainting'. Sometimes the word is used as an euphemism for epilepsy, in order not to pronounce the dreaded word *tordíp*.

Dérwout: A mixture of herbs, butter oil and *adal óot* stone (see below) used as protection against *tesérimt* (see below) as well as treatment for this sickness.

Diwáb: Smallest segment of the Beja lineage system. Although part of a patrilineal lineage system, this smallest segment has in practice an ambilineal recruitment.

Door érr: Meaning 'cousin'. Used in a broad sense as to cover classificatory cousins.

Gúrda: A sickness characterized by fever, pain all over

316

	the body and laziness. Thought to be caused by green vegetation after rich rain.
Hāf:	A serious stomach sickness often causing death. The stomach is swollen and thought to contain 'solid parts'.
Hāf masóob:	A children's sickness which is less severe than *hāf*. Swollen stomach and diarrhea are typical symptoms.
Háale:	Meaning 'mad' or 'madness'.
Hamash-ragadíd:	Equivalent to the Sudanese Arabic word *junūn* (pl. of *jinn*), meaning spirits.
Hemiéf:	The concept strictly means 'delayed breakfast'. It designates as well a non-serious sickness condition resulting from not having breakfast in time.
Heminéit:	Both a name for a conceived stomach fluid (stomach in a broad sense) and a bad stomach condition (see discussions)
Herár:	Common term for various conditions leading to yellow discoloring of the skin and the sclera of the eyes.
Héequal:	A concept denoting both good luck, holiness and fertility.
Hindíib (pl.híndib):	A broad concept covering herbs, bushes and trees.
Hūm:	Brain.
'Ikwib:	Meaning 'overgrounds', referring to spirits inhabiting the space over the ground.
Imérar:	Blood vessels. The term sometimes include the nerves.
Ináwa:	Nerves.
'Iwhib:	Meaning 'undergrounds', referring to spirits dwelling underground.
Kalawáb:	Literally means 'inside' of anything, like the inside of a cup. It is also used to denote the inside of the stomach (in a broad sense).
Kelay ťáat:	Literally the expression means 'the bird stroke'. A special kind of spirit bird is thought to cause half side facial paralysis by slapping the face with one of its wings.
Kosúlt:	Also called *yáanat* in Beja language.

317

Kusháabe: Meaning 'circumcision'. The concept is also often used for sickness resulting from lack of circumcision.

Mírquay: Meaning both 'fright' and 'sickness from fright'. In the latter case it denotes a child sickness caused by a sudden shocking experience (see discussion). The Arabic word *khoof* is sometimes used by Beja.

Míngay: Strictly meaning 'left alone'. It is often used for 'fright sickness', implying that the sickness results from the child being left alone.

O'tám: Porridge made of sorghum and water. Usually sour milk is added to this traditional Beja staple food.

'Oogna: Heart.

Ogwéb: A kind of eye inflammation.

Saríit: A back sickness characterized by severe pain in the lower lumbaric region.

Sirr: Stomach sickness with sudden onset of vomiting.

T'háasimt: Skin sickness with small rashes and no wounds. The name of it strictly means 'spider'. The sickness may be caused by a natural or a spirit spider.

T'hélat: Used for camels or cows made *héequal* (see above) by ritually making special marks in their ears and let them roam around freely as a 'property of God'.

Táflam: Stomach sickness with severe diarrhea, which sometimes contains blood. Stomach pain with a kind of 'knocking' sensation is often described.

Tesérimt: A child sickness characterized by rashes and circular discoloring of the skin. Often infected wounds appear. The sickness, which often causes death, is thought to stem from a mystical influence from special types of animals and food (see discussions).

Toodíh: Breast infection often occurring in lactating women.

Toordíp: Beja term for epilepsy. The Arabic term *sara'a* is also used by some Beja.

Waswás: Slight psychological disturbance which is not serious enough to be perceived as madness.

Watáb: A non-serious sickness characterized by headache, tiredness and laziness.

APPENDIX 3

Al-KHATMIYYA: ITS ORIGIN AND DEVELOPMENT IN THE SUDAN

Introduction: Ibn Idris and 'the Neo-Sufis'[1]

I think it to be senseless to say something meaningful about the origin and development of al-Khatmiyya without starting out with some commentaries about Ahmad b. Idris, the Moroccan mystic and teacher. He was born in 1787 in Maysur, Morocco and moved to Fez 20 years later (Karrar 1992, O'Fahey 1990, *Vikør* 1991). Little is known about his first 20 years except that he came from a very pious family and was taught the Quran by two elder brothers (ibid.).

Shortly after arriving in Fez, Ahmad began to hold circles on Sufism and *'ilm*[2] where he showed clear opposition to the veneration of saints (Karrar 1992). The last point is interesting, since his point of view on this matter is representative of his efforts towards establishing a *ṭarīqa*[3] purified of superstitions and more in accordance with Sunna and the Quran than he felt was the case with many of his Sufi forerunners (O'Fahey 1990). Indeed, the *ṭarīqa* he established represents the kind of *ṭarīqa* for which Fazlur Rahman uses the term 'Neo-Sufism' which he says stripped traditional Sufism of ' . . . its ecstatic and metaphysical character and content which were replaced by a content which was nothing else than the postulates of the orthodox' (In: O'Fahey 1990:1–2). A similar point is made earlier by Trimingham (1949).

Later on Ahmad ibn Idris made his pilgrimage to Mecca. He arrived there in 1798 and stayed in Mecca for 14 years together with students of al-Mighani. In Mecca he founded a new *ṭarīqa* called *al-ṭarīqa* al-Muhammadiyya al-Ahmadiyya to stress its direct link to the Prophet (Karrar 1992). This is of symbolic importance in many ways, since he considered himself a reformer with the aim to restore 'the original Islam.' He was strongly inspired by the Salafiyya[4] or Wahabiyya,[5] and he, like the followers of al-Wahhab, stood in opposition to the official law schools. As Karrar (1992:51) puts it, he 'rejected *qiyas* (analogy) and *'ijma* (consensus), except that of the Prophet's companions as sources of Islamic law.'

In 1813 the Turco-Egyptian regime occupied Mecca, and Ahmad went, together with his student al-Mighani, to what was then called Upper Egypt. Two years later, in 1815, Ahmad ibn Idris went as a missionary to the Sudan, while his master remained in Egypt. Previously he had been sent by Ahmad to Ethiopia on a mission journey (Karrar 1992, O'Fahey 1990).

Whether or not the label 'Neo-Sufism' can be justified for movements like those originating from Ahmad ibn Idris, the *ṭarīqas* covered by the term have one important common trait in that they all operated on the frontiers of Islam, specifically in Northern Africa[6] (O'Fahey 1990, Vikør 1991, Voll 1969). In the whole of this region the movements cross-cut ethnic boundaries. They put heavy weight upon missionary activities, both among Muslims and non-Muslims (O'Fahey 1990). What one can, in addition, say for all of these movements, is that their social organization is more formalized than earlier *ṭarīqas*, with for example more formal authority of their leader and a tendency towards inheritance of the leader function (Karrar 1992, O'Fahey 1990, Vikør 1991). When one leader died, it often resulted in a struggle between different potential inheritors of his position. This was what happened when Ahmad died, and several of his sons and followers claimed to be his successor. Some of them, like his close followers Muhammad b. ʿAli **al-Sanusi and Muhammad** ʿUtman al-Mighani, came to establish their own *ṭarīqas* (ibid.).

Muhammad ʿUtman al-Mighani and the Sudan mission

Of these two followers, al-Sanusi had the closest bond to his teacher ibn Idris. The relationship between al-Mighani and his master seems to have been more strained.[7] Muhammad ʿUtman al-Mighani, who I from now on will call only

Muhammad, was sent by his teacher as a missionary to Ethiopia, probably in what now is Eritrea (Karrar 1992; O'Fahey 1990; Trimingham 1949). From Eritrea he traveled on to the Sudan against the warnings of his master, who possibly was afraid of what was going to happen to his slightly unruly, young and enthusiastic pupil who in some respects tended to act as a political leader toward the Ethiopian authorities as well as a religious leader (O'Fahey 1990).

Muhammad was born in Hejaz and came from a Sharifian family. He grew up in Mecca with an uncle, Muhammad Yasin b.Abd Allah al-Mahjub al-Mighani, a famous Sufi and 'alim.[8] His uncle considered him a brilliant pupil, and by the age of thirteen he had good knowledge of the most important Islamic sciences like grammar, rhetoric, law and Quranic exegesis. He later on affiliated himself with five different Sufi-orders.

It seems that the trigger for the establishment of these new orders is not to be searched for in the Western world, but rather within the Islamic world itself. But, later on, during the nineteenth century, European control and colonization of much of the Islamic world caused a certain transformation of the new ṭarīqas (Vikør 1991; Voll 1969). The change was not so much a change in philosophy and religion, but primarily a political and organizational change in the way the ṭarīqas functioned. Voll (1969:651) put it this way: ' . . .the major concern, in a sense, shifted from reform to defense, from ideology to power.' As a result, most brotherhoods, with more or less success, tried to establish small states in India, Algeria, West-Africa, Libya and the Arabian Peninsula (Voll 1969). Khatmiyya, as I will discuss later on, represented an important exception.

Islamization of Sudan and the spread of Sufism

The Islamization of the Sudan[9] was a slow process and was conducted rather late in history compared with other Muslim areas. After the Byzantine province of Egypt was conquered by Muslim Arabs between A.D. 639 and 641, the Nubian territories south of the First Cataract survived as two Christian states until the time of Muhammad Ali Pasha. He was, as an Ottoman ruler, the first to succeed in making a permanent conquest of the Christian territories of the Sudan in 1820 (Holt 1977; Trimingham 1949).

Long before this time, Muslim Arabs, first and foremost traders, had traveled into the Sudan. Many of them were active as proponents of Islam, and some of them intermarried with local women. All the same, their kind of Islam is described as rather superficial, and 'the true Islamization' was first and foremost spread by individual teachers (Holt 1977). A great number of those people were proponents of Sufism and established different Sufi orders alongside of teaching Islam.

The first Sufi-orders established themselves in the Sudan in the sixteenth century. The first of them were the decentralized and localized movements Qadirriyya[10] and Shadhiliyya. This happened at the same time as greater political stability was achieved through the foundation of the Funj and Abdallah kingdoms. Those and other movements from this first 'wave,' however, never gained a strong foothold and never obtained many followers. The movements exist today, but they are relatively small (Holt 1977; Karrar 1992).

The 'second wave' took place in the eighteenth and nineteenth centuries. Four organizationally centralized *turuq* spread throughout the country, two of which originated from the teachings of Ahmad Ibn Idris, namely the Khatmiyya and the Idrisiyya (Karrar 1992).

As in other north African countries, the Sufi-movements in the Sudan operated on two different levels. Firstly, they converted people who were already Muslims to Sufism. Secondly, they operated in areas on the frontiers of Islam. In Sudan this meant western Sudan and the southern parts of the Gezira (Karrar 1992).

The religious and political success of the Khatmiyya movement

Muhammad's missionary work was especially successful in Northern and Eastern Sudan. He won the support of several local leaders of established *khalwas*,[11] important religious families and some tribal leaders. Besides, the fact that people held him to be related to the prophet Muhammad and to be a great scholar contributed unquestionably to his success among these local political and religious leaders. And, not least, he also won the support of the merchant class (Karrar 1992). This last fact is very important and, I believe, is often ignored or only lightly commented upon by most scholars.[12]

One other factor contributing to the success of the Khatmiyya in the Sudan was what can be called 'the Sudanization' of the movement. Although the teaching of Mohammad had its background in the Sufi thought of his day,[13] and, as we have seen, in the teaching of al-Wahhab and what can be called *ahl al-Sunna*, the order he established did not remain an abstract reformist group. The type of leadership became heavily influenced by Sudanese custom. For example, the leader of the movement became recognized as a *wali*[14] of the kind revered and respected in the Sudan, as part of popular Islamic conceptions. This is important, since loyalty toward persons always has had a great appeal to Sudanese Muslims. A *wali* leader was and is a focus for great respect and devotion.

In the same manner local *ṭarīqa* practices became assimilated into Khatmiyya (Voll 1969). As an example, there was no distinction between the *faqīr* as a Khatmiyya *khalīfa* and his other local functions. As one can also witness today, this relates to areas such as healing practices.[15] Many old Sudanese practices, such as those related to shrine visiting, were incorporated into the movement. In the town of Sinkat, veneration of Sitta Maryam, a local female Muslim saint, still plays a very important role in the Khatmiyya movement.

All so-called 'Neo-Sufi' movements have throughout their history kept close links with secular power holders in the areas they operated. In return for their willingness to co-operate and act as middle parties between rulers and the people, they gained recognition and protection. This is also the case of the Khatmiyya movement, although it, as mentioned, never directly came to hold recognized power.

Mohammad came to ally himself closely with the Turco-Egyptians. The Turco-Egyptians were regarded by many Sudanese as alien, oppressive intruders, and Mohammad's alliance with them was probably the reason why some of his principal and powerful adherents defected from the movement. All the same, this alliance was well suited to the thought maintained by leaders of the Khatmiyya movement that one should work toward the unity of all Muslims, also on the political level.

One can perhaps trace here a certain influence from the Wahabiyya movement. Up to the period of independence, followers of the Khatmiyya had been more positive about a political unity with Egypt, some of them were even proponents of a common government (Karrar 1992; Voll 1969). At the same time, as we have seen, 'the Sudanization of the movement' had been very important in regard to the movement gaining a strong foothold in the Sudan. This attitude stood in sharp contrast with the viewpoints held by followers of the Mahdia, a 'messianic' movement which got its name from its leader, Mohammad Ahmad ibn 'Abdallah, a strong and charismatic religious *wali* and *'imam* from Dunqula.

The Mahdist revolution and the Khatmiyya

For quite a long period there had been a popular expectancy in the Sudan that in the future a 'leader chosen by God at the end of time [would arrive] and fill the earth with justice and equity, even as it had been filled with oppression and wrong' (Holt 1977:78–79).

Mohammad Ahmad, in 1881, announced himself as the expected Mahdi and almost immediately gained a large following,[16] at first in central Sudan, and later in the north, and to a certain extent, in western Sudan. He soon after established a Mahdist state extending from Darfur in the west, Dongola in the north, Bahr al-Ghasal in the south and, after several military clashes among others with followers of Khatmiyya, the Suakin Province in the East (Holt 1977; Voll 1969).

The Mahdi preached strongly against allowing any foreign influence in the Sudan. A unity with Egypt was also considered out of question. The political affiliation by Khatmiyya leaders with the Turco-Ottoman rulers was unacceptable to him and his followers, and this issue was one of the main reasons why there were severe confrontations amongst followers of the two movements.

Developments of Khatmiyya in the 20th century

Khatmiyya remained a highly centralized movement after the defeat of the Mahdist state by Egyptian and British military forces in 1898, and the process of 'Sudanization' of the movement continued at the same time as the organization operated both on the level of popular religion and that of politics (Voll 1969). The leaders continued to act as popular *walis* with *karāma* originating from God and continued to act as religious healers.

In the early years of the Anglo-Egyptian Condominium (1899–1956), the British, who lacked legitimacy among the Sudanese people, looked for a strong Sudanese organization which could act as an intermediate group between them and the people. Khatmiyya seemed well suited for this task, and the leaders of the movement were more that willing to go into this type of partnership. In this way they became the most important intermediary group for the British throughout the whole period of the Condominium. After the First World War, however, the importance of the Khatmiyya mode of participation became less important. The reason for this was the growing recruitment of native Sudanese into administrative offices. This created a declining need for informal religious intermediaries (Dhaher J. Mohamed 1988; Holt 1977; Voll 1969)

During and after the Second World War the development of political parties created new opportunities for religious leaders. Some religious leaders did not themselves want to act officially as political leaders in a secular arena,[17] but their political influence through the parties has been enormous. While the Umma party originated from the Mahdia, the Khatmiyya movement inspired the establishment of political parties such as National Unionist Party (NUP) and, later, immediately after the independence of the Sudan in 1956, the People's Democratic Party (Holt 1977).

The leaders of the Khatmiyya acted as intermediaries between rulers and people, as proponents of new ideas and programs[18] and as advisers in international questions. The economic wealth of the organization also grew enormously up to independence.

Immediately after independence, a new coalition between the Ansar and Khatmiyya took place. This was, among other things, made possible by the emergence of secularist politicians as an, at least in theory, independent political force. But, soon, the Khatmiyya realized that if their influence was to be maintained, they had to follow their own political course. This resulted in the organization of the People's Democratic Party in 1956, which is still, although illegal for the time being, the political party with most adherents in eastern Sudan.

NOTES

1 The word 'Sufi' is said to mean 'clothed in wool,' alluding to the fact that early Islamic mystics used to wander around in wool clothes.

2 Arabic word meaning 'knowledge,' 'science,' 'doctrine,' 'art' or 'profession' (Catafago 1975). Here it implies religious learning.

3 *Tarīqa* strictly means 'way' or 'path' in Arabic. It is as well used to describe different directions in mystical Islam, speaking about different Sufi orders as differnt *tarīqa* as different Sufi orders.

4 Meaning 'the followers' in Arabic, here in the sense of 'the followers of the prophet Mohammad.'

5 The movement got its name from its founder Mohammad b.Abd al-Wahhab (1703–92) who called for a 'return to the sources,' that is to say the Quran and the Sunna. He managed to establish for a while a small kingdom in the desert of the Arabian Peninsula.

6 For example the *tarīqa* of Ahmad al-Tijani, Mohammad al-Sanusi and Mohammad 'Utman al-Mighani.

7 It seems that what is left of the written correspondence between them gives an indication of this.

8 Scholar.

9 It would of course be more correct to say 'the territories which were later to become the Sudan.' But, as one cannot even today say that the whole of the Sudan is totally Islamized, this expression would also be an inaccurate one.

10 Also known as Jilaniyya after its founder Abd al-Qadir al-Jilani (1077–1166), who was born in Persia.

11 The term 'khalwa' has been used with several different meanings within the Islamic tradition. Idris Salim El Hassan (1991:1) writes: 'It means either, first, the state or, second, place of solitude for purposes of worship. Third, it applies to a place which might combine both religious and social functions that involve public events ... Fourth, it may simply mean 'men's house' ... as a guest house for the unmarried youth of the group concerned or a stop-over for passers-by. Sixth, *khalwa* ... could refer to the place where Quran is taught ...'

12 While this fact sometimes has been commented upon in writings of historians related to historical periods like the Condominium period (Anglo/Egyptian rule), it is certainly overlooked or ignored, I think, in literature which treats the period, or parts of it, after the independence of the Sudan.

13 Mohammad 'Utman was initiated into five different turuq before establishing his own *tarīqa*, namely the Nashbandiyya, the Qadiriyya, the Shadiliyya, the Junaydiyya and the Mirghaniiya. In fact, after being initiated into those orders, his master Ibn Idris initiated him into them again for the second time. (Karrar 1992)

14 Arabic word meaning 'a favorite of God,' 'a favorite of the King' or 'an intimate friend' (Catafago 1975). Within Sufi Islamic movements the term is often used in the sense 'a close friend of God' or 'a favorite of God.'

15 My own experience from fieldwork in the Red Sea Hills.
16 Some historians have ascribed the success of the Mahdia to the faults of Turco-Egyptian rule. But this statement fails clearly to account for the reason why this revolution did not occur before 1881. It seems more reasonable to look beyond Sudan and relate it to the khedival autocracy as a whole, which after the removal of Isma'il in 1879 had lost much of its prestige and grip on people under its rule.
17 The Ansar Mahdi and its leader, Sayyid Abd al-Rahman, are important exceptions, as they took a relatively direct role in politics.
18 Sayyid Ahmad in Kassala was one of the leaders in introducing new agricultural methods in the Sudan.

APPENDIX 4

QUESTIONS FROM THE FIRST ROUND OF
SEMI-STRUCTURED INTERVIEWS 1993

The numeric order of the questions was not persued strictly, since we wanted the interview to run as smoothly and natural as possible. The respondents were encouraged to make associations freely to the questions. As well, we provided enough time to allow for telling personal stories in between or for greeting new arriving guests etc.

A. Administered individually:

1. How many children do you have?
2. What are their age and sex?
3. Are all of them well?
4. If not, what kind of symptoms do they have?
5. Have any of your children died?

B. Administered to women in group (or singular women, if they are alone when the interview takes place):

What is the a. name of the sickness, b. the cause of it and c. the best treatment when your child:

1. cry and cry without stopping, with no other symptom?
2. is coughing very bad without any other symptom?
3. is coughing and spitting blood?
4. is very hot/has fever?
5. has diarrhea?
6. is getting thinner and thinner all over the body?
7. has a big, swollen stomach, swollen over the ankles and is thin over the rest of the body?

329

8. suddenly cannot stand on its feet any longer?
9. complains about pain in the stomach without any other symptom?
10. breaks a bone (an arm or a leg)?
11. has a wound?
12. faints suddenly?
13. complains about headache?
14. is bitten by a snake/scorpion?
15. has a running nose?

C. For the interpreter: to state whether the household seems to be poor, middle or well off economically.

Preparations and administration of the interview

Since I initially was to carry out the interviews of mothers in a social milieu characterized by severe segregation between the sexes, I was recommended by local health workers to find a female interpreter. Luckily I found a female nutritionist Falna Mohammad, who speaks fluently Tu Bedawie, Arabic and English. She is a Hadandowa and has been living in the mountain area near where we carried out our interviews until she moved out for higher education. She has been working for some periods for different relief organizations like Oxfam and Red Crescent and has earlier carried out interviews herself in connection with nutrition planning work.

When preparing the questions, we worked together to eliminate questions which would be culturally improper to ask or to change the style of questions which could be misunderstood. Afterwards we sometimes made an agreement that she should go alone into the different households together with a local representative for Sudanese Red Crescent who was known to the people. I sat nearby in a 'men's hut' so that we could communicate if problems arose considering the administration of the interviews. At other points of time I was allowed to be present during the interview, which gave me an opportunity to ask additional questions related to their answers.

The questions were not necessarily posed in the same order as in my outline. The question about dead children, for example, which of course made the women very sorrowful, was administrated rather late in the interview and preceded and followed by all the culturally appropriate words of sympathy and the help and assistance from God both at present time and for the future.

We also made some adjustments of the procedure after the first round of interviews. At first we made a distinction between deep and shallow wounds (question 11), which seemed a meaningless distinction for the mothers we interviewed, so we ended up with asking about wounds in general. After the first round we also found out that we had to be more explicit in asking about what the women thought caused the different symptoms in their children. So for the rest of the interviews the interpreter used some time for each question to encourage them to say something about that. My interpreter herself uses some 'traditional' devices when she or her children are sick, and she is genuinely interested in folk medicine. I think myself that this enabled her to create an atmosphere of confidence when carrying out interviews with the women. She is also a devout Muslim, which made her respected by the people she encountered.

The interpreter was taking notes through the whole interviews. This was not a simple task, since most of the questions gave rise to discussions among women present and, as well, often several of them tried to answer at the same time! After completing each round of interviews we went through the written material together to see if we should do some adjustments in our strategies.

After all the interviews were completed, we sat together for three days going through her notes and writing them out in full sentences. While doing this she added much useful information about the labels the women used for describing different symptoms, the different means for healing they used and ideas she knows about which could lie behind their labeling and choices of solutions. She also consulted relatives and friends to voice their opinions on translation of words and expression. In addition, she provided me with valuable information regarding her own sickness experiences and sickness experiences in her close relatives.

When the written material was completed, I used some time with her discussing different ideas about peoples cultural world that I could get out of this material. She commented upon it and also discussed this together with her mother and other old women in her native village.

APPENDIX 5

SECOND ROUND OF SEMI-STRUCTURED INTERVIEWS 1994

In a new round of questions, I performed questions with male as well as female respondents. Hence, I was variously working together with a male and a female research assistant. Like in the earliest interview, we let the informants freely give associations to the questions as well as allowing them the time to tell personal stories.

The questions

What are the a. symptoms, b. causes and c. treatment for:

1. a. *hāf*, b. *hāf masóob* and c. *táfram*?
2. a. *Alíib*, b. *yáanat/kosúlt* and c. *eratiót*?
3. a. *tórdip*, b. *hilatéit* and c. *dérwou* (in some interviews d. *illowéen*)?
4. *sírr*?
5. a. *watáb*, b. *sáfra* and c. *itrásh* (since *itrásh* turned out to be *watáb*, in some interviews instead asked about *heminéit*)?
6. a. *khoof*, b. *míngay*, c. *nighíib*, d. *mírquay* and e. *qast*?

This initial round of interviews soon gave rise to a more extensive list of native diagnoses, as given below. The same questions of symptoms, etiology and means of treatment were asked as above.

The new and final list of diagnostic labels for interview

1. a. *Hāf*
   b. *Hāf masóob*
   c. *Táfram*
   d. *Gábda*[1].
2. a. *Toordíp*[2].
   b. *Hilaléit*
   c. *Dérwou*
3. *Sírr*[3]
4. *Tesérim/sérimt*
5. a. *Watáb*
   b. *Sáfra*
   c. *Heminéit*[4]
6. *Tifáfy*[5]
7. a. *Tháasim/háasimt*
   b. *Tanqáabe*
   c. *Tóy'éh*
8. a. *Lámlam*[6]
   b. *Timishúuwi*
   c. *Balámiet óot*[7]
   d. *Mahfúura*[8]
9. *Tunqúilat*[9]
10. *Shaqíiqa*
11. a. *Aay*
    b. *Boyée*[10]

NOTES

1 Arabic, same as *táqwuri* in Bedawiet, meaning a knot.
2 Same as *sára'a* in Arabic. The word *díbia* means 'fallen down' in Beja language.
3 Bedawiet, same as *síhir* in Arabic.
4 Bedawiet, adjective *'hemíib'*, meaning the same as *'murr'* in Arabic, used for salt water or coffee without sugar.
5 Means 'to flow over' (like a cup filled up with fluid and then more is added)
6 Something called *náfil* (serious type, 'big roots', spreading from the *náfil*) is mentioned in one interview when asking about *lámlam*-> try to open it by every means so as to get rid of the dirty blood within it, try snuff, try leaves of *nábak*. If not OK, take him to doctor for operation. (The word *khorāj* in Arabic is said to mean a disease stemming from injections.)
7 *Balámiet* means 'wind' and *oot* means 'girl' in Beja language.

8 Arabic word meaning something like 'to make a hole in something.'
9 Bedawiet word for 'kidney', meaning both the disease and the organ itself.
10 Meaning 'something from blood (*boy*).'

APPENDIX 6

MARRIAGE PATTERNS AMONG HADANDOWA BEJA

Data from Musai Diwab, a subsection of Rabba Maq, a Hadandowa Beja subtribe.

Explanations:
Mo = mother
Fa = father
Da = daughter
So = son
Si = sister
Br = brother

The ideal marriage partner for Beja men is said to be FaBrDa. As is evident from the material below, this aim is only occasionally achieved. In most cases, however, people will seek a marriage partner within their own *diwáb*. Beja people are usually explicit in stating that their way of reckoning relatives is patrilineal. Nevertheless, the lowest level of their lineage system, the *diwáb*, is amibilinial in its recruitment. Since it has been the convention in anthropology, for the sake of simplicity I have reckoned relationships from the man's point of view. Men often tend to be considerably older than their wives. For this reason, as will appear below, there is sometimes a one generation gap between husband and wife.

Man 1: FaFaSiDaDa
Man 2: MoFaFaMoSiSoSoSo
Man 3: From the same *diwáb*, but not closely related.

Man 4: MoBrDa and FaSiDa[1].
Man 5: MoSiDaDa
Man 6: FaBrDa
Man 7: FaFaSiDaDa
Man 8: FaBrDa
Man 9: MoBrDa
Man 10: MoBrDa
Man 11: FaFaFaSiDa
Man 12: MoBrDa
Man 13: From the same *diwáb,* but not closely related.
Man 14: From the same *diwáb,* but not closely related.
Man 15: FaFaFaBrSoSoSoDa
Man 16: From the same *diwáb,* but not closely related.
Man 17: FaBrDa
Man 18: From the same *diwáb,* but not closely related.
Man 19: a. FaBrDa. b. Second marriage: FaBrDa.
Man 20: FaBrDa
Man 21: FaBrDa
Man 22: From the same *diwáb,* but not closely related.
Man 23: From the same *diwáb,* but not closely related.
Man 24: From the same *diwáb,* but not closely related.
Man 25: From the same *diwáb,* but not closely related.
Man 26: From the same *diwáb,* but not closely related.
Man 27: From the same *diwáb,* but not closely related.

Since one man from this sample married twice, the total number
of marriages amounts to 28. Of those 28 marriages, only 7 men,
or only 25% married according to the pronounced ideal, that is,
marrying their FaBrDa. 4 men, or 14.3 % married their MoBrDa.
Only in one instance a man married his FaSiDa. In this case, his
wife was also his MoBrDa. In 11 of the samples, or in 39.3 % of
the marriages, the man married a woman whose relationship to
him was not known, except from the fact that she belonged to his
own *diwáb.* Perhaps most noteworthy, in no cases a man married
a wife outside his own *diwáb.*

NOTE

1 His father and her mother are siblings, and his mother and her father
  are siblings.

APPENDIX 7

CHILD MORTALITY IN THE AFTERMATH OF DROUGHT

Since the health and well-being of infants and small children tend to be immediately affected by changes in the living situation, the rate of mortality of children may be a good indicator of the present precarious adaptation of Hadandowa Beja people to their natural environment. To obtain reliable data regarding child births and mortality among the Beja, however, is not an easy task. Since, as already discussed, Beja people try to keep the number of children a secret, it is difficult to make an assessment of the number of living children. The Beja also do not find it appropriate to remember and talk about dead children or dead persons in general. 'God's will happened,' they will say after the death of a relative or family member. In addition, speaking about deceased children is always a tough subject for parents.

All this requires a good strategy, carefulness and cultural sensitivity from the researcher and the assistants. However, by receiving support from local Red Cross staff in Sinkat and Derudeb, and by making it clear to informants that we were exclusively looking for factors related to the general development of the health situation, we established some confidence in people. We hoped that this contributed to giving us relatively reliable information. The questions about child births and deaths were asked after we conducted a general interview for about one hour with each informant. In this way we tried to establish some degree of social contact before trying to obtain this difficult information. The results are presented in the table below:

337

Table 10. *Fertility and mortality. N=284*

	Living Girls	Living Boys	Living Children	Dead Children	Total Children Born
Number	84	128	212	72	284
% of Total			74.6	25.4	
% of Living	39.6	60.4			

Thirty of the 85 households were randomly chosen from various sites within the towns of Sinkat and Derudeb and the rural areas of Baramio and Odrus. The informants were all mothers still caring for children. Fifty-five of the households represent a total sample from close studies of two small localities.[1] The living children are all under the age of 15 years.[2]

The child mortality proved relatively high, around 25.4 % of the total number of children born in those thirty families. This gives a mean number of 0.9 dead children per family out of a mean total number of 3.3 born into each family. Most of the deceased children died following the droughts of 1984 and 1991. The mean number of living children is 2.5. Unfortunately, in most cases it was impossible to ask about the sex of the deceased children.

Saghayroun & Farah (in Ertur & House 1994:55) estimate the probability for a child dying before the age of two years in all Sudan to be 17%. Of the provinces, Khartoum ranks lowest with 12.1%, while the Red Sea Province ranks highest with 25.3%. Given that my data includes children up to approximately 15 years of age, my estimate is probably a conservative one. However, most childhood deaths among the Hadandowa informants tend to have occurred before the age of two years. While the total number of children born in each family, on average, turned out to be 3.3 from my data, Saghayroun & Farah (ibid.) suggests 6.4 as the Total Fertility Rate for the Red Sea Province in 1973. Their data of course includes town dwelling non-Bejas, who may make up a greater proportion of the population of the Red Sea Province than the Beja.[3]

An astonishing discovery is that the number of living boys (128) is significantly higher than living girls (84). This gives a mean number of 1.0 girls and 1.5 boys pr. family, which corresponds to 39.6% girls and 60.4% boys. In other words, in the 85 households there are, on average, half again as many boys as girls. Admittedly, the number of households for investigation is quite low. However, the difference is significant enough to account for a general trend. Submitting the data to a chi-square test yields the result of X2-obt = 9.13.[4] Since the critical value of X2 is 6.635 for one degree of freedom (df) and an alpha level at 0.01,[5] the null hypothesis, that there is equally as many girls as boys in the population,[6] may quite safely be rejected.[7]

A practical point may be added to this. The average age for men is considerably higher than the average age for women in married couples. Some of my informants explained this by pointing to the high economic expenditure in connection with the marriage ceremony and establishing a new household in the present precarious situation, an explanation which Ausenda (1987) also supports. If the difference in the sex ratio was similar in the previous generation and the population is increasing, however, this may naturally account for this age difference to some degree, since polygamy is very rarely practiced among Beja, in contrast to Somali pastoralists (Lewis 1962). A significant increase in the Beja population has most probably taken place since national censuses were introduced in 1956.[8] However, how may such a difference in sex ratio in Beja children be explained?

Since Beja do not give dowries, the possibility that girls are sometimes killed off because of higher marriage costs for the bride's family, as occurs in parts of India, can be ruled out. Since Beja usually marry close relatives, the transfer of goods between groups of relatives tends to be both reciprocal and relatively small (Ausenda 1987). Although boys tend to be valued over girls (Vågenes 1990), the initial period of matrilocality means that the parents of a bride will enjoy the help and co-operation from her husband and his relatives for at least a time (Ausenda 1987; Dahl et al. 1991; Salih 1971). Several informants also pointed out that daughters tended to be a more reliable support for parents in old age than sons.

A second explanation is that some informants distrusted our motives and thought that we were doing registrations for the authorities. Each family receives an official sugar ration according to the number of household members. For this reason, some informants may have exaggerated the total number of children. However, having boys is no prerogative over having girls in relation to the official authorities. In other words, this explanation does not account for a higher number of boys than girls.

A third explanation may be parental neglect based on folk diagnosis of the kind described by Scheper-Hughes (1990, 1992) from Northeastern Brazil where parents left their children to die in cases where they perceived the children as 'having the marks of death.' Culturally determined constellations of perceived symptoms made parents end their care of some children in order to care for children who were seen as more fit to survive. However, such a mechanism will also not account for a difference in sex ratio.

Another possible explanation for the difference in the sex ratio of children could be that people simply gave the wrong number. Since it is not considered any shame to have many daughters, however, there is no reason why people should under-estimate their number of daughters. However, it is considered a social deficit to beget no sons. For this reason it is a possibility that the informants exaggerated the number of sons or stated that they had a son when they had only daughters. Since both my assistant and I were totally unrelated to them, however, it is difficult to see why anybody should try to impress us in this regard. Moreover, the informants were usually not alone, but surrounded by close relatives who served as a check on the information given.

A fifth explanation relates to the fear of the 'evil eye' among the Beja people. Many of them believe that by giving away information about the correct number of children the health and well-being of these children may be affected. Although it is difficult to see how this may account for the difference in reported sex ratio, this precaution may account for a general low number of reported living children.

A final point may partly explain the difference in sex ratio, although I have no real evidence for its truth. It could be the case that in households with very scarce economic resources, like most Hadandowa households, more efforts are directed toward feeding and caring for boys as well as treating them when they are sick. Several of my closest informants in Sinkat told me that boys generally were more spoiled by their parents than girls, which is in accord with my own observations.[9] As an example, the *faqīr* Ahmad, when telling me about the usefulness of getting enough sleep, added:

'Boys should sleep as long as they like to as children. Girls you can wake up! The sleeping cleans the blood. Also, the child ought to lay on the right side so as to support the rhythm of the heart.'

Although enough sleep and sleeping in the right position are seen as generally important for the health of children, it is most important for boys. His statement is not untypical. When people were asked directly, however, they usually stated that they would do as much for a sick girl as a sick boy. Most of my informants voiced the opinion that boys generally need more food and more nutritious food than girls. The culturally highly valued butter oil from milk, for example, is seen as making boys strong, good-looking and virile.

If my explanation is correct, there are at least two ways of seeing this cultural mechanism. As well as seeing it as a culturally shaped neglect of girls, it might instead be seen as placing cultural value on providing extra efforts in order to secure the health and well-being of boys, since they are the future protectors and sources of income (as culturally evaluated) of the households they will head. An additional point is worth making. Having no living sons is a very usual factor leading to divorce (Vågenes 1990). In some cases I encountered, men divorced themselves from their wives because they had no sons or after their only son died. Clearly, the impetus for parents to care for their sons is great.

I doubt, however, the validity of my data as reflecting true rates of fertility and mortality. Firstly, the mortality rate is very low compared with data obtained from adjacent areas in Eritrea and Ethiopia after the drought of 1984.[10] It is possible that Beja parents interviewed did not report all cases of child death, since Beja people are culturally expected to forget and not talk about deceased relatives in general. Secondly, as already discussed, the average number of living children is surprisingly low. Thirdly, the difference in sex ratio does not match similar investigation in the wider region of East Africa.[11] For this reason, in addition to the nutritional aspect already commented upon, a cultural preference in the parent's report cannot be ruled out.

More thorough investigations, for example longitudinal surveys of selected households over several years, are needed in order to confirm or disconfirm the trends in my material as reflecting a true state of fertility and mortality in the Red Sea Hills. Even if eventually disconfirmed, however, my data are of interest as a point of departure for investigating why Beja parents are reporting in particular biased ways.

NOTES

1 One of them was a neighborhood section representing one *diwáb* in Dinayet (suburb of Sinkat), and the other one was a rural village in Odrus.

2 People in the Red Sea Hills mostly do not keep track of their age. However, I suppose that I am relatively safe in estimating the age of the oldest children to between 13 and 15 years.

3 Reliable data on ethnic composition of the population is difficult to obtain.

4 See Pagano (1990:402–405) for details of the argument. My reason for utilizing a nonparametric test is that it has fewer requirements or assumptions about population characteristics. I admit that is less robust than paradigmatic tests. However, given that the value of X2 is far beyond the critical value, I hold it to be a reasonable safe test to reject the null hypothesis.

5 Pagano (1990:430) defines the alpha level as 'the threshold probability level against which the obtained probability is compared to determine the reasonableness of the null hypothesis. It also determines the critical region for rejection of the null hypothesis. Alpha is usually set at 0.05–0.01. The alpha level is set at the beginning of an experiment and limits the probability of making an error.'

6 The expected frequency of boys out of a total of 212 will be 106 under the assumption that sampling is random from the null hypothesis population.

7 According to Eltay & Hashmi (in: Ertur & House 1994:39) the distribution of males and females in the age group of 0–4 years is 13.54% for males and 13.99% for females in the Sudan in 1983. For the age group 5–14 years the percentage is 31.03 for males and 29.44 for females. From their data no marked sex ratio difference is evident from their all Sudan survey. My data is clearly at variance with their findings at this point.

8 I have unfortunately not come across any reliable censuses registering the tribal affiliation of the population of Eastern Sudan. However, four general censuses which account for specific regions have been carried out for the whole of the Sudan since 1956. From 1956 and to 1993 the population of Eastern Sudan has increased from around 941,000 to around 3,052,000 (Eltay and Hashmi, in Ertur and House 1994; Modawi and Siddig 1995). This represents an increase of 324%. Although the quality of the census techniques may be put into question (ibid.), they nevertheless point clearly towards a general trend. Most development and relief workers I spoke to in

Eastern Sudan were of the opinion that the general increase in population size is also a feature of the Beja population.

9 During my chats with the old *fagīr*, Mohammad, several times some of his grandchildren came and asked for sugar. Whilst he often gave in to the boys, especially his youngest grandson, he generally waved the girls away. This is just one example of episodes I encountered where boys seemed generally to be more easily spoiled by parents or grandparents. I admit, however, that I was mostly not able to make observances from female settings, where I have had to rely on reports from female assistants.

10 Dr. med. Bernt Lintjørn, University of Bergen, personal communication.

11 Same source as footnote 10 above.

BIBLIOGRAPHY

Abu-Lughod, L. 1986. *Veiled Sentiments: Honor and Poetry in a Bedouin Society.* Berkeley and Los Angeles: University of California Press.

Alver, B. G. 1971. *Heksetro og trolldom: en studie i norsk heksevesen.* Oslo, Norway: Universitetsforlaget.

Al-Safi, Ahmad. 1970. *Native Medicine in the Sudan: Sources, Conceptions, and Methods.* Khartoum, Sudan: Khartoum University Press.

Ausenda, G. 1987. *Leisurely Nomads: The Hadendowa Beja of Gash Delta and their transition to sedentary village life.* Unpublished doctoral thesis, Columbia University.

Austen, R. A. 1993. The Moral Economy of Witchcraft: An Essay in Comparative History. In Jean and John Comaroff (eds.): *Modernity and Its Malcontents. Ritual and Power in Postcolonial Africa.* Chicago: The University of Chicago Press, pp. 89–110.

Austin, J. L. 1962. *How to do Things with Words. The William James Lectures delivered at Harvard University in 1955.* Oxford and New York: Oxford University Press.

Bailey, F. G. 1994, *The Witch-Hunt; or, The Triumph of Morality.* Ithaca and London: Cornell University Press.

Bailey, F. G. 1971. *Gifts and Poison.* Oxford: Basil Blackwell & Mott, Ltd.

Balfour, Sir Andrew. Different letters, notes, research papers and drafts from the period of 1897–1931. Found in the archive of London School of Hygiene and Tropical Medicine, London.

Barth, F. 1961. *Nomads of South Persia: The Basseri Tribe of the Khamseh Confederacy.* Boston: Little, Brown and Co.

Barth, F. 1965. *Political Leadership among the Swat Pathans.* New York: Humanities Press.

Bastien, M. L. 1993. 'Bloodhounds Who Have No Friends': Witchcraft and Locality in the Nigerian Popular Press. In Jean and John Comaroff (eds.): *Modernity and Its Malcontents. Ritual and Power in Postcolonial Africa*. Chicago: The University of Chicago Press, pp. 129–166.

Bastien, J. W. 1989. Differences between Kallawaya-Andean and Greek-European humoral theory. *Social Science and Medicine 1*, Vol. 28, pp. 45–51.

Baxter, P. T. W. 1972. Absence makes the heart grow fonder. Some suggestions why witchcraft accusations are rare among East Africa pastoralists. In Max Gluckman: *The allocation of responsibility*. Manchester: Manchester University Press, pp. 163–191.

Becker, R. and Ward, T. B. 1991. Children's use of shape in extending novel labels to animate objects: Identity versus postural change. *Cognitive Development 6*, pp. 3–16.

Beidelman, T. O. 1963. Witchcraft in Ukaguru. In Middleton & Winter (eds.): *Witchcraft and Sorcery in East Africa*. London: Routledge & Kegan Paul Ltd.

Bilu, Y. and Ben-Ari, E. 1992. The making of modern saints: Manufactured charisma and the Abu-Hatseiras of Israel. *American Ethnologist 4*, Vol. 19, pp. 672–687.

Bishaw, M. 1991. Promoting Traditional Medicine in Ethiopia: A Brief Historical Review of Government Policy. *Social Science and Medicine 2*, Vol. 33, pp. 193–200.

Bloch, M. 1986. *From Blessing to Violence*. Cambridge: University of Cambridge.

Bloch, M. 1994. Language, Anthropology, and Cognitive Science. In R. Borofsky (ed.): *Assessing Cultural Anthropology*. New York: McGraw-Hill, Inc.

Bloss, J. F. E. 1948. *The Experiences of a Medical Inspector: Reports from Different Parts of Sudan. Malakal 1948*. Unpublished book manuscript 1948, Sudan Archive, Durham, England.

Boddy, J. 1988. Spirits and Selves in Northern Sudan: The Cultural Therapeutics of Possession and Trance. *American Antropologist 1*, Vol. 15, pp. 4–27.

Boddy, J. 1989. *Wombs and Alien Spirits*. Wisconsin: The University of Wisconsin Press, Madison.

Bonsaksen, S. R. 1993. Beja-folket i det østlige Sudan. Gammel islams nomade-kultur i ferd med å forsvinne. *Midtøsten Forum 1*, March 1993

Bonsaksen, S. R. 1991. *Living Today on Tomorrow's Resources. Coping with Drought among the Hadendowa of Eastern Sudan.* Unpublished Cand. Polit. Thesis, University of Bergen, Bergen, Norway.

Bourdieu, P. 1977. *Outline of a Theory of Practice.* Cambridge: Cambridge University Press.

Bousefield, L. 1908. The Native Methods of Treatment of Diseases in Kassala and Neighbourhood. *Third Report of the Wellcome Research Laboratories at the Gordon Memorial College.* Khartoum, 1908, pp. 273–276. Found in London School of Hygiene and Tropical Medicine, London

Boyer, P. 1993. Pseudo-Natural Kinds. In Boyer (ed.): *Cognitive Aspects of Religious Symbolism.* Cambridge, Massachusetts: Cambridge University Press.

Boyer, P. 1996a. *Religious Ontologies and the Bounds of Sense: A Cognitive Catalogue of the Supernatural.* Unpublished paper presented at The Center for Advanced Study in the Behavioral Sciences, Stanford.

Boyer, P. 1996b. What makes Anthropomorphism Natural: Intuitive Ontology and Cultural Representations. *J.Roy.antrop.Inst. (N.S.) 2,* pp. 83–97.

Brandes, S. 1980. *Metaphors of Masculinity. Sex and Status in Andalusian Folklore.* University of Pennsylvania Press.

Brøgger, J. 1971. *Montevarese. A Study of Peasant Society and Culture in Southern Italy.* Bergen, Norway: Universitetsforlaget.

Brøgger, J. 1989. *Pre-bureaucratic Europeans. A Study of a Portuguese Fishing Community.* Oxford: Norwegian University Press.

Bruner, J. 1990. *Acts of Meaning.* Cambridge, Massachusets: Harvard University Press.

Carneiro, R. L. 1988. The Circumscription Theory: Challenge and Response. *American Behavioral Scientist* 4, Vol. 31, pp. 497–511, March/April 1988.

Catafago, J. 1975. *An Arabic and English Literary Dictionary.* Beirut: Libraire Du Liban, Beirut.

Chand, A. D., *et al.* 1994. The Marathi 'Taskonomy' of Respiratory Illnesses in Children. *Medical Anthropology,* Vol. 15, pp. 395–408.

Ciekawy, D. 1990. Utsai and the State: The Politics of Witchcraft Eradication in Coastal Kenya. Unpublished Paper, African Studies Workshop, University of Chicago.

Classen, C., *et al.* 1994. *Aroma. The Cultural History of Smell.* London and New York: Routledge.

Cloudsley, A. 1984. *Women of Omdurman. Life, Love and the Cult of Virginity.* London: Ethnographica.

Constantinides, P. 1977. Ill at Ease and Sick at Heart: Symbolic Behavior in a Sudanese Healing Cult. In I. M. Lewis (ed.): *Symbols and Sentiments*, pp. 61–83, New York: Academic Press.

Constantinides, P. 1982. Women's Spirit Possession and Urban Adaption in the Muslim Nothern Sudan. In P. Caplan and D. Burja: *Women United, Women Divided: Comparative Studies of Ten Contemporary Cultures*, pp. 185–206, Bloomington: Indiana University Press.

Corbin, A. 1986. *The Foul and the Fragrant. Odor and the French Social Imagination.* Cambridge, Massachusetts: Harvard University Press.

Crapanzano, V. 1973. *The Hamadsha: A Study in Moroccan Ethnopsychiatry.* Berkeley: University of California Press.

D'Andrade, R. 1995. *The Development of Cognitive Anthropology.* Cambridge, Massachusetts: Cambridge University Press.

D'Andrade, R., *et al.* 1972. Categories of Disease in American-English and Mexican-Spanish, in *Multidimensional Scaling*, Vol. II.

Dahl, G. 1989. *Who can be blamed? Interpreting the Beja Drought.* Paper presented at the International Conference on Environmental Stress and Security, 13–15 December 1988, Stockholm, Sweden.

Dahl, G. 1991. The Beja of the Sudan and the Famine of 1984–1986. *Ambio 5*, Vol. 20, pp. 189–191.

Dahl, G., *et al.* 1991. *Responsible Man. The Atmaan Beja of Northeastern Sudan.* Uppsala, Sweden: SSSA and Nordiska Afrikainstitutet, 1991

Dhaher, Jasim Mohamed. 1988. *The Contribution of Sayed Ali al-Mighani, Leader of the Khatmiyya, to the Political Evolution of the Sudan 1884–1968.* Unpublished doctoral dissertation, University of Exeter.

Dundes, A. (ed.). 1981. *The Evil Eye. A Folklore Casebook.* New York & London: Garland Publishing, Inc.

Duranti & Goodwin. 1992. *Rethinking Context. Language as an Interactive Phenomenon.* Cambridge, Massachusetts: Cambridge University Press.

Dougherty, J. and Keller, C. 1982. Taskonomy: A Practical Approach to Knowledge Structures. *American Ethnologist 4*, Vol. 9, pp. 763–774.

Douglas, M. 1970. Thirty years after 'Witchcraft, Oracles and Magic.' In M. Douglas: *Witchcraft confessions and accusations. ASA Monograph, 9*. London: Tavistock Publications.

Early, E. A. 1985. Catharsis and Creation: The Everyday Narratives of Baladi Women of Cairo. *Anthropological Quarterly 58*, pp. 172–181.

Early, E. A. 1988. The Baladi Curative Systems of Cairo, Egypt. *Culture, Medicine and Psychiatry 12*, pp. 65–83.

Edgerton, R. B. 1971. *The Individual in Cultural Adaption. A Study of Four East African Peoples*. Berkeley: University of California Press.

Eickelman, D. F. 1981. *The Middle East. An Anthropological Approach*. New Jersey: New York University Press.

El-Dareer, Asma. 1982. *Woman, Why Do You Weep? Circumcision and it's Consequences*. London: Zed Press.

Elster, J. 1978. *Logic and Society. Contradiction and Possible Worlds*. New York: John Wiley & Sons.

Ertur, O. S. and House, W. J. 1994. *Population and Human Resources Development in the Sudan*. Ames, Iowa: Iowa State University Press.

Evans-Pritchard, E. E. 1985 (1937). *Witchcraft, Oracles and Magic among the Azande*. Oxford: Clarendon Press.

Eysenck & Keane. 1995. *Cognitive Psychology. A Student's Handbook*. Hillsdale, USA: Lawrence Erlbaum Associates Publ.

Fadlalla, A. H. 1992. *The Hadendowa Woman: an Honourable Subordinate*. Master of Science Thesis in Social Anthropology, Department of Sociology and Social Anthropology, The University of Khartoum, Khartoum.

Feierman & Janzen (eds.). 1992. *The Social Basis of Health and Healing in Africa*. Berkeley: University of California Press.

Fortes, M. 1976. Foreword. In J. Loudon (ed.): *Social Anthropology and Medicine*, pp.ix-xx. London: Academic Press.

Foster, G. M. 1976. Disease Etiologies in non-Western Medical Systems. *American Anthropologist*, Vol. 78, pp. 773–782.

Foster, G. M. 1987. On the Origin of Humoral Medicine in Latin America. *Medical Anthropology Quarterly 4*, Vol. 1, December 1987.

Foster, G. M. 1984. The Concept of Neutral in Humoral Medical Systems. *Social Science and Medicine 3*, Vol. 8, Summer 1984.

Frankenberg, R. 1980. Medical Anthropology and Development: A Theoretical Perspective. *Soc.Sci.Med.* Vol. 14B, pp. 197–207.

Frazer, J. G. 1951. *The Golden Bough: A Study in Magic and Religion*. New York: Macmillan (original work published in 1890).

Gallagher, N. E. 1983. *Medicine and Power in Tunisia, 1780–1900*. Cambridge: Cambridge University Press.

Geertz, C. 1968. *Islam Observed*. New Haven, CT: Yale University Press.

Gellner, E. 1969. *Saints of the Atlas*. Chicago: University of Chicago Press.

Gelman, S. & M. 1986. Categories of Induction in Young Children. *Cognition 23*, pp. 183–209.

Geschiere, P. 1988. Sorcery and the State: Popular Modes of Action among the Maka of Southeast Cameroon. *Critique of Anthropology*, Vol. 8, pp. 35–63.

Gmelch, G. 1996. Superstition and Ritual in American Baseball. *Anthropology 95/96, Annual Editions*, 18th edition pp. 195–199, 1996. Originally appearing in Elysean Fields Quarterly: The Baseball Review, All Star Issue, Vol. 11, No. 3, pp. 25–36.

Goffman, E. 1972. *Relations in Public. Microstudies of the Public Order*. Middlesex: Penguin Books.

Good, B. J. 1994. In the Subjunctive Mood: Epilepsy Narratives in Turkey. *Social Science and Medicine 6*, Vol. 38, pp. 835–842.

Good, B. J. 1992. The Comparative Study of Greco-Islamic Medicine: The Integration of Medical Knowledge into Local Symbolic Contexts. In Leslie, C. and Young, A. (eds.): *Paths to Asian Medical Knowledge*. Berkeley: University of California Press.

Goody, J. (ed.). 1968. *Literacy in Traditional Societies*. Cambridge, Massachusetts: Cambridge University Press.

Goody, J. 1977. *The Domestication of the Savage Mind*. Cambridge, Massachusetts: Cambridge University Press.

Greenwood, B. 1981. Cold or Spirits? Choice and Ambiguity in Morocco's Pluralistic Medical System. *Social Science and Medicine*, Vol. 15B, pp. 219–235.

Grønhaug, R., *et al.* 1991. *The Ecology of Choice and Symbol*. Bergen, Norway: Alma Mater Forlag.

Haaland, G. 1990. Øl og morsmelk. Symbol, moral og valg i Fursamfunnet. *Norsk Antropologisk Tidsskrift 1*, pp. 3–16.

Hall, M. J., et al. 1981. *Sisters under the Sun. The Story of Sudanese Women.* London: Longman

Hannerz, U. 1969. *Soulside: Inquiries into Ghetto Culture and Community.* New York: Colombia University Press.

Hirschfeld, L. A. 1995. Do children have a theory of race? *Cognition 54*, pp. 209–252.

Holland, D. and Quinn, N. 1987. *Cultural Models in Language and Thought.* New York: Cambridge University Press.

Holt, P. M. 1977. *A Modern History of the Sudan.* London: Weidenfeld and Nicolson.

Holt, P. M. and Daly, M. W. 1979. *The History of the Sudan from the Coming of Islam to the Present Day.* London: Weidenfeld and Nicolson.

Holy, L.: *Religion and Custom in a Muslim Society.* Cambridge, Massachusetts: Cambridge University Press, 1991.

Huber, B. R. and Anderson, R. 1996. Bonesetters and Curers in a Mexican Community: Conceptual Models, Status, and Gender. *Medical Anthropology,* Vol. 17, pp. 23–38.

Hunwick, J. 1992. *Religion and National Integration in Africa.* Evanston, Illinois: Northwestern University Press.

Hutchins, E. 1980. *Culture and Inference. A Trobiand Case Study.* Cambridge, Massachusetts: Harvard University Press.

Hutchins, E. 1978. *Reasoning in Discourse: An Analysis of Trobiand Land Litigation.* PhD dissertation, Univ. of California, San Diego.

Hutchins, E. 1995. *Cognition in the Wild.* Cambridge, Massachusetts: The MIT Press.

Idris Salim El Hassan. 1991. Technical paper. Center for Developmental Studies, University of Bergen, Norway.

Ismail, Abd al-Rahman. 1934. *Folk Medicine in the Modern Egypt* (1892–4). Translated by John Walker. London: Luzac & Co.

Jacobs, A. H. 1979. Maasai Inter-Tribal Relations: Belligerent Herdsmen or Peaceable Pastoralists? *Senri Ethnological Studies 3,* pp. 33–52.

Jakobson & Halle. 1956. *Fundamentals of Language.* The Hague: Mouton Press.

James, W. 1988. *The Listening Ebony. Moral Knowledge, Religion, and Power Among the Uduk of Sudan.* Oxford: Clarendon Press.

Johansen, A. 1984. *Tid är makt. Tid är pengar.* Gothenburg, Sweden: Röda Bokförlaget.

Johnson, G. 1987. *The Body in the Mind: The Bodily Basis of Meaning,*

Imagination, and Reasoning. Chicago: University of Chicago Press.

Karrar, A. S. 1992. *The Sufi Brotherhoods in the Sudan*. London: C. Hurst & Company.

Keesing, R. M. 1977. *Cultural Anthropology. A Contemporary Perspective*. New York: Holt, Rinehart and Winston.

Keesing, R. M. 1982. *Kwaio Religion: The Living and the Dead in a Solomon Island Society*. New York: Columbia University Press.

Kenyon, S. M. 1991. *Five Women of Sennar. Culture and Change in Central Sudan*. Oxford: Clarendon Press.

Kinsley, D. 1995. *Health, Healing and Religion. A Cross-Cultural Perspective*. Upper Saddle River, New Jersey: Prentice Hall.

Kleinman, A. 1978. Concepts and a Model for the Comparison of Medical Systems as Cultural Systems. *Social Science and Medicine 12*, Vol. 85.

Kleinman, A. 1980. *Patients and Healers in the Context of Culture*, Berkeley: University of California Press.

Labov, W. 1982. Speech Actions and Reactions in Personal Narrative. In D. Tannen (ed.): *Analyzing Discourse: Text and Talk*. Washington D.C.: Georgetown University Round Table on Languages and Linguistics 1981, Georgetown University Press.

Labov, W. and Fanshel, D. 1977. *Therapeutic Discourse. Psychotherapy as Conversation*. New York, San Francisco and London: Academic Press.

Labov, W. and Waletsky, J. 1967. Narrative Analysis. In June Helm (ed.): *Essays on the Verbal and Visual Arts*. Seattle: University of Washington Press.

Laderman, C. 1992. A Welcoming Soil: Islamic Humoralism on the Malay Peninsula. In C. Leslie and A. Young (eds.): *Paths to Asian Medical Knowledge*. Berkeley: University of California Press.

Laderman, C. 1981. Symbolic and Empirical Reality: A New Approach to the Analysis of Food Avoidance. *American Ethnologist 8*, pp. 468–493.

Lakoff, G.: *Women, Fire, and Dangerous Things. What Categories Reveal about the Mind*. Chicago and London: The University of Chicago Press, 1987.

Lakoff, G. and Johnson, M.: *Metaphors We Live By*. Chicago: University of Chicago Press, 1980.

Lakoff, G. and Kovecses, Z. 1987. The Cognitive Model of Anger

Inherent in American English. In Holland & Quinn (eds.): *Cultural Models in Language and Thought*. Cambridge, Massachusetts: Cambridge University Press.

Leach, E. 1981 (1976). *Culture and communication. The Logic by which Symbols are Connected*. London: Cambridge University Press.

Leslie, C. and Young, A. (eds.). 1992. *Paths to Asian Medical Knowledge*. Berkeley: University of California Press.

Lewis, D.: *Counterfactuals*. Oxford: Basil Blackwell, 1973.

Lewis, I. M. 1989. *Ecstatic Religion. A Study of Shamanism and Spirit Possession*. London and New York: Routledge.

Lewis, I. M. 1968. Literacy in a Nomadic Society: The Somali Case. In J. Goody (ed.): *Literacy in Traditional Societies*. Cambridge, Massachusetts: Cambridge University Press.

Lewis, I. M. 1962. *Marriage and the Family in Northern Somaliland*. Kampala, Uganda: East African Institute of Social Research.

Lewis, I. M. 1955. *Peoples of the Horn of Africa. Somali, Afar and Saho*. London: International African Institute.

Lewis, I. M. 1986. *Religion in Context. Cults and Charisma*. Cambridge, Massachusetts: Cambridge University Press.

Lewis, I. M. 1981. *Somali Culture, History and Social Institutions. An Introductory Guide to the Somali Democratic Republic*. London: The London School of Economics and Political Science.

Lewis, I. M. 1966. Spirit Possession and Deprivation Cults. *Man (N.S.) 3*, Vol. 1, pp. 307–329, 1966.

Lewis, I. M. 1971. Spirit Possession in North-East Africa. In Y. F. Hassan (ed.): *Sudan in Africa*. Khartoum: Khartoum University Press.

Lewis, I. M. 1969. Spirit Possession in Northern Somaliland. In J. Beattie, *et al.* (eds.): *Spirit Mediumship and Society in Africa*, London: Routledge and Kegan Paul.

Lewis, I. M., *et al.* 1991. *Women's Medicine. The Zar-Bori Cult in Africa and Beyond*. Edinburgh: Edinburgh University Press.

Logan, M. H. 1993. New Lines of Inquiry on the Illness of Susto. *Medical Anthropology*, Vol. 15, pp. 189–200.

Loudon, J. B. 1976. *Social Anthropology and Medicine*. A.S.A. Monograph 13, London: Academic Press.

Luhrmann, T. M. 1989. *Persuasions of the Witch's Craft. Ritual Magic in Contemporary England*. Cambridge, Massachusetts: Harvard University Press.

Lyons, J. 1977. *Semantics: Vol. 2.* Cambridge: Cambridge University Press.

Makris, G. 1991. *Social Change, Religion, and Spirit Possession: The Tumbura Cult of the Sudan.* Unpublished doctoral dissertation in social anthropology, LSE, University of London, October 1991.

Mandler, J. M. 1984. *Stories, Scripts and Scenes: Aspects of a Schema Theory.* Hillsdale, New York: Lawrence Erlbaum Associates, 1984.

Mandler, J. M. and DeForest, M. 1979. Is There More than One Way to Recall a Story? *Child Development 50*, pp. 886–889.

Mandler, J. M. *et al.* 1980. Cross-cultural Invariance in Story Recall. *Child Development, 51*, pp. 19–26.

Massey, C. and Gelman, R. 1988. Preschoolers' Ability to Decide whether Pictured Unfamiliar Objects can Move Themselves. *Developmental Psychology 24*, pp. 307–317.

Mathews, H. F. 1992. The Directive Force of Morality Tales in a Mexican Community. In R. D'Andrade and C. Strauss (eds): *Human Motives and Cultural Models.* Cambridge, Massachusetts: Cambridge University Press 1992.

Mauss, M. 1972. *A General Theory of Magic.* New York: W. W. Norton (original work published in 1902).

Mauss, M. (1925) 1954. *The Gift: Forms and Functions of Exchange in Archaic Societies.* London: Cohen and West.

Medin, D. L. 1989. Concepts and Conceptual Structure. *American Psychologist 12*, Vol. 44, pp. 1469–1481, December 1989.

Medin, D. L. and Shoben, E. J. 1988. Context and structure in conceptual combination. *Cognitive Psychology 20*, pp. 158–190.

Migliore, S. 1983. Evil Eye or Delusions? On the Consistency of Folk Models. *Medical Anthropology Quarterly 2*, Vol. 14, Febr. 1983.

Miller, P. J. and Moore, B. B. 1989. Narrative Conjunctions of Caregiver and Child: A Comparative Perspective on Socialization through Stories. *Ethos 4*, Vol. 17.

Miller, P. J., *et al.* 1990. Narrative Practices and the Social Construction of Self in Childhood. *American Ethnologist 17*, pp. 292–311.

Modawi, A. W. A. and Siddig, K. E. H. 1995. *Population Distribution in the Sudan.* Paper presented at the the Seminar on Advance Census Results, Khartoum January 29–30, 1995. Khartoum: Central Bureau of Statistics.

Morsy, S. 1980. Body Concepts and Health Care: Illustrations from an Egyptian Village. *Human Organization 1*, Vol. 39, Spring 1980.

Morton, J. and Fre, Z. 1986. *Red Sea Province and the Beja*. Oxford: A prelimary report for Oxfam.

Murdock, G. P. 1959. *Africa. Its Peoples and Their Culture History.* New York: McGraw-Hill Book Company, Inc.

Murdock, G. P. 1980. *Theories of Illness. A World Survey.* Pittsburgh, USA: University of Pittsburgh Press.

Nadel, S. F. 1952. Witchcraft in Four African Societies: An Essay in Comparison. *American Anthropologist 54*, pp. 18–29.

Nasr, S. H. 1972. *Ideals and Realities of Islam*. Boston: Beacon Press.

Natvig, R. 1992. Liminal Rites and Female Symbolism in the Egyptian Zar Possession Cult. *Numen 1*, Vol. XXXV.

Newbold, D. 1935. The Beja Tribes of the Red Sea Hinterland. In J. A. de C. Hamilton (ed.): *The Anglo-Egyptian Sudan from Within*. London: Faber and Faber.

Nichter, M. 1989. *Anthropology and International Health. South Asian Case Studies*. Dortrecht, Boston and London: Kluwer Academic Publishers.

Nichter, M. 1992. Of Ticks, Kings, Spirits, and the Promise of Vaccines. In Leslie, C. and Young, A. (eds.): *Paths to Asian Medical Knowledge*. Berkeley: University of California Press.

Nisbett, R. E., *et al.* 1995. Homicide and U.S. Regional Culture. In Weiner, N. A. *et al.* (eds.): *Interpersonal Violent Behavior and Cultural Aspects*. New York: Springer.

O'Fahey, R. S. 1990. *Engimatic Saint. Ahmad Ibn Idris and the Idrisi Tradition.* London: Hurst & Co.

O'Fahey, R. S. 1980. *State and Society in Dar Fur.* London: C. Hurst & Company.

Ong, W. J. 1990. *Muntlig og skriftlig kultur: teknologiseringen av ordet*. Gothenburg, Sweden: Anthropos.

Pagano, R. R. 1990. *Understanding Statistics in the Behavioral Sciences*. New York: West Publishing Company.

Paul, A. 1954. *A History of the Beja tribes of the Sudan*. London: Frank Cass & Co.

Paul, S. 1975. *Ethnomedicine and Social Medicine in Tropical Africa*. Arbeitsgemeinschaft für Ethnomedicine Hamburg 1975. Munich: In Kommission Klaus Renner Verlag.

Pool, R. 1994. On the Creation and Dissolution of Ethnomedical

Systems in the Medical Ethnography of Africa. *Africa 1*, Vol. 64.

Pool, R. 1989. *There Must Have Been Something . . . Interpretation of Illness and Misfortune in a Cameroon Village.* Amsterdam.

Popper, K. R. 1992. *In Search of a Better World. Lectures and Essays from Thirty Years.* London and New York: Routledge.

Quinn, N. 1992a. *How Love and Marriage go Together.* Paper delivered at the 91st Annual Meeting of the American Anthropological Association, San Francisco, December 1992.

Quinn, N. 1991. The Cultural Basis of Metaphor. In J. W. Fernandez (ed): *The Theory of Tropes* in *Anthropology.* Stanford, California: Stanford University Press.

Quinn, N. 1992b. The Motivational Force of Self-understanding: Evidence from Wives' inner Conflicts. In R. D'Andrade & C. Strauss (eds.): *Human Motives and Cultural Models.* Cambridge, Massachusetts: Cambridge University Press.

Quirk, R. S., *et al.* 1972. *A Grammar of Contemporary English.* London: Longman.

Rack, P. 1986. *Innvandrere, kultur og psykiatri.* Oslo, Norway: Tano.

Rahim, S. I. 1991. *Zar* among Middle-aged Female Psychiatric Patients in the Sudan. In I. M. Lewis, *et al.: Women's Medicine. The Zar-Bori Cult in Africa and Beyond.* Edinburgh: Edinburgh University Press.

Rekdal, O. B. and Blystad, A. Forthcoming. 'We are sheep and goats'. Iraqw and Datooga discourses on fortune, failure and the future. In D. M. Anderson and V. Broch-Due, eds.: *Poverty matters: Rich and poor among pastoralists in eastern Africa.* London: James Currey.

Roper, E. M. 1928. *Tu Bedawie. An Elementary Handbook for the Use of Sudan Government Official.* Hertford, Herts, England: Stephen Austin and Sons, Ltd., Oriental and General Printers.

Rozin & Fallon. 1987. A Perspective on Disgust. *Psychological Review 94*, pp. 23–41.

Rozin & Nemeroff. 1994. The Contagion Concept in Adult Thinking in the United States: Transmission of Germs and of Interpersonal Influence. *Ethos 2*, Vol. 22, pp. 158–186.

Rozin & Nemeroff. 1990. The Laws of Sympathetic Magic. A Psychological Analysis of Similarity and Contagion. In Schweder, Stigler & Herdt (eds.): *Essays on Comparative*

355

Human Development. New York: Cambridge University Press.

Rozin, P. L. *et al.* 1986. Operations of the Laws of Sympathetic Magic in Disgust and other Domains. *Journal of Personality and Social Psychology 50*, pp. 703–712.

Rumelhart, D. E. 1975. Notes on a Schema for Stories. In D. G. Bobrow and A. Collins (eds.): *Representation and Understanding: Studies in Cognitive Science*. New York: Academic Press.

Rumelhart, D. E. 1977. Understanding and Summarizing Brief Stories. In D. LaBerge and S. J. Samuels (eds.): *Basic Processes in Reading: Perception and Comprehension*. Hillsdale, NJ: Lawrence Erlbaum Associates.

Sachs, L. 1983. *Evil Eye or Bacteria. Turkish Migrant Women and Swedish Health Care*. Stockholm, Sweden: Stockholm Studies in Social Anthropology.

Safa, K. 1988. Reading Saedi's *Ahl-e-Hava:* Pattern and Significance in Spirit Possession Beliefs on the Southern Coasts of Iran. *Culture, Medicine and Psychiatry 12*, pp. 85–111.

Salih, Al-Tayyib. 1968. *The Wedding of Zein and Other Stories*. London: Heinemann Educational.

Salih, H. M. 1980. Hadendowa Traditional Territorial Rights and Inter-Population Relations within the Context of the Native Administration System 1927–1970. *Sudan Notes and Records*, Vol. 61, pp. 118–133, 1980.

Salih, H. M. 1971. *Some Aspects of Hadendowa Social Organization*. M. Sc. Thesis in Social Anthropology, University of Khartoum, Khartoum, Sudan.

Sarbin, T. R. (ed.). 1986. *Narrative Psychology. The Storied Nature of Human Conduct*. New York: Praeger Special Studies.

Schank, R. C. 1982. *Dynamic memory. A Theory of Reminding and Learning in Computers and People*. Cambridge, Massachusetts: Cambridge University Press.

Schank, R. C. and Abelson, R. P. 1977. *Scripts, Plans, Goals and Understanding. An Inquiry into Human Knowledge Structures*. Hillsdale, New Jersey: Lawrence Erlbaum Associates.

Scheper-Hughes, N. 1992. *Death without Weeping: The Violence of Everyday Life in Brazil*. Berkeley: University of California Press.

Scheper-Hughes, N. 1990. Mothers' Love and Child Death in Northeast Brazil. In J. Stigler, *et. al.* (eds.): *Cultural Psychology*.

Essays on comparative human development. Cambridge, Mass.: Cambridge University Press.

Schneider, A. 1988. Bemerkungen zum sog. Zar und zu anderen Krankenhellungs-zermonien in Africa. In Karl Hornman (ed.): *Musik- und Tanztherapie*, Munster: F. Hettyen Verlag.

Sharif Harir. 1995. *The Mosque and the Sacred Mountain: Duality of Religious Beliefs among the Zaghawa of Northwestern Sudan*. Bergen, Norway: Unpublished paper, Center for Development Research, University of Bergen, 1995.

Siegel, R. E. 1970. *Galen on sense perception: His doctrines, observations and experiments on vision, hearing, smell, taste, touch and pain and their historical sources*. Basel: Karger.

Slikkerveer, L. J. 1990. *Plural Medical Systems in the Horn of Africa*. London and New York: Kegan Paul International.

Sontag, S. 1989. *AIDS and its Metaphors*. New York: Farrar, Strauss and Giroux.

Sontag, S. 1978. *Illness as Metaphors*, New York: Farrar, Strauss and Giroux.

Spiro, M. 1952. Ghosts, Ifaluk, and Teleological Functionalism. *American Anthropologist 4*, Vol. 54.

Spiro, M. 1993. Is the Western Conception of Self Peculiar within the Context of the World Cultures? *Ethos 2*, Vol. 21, pp. 107–153.

Stein, H. F. 1990. *American Medicine as Culture*. London: Westview Press.

Storås, F. 1996. *Being a Nomad in Turkana, Kenya*. Doctoral dissertation, Department of Social Anthropology, University of Bergen, Norway.

Strauss, C. 1992. What Makes Tony Run? Schemas as Motives Reconsidered. In R. D'Andrade and C. Strauss (eds): *Human Motives and Cultural Models*. Cambridge, Massachusetts: Cambridge University Press.

Strauss, C. and Quinn, N. 1992. Preliminaries to a Theory of Culture Aquisition. In D. C. Knill and P. van der Broeck Pick (eds.): *Conceptual and Methodological Inquiries*. Washington D.C.

Swartz, M. J. 1991. *The Way the World Is. Cultural Processes and Social Relations among the Mombasa Swahili*. Berkeley: University of California Press.

Trimingham, J. S. 1976. *Islam in Ethiopia*. London: Frank Cass.

Trimingham, J. S. 1949. *Islam in the Sudan*. London: Frank Cass.

Turner, V. 1989. *The Forest of Symbols. Aspects of Ndembu Ritual.* London: Cornell University Press.

Turner, V. 1967. Witchcraft and Sorcery: Taxonomy versus Dynamics. In V. Turner: *The Forest of Symbols. Aspects of Ndembu Ritual.* Ithaca: Cornell University Press.

Tuzin, D. 1986. *Sensory Contact and Moral Contagion in Ilahita.* Paper presented at the 85th annual meeting of the American Anthropological Association, Philadelphia, December 3–7, 1986.

Tylor, E. B. 1924. *Primitive Culture: Researches into the Development of Mythology, Philosophy, Religion, Art and Custom.* New York: Brentano's Publishers (originally published in 1871).

Ullmann, M. 1978. *Islamic Medicine.* Edinburgh: At the Edinburgh University Press.

Vågenes, V. 1995. Male Outside and Female Inside – Spatial Orientation in the Gender System of Hadendowa, Northeastern Sudan. *Norsk Geografisk Tidsskrift,* Vol. 49, pp. 91–104.

Vågenes, V. 1990. *Women Going Public. Social Change and Gender Roles in the Red Sea Hills, Sudan.* Cand.Polit. Thesis in geography, Dept. of Geography, University of Bergen, Bergen, Norway.

Vikør, K. 1991. *Sufi and Scholar on the Desert Edge. Muhammad b. 'Ali al-Sanusi (1787–1859).* Unpublished doctoral dissertation, University of Bergen, Norway.

Voll, J. O. 1969. *A History of the Khatmiyyah Tariqah in the Sudan.* Unpublished doctoral dissertation, Harvard University, Cambridge, Massachusetts.

Walker, P. 1987. *Food for Recovery. Food Monitoring and Targeting in the Red Sea Province, Sudan 1985–87.* Oxford: Oxfam Report, 1987.

Wehr, H. 1961. *A Dictionary of Modern Written Arabic.* Ithaca: Cornell University Press.

Westermarck, E. 1926. *Ritual and Belief in Morocco.* London: Macmillan.

Whiting, B. B. 1950. *Paiute Sorcery.* New York: Viking Fund Publications in Anthropology No. 15.

Wikan, U. 1982. *Behind the Veil in Arabia – Women in Oman.* Baltimore: Johns Hopkins University Press.

Wikan, U. 1989. Illness from Fright or Soul Loss: A North Balinese Culture-bound Syndrome? *Culture, Medicine and Psychiatry* 13, pp. 25–60.

Wolff, M. E. and G. L. Personal letters, annual reports, work diaries and staff reports 1914–37. In Sudan Archive, Durham, England.

Yoder, P. S. 1982. Introduction. In P. S. Yoder (ed.): *African Health and Healing Systems: Proceedings of a symposium,* pp. 1–20, Los Angeles: Crossroad Press.

SUBJECT INDEX

Al-Khatmiyya, 320–8

Baraka, see Héequal
Beja
  and concepts of honor, 29–35
  and explanations for sickness
    and misfortune, 34–5, 36–43
  and gender roles, 26–9
  and Islam, 21–3, 320–8
  and literacy, 20
  marriage patterns, 24–5, 38–9,
    335–6
  and pastoral adaptation, 20, 21,
    29–35
  and social and environmental
    changes, 35–6, 43–6
  and the *diwáb*, 24–7, 36, 39–43,
    257, 310–11
  and tribal organization, 23–7
Beni Amer, 23, 166, 256

Case studies, 204–13
Circumcision
  lack of, and sicknesses, 112, 125,
    178–9
  performance of, 27, 28, 62
Cognitive anthropology, 7–15
Cognitive psychology, 8, 10, 11
Cognition
  distributed, 11
Cognitive science, 7–8
Cultural models, 10, 11, 20, 80,
  139, 143, 157, 171, 191, 205, 235,
  247, 257, 259, 262, 266, 307

Emotions
  and cognition, 11
Essence theories, *see* Theories of
  essence
Evil eye, 33, 35, 40, 41, 168–72, 211

Feature analyses, 10
Fertility and mortality, 337–43
Folk theories
  and classification, 12, 13

Healers
  The *basur*, 62–5, 68–9, 93, 97,
    128–9, 205, 208, 250, 255, 265,
    267–78, 285, 308
  The cowry-shell woman, 65–6
  The *fagur*, 21, 47, 58–60, 66–9,
    97, 133–4, 147–8, 150, 154–5,
    162, 169–70, 174, 205, 208–12,
    219–20, 223–5, 228–9, 231–3,
    237–50, 254–5
  The *táflam basur*, 70
  The *zār* doctor, 71–3, 147, 205,
    211, 219, 225
Héequal,
  analyzed, 157–64
  and *busarār*, 65
  and fertility, 158–64, 186, 205
  and *fugarā*, 22, 66, 154–5, 225,
    229, 234
  and metonomy, 175
  and sicknesses, 158–60, 258–9
  defined, 22

360

Karāma, 87, 88, 148, 161, 178–9, 223–4, 226

Linguistics, 10
Logics, types of
  Denial of the antecedent, 183
  Modus ponens, 181, 186, 309
  Modus tollens, 181–2, 186, 309
  Plausible inference, 182–3, 309

Metaphors, 10, 106–8, 143, 152, 154, 177, 189–96, 307
Metonyms, 142–3, 171, 175, 189–96, 307
Mothers work and health, 175–8, 227
Motivation
  and cognition, 11

Narratives
  analyses of, 215–304
  and folk model of mind, 296–9, 308
  and implicit knowledge, 3, 16, 18, 75–9, 214–15, 307, 309
  and 'open slots,' 12, 137–8, 188, 214, 245
  and pragmatics, 18, 245–6, 248, 266–7, 298–300
  and reflexivity, 230–1, 247, 266–7, 309–10
  and schema theories, 11, 16–17
  and story grammar, 279–98
  and subjunctiveness, 251, 253–6, 285
  mythical, 267–304, 308
  personal, 215–67, 307–8
Neurology, 10

Philosophy
  cognitive, 10
  of science, 9
Prototypes
  and theories of essence, 14
  defined, 10
  theories of, 14

Schemata

and cultural propositions, 12, 80–203, 184–5, 187–8
and cultural theories, 13, 80–203, 184–5, 187–8
and scripts, 185
defined, 10
theories, 10, 11
universialistic, 11

Sicknesses
  ablága, 232
  áfram, 57, 96
  alíb, 173, 205, 208, 254
  and anthropological theories, 83–6
  and 'bad blood,' 118–20, 124–6, 128, 185
  and blood-letting, 64
  and brandings, 127–9
  and compatibility, 138–43, 222–3
  and envy, 168–72, 210–11
  and herbs, 63, 86–92
  and human conduct, 178–9
  and microbes, 130–2
  and nutrition, 39, 51–3, 134–43, 165–6
  and olfaction, 121–7, 187, 228–9
  and personalistic traits, 104–9
  and substances, 92–104
  and the laws of sympathetic magic, 109–16, 127, 132–3, 138, 141–3, 155, 163–6, 174–5, 178, 189–96, 225
  and theories of human physiology, 116–32
  and unfulfilled wishes, 166–8, 228
  anemia, 51
  bájal, 96
  berudéit, 93
  bleeding, 111, 146
  boyée, 124
  broken bones, 62–3, 128
  common cold, 93, 124
  dalil óob, 93, 111
  depression, 146
  dérwou, 93
  eratiót, 111

eye inflammation, 88, 124
fainting, 125
fever, 95
fright sickness, *see* mírquay
gastroenteritis, 52
gúrda, 55, 94, 111, 118, 119, 124
háale, 60–1, 145–6, 210
hãf, 56–7, 82, 88, 93, 95, 98,
    102–7, 109, 128, 140, 182, 205,
    306–7
hãf masóob, 56–7, 94–5, 107, 119,
    128, 140, 176, 205
hallíg, 96
headache, 125–6
heminéit, 55, 88, 94–5, 106, 118,
    119, 140
herár, 56, 95, 124, 128–9, 146, 198
hot and cold, 53–7, 92, 94–104
kássar, 106
kelay t'áat, 60
khoof, see mírquay
koléit, 55, 95–6
kosúlt, 54, 81, 88, 93, 94, 95–6, 98,
    100–2, 104, 106, 107–9,
    118–19, 140, 141, 182, 185,
    233, 306–7
lung infections, 52, 124, 126, 223
measles, 52, 93, 124, 129, 130,
    140
milaria, 55, 94, 119, 124
mírquay (khoof), 59, 87, 94, 112,
    124, 125, 172–6, 205, 208, 232
na'éh, 94
occurrence of, 51–2
of mystical influence, 57–62,
    144–75
ogwéb, 118
paralysis, 146
respiratory tract infection
sarít, 125–6, 129
scorpion bit, 94, 119, 133
shagîga, 59, 95, 124, 125
sirr, 57, 168, 265
smallpox, 126
snake bite, 94, 119, 133
swellings, 146
táflam, 56–7, 70, 87, 93, 105, 112,
    128, 129, 151, 176, 196, 204
tesérimt, 57, 93, 105, 110, 114,

    159–62, 164, 166, 189, 205,
    208–10, 248–52, 255–66, 224,
    246, 306
tetanus, 52
t'háasimt, 58, 88, 105, 110, 124,
    176
toodíh, 70, 105, 129
toordíp, 59–60, 105, 232
tuberculosis, 57, 129
uáy, 125
vitamin deficiencies, 52
waswás, 61, 145, 146
watáb, 56, 93, 95–6, 98, 128
whooping cough, 52, 87, 105
woréeb, 124
wounds, 63, 128, 168
yambírir, 95
zãr, 61–2, 69, 94, 125, 156–7,
    211–12, 216–46
Sorcery
    accusation of, 38–9, 46, 50, 162,
        171–2
    theories of, 34, 36–7, 40, 42, 46,
        111, 169
    treatment of, 88, 111, 169–70
Spirits
    and brandings, 128
    and odors, 124–5, 149, 228–9
    and pollution, 148–9, 223
    nature of, 144–57
    possession and aggression, 34,
        40–2, 46, 145–6, 148–51, 223,
        254
    protection against, 111, 149–50,
        176, 221, 225, 230
    types of, 112, 144, 148, 151,
        155–7, 163
Sympathetic magic, laws of,
    112–16, 175, 189, 192, 225, 265
    defined, 109–10

Taxonomies, 10
Theories of essence
    and classification, 14, 15,
        98–104, 186–7, 305
    and contagion, 12, 110, 115–16,
        129–33, 136, 142–3, 154–5,
        166, 177–8, 186–96, 225, 307,
        310–11

and metonyms and metaphors,
106–8, 142–3, 152, 154, 175,
177, 189–96, 229, 307
and predicate restrictions, 15,
305
and prototypes, 14
and 'pseudo-natural' kinds, 15,
89–92, 153, 186, 306
Tigré, 23

Traditional knowledge
description of, 180–1, 269, 272,
276
value of, 180, 269, 273, 276

Witchcraft
accusations of, 46, 50, 89
theories of, 34, 36–8, 40–2,
168–9

AUTHOR INDEX

Abelson, R. P., 16, 184
Abu-Lughod, L., 151
Al-Safi, Ahmad, 216
Alver, B. G., 107
Anderson, R., 62
Atran, S., 14, 15
Ausenda, G., 23–5, 27, 34–5, 37–9,
    43, 47, 65, 119, 177, 222, 339
Austin, J. L., 312

Bailey, F. G., 171
Balfour, Sir A., 21
Barth, F., 24, 25, 40, 171
Bastien, J. W., 44, 96, 97
Baxter, P. T. W., 49
Becker, R., 15
Beidelman, T. O., 171
Bell, J., 74
Ben-Ari, E., 157
Berentzen, S., 253
Bilu, Y., 157
Bishaw, M., 62
Bloch, M., 7, 266
Bloss, J. F. E., 21, 62
Blystad, A., 50, 303
Boddy, J., 62, 132, 154–5, 172, 216,
    241, 255, 277, 301
Bonsaksen, S. R., 37, 43, 46, 256
Bourdieu, P., 151
Bousefield, L. 21
Boyer, P., 8, 14–15, 89–91, 153, 163,
    190, 306
Brandes, S., 177
Brøgger, J., 49, 171

Bruner, J., 247–8, 253, 263, 279,
    285, 297

Carneiro, R. L., 42
Catafago, J., 47, 327
Chand, A. D., 196
Ciekawy, D., 44
Classen, C., 122
Cloudsley, A., 62, 155
Collins, A., 309
Constantinides, P., 62, 155, 216
Corbin, A., 122
Crapanzano, V., 157
Crawley, E., 127
Crites, S., 216

Dahl, G., 23–7, 32, 35, 38, 39, 44,
    46, 222, 339
Daly, M. W., 22
D'Andrade, R., 7, 10–12, 14–15,
    115, 130, 203, 262, 296, 298, 309
DeForest, M., 285
Dhaher J. Mohammad, 326
Dougherty, J., 196
Douglas, M., 49
Dundes, A., 49
Duranti, A., 253

Early, E. E., 121, 131–2, 252
Edgerton, R. B., 30
Eickelman, D. F., 69
El-Dareer, A., 27, 179
Elster, J., 253
Eltay, Omer, 35, 342

Ertur, O. S., 35, 338, 342
Evans-Pritchard, E. E., 34, 42, 192
Eysenck, M. W., 184

Fadlalla, A. H., 177
Fallon, A. E., 109, 132, 175, 190
Fanshel, D., 301
Farah, Abdul-Aziz M., 338
Feierman, S., 121, 302
Fortes, M., 83
Foster, G. M., 83, 89, 96, 97
Frankenberg, R., 86
Frazer, J. G., 109, 113–14, 174, 189, 192
Fre, Z., 32

Gaik, F., 253
Gallagher, N. E., 62, 64, 67, 92, 122, 128
Geertz, C., 157
Gellner, E., 157
Gelman, M., 15
Gelman, R., 15
Gelman, S., 15
Geschiere, P., 44
Ghazali, J., 74
Gmelch, G., 194
Goffman, E., 194
Good, B. J., 60, 117, 120–1, 132, 248, 254, 255, 263, 303
Goodwin, C., 253
Goody, J., 233
Greenwood, B., 144
Grønhaug, R., 253

Haaland, G., 175, 177
Hall, M. J., 45, 62, 155–6
Halle, M., 189
Hannerz, U., 49
Haram, L., 303
Harir, Sharif, 74, 151
Hashmi, Sultan, 35, 342
Hirschfeld, L. A., 306
Holland, D., 11, 143
Holt, P. M., 22, 322–3, 325–6
Holy, L., 34, 67, 69, 113, 154, 157, 162, 171–2, 175, 179
House, W. J., 35, 338, 342
Huber, B. R., 62

Hunwick, J., 154
Hutchins, E., 9, 11, 186, 203, 309

Ibn Qayan al-Juwziyya, 54, 180
Idries Shah, 279
Idris Salim El Hassan, 327
Ingstad, B., 50

Jacobs, A. H., 48
Jakobson, R., 189
James, W., 89
Janzen, J. M., 121, 302
Johansen, A., 187
Johnson, G., 11, 107, 143, 154, 177, 190

Karrar, A. S., 22, 157, 320–3, 325, 327
Keane, M. T., 184
Keesing, R. M., 163, 171, 177, 266
Keil, F. C., 15
Keller, C., 196
Kenyon, S. M., 62, 155, 216
Kinsley, D., 157
Kleinman, A., 5, 62, 85, 255
Kovecses, Z., 11, 143, 154, 190

Labov, W., 296, 301
Laderman, C., 97, 120, 132, 139
Lakoff, G., 11, 107, 143, 154, 177, 190
Last, M., 84
Leach, E., 189, 190, 192
Leslie, C., 97
Lewis, D., 253
Lewis, I. M., 22, 62, 75, 155, 157, 233, 238, 241, 301, 339
Lintjørn, B., 343
Logan, M. H., 172
Loudon, J. B., 83, 302
Luhrmann, T., 195
Lyons, J., 253

Makris, G., 62, 155, 216
Mandler, J. M., 11, 277, 279, 281–2, 285, 293, 296, 298, 304
Massey, C., 15
Mathews, H., 10, 11, 287, 297
Mauss, M., 20, 109

Medin, D. L., 10, 11, 14
Michalski, R., 309
Migliore, S., 171
Miller, P. J., 243, 247, 276
Modawi, A. W. A., 342
Moore, B. B., 247
Morsy, S., 121
Morton, J., 32
Murdock, G. P., 25, 34, 41, 49, 129, 171, 172

Nadel, S. F., 37, 40, 43, 171
Nasr, S. H., 69, 154
Natvig, R., 62, 155
Nemeroff, C, 15, 109, 110, 114, 116, 122, 127, 132, 136, 142, 143, 166, 174, 175, 190, 191, 192
Nerlove, S., 12
Newbold, D., 21
Nichter, M., 97, 255
Nisbett, R. E., 31, 33, 41, 48

O'Fahey, R. S., 320, 321, 322
Ong, W. J., 233

Pagano, R. R., 342
Paul, A., 21, 23, 33, 35, 37, 44, 64, 68, 256
Pool, R., 83, 84
Popper, K. R., 1, 2

Quinn, N., 10–12, 143, 190
Quirk, R. S., 253

Rack, P., 297
Rahim, S. I., 216
Rekdal, O. B., 50
Romney, A., 12
Roper, E. M., 24–5, 47
Rosch, E., 10, 14
Rozin, P., 15, 109–10, 114–16, 122, 127, 132, 136, 142–3, 166, 174, 175, 190, 191, 192
Rumelhart, D. E., 279, 304

Sachs, L., 49, 171

Safa, K., 62, 155
Saghayroun, Atif A., 338
Salih, H. M., 24, 25, 39, 47, 339
Sarbin, T. R., 300, 301
Schank, R. C., 16, 184, 187
Scheper-Hughes, N., 340
Schneider, A., 62, 155, 216, 262
Shams ad-Din Mohd. Ibrahim Abi Bakri, 196
Shoben, E. J., 14
Siddig, K. E. H., 342
Siegel, R. E., 121
Slikkerveer, L. J., 63, 67, 126, 302
Sommers, F., 15
Sontag, S., 107, 177, 310
Spiro, M., 41, 42, 216, 300
Stein, H. F., 85, 107, 130
Storås, F., 33, 233
Strauss, C., 10, 11
Swartz, M., 28, 29

Trimingham, J. S., 21–3, 44, 47, 67, 150, 157, 170, 172, 256, 320, 322
Turner, V., 49, 112–13
Tuzin, D., 116, 127, 193, 196
Tylor, E. B., 109, 115

Ullmann, M., 98, 120, 132, 138, 139

Vågenes, V., 26–7, 36, 43–4, 179, 256, 322, 339, 341
Vikør, K., 320, 321
Voll, J. O., 21, 22, 157, 321, 322, 324–6

Wagner, R., 264
Waletsky, J., 301
Walker, P., 46, 174
Ward, T. B., 15
Weber, M., 28
Westermarck, E., 157
Whiting, B. B., 37, 40
Wikan, U., 67, 172

Yoder, P. S., 83
Young, A., 97